Thinking and Speaking in Two Languages

FSC
www.fsc.org

BILINGUAL EDUCATION & BILINGUALISM
Series Editors: **Nancy H. Hornberger** *(University of Pennsylvania, USA)* and **Colin Baker** *(Bangor University, Wales, UK)*

Bilingual Education and Bilingualism is an international, multidisciplinary series publishing research on the philosophy, politics, policy, provision and practice of language planning, global English, indigenous and minority language education, multilingualism, multiculturalism, biliteracy, bilingualism and bilingual education. The series aims to mirror current debates and discussions.

Full details of all the books in this series and of all our other publications can be found on http://www.multilingual-matters.com, or by writing to Multilingual Matters, St Nicholas House, 31-34 High Street, Bristol BS1 2AW, UK.

BILINGUAL EDUCATION & BILINGUALISM
Series Editors: Nancy H. Hornberger *(University of Pennsylvania, USA) and* Colin Baker *(Bangor University, Wales, UK)*

Thinking and Speaking in Two Languages

Edited by
Aneta Pavlenko

MULTILINGUAL MATTERS
Bristol • Buffalo • Toronto

Library of Congress Cataloging in Publication Data
A catalog record for this book is available from the Library of Congress.
Thinking and Speaking in Two Languages/Edited by Aneta Pavlenko.
Bilingual Education & Bilingualism
Includes bibliographical references and index.
1. Bilingualism. 2. Second language acquisition. 3. Language and languages–Study and teaching.
I. Pavlenko, Aneta
P115.T55 2011
404'.2–dc222010041225

British Library Cataloguing in Publication Data
A catalogue entry for this book is available from the British Library.

ISBN-13: 978-1-84769-337-2 (hbk)
ISBN-13: 978-1-84769-336-5 (pbk)

Cover image: Oppenheim, Meret (1913–1985): Object (le déjeuner en fourrure), 1936. New York, Museum of Modern Art (MoMA). Fur covered cup, saucer and spoon, 4 3/8' (10.9 cm) diameter; saucer, 9 3/8' (23.7 cm) diameter; spoon, 8' (20.2 cm) long; overall height 2 7/8' (7.3 cm). Purchase. Acc. n.: 130. 1946. a-c © 2010. Digital image, The Museum of Modern Art, New York/Scala, Florence

Multilingual Matters
UK: St Nicholas House, 31-34 High Street, Bristol BS1 2AW, UK.
USA: UTP, 2250 Military Road, Tonawanda, NY 14150, USA.
Canada: UTP, 5201 Dufferin Street, North York, Ontario M3H 5T8, Canada.

The policy of Multilingual Matters/Channel View Publications is to use papers that are natural, renewable and recyclable products, made from wood grown in sustainable forests. In the manufacturing process of our books, and to further support our policy, preference is given to printers that have FSC and PEFC Chain of Custody certification. The FSC and/or PEFC logos will appear on those books where full certification has been granted to the printer concerned.

Typeset by Datapage International Ltd.
Printed and bound in Great Britain by Short Run Press Ltd.

Contents

Contributors

Eef Ameel (PhD in Psychology, University of Leuven, Belgium, 2007) is a Postdoctoral Fellow at the University of Leuven, Belgium. Her research focus is on lexical development during later first language acquisition and on the development of and representation in the bilingual lexicon.

Panos Athanasopoulos (PhD in Linguistics, University of Essex, UK, 2006) is a lecturer in applied linguistics at the School of Education, Communication, and Language Sciences, Newcastle University, UK. His research interests are in bilingualism and cognition, language and thought, and language acquisition. He is particularly interested in language acquisition and conceptual development, and the extent to which learning novel lexical and/or grammatical categories leads to cognitive restructuring in the bilingual mind.

Emanuel Bylund (PhD in Bilingualism Research, 2008, and PhD in Spanish Linguistics, 2009, Stockholm University, Sweden) is an associate professor at the Centre for Research on Bilingualism, Stockholm University, Sweden. He is currently a post-doctoral fellow at University of the Western Cape, South Africa. His research concentrates on crosslinguistic differences in event cognition, and age effects in first language attrition and second language acquisition.

Mary Carroll (Dr Phil in Linguistics, University of Heidelberg, Germany, 1982) is a Research Fellow at the University of Heidelberg, Germany. Her research interests include the following areas: how languages structure space and time, with a focus on grammaticized concepts and their role in determining frames of reference; information structure and associated processes in language production; adult second language acquisition.

Marianne Gullberg (PhD in Linguistics, Lund University, Sweden, 1998) is Professor of Psycholinguistics at Lund University, Sweden. She has headed a research group at the Max Planck Institute for Psycholinguistics, Nijmegen, the Netherlands, and co-founded and co-directed the Nijmegen Gesture Centre. She is Associate Editor of *Language Learning* and *Language, Interaction, and Acquisition*, and Information Editor of *Gesture*. Her research targets second language acquisition and multilingual processing and language use, with particular attention to implicit learning, discourse and the semantic-conceptual interface.

Barbara Malt (PhD in Cognitive Psychology, Stanford University, USA, 1982) is Professor of Psychology at Lehigh University, USA. She is interested in how people understand the world, how they talk about the world and what the relation is between the two. She has published on concepts, word meaning and word use, the interface of language and thought, and implications for bilingualism. She is co-editor with Phillip Wolff of *Words and the Mind: How Words Capture Human Experience* (Oxford University Press, 2010). She has served as Associate Editor for the *Journal of Experimental Psychology: Learning, Memory, and Cognition* and as Chair of the Psychology Department at Lehigh.

Aneta Pavlenko (PhD in Linguistics, Cornell University, USA, 1997) is Professor at the College of Education, Temple University, Philadelphia, USA. She is the author of *Emotions and Multilingualism* (Cambridge University Press, 2005, winner of the BAAL Book Prize), editor of *Bilingual Minds* (Multilingual Matters, 2006) and *The Bilingual Mental Lexicon* (Multilingual Matters, 2009) and co-author (with Scott Jarvis) of *Crosslinguistic Influence in Language and Cognition* (Routledge, 2008). Her research examines the relationship between language, emotions and cognition in bilingualism and second language acquisition.

Barbara Schmiedtová (PhD in Psycholinguistics, Max Planck Institute of Psycholinguistics and Radboud University Nijmegen, Netherlands, 2004) is Associate Professor of Linguistics at the University of Heidelberg, Germany. Her research interests include the relationship between language and cognition, first and second language acquisition, bilingualism, language typology, language pathology, experimental design and methodology. Currently, she is focusing on the role of aspectual distinctions in event realization.

Christiane von Stutterheim (PhD in Linguistics, Free University, Berlin, Germany, 1984) is Full Professor at the University of Heidelberg, Germany. She is Director of the Linguistics Department at the Institute for General and Applied Linguistics and currently Dean of the Faculty of Modern Languages. Her research interests cover psycholinguistics, particularly crosslinguistic aspects of language production, second language acquisition and cognition of space and time. Over the last years, she has directed a number of interdisciplinary crosslinguistic research projects, funded by the German Science Foundation.

Acknowledgments

Meret Oppenheim's iconic *Le Déjeuner en fourrure* provides a perfect illustration of the many purposes of this volume. Oppenheim's fur-covered teacup had challenged the canons of classical sculpture and the invisibility of women in art, and showed how even the slightest twist – in this case, the addition of the pelt of a Chinese gazelle – could transform the nature of the most mundane objects and the associations they summon in our minds. In a similar vein, the contributors to this volume question the ingrained assumptions in the study of language and cognition and the invisibility of bi- and multilingual speakers, and show how the application of a bilingual lens reveals new facets of the interaction between languages and cognitive processes in the human mind. I am thankful to the SCALA Group for permission to reproduce this picture. I am equally grateful to publishers who allowed us to reproduce the images in individual chapters.

The work on this volume has been a wonderful journey of learning and inspiration. I thank all the volume contributors whose exciting ideas, superb professionalism and unfailing promptness made my editorial tasks a pleasure and a privilege. I am equally grateful to Rafael Berthele, Scott Jarvis and Monika Schmid, who, together with the authors, contributed their time and expertise to the anonymous peer-review process. Last but not least, I want to thank the Multilingual Matters team, and in particular Colin Baker, Tommi Grover, Anna Roderick and Sarah Williams, who make author–publisher collaboration a truly enjoyable experience.

Chapter 1
Introduction: Bilingualism and Thought in the 20th Century

ANETA PAVLENKO

I still remember it as if it happened yesterday: the unseasonably chilly October morning, the immense line outside the warehouse, and our excitement and anticipation of the treasures we might discover inside. It was the fall of 1992 and my friends and I were first year graduate students in Linguistics at Cornell University, waiting for the opening of Ithaca's famous Friends of the Library book sale. It turned out that true aficionados had camped overnight outside the warehouse on Esty Street and so, for the first hour after the opening, we could only screen the people exiting triumphantly with their brown paper bags full of books, and hope that they were not carrying all the prizes away. Then, finally, we were at the door. Checking the book sale's map, we raced through the crowded floor to the linguistics bookcase and began raiding its holdings. And there it was: a caramel brown binding with golden letters announcing that this volume, published in 1949, contained *Selected Writings of Edward Sapir*. Two decades later, I still remember the thrill of lifting the book off the shelf, of finding the *ex libris* of emeritus Psychology Professor Robert MacLeod (Cornell professors regularly donated books to the book sale), of reverently looking through its well-thumbed pages and of coming across this mysterious comment:

> To pass from one language to another is psychologically parallel to passing from one geometrical system of reference to another. The environing world which is referred to is the same for either language; the world of points is the same in either frame of reference. But the formal method of approach to the expressed item of experience, as to the given point of space, is so different that the resulting feeling of orientation can be the same neither in the two languages nor in the two frames of reference. Entirely distinct, or at least measurably distinct, formal adjustments have to be made and these differences have their psychological correlates. (Sapir, 1949 [1924]: 153)

These words beautifully captured the disorientation of my own transition from Russian to English and I could not wait to see what Sapir meant by the psychological correlates. But when I scanned the following text, I realized, with great disappointment, that this was just a

1

cryptic aside in a discussion of the relationship between grammar and the lexicon. I was left alone, like a particularly clumsy Alice, who saw a tantalizing glimpse of another world and then failed to cross through the looking glass. What did Sapir mean? Why didn't he examine the phenomenon of bilingualism any further? What is the relationship between bilinguals' languages and thought? These questions haunted me ever since, but the answers continued to be elusive because, until now, the history of debates about language and thought has been a history of thinking of language in the singular, of disengagement with bilingualism.

The purpose of this volume is to reverse this trend and to begin unlocking the mysteries surrounding thinking and speaking in bi- and multilingual speakers. In doing so, some of the chapters in this collection will engage with the theory of linguistic relativity, also known as the Sapir-Whorf hypothesis. The goal of this engagement, however, is to understand the implications of Sapir's and Whorf's ideas for speakers of multiple languages, not to 'prove' or 'contest' the hypothesis commonly formulated as follows:

> the famous Sapir-Whorf hypothesis of linguistic determinism, stating that people's thoughts are determined by the categories made available by their language, and its weaker version, linguistic relativity, stating that differences among languages cause differences in the thoughts of their speakers. (Pinker, 1994: 57)

I have made the editorial decision to side-step the debates about the Sapir-Whorf hypothesis for three interrelated reasons. The first is my deep conviction that the articulation of the so-called Sapir-Whorf hypothesis and the research based on this articulation represent a departure from Sapir's and Whorf's original ideas. In Section 1.3 of this chapter, I will trace the transformation of Sapir's and Whorf's complex arguments into the sound-bite juxtaposition of 'strong' linguistic determinism to 'weak' linguistic relativity and reveal the real authors of the Sapir-Whorf hypothesis – North American psychologists Roger Brown and Eric Lenneberg.

The second reason for side-stepping the debates involves a limited and limiting set of questions inspired by the Brown-Lenneberg hypothesis, questions that presuppose monolingualism as the norm. Only in the world imagined to be monolingual could one consider the possibility of languages 'determining' people's thoughts, without asking what happens with those who grow up speaking two or more languages, or those who learn other languages later in life. Consequently, instead of reviewing studies easily accessible to the readers, I will provide a historic overview of lesser-known research on bilingualism and thought.

The third reason involves constraints placed on research design by the current articulations of linguistic relativity. Instead of asking when, how, why and to what degree languages may influence cognitive categories and processes, current research privileges investigations of non-verbal behaviors that provide 'true' evidence 'for' or 'against' linguistic relativity. Lucy (1992a), Slobin (1996) and Levinson (2003) criticized this oversimplification and offered convincing arguments in favor of combining laboratory and naturalistic, as well as verbal and non-verbal, tasks in the study of linguistic relativity. Their arguments, however, have not been fully heeded by researchers in psychology, where 'habitual thought' is examined through experiments that measure reaction times to artificial tasks in laboratory conditions (e.g. Boroditsky, 2001; Chen, 2007; January & Kako, 2007; Tse & Altarriba, 2008).

To sum up, then, the present volume as a whole does not aim to take a position on or to provide any evidence 'for' or 'against' the Sapir-Whorf hypothesis in its current formulation (but see Chapter 2). Rather, it contributes to the scholarship on language and cognition by expanding its range to bilingual speakers as a focus of a systematic and sustained inquiry. This is particularly important because in today's globalized urban environments, it is more and more difficult to locate monolingual speakers of languages other than English (cf. Chapter 2). Unfortunately, some researchers studying language and cognition have not yet come to grips with this fact and continue to perpetuate the illusion of the monolingualism of their participants, while others simply do not know how to deal with the 'messiness' of bilingualism. Thus, the first aim of this volume is to introduce research designs that allow for rigorous examination of language and cognition in bilingual speakers.

Its second aim is to return to Sapir's and Whorf's original focus on everyday life and linguistic thought and to highlight a range of context-sensitive and ecologically valid methods of psycholinguistic inquiry. Consequently, the studies discussed here examine language and cognition, or thinking and speaking, in the bilingual mind across a range of verbal and non-verbal behaviors. The chapter by Athanasopoulos will focus on 'thinking' and thus more directly on the Whorfian ideas, the following two chapters, by Schmiedtová, v. Stutterheim and Carroll, and by Bylund, will involve 'thinking, seeing, and speaking'; the next chapter by Gullberg involves 'thinking, speaking and gesturing'; and the remaining two chapters by Malt and Ameel, and by Pavlenko, 'speaking' and more specifically, 'naming'.

These chapters depart from the usual scholarly genres – they are neither argumentative essays nor empirical studies proper. Rather, the contributors were invited to discuss the programmatic work that they – and their research teams – have been conducting on thinking and speaking in two languages and whose primary results have already appeared in peer-reviewed journals. Given the fact that these publications came out in a variety of disciplinary fields, and sometimes in languages other than English, we decided that it would be worthwhile to synthesize and analyze – and in some cases reanalyze – the results of the studies, thus engaging in a scholarly dialog that goes beyond a single study at a time.

To provide a social context for these chapters, I will begin by examining what bilinguals themselves say about thinking and speaking in two languages. To provide a historical context, I will then continue with an overview of ways in which the relationship between bilingualism and thought had been conceived of in the 20th century.

1.1 Thinking and Speaking in Two Languages: An Insider's View

One of the ways in which ecological validity is commonly established is to see whether the subject of inquiry is of interest and importance to the population in question. In the case of thinking and speaking in two languages, the answer appears to be a resounding 'yes'. Even the most superficial perusal of immigrant memoirs and bilinguals' autobiographies uncovers a wealth of reflections on thinking and speaking in two languages, with 'thinking' understood broadly as inner speech and as ways of perceiving, conceptualizing and framing objects, actions, events and phenomena.

In my own corpus of autobiographic writing by bi- and multilingual speakers, which includes texts in four languages (English, French, Spanish and Russian) and spans more than a century, these references appear throughout, starting with the turn of the 20th century memoirs of European immigrants who document the process of their assimilation in the USA (Pavlenko, 2004). For instance, Mary Antin, a Jewish woman whose family escaped tsarist Russia, writes joyfully in her celebrated autobiography, *The Promised Land*, that as a student at Barnard College, she 'learned at least to think in English without an accent' (Antin, 1912: 360). For Antin, this does not mean simply reaching a level of proficiency sufficient to express her thoughts – she talks about gaining new concepts, such as privacy (Antin, 1912: 289), and new perspectives, such as women's rights and individual fulfillment (Antin, 1912: 277).

Given the common theme of linguistic assimilation in immigrant and expatriate memoirs, it is not surprising that they paint a very similar trajectory where the new arrival continues to 'think' in the first language (L1) for a while and, only with time, shifts to 'thinking' in the second language (L2). Foreign language knowledge, on the other hand, does not appear to influence the thought process. For instance, Veronica Zhengdao Ye, a Chinese expatriate in Australia, states:

I had a fairly good command of basic English, but it had never influenced my way of thinking and experiencing the world until I moved to Australia. (Zhengdao Ye, 2007: 69)

According to bilinguals' autobiographies in my corpus, it is only when speakers move to the country where the language is spoken that this language begins to exert influence on their thinking, and even then the influence is not immediately apparent. A German immigrant in the USA, Gerda Lerner, recalls that in her first years in the country, she experienced a dissociation between her thinking processes and the language of the environment:

For nearly two years, I managed on that level of crude communication [in English], while my thoughts and dreams went on unperturbed in German. (Lerner, 1997: 35)

A similar reminiscence comes from Jade Snow Wong, who grew up in the USA speaking Chinese:

At this time [second year of college] Jade Snow still thought in Chinese, although she was acquiring an English vocabulary. (Wong, 1945: 132)

Eventually, however, the native language appears to suffer from disuse, and some immigrants, like the Polish-English bilingual, Eva Hoffman, experience what contemporary psycholinguists may characterize as deactivation or inhibition of the L1 and perhaps even language attrition, and the speakers themselves experience as an acute loss of inner speech:

The worst losses come at night. As I lie down in a strange bed in a strange house... I wait for that spontaneous flow of inner language which used to be my nighttime talk with myself... Nothing comes. Polish, in a short time, has atrophied, shriveled from sheer uselessness. Its words do not apply to my new experiences... (Hoffman, 1989: 107)

For Hoffman, inner speech is the key vehicle of thought and its loss is tantamount to losing an important means of interacting with one's environment, as important as the eyes are to visual and the ears to aural perception:

I understood how much our inner existence, our sense of self, depends on having a living speech within us. To lose an internal language is to subside into an inarticulate darkness in which we become alien to ourselves; to lose the ability to describe the world is to render that world a bit less vivid, a bit less lucid. And yet the richness of articulation gives the hues of subtlety and nuance to our perceptions and thought. (Hoffman, 1999: 48)

Hoffman is not alone in her experience of the in-between world where one language has vanished and the other has not yet stepped up to the plate. Elaine Mar and Helen Kim, who came to the USA as children of immigrant families, respectively, from China and Korea, recall a similar time in their teenage years, when being caught between languages meant not being able to render one's thoughts in either:

> I felt trapped inside my body. Language seemed a purely physical limitation. Thoughts existed inside my head, but I wasn't able to make them into words. (Mar, 1999: 66)

> At the age of twelve, I started writing poems and short stories in Korean, but I wasn't learning any more Korean, and my English wasn't good enough to describe the complex emotions I was beginning to experience. I remember sometime around age fourteen visualizing what I wanted to express and consciously leaving out the words because they were inadequate. (Kim, 2000: 122)

Similar to Kim, Zhengdao Ye experienced the in-between time as a competition between the two languages for control of the thought processes and also as a time of frustration when the precision of self-expression is getting lost in the native language and is not yet found in the newly learned one:

> the struggle between English and Chinese is constant. When speaking English, I may think in English, but only partially; the next moment, it flicks back to Chinese. Sometimes I get confused and the two languages merge – one on top of the other. I can hear myself speaking in English, but the substance seems to be in Chinese. It is my thoughts wrapped in a loose mantle of another language. I am desperate in trying to find the perfect fit, the best expression. But often, after a careful search of an array of synonyms, I still fret about that word. It pains, distresses, and angers me not being able to fully express myself in another language. (Zhengdao Ye, 2004: 138)

In their attempts to appropriate the new language, some immigrants may appeal to writing, oftentimes private writing, in the form of poetry or diaries. Hoffman (1989) talks about opening her first diary and forcing herself to make a decision between Polish, which was quickly becoming 'a dead language' (Hoffman, 1989: 120), and English, 'the language of the present, even if it's not the language of the self' (Hoffman, 1989: 121). 'My journals, which are filled with Korean, Konglish, bad English, and English, chronicle the frustration of this language transition', recalls Kim (2000: 122). Lerner (2002: 170) remembers writing poetry in English in order to bridge 'the difference between the German in which I thought and the English in which I attempted to write'. It is only with the passage of time and through deep immersion that the new language becomes the dominant language of immigrants' thoughts:

> It took several years before I began to think in English. It was exciting when it actually happened and it made a qualitative difference in the way I lived. I began to be able to express myself with the speed and precision characteristic of me and most of the time I could find the word I needed without resorting to a dictionary. (Lerner, 1997: 40)

This ability to fully express oneself cannot be captured by the dominant second language acquisition (SLA) constructs of fluency and proficiency, because it involves something that goes far beyond lexical richness or speedy lexical retrieval, namely, the skill of selecting the word, the expression, the perspective that fits the new circumstances best. In other words, the speakers have to adopt a new way of seeing and perceiving. Some, like the Spanish-English bilingual, Ariel Dorfman, may recall the exact day when they realized that they were thinking, unconsciously, in the new language:

> A day comes back to me – I must have been sixteen – the first time I realized that Spanish was beginning to speak me, had infiltrated my habits. It was in carpentry class and I had given a final clumsy bang with a hammer to a monstrous misshapen contraption I had built and it broke, fell apart right there, so I turned to the carpentry teacher and *"Se rompió"*, I said, shrugging my shoulders. His mouth had twisted in anger. *"Se, se, se."* he hissed. "Everything in this country is *se*, it broke, it just happened, why in the hell don't you say I broke it, I screwed up. Say it, say, *Yo lo rompí, yo, yo, yo*, take responsibility, boy." And all of a sudden I was a Spanish speaker, I was being berated for having used that form of the language to hide behind, I had automatically used that ubiquitous, impersonal *se*... (Dorfman, 1998: 114–115)

Eventually, this new language becomes not only the language of the outside, but also the language of the inner speech and communication with the self:

> When I talk to myself now, I talk in English. ...If I tried talking to myself in my native tongue, it would be a stumbling conversation indeed, interlaced with English expressions. So at those moments when I am alone, walking, or letting my thoughts meander before falling asleep, the internal dialogue proceeds in English. (Hoffman, 1989: 272)

For immigrants, this achievement may come at the price of a loss – the loss of the native language as a meaningful vehicle of thought, emotion and communication (Pavlenko, 1998). This loss, so acutely felt by

Hoffman (1989), is also mourned by Lerner, who recalls her inability to communicate in German, the family language, with her sister Nora:

> I no longer thought in German and therefore could not express anything significant in that language. I lacked the facility, I said. I would often start a letter to Nora in German and give it up after a few lines, switching to English. (Lerner, 1997: 44)

For Kyoko Mori, who was born and grew up in Japan but now resides in the USA, this inability to translate oneself into her native Japanese became the dominant source of anxiety during her visits to Japan:

> Trying to speak Japanese in Japan, I'm still thinking in English. I can't turn off what I really want to say and concentrate on what is appropriate. Flustered, I try to work out a quick translation, but my feelings are untranslatable and my voice is the voice of a foreigner. The whole experience reminds me of studying French in college and being unable to say or write what I thought. (Mori, 1997: 17)

It is not surprising that the transition from one 'language of thought' to another is acutely perceived and dramatically described by the global nomads – immigrants, travelers, expatriates – who change languages as teenagers or adults and witness all the stages of this transition. Yet, the relationship between languages and thought is also pondered on by childhood bilinguals who, like Julian Green, bilingual in French and English, wonder: 'Does one think in the same way in both languages and in terms, which are, so to speak, interchangeable?' (1993 [1941]: 83). His own experience provides a negative answer to the question. In particular, Green recalls a time when he started writing an autobiography in French, only to shift to English because he found an English-language publisher. Shortly afterward, he realized that he was

> writing another book, a book so different in tone from the French that a whole aspect of the subject must of necessity be altered. It was as if, writing in English, I had become another person. I went on. New trains of thought were started in my mind, new associations of ideas were formed. There was so little resemblance between what I wrote in English and what I had already written in French that it might almost be doubted that the same person was the author of these two pieces of work. (Green, 1993 [1941]: 62)

His experience mirrors that of other bilingual writers and scholars who learned their second languages later in life and found themselves writing the same book or the same paper differently in different languages (Todorov, 1994; Ward Jouve, 1991). It also reflects the experience of writers, like the Spanish-English bilingual, Rosario Ferré, or the French-Spanish bilingual, Claude Esteban, who grew up with two languages and perceive themselves as different people and different writers in these languages:

> Writing in English is like looking at the world through a different pair of binoculars: It imposes a different mind-set. (Ferré in Kellman, 2003: 138)

> Non, je n'étais pas le même, dès lors que je m'exprimais en français et en espagnol, et il me fallait vivre avec ce dédoublement de la conscience, des mots, des gestes de chaque jour, sans parvenir jamais à les réduire.

> [No, I was not the same when I expressed myself in French and Spanish, and I have had to live with this doubling of consciousness, words, everyday gestures, without being able to reduce them.] (here and further on author's translation; Esteban, 2004)

What are we to make of these disquisitions about ways in which languages shape – and re-shape – thought? Long ago, a prominent North American psychologist, Roger Brown, advocated mistrust in such testimony from bilinguals because 'there is a familiar inclination on the part of those who possess unusual and arduously obtained experience to exaggerate its remoteness from anything the rest of us know' (Brown, 1958: 233). Following his argument, we could dismiss these statements as individual affectations or exaggerations – if not for the systematicity with which the theme of different languages linked to different ways of thinking reappears across time and space.

One could also argue that the views of people without academic training on such a complicated subject as thought are simply uninformed and unsophisticated. And yet, this argument does not hold because self-reports linking languages with different ways of thinking come also from linguists (e.g. Wierzbicka, 1985, 1997) and from bilingual writers, who spend even more time than linguists thinking about ways in which different sets of words and structures capture, transform and distort the reality that they are trying to convey. Miller (1996: 275) argues that as writers, they 'have needed to develop knowledge about language and, as a rule, an ear for its meanings that is more acute and subtler than that possessed by the rest of us'.

Alternatively, we could try to dismiss their views as a writerly trope – if not for the fact that this trope emerges not only in the work of writers, but also in the testimonies of scholars and laypeople from a variety of linguistic and socioeconomic backgrounds. For instance, several respondents to the questionnaire that Jean-Marc Dewaele and I have administered on-line to 1039 bi- and multilinguals, replied along the same lines:

> Yes when I am in the country where the language is spoken. I think differently. (Monica, 33, Italian-French-English-Spanish-Amharic) (Pavlenko, 2006: 13)

> Different languages allow me different thought structures and possibly different ways of feeling too. (Erica, 38, German-English) (Pavlenko, 2006: 24)

Thus, I side with Haiman, who sees great intrinsic value in bilinguals' self-reports:

> From a scientific point of view, using native testimonials is perhaps like "making an elephant a professor of zoology", but it may be that on this kind of subject "elephants" who do not pretend to transcend their species are more reliable authorities than "human professors of zoology" who delude themselves that they are able to transcend theirs. To put this another way, the inner self is a subject that can be approached only from within. (Haiman, 2005: 114–115)

These reports 'from within' tell us that for many, albeit not all, bi- and multilinguals, a change in the language of interaction results in changes in self-expression and ultimately in ways of seeing and perceiving (Pavlenko, 2006). From this perspective, in the view of Pérez-Firmat:

> the ultimate validity of the Sapir-Whorf hypothesis is irrelevant. What is crucial is that many bilinguals relate to their languages in ways that enact some version of this hypothesis. (Pérez-Firmat, 2003: 13)

What this means, in other words, is that for many bi- and multilingual speakers, both the idea of linguistic determinism and the opposition to linguistic relativity are absurd because their own linguistic experience illuminates ways in which languages shape and affect thought and, simultaneously, provides an escape from these influences through the learning and use of additional languages. Consequently, as already mentioned earlier, this volume will side-step the linguistic relativity debate and explore instead the linguistic and cognitive processes that lead so many speakers to live out linguistic relativity as their everyday reality. To ensure the success of this research venture, it is critical to understand why two previous attempts to engage in the study of bi- and multilingualism and thought – Epstein (1915) and Ervin(-Tripp) (1954, 1964, 1967) – did not generate any follow-ups. In what follows, I will consider these studies in their historical and sociopolitical contexts.

1.2   Bilingualism and Thought in the 20th Century: 1900s–1940s

The idea that languages are linked to the culture and possibly even thought of their speakers is by no means new – it achieved prominence in the 18th century in the work conducted within the Western Classical and German Romantic traditions by Leibniz, Herder and, most notably,

Wilhelm von Humboldt (1767–1835) (Allan, 2007; Joseph, 2002; Koerner, 2002). It was Humboldt who permanently linked languages with world views [Weltanschauung], arguing that 'the differences between languages are not those of sounds and signs but those of differing world views' (1836, translated in Humboldt, 1963: 246).

Humboldt's views, shared by other 19th and early 20th-century scholars, such as Steinthal, Whitney and Boas, inspired the first systematic scholarly investigation of the relationship between multilingualism and thought – Izhac Epstein's (1862–1943) doctoral dissertation, *La pensée et la polyglossie* (Epstein, 1915), carried out at the University of Lausanne. The key research questions posited in the study involved the relationship between multilingualism and thought, with the latter operationalized as different types of mental operations, including inner speech, mental translation and calculations. The data collected by the researcher included: (a) a study of school students' perception and memory for foreign language words; (b) responses to a questionnaire distributed to 23 multilingual participants in and outside Switzerland; and (c) the author's introspections and observations of other multilingual children and adults. The questions asked in the questionnaire touched on perceptions of translation (non-)equivalence in the respondents' languages, crosslinguistic influence, verbal imagery invoked by particular languages, language choice, language of mental calculations and the language of the participants' dreams. Epstein (1915: 11) also directly asked: 'Pensez-vous quelquefois en langue étrangère et à quelle occasion?' [Do you ever think in a foreign language and when (on what occasion)?]. His underlying assumption was that 'chaque peuple a une façon particulière et caractéristique de grouper, afin de les nommer, les choses et leurs propriétés, les actes et les rapports' [every nation has a particular and characteristic manner of grouping things and their properties, actions and relations, in order to name them] (Epstein, 1915: 115) and that these differences may affect multilinguals' thought processes.

Using his data, largely consisting of self-reports, Epstein (1915) concluded that multilinguals associate languages with particular people, contexts and domains, and spontaneously adjust inner speech, or the language of the mental dialog, depending on the topic, and imagined settings and interlocutors. Mental calculations, he found, are conducted in the L1 or in the language in which mathematical instruction took place. Regarding learning modes, he argued that if foreign languages are learned in communicative settings, 'les diverses langues peuvent, chez le polyglotte, s'associer chacune directement à la pensée et fonctionner, sous toutes les formes impressives et expressives, indépendamment de Lm' [different languages may, in a multilingual, attach themselves directly to thought and function, in all modes of perception and expression, independently of the mother tongue] (Epstein, 1915: 35). In contrast, languages learned through the grammar-translation method will be attached to translation equivalents and require mental translation. The type of linkage will depend on the instruction method, the level of proficiency (direct linkage requiring a higher level of proficiency), the mode of expression (direct linkage being more common in speaking) and individual differences. Furthermore, even when multilinguals 'think' in the L2, they may borrow terms from the L1 that are non-existent in the L2.

While Epstein's (1915) views of what constitutes 'thought' and linguistic influences on thought were not particularly sophisticated, some of his ideas about bilingualism appear strikingly contemporary. His views of the relationship between the L1, the L2 and the conceptual store are reminiscent of later distinctions between coordinate and subordinate bilingualism, his ideas about 'une influence négative ou inhibitrice' of the previous language of conversation in the case of an abrupt language change predate by almost a century our notions of language activation and inhibition, while his reflections about 'l'interférence' and 'l'intercalation' invoke our own ideas about language transfer, code-switching and lexical borrowing. To assist the formation of direct links between 'thoughts' and L2 words, Epstein (1915) advocated the Direct Method that had eliminated translation exercises and the mother tongue of the pupils from the classroom, and this recommendation, once again, is echoed in later support for immersion approaches.

The parallels with contemporary thinking on the interaction between languages render the conclusion reached by Epstein (1915) at the end of his monumental thesis a complete surprise to the present-day reader. Arguing that bilingualism slows down the thought process through activation of alternative options available in other languages, Epstein (1915: 210) concluded that 'La polyglossie est une plaie sociale' [Multilingualism is a social ill]. Consequently, his recommendation was to limit foreign language instruction to reading and basic everyday expressions, the only two skills an educated person really needed. And since bilingualism could be particularly harmful for young children whose thought processes were still developing, his recommendation was to begin foreign language instruction in later childhood, at an age experimentally determined. Regarding instruction per se, he recommended an oral beginning followed by a greater engagement with literary modes.

Surprising to us, the conclusion reached by Epstein (1915) was in line with the Western European trend of the era to see bilingualism – at least that of the lower classes and ethnic minorities – as an intellectual impediment and a site of a cognitive, linguistic and emotional conflict. A negative view of bilingualism was particularly prominent in multilingual countries and areas torn by language conflicts, such as Belgium,

Catalonia, Czechoslovakia, Luxembourg, Switzerland and Wales, where arguments about the negative cognitive consequences of bilingualism were martialled in defense of particular nationalist positions and educational curricula (for discussion, see Weinreich, 1953: 71–73, 115–122). In Belgium, for instance, monolingual Flemish and Walloon children were shown to outperform French-Flemish bilinguals (Toussaint, 1935). Similarly, in Wales several studies documented the superior test performance of monolingual children over Welsh-English bilinguals, providing support for English-only instruction (Saer, 1924; Saer *et al.*, 1924; Smith, 1923). Among the key arguments in these studies were the monolinguals' superior 'accuracy of thought' (Smith, 1923: 282) and delays caused by the recall of alternate word symbols in the two languages (Saer, 1924: 38). Concerns about bilingualism were also expressed by Jespersen, one of the best-known European linguists of the era:

> It is, of course, an advantage for a child to be familiar with two languages: but without doubt the advantage may be, and generally is, purchased too dear. First of all the child in question hardly learns either of the two languages as perfectly as he would have done if he had limited himself to one. It may seem, on the surface, as if he talked just like a native, but he does not really command the fine points of the language. Has any bilingual child ever developed into a great artist in speech, a poet, or orator? (Jespersen, 1922: 148)

In Nazi Germany, bilingualism, associated with Jews, Poles and other ethnic minorities, was seen as a cause of 'mercenary relativism', intellectual deterioration and mental inferiority (Henss, 1931; Müller, 1934; Sander, 1934; Schmidt-Rohr, 1933; Weisgerber, 1933). Sander, for instance, adopted a Humboldtian view of languages as embodiments of different world views to make the following argument:

> Bilingualism leads not only to harmless speech errors, but it goes deeper, especially when it is imposed by force in early childhood, and endangers the closed and self-centered wholeness of the developing structure... Every language establishes, as an articulated system, a very definite, relatively uniform and closed orientation of perception, feeling, and thinking in those who speak it. The consequence [of bilingualism in children] is that the inner attitudes which are conditioned by language will not stand unconnectedly beside one another, but will enter into conflicting tensions in the child's soul... This functional opposition of two language formations can lead to shake-ups of the structure. (Sander, 1934, translated by Weinreich, 1953: 119–120)

The only exception was made for the harmless bilingualism of German-speaking children who learned a dialect at home and the standard at school (Schmidt-Rohr, 1933).

In the USA, immigrant and minority children were also considered to be in particular 'danger' of a bilingual upbringing (Hakuta, 1986; Weinreich, 1953: 115–118). This view is best understood within the context of the dramatic demographic changes that took place between 1880 and 1924. During this period, often termed the Great Migration, approximately 24 million immigrants entered the USA. This overwhelming influx of new arrivals raised numerous concerns about national unity and the capacity of the American society to assimilate such a large body of newcomers (Pavlenko, 2002). The First World War further heightened the sense of American nationalism and highlighted the persistence of Old World ties among the European-born immigrants, including but not limited to language. And when in 1917 the USA declared war on Germany, the anti-immigrant sentiments found an outlet in a strong anti-German movement.

Prior to the war, German speakers were among the most numerous and visible immigrants; as a result, German was a widespread language of literature, newspapers and theater in immigrant communities and also the most widely taught foreign language (Pavlenko, 2002; Schlossman, 1983; Wiley, 1998). German-medium instruction also attracted Central and Eastern European immigrants who spoke German, while German-English bilingual programs drew in children from non-German-speaking families (Schlossman, 1983). By 1917, however, German became 'the language of the enemy': German books were removed from libraries and destroyed, German-language theaters and publications closed and German speakers became subject to threats, intimidations and beatings (Luebke, 1980; Pavlenko, 2002; Wiley, 1998). Together with the Americanization movement, these developments precipitated a rapid shift to English within many immigrant communities.

The advisability of German instruction in US schools was also in question and some educators argued that there was no place in American education for the language that upheld the Teutonic philosophy that 'prides in its inhumanity' (Gordy, 1918: 262). Gordy (1918) also argued that American students should be protected from other languages that could 'contaminate' them, notably Russian, Japanese, Chinese and Italian. These attitudes were amplified in the pamphlets of the American Defense League, which asserted that a 'language which produces a people of ruthless conquestadors [sic] such as now exists in Germany, is not a fit language to teach clean and pure American boys and girls' (Luebke, 1980: 5).

Not surprisingly, many prominent American intellectuals – some of them foreign born – stood up in defense of German and other foreign languages (Barnes, 1918). As a result, foreign languages retained their positions in high schools and colleges, but gave way at the elementary level, where the children were judged to be most vulnerable. Incidentally, this was also the level at which 80% of the students ended their education (Gordy, 1918), thus making foreign language instruction an upper-class privilege. Between 1917 and 1922, Alabama, Colorado, Delaware, Iowa, Nebraska, Oklahoma and South Dakota passed legislation that prohibited foreign language instruction in grades I through VIII; Wisconsin and Minnesota restricted it to one hour a day; and Louisiana, Indiana and Ohio made the teaching of German illegal at the elementary level, as did several cities with large German-speaking populations (Luebke, 1980; Pavlenko, 2002). And as time went by, North American scholars, just like their European colleagues, 'identified' adverse effects of bilingualism on children's cognitive development (e.g. Smith, 1931, 1939; Spoerl, 1943; Yoshioka, 1929).

It is in this public climate, hostile to bilingualism in general and to German in particular, that two German immigrants in the USA,[1] Franz Boas and Edward Sapir, articulated their ideas about the relationship between language, culture and thought. Drawing on the German Romantic tradition of Herder, Humboldt and Steinthal, Boas (1858–1942) argued that cultures are reflected in the languages of their speakers and that

> the groups of ideas expressed by specific phonetic groups show very material differences in different languages, and do not conform by any means to the same principle of classification. (Boas, 1966a [1911]: 21)

Humans, however, are unaware of the ways in which their languages classify experience differently because of the automatic nature of language use:

> the categories of language compel us to see the world arranged in certain definite conceptual groups which, on account of our lack of knowledge of linguistic processes, are taken as objective categories, and which, therefore, impose themselves upon the form of our thoughts. (Boas, 1966b [1920]: 289)

Boas' student at Columbia, Sapir (1884–1939), shared his ideas about cultural influences on language and about implicit classification of experience and showed ways in which vocabularies reflect the social environments of the speakers and aspects of the physical environments important to them (e.g. Sapir, 1949 [1912]). Sapir also went further than Boas, arguing that linguistic classifications reflected and channeled thought, whereby the relativity of concepts could be called 'the relativity of the form of thought' (Sapir, 1949 [1924]: 159). His fullest statement of what came to be seen as linguistic relativity appeared in his well-known paper 'The status of linguistics as a science':

> Language is a guide to "social reality". Though language is not ordinarily thought of as of essential interest to the students of social science, it powerfully conditions all our thinking about social problems and processes. Human beings do not live in the objective world alone, nor alone in the world of social activity as ordinarily understood, but are very much at the mercy of the particular language which has become the medium of expression for their society. It is quite an illusion to imagine that one adjusts to reality essentially without the use of language and that language is merely an incidental means of solving specific problems of communication or reflection. The fact of the matter is that the "real world" is to a large extent unconsciously built up on the language habits of the group. No two languages are ever sufficiently similar to be considered as representing the same social reality. The worlds in which different societies live are distinct worlds, not merely the same world with different labels attached. ... We see and hear and otherwise experience very largely as we do because the language habits of our community predispose certain choices of interpretation. (Sapir, 1949 [1929]: 162)

Having articulated this view, Sapir carefully tried to avoid any oversimplification of his ideas, pointing out, for instance, that the absence in a language of formal devices that express causal relations is not in any way indicative of the speakers' ability to conceive of and express causation as such (Sapir, 1949 [1924]: 155).

Benjamin Lee Whorf (1897–1941), who studied with Sapir at Yale, articulated a more precise approach to the study of the influence of language on thought, illustrating it with detailed case studies. His own version of the linguistic relativity principle states that

> users of markedly different grammars are pointed by their grammars towards different types of observations and different evaluations of externally similar acts of observation, and hence are not equivalent as observers but must arrive at somewhat different views of the world. (Whorf, 1956 [1940]: 221)

This statement shows that, on the linguistic side, Whorf was primarily interested in grammar, or structural patterns, and on the cognitive side, 'in the fundamental conceptual ideas habitually used by speakers of those languages' (Lucy, 1992a: 39). To specify the scope of linguistic influence, Whorf developed new conceptualizations of grammatical categories: overt categories marked systematically (e.g. plurals) and covert categories marked only in certain contexts (e.g. intransitive verbs). He was also interested in the lexicon: in fact, several of Whorf's (1956 [1941]) famous examples of the influence of language on habitual thought involve lexical items that obfuscate a potentially dangerous situation for English speakers: 'empty gasoline drums' perceived as harmless even though they contain explosive vapor, 'limestone' coverings perceived as incombustible because they contain 'stone', or 'a blower' whose perceived function is to blow air but which can also blow flames and sparks.[2]

The contributions of Humboldt, Boas, Sapir and Whorf to the debate on language and thought are well known and have been summarized, examined and discussed in numerous sources (e.g. Joseph, 2002; Koerner, 2002; Lee, 1996; Lucy, 1992a). What remains unexamined and puzzling is the fact that these scholars – bi- or multilingual themselves[3] – said so little about the interaction of two or more languages in a single mind. One of the more precise statements describing this relationship can be found in Humboldt's work:

> each language draws a circle around the people to whom it adheres which it is possible for the individual to escape only by stepping into a different one. The learning of a foreign language should therefore mean the gaining of a new standpoint toward one's world-view, and it does this in fact to a considerable degree, because each language contains the entire conceptual web and mental images of a part of humanity. If it is not always purely felt as such, the reason is only that one so frequently projects one's own world-view, in fact one's own speech habits, onto a foreign language. (Humboldt, 1836: LXVI; translated in Humboldt, 1963: 294)

Boas (1966a [1911]: 55–59) underscored the need for ethnologists to have command of American Indian languages, because information received through interpreters may not reflect the local point of view. As to Sapir, all I have been able to locate is the cryptic paragraph, cited earlier and preceded by an image of a poor man who 'is haunted by the form-feeling of another language and is subtly driven to the unconscious distortion of the one speech-system on the analogy of the other' (Sapir, 1949 [1924]: 153). Whorf was not particularly vocal on the subject either. His comments show that he believed that one could understand alternative world views through learning and/or analysis of other languages and that he found such metalinguistic awareness extremely beneficial (see also Lee, 1996). In one case, he ends his comparative analysis of English, Shawnee and Nootka by stating that 'we handle even our plain English with much greater effect if we direct it from the vantage point of a multilingual awareness' (Whorf, 1956 [1941]: 244). It is not clear, however, at what point such multilingual awareness may kick in or what it may mean for the everyday thought processes of a multilingual individual.

Despite their brevity, these remarks show that neither Sapir nor Whorf entertained the idea of languages determining world views – both saw human minds as capable of acquiring new perspectives and frames of reference through learning of additional languages. If they had said more, then perhaps scientists would not have wasted decades debating the idea of linguistic determinism. But they didn't and we might never know the exact reasons why. It is possible that they considered this view obvious and thus did not deem further elaboration or inquiry worthy of their time and attention. It is also possible that the anti-German climate of the inter-war USA discouraged explicit engagement with bilingualism on the part of German-Americans, such as Boas and Sapir. Darnell (1990: 168), in her biography of Sapir, mentions that Boasians were commonly perceived as Germans or German sympathizers. It is also possible that these scholars may have been concerned about the interpretation of their ideas about bilingualism by the non-academic audience. The discussion above shows that such concern would have been fully legitimate – both in Western Europe and in North America, the opponents of bilingualism did argue that alternative thinking patterns made available by respective languages slow down thought processes, create mental confusion and conflict, and 'contaminate' thinking.

1.3 Bilingualism and Thought in the 20th Century: 1950s–1990s

Now, given the anti-deterministic stance in both Sapir's and Whorf's writings, how did the idea of linguistic determinism come into existence? By the 1950s, Sapir and Whorf were gone, but their publications became widely available through newly published collections (Sapir, 1949; Whorf, 1956). These collections – as well as previous publications that were already widely circulated – inspired the new field of psycholinguistics that came together through a series of summer seminars sponsored by the Social Science Research Council (Osgood & Sebeok, 1954). Yet, there was a major problem in dealing with Sapir's and Whorf's ideas – the two were linguistic anthropologists, not experimental psychologists, and it had never occurred to them to put forth testable hypotheses. The follow-up discussion attempted to correct this 'oversight' and to 'systematize' the ideas, an attempt that led to the development of the Sapir-Whorf hypothesis.

Because many of the scholars engaged in the initial discussion interacted with each other in ethnolinguistic and psycholinguistic forums, the authorship of the Sapir-Whorf hypothesis appears to be distributed. The term 'the Sapir-Whorf hypothesis' was used in a conference paper by Hoijer (1954) and then adopted and popularized by Carroll (1956: 27) and others (Koerner, 2002). The term 'linguistic determinism' appears to have been put forth – or at least made its first prominent appearance – in Brown's (1958) book, in the chapter entitled 'Linguistic relativity and determinism'.[4] Brown and his pupil, Eric Heinz Lenneberg, incidentally another German-American uninterested in bilingualism, have also made a major contribution toward articulating the determinism/relativity dichotomy and translating Sapir's and Whorf's ideas into testable research designs and hypotheses (Brown, 1958; Brown & Lenneberg, 1954; Lenneberg, 1953).

These attempts have undoubtedly played an important role in moving the study of language and cognition forward. At the same time, in their haste to make complex linguistic notions fit experimental paradigms in psychology, Lenneberg (1953), Brown (1958) and their followers departed from the original arguments in three important ways (see also Lee, 1996; Lucy, 1992a). To begin with, they shifted the focus of the inquiry from interpretive categories of thought or concepts to cognitive processes, such as perception or memory, which Sapir and Whorf were not particularly interested in, and to domains, such as color, that had only a tenuous relationship to the original idea of Weltanschauung or world view. Secondly, they privileged the idea of thought potential (and, by implication, what *can* be said) over Whorf's concerns with habitual thought (and thus by definition with what *is* said). Most importantly, they replaced relativity as a way of thinking about languages with the 'testable' idea of linguistic determinism, which does not appear in either Sapir's or Whorf's writings. The resulting 'strong' determinism/'weak' relativity dichotomy should have been rightly called the Brown–Lenneberg hypothesis because it had little in common with Sapir's and Whorf's ideas about language and thought.

However, the new hypothesis had one major advantage – it was much easier to digest and argue about than the original work, and the resulting uptake was almost immediate. Black (1959: 236) still acknowledges that the idea of determinism may not come from Whorf and states: 'I have chosen to say "partially determines" in both cases [conceptual system and associated world-view], though it is hard to decide what Whorf's final opinion was about the relation'. Yet, Gastil (1959), writing in the same year, does not offer such a caveat when discussing linguistic determinism. Fishman's (1960: 336) attempt to 'systematize' Whorf's ideas, states that 'the impact of language *determinism* on cognition ought to be more pervasive and more difficult to counteract than that of language *relativity*'. Soon, the newly minted Sapir-Whorf hypothesis took on a life of its own, multiplying and reproducing itself in myriads of psychology textbooks, linguistics articles, introductory lectures and popular media, and moving the discussion further and further away from Sapir's primary interest in 'social reality' and Whorf's central concern with linguistic categories and 'habitual thought'.

An intriguing feature of the publications of that period is the tension in articulating the relationship between bilingualism and linguistic relativity. In Brown's (1958: 232) view, the presence of 'numerous bilingual persons and countless translated documents' serves as evidence that the German mind is 'very like our own'. He has a little more difficulty dealing with those who are bilingual in Native American languages, especially because these bilinguals 'have often said that thinking is different in the Indian language' (Brown, 1958: 232). In this case – as already mentioned earlier – Brown's recommendation is to distrust those who have the 'unusual' characteristic of being bilingual:

> There are few bilinguals, after all, and the testimony of those few cannot be uncritically accepted. There is a familiar inclination on the part of those who possess unusual and arduously obtained experience to exaggerate its remoteness from anything the rest of us know. This must be taken into account when evaluating the impressions of students of Indian languages. In fact, it might be best to translate freely with the Indian languages, assimilating their minds to our own. (Brown, 1958: 233)

The tendency to use mutual translatability of languages and bilingualism as phenomena that refute linguistic relativity has persisted ever since. Macnamara (1970, 1991) repeatedly argued that if the Whorfian hypothesis were true, bilinguals would be doomed, having to conform to one of the three patterns: (a) 'think' in language A when speaking either A or B, and as a result fail to understand or be understood by speakers of language B; (b) 'think' in a 'hybrid' manner, appropriate to neither language, and risk understanding no one and being understood by no one; (c) 'think' differently depending on the language used and as a result having difficulties in communicating with themselves and in translating into one language what was said in another. In a later paper, Macnamara (1991) took a less radical view and suggested that in the third case, bilinguals would be able to translate and to communicate with speakers of either language. Nevertheless, he argued that these implications ran afoul of the guiding principles of natural language semantics: whatever can be expressed in one language, can be translated into another.

Paradis (1979), in his reply to Macnamara (1970), argued that the first two options and difficulties with translation are indeed the case, and that none of the three cases could be used to refute the Whorfian hypothesis *ad absurdo*. The first case, described by Macnamara, refers to the phenomenon of L1 transfer that may indeed impede cross-cultural communication. The second case is reminiscent of speakers who develop categories distinct from those of the L1 and the L2, as is commonly seen in contact varieties. The third case describes bicultural bilinguals who adjust their linguistic and conceptual repertoires, depending on their interlocutor and, as we have seen earlier, experience difficulties in translation and communication with the self.

A different view of bilingualism appeared in the influential state-of-the-art survey of the emerging discipline of psycholinguistics (Osgood & Sebeok, 1954), collectively authored by some of the most prominent linguists, psychologists and anthropologists of the era. Walker *et al.* (1954: 201), who co-authored the section on language, culture and cognition, stated that bilingual individuals constitute 'an exceptionally favorable ground for testing this [Whorfian] hypothesis', and put forth hypotheses that might be tested in bilinguals (e.g. differences between compound and coordinate bilinguals) and research design proposals (e.g. semantic differential scales, verbal responses to non-verbal stimuli and the Thematic Apperception Test (TAT)). This acknowledgment should not, however, be interpreted as a sign of a general interest in bilingualism on the part of the North American psycholinguistic community. Rather, these ideas and research design proposals are easily traced to a single member of the group that authored the monograph, the only member who was, at the time, interested in bilingualism and engaged in bilingualism research, the young scholar Susan Ervin.

Ervin's ideas were further developed in the section of the report co-authored by Ervin and Osgood (1954), which reframed Weinreich's (1953) arguments about the organization of the bilingual mind. Trying to capture the relationship between languages and concepts, Weinreich (1953) suggested that there are three basic types of bilingual memory – coexistent, merged and subordinative – and that representations could be different for different individuals and even for different words within an individual's vocabulary. Ervin and Osgood (1954) changed the terms to 'coordinate', 'compound' and 'subordinate', and linked them to language learning histories, and it is their definitions that have been adopted by the field. Coordinate bilinguals, in this view, are speakers who learned their languages in distinct environments and have two conceptual systems associated with their two lexicons. Compound bilinguals learned their languages in a single environment and, conse-quently, have a single underlying and undifferentiated conceptual system linked to the two lexicons. In turn, subordinate bilinguals, typically classroom learners who learned the L2 via the L1, have a single system where the L2 lexicon is linked to conceptual representations through the L1 words. Ervin and Osgood (1954) also argued that only coordinate bilinguals can provide truly cross-cultural translation, yet the translation process would be marred by difficulties, because translation equivalents may have contextual or connotational differences and non-equivalents may have only partially adequate translations.

Lambert and associates (Jacobovits & Lambert, 1961; Lambert *et al.*, 1958; Lambert & Rawlings, 1969) soon provided empirical support for these hypotheses, showing that coordinate bilinguals made more semantic distinctions between translation equivalents, had relatively independent association networks linked to translation equivalents, and experienced greater difficulty with translation than compound and subordinate bilinguals. Other studies, however, did not find any differences between compound and coordinate bilinguals (e.g. Kolers, 1963) and, as time went by, the focus of psycholinguistic inquiry in the field of bilingualism shifted from the contents of conceptual categories to lexical processing (for an informative overview of the history of this research, see Keatley, 1992). Lambert and associates also undertook studies of the influence of bilingualism on cognitive development, legitimizing this area of research and turning it into a thriving area of study, in particular in Canadian academia (e.g. Bain & Yu, 1980; Bialystok, 2001; Lambert, 1972).

Meanwhile, Ervin(-Tripp) – four decades after Epstein's (1915) initial inquiry – carried out several empirical studies that directly tested the relationship between languages and thought in bilingual speakers, with thought operationalized as ways of classifying and interpreting non-verbal and verbal stimuli. Ervin(-Tripp) developed a research design where bilinguals were tested twice on the same set of materials – TAT cards, semantic differentials, word associations, and sentence and story completion tasks, with the sessions in their respective languages taking place six weeks apart. Her studies with Japanese-English (Ervin, 1954; Ervin-Tripp, 1967) and French-English (Ervin-Tripp, 1964) bilinguals showed that the content of the responses shifted with the change in language. The researcher put forth a number of explanations for her findings, including differences in prominent cultural themes, but also possible language influence on the classification of the stimuli and resulting differences in recall of past experiences in the language in question (Ervin-Tripp, 1964). She also conducted studies of color vocabu-lary, showing that Navaho-English bilinguals' color categories differed from those of monolingual speakers of English and Navaho (Ervin, 1961).

Despite the interest generated by Ervin(-Tripp)'s studies, they did not inspire much uptake or follow-up. The rise of Chomskian linguistics with its innatist view of language and the search for universals spelled the demise of the Whorfian hypothesis. By the 1970s, Whorfianism 'has become a bête noire, identified with scholarly irresponsibility, fuzzy thinking, lack of rigor, and even immorality' (Lakoff, 1987: 304). The study of bilingualism, thriving by then in Europe and Canada, also did not generate much interest in the USA, the country that continued to imagine itself as staunchly monolingual. And Ervin-Tripp moved on, to study child language development.

1.4 Conclusions

The late 1980s and early 1990s witnessed a renewed interest in linguistic relativity and in Sapir's and Whorf's original ideas, seen in the work of Lakoff (1987), Lucy (1992a, 1992b), Slobin (1996, 2000, 2001), Levinson (1996, 1997, 2003) and their associates. This work engendered a heated debate, with strident opposition to neo-Whorfianism from several prominent linguists and psychologists (e.g. Li & Gleitman, 2002; Pinker, 1994, 2007). This debate has continued ever since with – once again – nary a thought given to the relationship between languages and thought in multilingual minds (but see Green, 1998; Hunt & Agnoli, 1991; Pavlenko, 1999, for concerns over the field's disregard for bilinguals).

It is only in the past decade that we have witnessed the beginning of a more focused and systematic examination of thinking and speaking in speakers of more than one language. This volume brings together the first results of a systematic inquiry that has rejected the artificial agenda created by Brown and Lenneberg and firmly placed linguistic thought, verbal processes – and bilingualism – at the center of the inquiry and not at the apologetic fringe.

Acknowledgments

I am deeply grateful to Panos Athanasopoulos, Colin Baker, Sarah Grosik, Scott Jarvis, John Lucy, Barbara Malt, Monika Schmid and students in my Bilingual Mind class for their critical and constructive feedback on this chapter. All remaining errors are exclusively my own.

Notes

1. This common perception of Boas and Sapir is, in fact, somewhat over-simplified. Boas, who came to the USA at the age of 29, was a German-speaking Jew who left Germany partially because of the rising anti-semitism, and Sapir, whose family settled in the USA when he was 6 years old, was a child of Yiddish-speaking Lithuanian Jews from Lauenberg, an area of Prussia that now belongs to Poland (Darnell, 1990).
2. Unfortunately, these examples have been misinterpreted by Lenneberg (1953), Pinker (1994) and others as arguments for language as the sole causal factor in the interpretation. In fact, Whorf had never intended such a reading, and in a letter to his editor, he considered adding a footnote explaining that language is not the sole or leading factor in the type of fire-causing behaviors he mentioned, but one of several factors (Lee, 1996: 153).
3. Sapir, for instance, dedicated himself to the study of languages from his earliest years. Trilingual in Yiddish, Hebrew and English, in high school and in college he had studied Latin, Greek, German, French and Spanish, as well as an array of other languages, and then proceeded to work on Native American languages (Darnell, 1990).
4. I thank John Lucy for suggesting Brown's (1958) book as a possible first instance of the appearance of the term.

References

Allan, K. (2007) *The Western Classical Tradition in Linguistics*. London: Equinox.

Antin, M. (1912, reprinted in 1969) *The Promised Land*. Princeton, NJ: Princeton University Press.

Bain, B. and Yu, A. (1980) Cognitive consequences of raising children bilingually: 'One parent, one language'. *Canadian Journal of Psychology* 34, 304–313.

Barnes, F. (1918) Shall German be dropped from our schools? *Modern Language Journal* 2, 187–202.

Bialystok, E. (2001) *Bilingualism in Development: Language, Literacy, and Cognition*. Cambridge: Cambridge University Press.

Black, M. (1959) Linguistic relativity: The views of Benjamin Lee Whorf. *Philosophical Review* 68, 228–238.

Boas, F. (1911, reprinted in 1966a) Introduction. In F. Boas (ed.) *Handbook of American Indian Languages* (pp. 1–79) (reprint edited by P. Holder). Lincoln, NE: University of Nebraska Press.

Boas, F. (1920, reprinted in 1966b) The methods of ethnology. In F. Boas (ed.) *Race, Language, and Culture* (pp. 281–289). New York: The Free Press/Macmillan.

Boroditsky, L. (2001) Does language shape thought? Mandarin and English speakers' conceptions of time. *Cognitive Psychology* 43, 1–22.

Brown, R. (1958) *Words and Things*. Glencoe, IL: The Free Press.

Brown, R. and Lenneberg, E. (1954) A study in language and cognition. *Journal of Abnormal and Social Psychology* 49, 454–462.

Carroll, J. (1956) Introduction. In J. Carroll (ed.) *Language, Thought, and Reality: Selected Writings of Benjamin Lee Whorf* (pp. 1–34). Cambridge, MA: MIT Press.

Chen, J-Y. (2007) Do Chinese and English speakers think about time differently? Failure of replicating Boroditsky (2001). *Cognition* 104, 427–436.

Darnell, R. (1990) *Edward Sapir: Linguist, Anthropologist, Humanist*. Berkeley, CA: University of California Press.

Dorfman, A. (1998) *Heading South, Looking North: A Bilingual Journey*. New York: Farrar, Straus & Giroux.

Epstein, I. (1915) *La pensée et la polyglossie: Essai psychologique et didactique* [Thought and Multilingualism: A Psychological and Didactic Essay]. Lausanne: Librarie Payot et Cie.

Ervin(-Tripp), S. (1954, reprinted in 1973) Identification and bilingualism. In A. Dil (ed.) *Language Acquisition and Communicative Choice. Essays by Susan M. Ervin-Tripp* (pp. 1–14). Stanford, CA: Stanford University Press.

Ervin(-Tripp), S. (1961, reprinted in 1973) Semantic shift in bilinguals. In A. Dil (ed.) *Language Acquisition and Communicative Choice. Essays by Susan M. Ervin-Tripp* (pp. 33–44). Stanford, CA: Stanford University Press.

Ervin(-Tripp), S. (1964, reprinted in 1973) Language and TAT content in bilinguals. In A. Dil (ed.) *Language Acquisition and Communicative Choice. Essays by Susan M. Ervin-Tripp* (pp. 45–61). Stanford, CA: Stanford University Press.

Ervin-Tripp, S. (1967, reprinted in 1973). An issei learns English. In A. Dil (ed.) *Language Acquisition and Communicative Choice. Essays by Susan M. Ervin-Tripp* (pp. 62–77). Stanford, CA: Stanford University Press.

Ervin, S. and Osgood, C. (1954) Second language learning and bilingualism. In C. Osgood and T. Sebeok (eds) *Psycholinguistics: A Survey of Theory and Research Problems*. Report of the 1953 Summer Seminar sponsored by the Committee on Linguistics and Psychology of the Social Science Research Council. Baltimore, MD: Waverley Press. *Journal of Abnormal and Social Psychology* supplement 49, 139–146.

Esteban, C. (2004) Interview. *Le nouveau recueil*, 71. On WWW at http://www.maulpoix.net/esteban.html. Accessed 29.10.09.

Fishman, J. (1960) A systematization of the Whorfian hypothesis. *Behavioral Sciences* 5, 323–329.

Gastil, R. (1959) Relative linguistic determinism. *Anthropological Linguistics* 1, 24–38.

Gordy, M. (1918) The German language in our schools. *Educational Review* October, 257–263.

Green, D. (1998) Bilingualism and thought. *Psychologica Belgica* 38, 253–278.

Green, J. (1993) *The Apprentice Writer*. New York/London: Marion Boyars.

Haiman, J. (2005) Review of Mary Besemeres' *Translating One's Self*. *Culture and Psychology* 11, 111–116.

Hakuta, K. (1986) *Mirror of Language: The Debate on Bilingualism*. New York: Basic Books.

Henss, W. (1931) Zweisprachigkeit als Pädagogisches Problem [Bilingualism as a pedagogical problem]. *Ethnopolitischer Almanach* 2, 47–55.

Hoffman, E. (1989) *Lost in Translation: A Life in a New Language*. New York: Penguin Books.

Hoffman, E. (1999) The new nomads. In A. Aciman (ed.) *Letters of Transit: Reflections on Exile, Identity, Language, and Loss* (pp. 35–63). New York: The New Press.

Hoijer, H. (1954) The Sapir-Whorf hypothesis. In H. Hoijer (ed.) *Language in Culture: Conference on the Interrelations of Language and Other Aspects of Culture* (pp. 92–105). Chicago, IL: University of Chicago Press.

Humboldt, W.v. (1963) *Humanist without Portfolio: An Anthology of the Writings of Wilhelm von Humboldt* (M. Cowan, trans.). Detroit, MI: Wayne State University Press.

Hunt, E. and Agnoli, F. (1991) The Whorfian hypothesis: A cognitive psychology perspective. *Psychological Review* 98, 377–389.

Jacobovits, L. and Lambert, W. (1961) Semantic satiation among bilinguals. *Journal of Experimental Psychology* 2, 576–582.

January, D. and Kako, E. (2007) Re-evaluating evidence for linguistic relativity: Reply to Boroditsky (2001). *Cognition* 104, 417–426.

Jespersen, O. (1922) *Language, its Nature, Development, and Origin*. London: Allen & Unwin.

Joseph, J. (2002) *From Whitney to Chomsky: Essays in the History of American Linguistics*. Amsterdam/Philadelphia: John Benjamins.

Keatley, C. (1992) History of bilingualism research in cognitive psychology. In R. Harris (ed.) *Cognitive Processing in Bilinguals* (pp. 15–49). Amsterdam: North Holland/Elsevier.

Kellman, S. (ed.) (2003) *Switching Languages: Translingual Writers Reflect on their Craft*. Lincoln/London: University of Nebraska Press.

Kim, H. (2000) Beyond boundaries. In M. Danquah (ed.) *Becoming American: Personal Essays by First Generation Immigrant Women* (pp. 113–125). New York: Hyperion.

Koerner, K. (2002) *Toward a History of American Linguistics*. London/New York: Routledge.

Kolers, P. (1963) Interlingual word associations. *Journal of Verbal Learning and Verbal Behavior* 2, 291–300.

Lakoff, G. (1987) *Women, Fire, and Dangerous Things: What Categories Reveal about the Mind*. Chicago, IL: University of Chicago Press.

Lambert, W. (1972) *Language, Culture, and Psychology: Essays by Wallace E. Lambert*. Selected and introduced by A. Dil. Stanford, CA: Stanford University Press.

Lambert, W., Havelka, J. and Crosby, C. (1958) The influence of language acquisition contexts on bilingualism. *Journal of Abnormal and Social Psychology* 56, 239–244.

Lambert, W. and Rawlings, C. (1969) Bilingual processing of mixed-language associative networks. *Journal of Verbal Learning and Verbal Behavior* 8, 604–609.

Lee, P. (1996) *The Whorf Theory Complex: A Critical Reconstruction*. Amsterdam: John Benjamins.

Lenneberg, E. (1953) Cognition in ethnolinguistics. *Language* 29, 463–471.

Lerner, G. (1997) *Why History Matters: Life and Thought*. New York/Oxford: Oxford University Press.

Lerner, G. (2002) *Fireweed: A Political Autobiography*. Philadelphia, PA: Temple University Press.

Levinson, S. (1996) Language and space. *Annual Review of Anthropology* 25, 353–382.

Levinson, S. (1997) From outer to inner space: Linguistic categories and non-linguistic thinking. In J. Nuyts and E. Pederson (eds) *Language and Conceptualization* (pp. 13–45). Cambridge: Cambridge University Press.

Levinson, S. (2003) *Space in Language and Cognition: Explorations in Cognitive Diversity*. Cambridge: Cambridge University Press.

Li, P. and Gleitman, L. (2002) Turning the tables: Language and spatial reasoning. *Cognition* 83, 265–294.

Lucy, J. (1992a) *Language Diversity and Thought: A Reformulation of the Linguistic Relativity Hypothesis*. Cambridge: Cambridge University Press.

Lucy, J. (1992b) *Grammatical Categories and Cognition. A Case Study of the Linguistic Relativity Hypothesis*. Cambridge: Cambridge University Press.

Luebke, F. (1980) Legal restrictions on foreign languages in the Great Plain states, 1917–1923. In P. Schach (ed.) *Languages in Conflict: Linguistic Acculturation on the Great Plains* (pp. 1–19). Lincoln: University of Nebraska Press.

Macnamara, J. (1970) Bilingualism and thought. In J. Alatis (ed.) *Georgetown University 21st Annual Round Table* (pp. 25–40). Washington, DC: Georgetown University Press.

Macnamara, J. (1991) Linguistic relativity revisited. In R. Cooper and B. Spolsky (eds) *The Influence of Language on Culture and Thought: Essays in Honor Joshua A. Fishman's 65th Birthday* (pp. 45–60). Berlin: Mouton De Gruyter.

Mar, E. (1999) *Paper Daughter: A Memoir*. New York: HarperCollins.

Miller, J. (1996) A tongue, for sighing. In J. Maybin and N. Mercer (eds) *Using English: From Conversation to Canon* (pp. 275–310). London: Routledge.

Mori, K. (1997) *Polite Lies: On being a Woman Caught between Cultures*. New York: Henry Holt.

Müller, K. (1934) *Die Psyche des Oberschlesiers im Lichte des Zweisprachen-Problems* [The Psyche of the Upper Silesian in the Light of the Problem of Bilingualism]. Bonn.

Osgood, C. and Sebeok, T. (eds) (1954) *Psycholinguistics: A Survey of Theory and Research Problems*. Report of the 1953 Summer Seminar sponsored by the Committee on Linguistics and Psychology of the Social Science Research Council. Baltimore, MD: Waverley Press. *Journal of Abnormal and Social Psychology* supplement, 49.

Paradis, M. (1979) Language and thought in bilinguals. In W. McCormack and H. Izzo (eds) *The Sixth LACUS Forum* (pp. 420–431). Columbia, SC: Hornbeam Press.

Pavlenko, A. (1998) Second language learning by adults: Testimonies of bilingual writers. *Issues in Applied Linguistics* 9, 3–19.

Pavlenko, A. (1999) New approaches to concepts in bilingual memory. *Bilingualism: Language and Cognition* 2, 209–230.

Pavlenko, A. (2002) "We have room for but one language here": Language and national identity in the US at the turn of the 20th century. *Multilingua* 21, 163–196.

Pavlenko, A. (2004) "The making of an American": Negotiation of identities at the turn of the 20th century. In A. Pavlenko and A. Blackledge (eds) *Negotiation of Identities in Multilingual Contexts* (pp. 34–67). Clevedon: Multilingual Matters.

Pavlenko, A. (2006) Bilingual selves. In A. Pavlenko (ed.) *Bilingual Minds: Emotional Experience, Expression, and Representation* (pp. 1–33). Clevedon: Multilingual Matters.

Pérez-Firmat, G. (2003) *Tongue Ties: Logo-eroticism in Anglo-Hispanic Literature.* New York: Palgrave Macmillan.

Pinker, S. (1994) *The Language Instinct.* New York: Harper Perennial.

Pinker, S. (2007) *The Stuff of Thought: Language as a Window into Human Nature.* New York: Viking.

Saer, D. (1924) The effect of bilingualism on intelligence. *British Journal of Psychology* 14, 25–38.

Saer, D., Smith, F. and Hughes, J. (1924) *The Bilingual Problem: A Study based upon Experiments and Observations in Wales.* Aberystwyth: University College of Wales.

Sander, F. (1934) Seelische Struktur und Sprache: Sturkturpsychologisches zum Zweitsprachen-problem [Psychic structure and language: Structural psychology of the problem of second languages]. *Neue Psychologische Studien* 12, 59.

Sapir, E. (1949) *Selected writings of Edward Sapir in Language, Culture, and Personality.* Edited by D. Mandelbaum. Berkeley/Los Angeles, CA: University of California Press.

Schlossman, S. (1983) Is there an American tradition of bilingual education? German in the public elementary schools, 1840–1919. *American Journal of Education* 91, 139–186.

Schmidt-Rohr, G. (1933) *Mutter Sprache: vom Amt der Sprache bei der Volkwerdung* [Mother Tongue: The Role of Language in the National Development]. Jena.

Slobin, D. (1996) From "thought and language" to "thinking for speaking". In J. Gumperz and S. Levinson (eds) *Rethinking Linguistic Relativity* (pp. 70–96). Cambridge: Cambridge University Press.

Slobin, D. (2000) Verbalized events: A dynamic approach to linguistic relativity and determinism. In S. Niemeier and R. Dirven (eds) *Evidence for Linguistic Relativity* (pp. 107–138). Amsterdam: Benjamins.

Slobin, D. (2001) Form-function relations: How do children find out what they are? In M. Bowerman and S. Levinson (eds) *Language Acquisition and Conceptual Development* (pp. 406–449). Cambridge: Cambridge University Press.

Smith, F. (1923) Bilingualism and mental development. *British Journal of Psychology* 13, 271–282.

Smith, M. (1931) A study of five bilingual children from the same family. *Child Development* 2, 184–187.

Smith, M. (1939) Some light on the problem of bilingualism as found from a study of the progress in mastery of English among pre-school children of non-American ancestry in Hawaii. *Genetic Psychology Monographs* 21, 119–284.

Spoerl, D. (1943) Binguality and emotional adjustment. *Journal of Abnormal and Social Psychology* 38, 35–57.

Todorov, T. (1994) Dialogism and schizophrenia. In A. Arteaga (ed.) *An Other Tongue: Nation and Ethnicity in the Linguistic Borderlands* (pp. 203–214). Durham & London: Duke University Press.

Toussaint, N. (1935) *Bilinguisme et education* [Bilingualism and Education]. Brussels.

Tse, Ch.-Sh. and Altarriba, J. (2008) Evidence against linguistic relativity in Chinese and English: A case study of spatial and temporal metaphors. *Journal of Cognition and Culture* 8, 335–357.

Walker, D., Jenkins, J. and Sebeok, T. (1954) Language, cognition, and culture. In C. Osgood and T. Sebeok (eds) *Psycholinguistics: A Survey of Theory and Research Problems*. Report of the 1953 Summer Seminar sponsored by the Committee on Linguistics and Psychology of the Social Science Research Council. Baltimore, MD: Waverley Press. *Journal of Abnormal and Social Psychology* supplement 49, 192–203.

Ward Jouve, N. (1991) *White Woman Speaks with Forked Tongue: Criticism as Autobiography.* London/New York: Routledge.

Weinreich, U. (1953) *Languages in Contact.* The Hague: Mouton.

Weisgerber, L. (1933) Die Stellung der Sprache im Aufbau der Gesamtkultur [The role of language in the constitution of national culture]. *Wörter und Sachen* 15, 134–224; 16, 97–236.

Whorf, B. (1956) *Language, Thought, and Reality. Selected Writings of Benjamin Lee Whorf.* Edited by John Carroll. Cambridge, MA: MIT Press.

Wierzbicka, A. (1985) The double life of a bilingual. In R. Sussex and J. Zubrzycki (eds) *Polish People and Culture in Australia* (pp. 187–223). Canberra: Australian National University.

Wierzbicka, A. (1997) The double life of a bilingual: A cross-cultural perspective. In M. Bond (ed.) *Working at the Interface of Cultures: Eighteen Lives in Social Science* (pp. 113–125). London/New York: Routledge.

Wiley, T. (1998) The imposition of World War I era English-only policies and the fate of German in North America. In T. Ricento and B. Burnaby (eds) *Language and Politics in the United States and Canada: Myths and Realities* (pp. 211–241). Mahwah, NJ: Lawrence Erlbaum.

Wong, J. (1945, reprinted in 1989) *Fifth Chinese Daughter.* Seattle, WA: University of Washington Press.

Yoshioka, J. (1929) A study of bilingualism. *Journal of Genetic Psychology* 36, 473–479.

Zhengdao Ye, V. (2004) La double vie de Veronica: Reflections on my life as a Chinese migrant in Australia. *Life Writing* 1, 133–145.

Zhengdao Ye, V. (2007) Returning to my mother tongue: Veronica's journey continues. In M. Besemeres and A. Wierzbicka (eds) *Translating Lives: Living with Two Languages and Cultures* (pp. 56–69). Queensland, Australia: University of Queensland Press.

Chapter 2
Cognitive Restructuring in Bilingualism

PANOS ATHANASOPOULOS

2.1 Introduction

Recent research has re-ignited the idea that our language may affect the way we think (Bowerman & Levinson, 2001; Gentner & Goldin-Meadow, 2003; Gumperz & Levinson, 1996; Lucy, 1992a). This chapter aims to extend that investigation to the domain of bilingualism. Throughout the chapter, a broad definition of bilingualism is adopted, including early and late bilingualism or second language (L2) acquisition. The terms 'bilingual' and 'L2 speaker' are used interchangeably throughout the chapter to refer to the knowledge and use of more than one language in the same mind. This view draws inspiration from Cook's (1991, 1992, 1999, 2003) multicompetence hypothesis, which views the person who speaks more than one language as an independent speaker/hearer/thinker rather than as an imperfect version of a monolingual native speaker ideal. It is also inspired by Grosjean's (1982, 1989, 1992, 1998) related argument that the bilingual person is not two monolinguals in the same body, but a unique language user with a complete language system. *A priori* distinctions, such as 'early' and 'late' bilingualism or 'true' bilinguals versus L2 learners, may hold the inherent danger of making distinct sets of assumptions and observations about essentially the same phenomena and interpreting them differently. For example, deviation from monolingual patterns in early bilinguals may be seen as convergence to a unitary norm, whereas deviation from monolingual patterns in late bilinguals may be seen as 'failure' to acquire or use the 'target' construction. That is not to say that age of acquisition is not an important factor. On the contrary, it is a factor that should be carefully measured and controlled, or directly investigated, in the study of bilingualism. But insofar as we are trying to understand the knowledge of two languages in the same mind, and how these may affect thinking, age of language acquisition should be one of many factors that lines of investigations may pursue. Other factors include, but are not limited to, language proficiency, sociocultural immersion, learning context, frequency and type of input, etc. (for a detailed discussion of factors affecting the multicompetent mind, see Jarvis & Pavlenko, 2008).

The chapter adopts Whorf's (1956: 221) original formulation of how language may affect cognition, namely, 'that users of markedly different grammars are **pointed** by their grammars toward different types of observations and different **evaluations** of externally similar acts of observation, and hence are not equivalent as observers but must arrive at somewhat different views of the world' (emphasis mine). It is clear from Whorf's original formulation of the linguistic relativity principle that he viewed language as an attention-directing mechanism, which influences higher-level cognitive processes, namely, conscious evaluation of the experienced world. Thus, the new enquiry into Whorf's principle of linguistic relativity focuses on specific grammatical and lexical categories, and on specific higher-level cognitive processes, such as reasoning, decision-making and similarity judgments.

For example, studies have shown that speakers of languages with obligatory grammatical number marking and a count/mass noun distinction are more likely to base their similarity judgments of objects based on common shape properties rather than common substance properties (e.g. matching a cardboard box with a plastic box rather than with a piece of cardboard) than speakers of languages where all common nouns are mass (Imai & Gentner, 1997; Imai & Mazuka, 2003; Lucy, 1992b; Lucy & Gaskins, 2001, 2003). Research has also shown that speakers of a language with a single term to refer to *blue* and *green* will judge blue and green stimuli as more similar than speakers of a language with a lexical blue/green distinction (Davidoff *et al.*, 1999; Kay & Kempton, 1984; Roberson *et al.*, 2000, 2005; Roberson, 2005). This research demonstrates that speakers of different languages do indeed evaluate differently objectively similar aspects of the experienced world. While such effects are more demonstrable in certain perceptual and cognitive domains than in others, at least Whorf's principle of linguistic relativity has become a matter of serious ongoing empirical investigation.

If speakers of different languages evaluate perceptual attributes of reality differently, does learning novel grammatical and lexical categories restructure cognition, or is cognition fixed once-and-for-all by the first language (L1) one is exposed to? Attempting to answer that question, this chapter presents an overview of a series of recent empirical studies by the author (Athanasopoulos, 2006, 2007, 2009; Athanasopoulos & Kasai, 2008). The studies in question aimed to specifically address the issue of whether knowing and using more than one language influences cognitive processing of the perceived world. These studies investigated categorical color perception and similarity judgments of objects in bilinguals with languages that differ in how they lexically partition color space, and in how they encode number grammatically.

The studies were motivated by the observation that surprisingly little research exists on the relationship between language and cognition in bilinguals (Green, 1998; Pavlenko, 1999, 2005), despite the fact that the majority of the world's population uses more than one language in order to communicate (Cook, 2002). In addition, bilingualism tends to be routinely overlooked in many studies in the field of linguistic relativity. This can sometimes yield inconsistent results across studies or cast serious doubt on previous findings. For example, Berlin and Kay (1969) found that native speakers of 20 different languages displayed similar color category prototypes to those of English monolinguals. The authors and others after them (Heider-Rosch, 1972; Heider & Olivier, 1972) interpreted these results as evidence for the universality of color categories. Berlin and Kay acknowledged that some speakers of languages other than English in their study were in fact US immigrants, fluent in English to different degrees, but they found it 'hard to believe that English could so consistently influence the placement of the foci in these diverse languages' (Berlin & Kay 1969: 12). A few years later, however, a study by Caskey-Sirmons and Hickerson (1977) did indeed show that color category prototypes of native speakers of five different L1s who had English as their L2, shifted from the L1 monolingual pattern toward the prototypes displayed by English monolinguals.

Laws *et al.* (1995) found no differences in similarity judgments of dark and light blue stimuli between Russian and English speakers, despite the fact that Russian has two terms to distinguish between light and dark blue. In contrast, a more recent study by Winawer *et al.* (2007) reported significant differences between populations in a similar task. In both studies, Russian participants were bilingual in English, with varying degrees of L2 proficiency, yet no measures controlled for any possible influence of their bilingualism on the results.

Munnich *et al.* (2001) found no differences in spatial cognition of English, Japanese and Korean speakers, despite crosslinguistic differences in how the languages in question encode spatial relationships. Japanese and Korean speakers were students in US universities. According to the authors, they were 'recent arrivals in the US' (no specific information given), and 'no participant had been exposed to languages other than their native language before the age of 12' (Munnich *et al.*, 2001: 180) (no specific ages were given, and as Pavlenko (2005) has rightly argued, 12 is by no means considered a standard threshold after which the potential to acquire other languages automatically shuts down). In addition, the authors believe that 'even with substantial exposure to English, participants would not be expected to gain a native-like proficiency in English' (Munnich *et al.*, 2001: 180). Overlooking the fact that the researchers did not formally measure the English proficiency of their participants at the time of testing, the issue at stake here is not whether these speakers would have gained 'native-like' L2 proficiency, but whether they would have gained enough proficiency in English to render their behavioral responses non-significantly different from those of English monolinguals (see Chapter 5, this volume, for evidence that L2 influence on L1 responses may occur even at lower levels of L2 proficiency).

Language proficiency may not even be the only crucial factor under-pinning bilingual cognitive behavior. In undertaking this investigation, the studies by Athanasopoulos and colleagues sought to elucidate the precise impact of a range of variables that may affect the way bi- or multilinguals process reality and the world around them. The variables under investigation included purely linguistic ones, such as language proficiency, as well as sociocultural ones, like length of stay in the L2-speaking country. A full list and a description of the variables that were investigated will be given in Section 2.3. Suffice it to say for now that careful measuring of variables such as L2 proficiency, acculturation, experimental setting and age of L2 acquisition allows for correlational analyses between cognitive performance and these variables, thus directly measuring the precise relationship between linguistic/socio-cultural variables and cognition in the human mind. This is a step never before taken in studies of this kind, and it has the potential to uncover a more precise picture of the relationship between language and thought.

In order to fully understand and appreciate what cognitive restructur-ing in bilingualism may entail, it is crucial to consider evidence from L1 acquisition, which shows that very early in life, cognition is influenced by 'prelinguistic', possibly innate, predispositions to perceptual attri-butes of reality. However, later on, after experience with language, cognitive patterns are restructured according to language-specific parti-tions of reality. Cognitive restructuring in L1 acquisition will be the concern of Section 2.2. Section 2.3 will then provide a theoretical backdrop to the question of how contrasting categorical aspects are reconciled in bilingual cognition, and what factors may play a role in bilingual cognitive processing. Sections 2.4 through to 2.8 will examine these issues empirically. Throughout Sections 2.4 to 2.8, I will discuss the methodological and theoretical significance of the recent findings for bilingualism and for the language and thought debate, identify several issues raised by the studies and suggest new avenues for the investiga-tion of these issues.

2.2 Cognitive Restructuring in Monolingualism

Category formation in infants is regarded as one of the building blocks of cognitive development (Oates & Grayson, 2004). It appears that infants have a predisposition toward categorization that precedes their language development (Mandler, 1997; Quinn, 1994). The question of how and according to which principles infants categorize has been the subject of a considerable amount of research. It is a relatively well-established finding in the literature that early, prelinguistic categorization is based on perceptual attributes intrinsic to the object (Mandler, 1997), and that infants are able to categorize even more abstract entities, such as spatial relations, relatively early in their development, and certainly well before acquisition of language is complete (i.e. as young as three months old; Quinn, 1994; Quinn *et al.*, 1996).

However, subsequent research has shown that once a child has acquired language, a certain amount of restructuring of previously formed categories occurs; in other words, language is a powerful tool for categorizing reality and the world. But how is the influence of language on cognitive categorization manifested? Until recently, no ready answer to this question existed. Certainly, empirical evidence demonstrated a tight link between the so-called vocabulary 'spurt', i.e. the rapid acquisition of words that occurs roughly at one year of age, and the ability to categorize. Children exhibit an extraordinary interest in naming things at the same time as they show increased development in their categorization abilities (Gopnik & Meltzoff, 1987, 1992). However, it remained unclear whether the nature of this relationship was causal, and if so, whether it was language development that caused changes in categorization behavior, or whether changes in the ability to categorize brought about the naming explosion. Cross-cultural evidence provided a key breakthrough: Gopnik and Choi (1995) and Gopnik *et al.* (1996) examined cognitive and linguistic development in Korean- and English-speaking children. They found that English-speaking children were superior to Korean-speaking children in categorization and naming tasks, while Korean-speaking children were superior to English-speaking children in means-ends abilities (e.g. retrieving a toy by removing or manipulating an obstacle). Gopnik and colleagues attribute these crosslinguistic differences in development to the observation that Korean-speaking mothers use more verbs and fewer nouns than English-speaking mothers (see also Gopnik, 2001).

Studies in the grammatical domain of number have demonstrated that a link exists between acquisition of this category and similarity judgments of objects and substances. Lucy (1992b) investigated this issue in Yucatec-speaking and English-speaking adults and children. In contrast to English, Yucatec has no obligatory grammatical number marking and no grammatical distinction between count and mass nouns, but instead implements a numeral classifier system that grammatically resembles the quantification of mass nouns in English (e.g. 'three candles' in Yucatec would be roughly translated in English as 'three-piece-wax'). Thus, in Yucatec all nouns would appear to be 'mass-like'.

One of the series of experiments that Lucy (1992b; Lucy & Gaskins, 2001, 2003) conducted was a triads matching task, with two conditions. In one condition, Yucatec and English speakers were presented with a standard solid object and then asked to match the object for similarity with one of two alternates. One alternate resembled the standard in shape but was made from a different material, and one alternate resembled the standard in material but had a different shape (e.g. matching a metal nail with either a wooden pencil or with a scrap of metal). In the other condition, the standard was a non-solid substance and participants were once again asked to make similarity judgments according to shape or material, exactly as in the solid object condition (e.g. matching hand cream arranged into a reverse c shape with either plasticine arranged into a reverse c shape or a pile of hand cream). Results showed that in the non-solid substance condition, Yucatec- and English-speaking adults performed similarly, that is, they both tended to select the material alternate (e.g. the pile of hand cream). This is a somewhat expected finding in light of the fact that both languages are similar with respect to mass nouns. In the solid object condition, however, English speakers tended to make a shape match (e.g. matching the metal nail with the wooden pencil rather than with the scrap of metal) significantly more than Yucatec speakers, who in turn continued to favor material in their similarity judgments (e.g. matching the metal nail with the scrap of metal rather than with the wooden pencil). This cognitive difference appears to be isomorphic to the grammatical difference between English and Yucatec: the former has count nouns and the latter does not. According to Lucy (1992b), count nouns in English encode an inherent unit of individuation, which nouns in Yucatec lack. The best perceptual correlate of this inherent unit of individuation is the shape of objects. Hence, English-speaking adults preferentially attend to shape, and Yucatec-speaking adults preferentially attend to material.

Crucially from a developmental point of view, Lucy and Gaskins (2001, 2003) conducted the aforementioned triads matching task with Yucatec- and English-speaking children aged seven and nine years old. The researchers found that the seven-year-olds in both language groups tended to match by common shape. Thus, the Yucatec-speaking 7-year-olds did not behave like their adult counterparts, who tended to match objects according to their material composition. By the age of nine, English-speaking children continued to favor shape. However, Yucatec-speaking nine-year-olds' behavior shifted dramatically, favoring material composition almost half of the time, and gradually approaching the adult Yucatec pattern. Lucy and Gaskins (2001, 2003) concluded that between the ages of seven and nine, some rather specific cognitive reorganization occurs whereby similarity judgment patterns diverge from a pre-existing 'innate' bias to a linguistically based one.

Lucy and Gaskins' (2001, 2003) developmental findings are supported by similar studies comparing cognitive and language development in

Japanese-speaking children. The Japanese grammatical pattern for marking number on nouns is very similar to that of Yucatec, i.e. all nouns are 'mass-like'. Imai and Gentner (1997) extended a study by Soja *et al.* (1991), which had shown that English-speaking children were perfectly capable of distinguishing between objects and substances in a triads matching task long before they had mastered the grammatical count/mass distinction in their language, suggesting that this distinction was certainly prelinguistic and possibly innate. Imai and Gentner (1997) presented English- and Japanese-speaking two-year-old children with substances, simple objects and complex objects, and asked them to match them with either a shape or material alternate. Both Japanese- and English-speaking children matched by common material in the substances condition, and by common shape in the complex objects condition. However, in the simple objects condition, the overwhelming majority (93%) of English-speaking children made a shape match, while the Japanese-speaking children performed at the level of chance. Japanese-speaking older children and adults showed a clear material preference in the simple object condition, contrary to English-speaking older children and adults who tended to favor shape. Imai and Gentner (1997, see also Imai & Mazuka, 2003) concluded that while children are able to distinguish cognitively between objects and substances prior to the acquisition of language (thus supporting the findings of Soja *et al.*'s (1991) study), similarity judgments in later childhood and adulthood rely to a large extent on the grammatical realization of the distinction in a speaker's particular language (thus supporting Lucy, 1992a, 1992b, and, ultimately, Whorf, 1956).

This transition from prelinguistic perceptual categorization to language-specific categorization has also consistently been found in the domains of color (Roberson *et al.*, 2004), space (Bowerman & Choi, 2001; Hespos & Spelke, 2004) and gender (Martinez & Shatz, 1996; Sera *et al.*, 1994). As Levinson (2001) puts it:

> When a child learns a language she is undergoing a cognitive revolution, learning to construct new macro-concepts. These macro-concepts which are part of our cultural baggage are precisely the contribution of language to our thinking. Language invades our thinking because languages are good to think with. (Levinson, 2001: 584; see also Vygotsky, 1934/1962)

In other words, language and cognition form a complex and unique bond early in life, characterized by children's progressively language-specific cognitive patterns as a function of acquisition of specific lexical and grammatical patterns in the ambient language. However, given that humans in the majority of cases are destined to learn more than one language in their lifetime, an investigation of this complex and unique bond only in monolinguals will surely yield an impoverished and incomplete picture of the intricate workings of the interaction between language and cognition in the human mind.

2.3 Cognitive Restructuring in Bilingualism

Recent studies provide evidence that at least for some domains, language affects cognition early in life, and this offers invaluable insights into how humans think. But the reality of the matter is that hardly anyone remains monolingual throughout their life. The vast majority of humans learn another language at some point in their lives, most commonly an international lingua franca, such as English, French or Spanish. Bilingualism is the norm rather than the exception in the majority of the world's countries (Cook, 1997, 1999, 2002). Even in traditionally monolingual countries, individual bilingualism is becoming increasingly prevalent, while the developed world is rapidly becoming multilingual through political and economic migration. If different languages encode reality and the world differently, and if linguistic experience may heavily impact on our cognitive outlook toward reality and the world, how are contrasting categorical aspects in languages reconciled in the cognition of bi- or multilingual speakers?

Green (1998), Cook (2002, 2003), Pavlenko (1999, 2005) and Jarvis and Pavlenko (2008) offer insightful discussions of the relationship between bilingual cognition and specific linguistic properties, and provide a methodological blueprint for testing several predictions pertaining to this relationship empirically. The authors stress the importance of integrating a range of investigative techniques, involving tasks that measure explicit linguistic competence and tasks that measure non-verbal behavior. Because of the dynamic and multi-varied nature of bi- and multilingualism, equally important, according to these authors, is a consideration of various factors that may affect bilingual linguistic and cognitive development. Some of these pertain to language expertise and knowledge itself, while others have more to do with the sociocultural environment that bilinguals operate in. This chapter takes the view that these two kinds of variables, far from being mutually exclusive, are inextricably linked and may manifest themselves in a variety of guises. We might usefully conceptualize these types of variables as points on a continuum, with linguistic knowledge at one end and sociocultural immersion at the other end. Figure 2.1 provides a graphic illustration of this continuum, presenting the variables that were investigated in the studies by Athanasopoulos and colleagues that follow.

A brief description of each variable is necessary in order to provide the reader with a more comprehensive understanding of the position of each variable on the continuum in Figure 2.1.

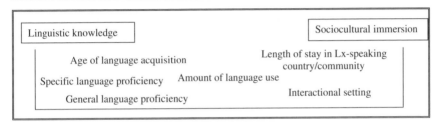

Figure 2.1 Continuum of linguistic and sociocultural variables that may affect bilingual cognition

- Specific language proficiency: Knowledge of the specific linguistic property under investigation. Elicitation of such knowledge may take several forms, ranging from free narratives to controlled conversations to picture descriptions designed to elicit the desired form, to written tasks such as grammaticality judgments and lexical retrieval tasks.
- General language proficiency: General level of competence in a language, ideally measured by independent language tests, which measure proficiency in a range of language areas. Alternatively, introspective techniques such as asking participants to judge their proficiency on a questionnaire may be used.
- Age of language acquisition: This variable has been placed toward the linguistic end of the continuum because development and mastery of language could well depend on maturational constraints, either because of a biologically determined 'sensitive' period for language acquisition, or due to a gradual decline of general learning mechanisms throughout the lifespan. For this reason, the influence of this variable may not be directly observable, but instead it may be a mediating variable in the relationship between language proficiency and degree of cognitive restructuring.
- Amount of language use: This variable sits in the middle of the continuum as it is characterized by both linguistic and sociocultural factors. The degree to which a multilingual individual will use one of the particular languages at their disposal is undoubtedly dependent on the interactional context and the degree of immersion in a specific community or country. Increasing the opportunity to use the language due to these factors will, in turn, lead to increases in expertise in the particular language and will potentially provide the individual with target-like examples of specific linguistic features.
- Interactional setting: According to Grosjean's (2001) idea of 'language mode', bilinguals may behave differently depending

on the particular social/interactional setting they are engaged in. In the context of evaluating perceptual distinctions, an L1 setting (e.g. receiving experiment instructions in the L1 by a native speaker of the L1) may promote a cognitive pattern that resembles that of monolingual speakers of the L1, and vice versa for an L2 setting.

• Length of stay in Lx-speaking community/country: Living in the country where one of the second/foreign languages (Lx) of the multilingual individual is spoken as a native language may promote and induce in the individual an inclination, conscious or unconscious, to emulate the linguistic, and crucially, the non-linguistic behavior of the target-language community.

It must be pointed out that due to the dynamic nature of multi-lingualism, all, none or some of these variables may be found to influence bilingual behavior to various degrees at different points of cognitive and linguistic development. If their influence is mediating or moderating rather than direct, then their impact may be very difficult to demonstrate in an experimental context. But to the extent that this is possible (e.g. through the use of language tests and biographical questionnaires), any study that wishes to address the relationship between language and thought in bi- or multilinguals should take linguistic and extra-linguistic variables into careful consideration. As will become clear in the sections that follow, the studies by Athanasopoulos and colleagues did not take into account all of these variables from the beginning. But as the picture started to become clearer with each study, more and more factors were considered, and this in turn yielded a more precise account of the interaction between these variables and bilingual cognition.

Heeding the calls of Pavlenko and others for research on bilingualism and thought, researchers are gradually taking seriously the possibility that bilinguals might have a different worldview from monolinguals as a result of using languages with contrasting linguistic categories. This chapter presents some of the first fruits of that research, in the grammatical domain of number and the lexical domain of color. If different linguistic categories yield different cognitive patterns, then examining bilinguals' cognitive patterns will uncover the precise impact of bilingualism on cognitive processing, thus elucidating the precise nature of the relationship between language and cognition in the human mind.

2.4 Effects of the Grammatical Representation of Number

Lucy (1992b) identifies two inherent properties of noun phrases as crucial for object classification preferences, namely, animacy and dis-creteness. Animacy refers to whether the referent of the noun is a human/animal or not. Discreteness refers to whether the referent of the noun is a discrete entity, with definable boundaries and usually solid form. For example, using these features, a 'cat' is [+ animate] (and thus by implication [+ discrete]), a 'shovel' is [− animate, + discrete] and 'water' is [− animate, − discrete]. Lucy (1992b) shows that there is an interaction between these two features and plural marking. In English, the plural is obligatorily applied to the first two groups (that is, [+ animate] and [− animate, + discrete], e.g. *cats, shovels*), but not to the third group ([− animate, − discrete], e.g. **waters*). In Yucatec (and Japanese for that matter), the plural is optionally applied to [+ animate] noun phrases, but not to the other two groups. Thus, English distinguishes grammatically between discrete and non-discrete entities, whereas Yucatec and Japanese distinguish grammatically only between animate and inanimate entities, but crucially not between discrete and non-discrete entities.

Based on these crosslinguistic differences, Lucy (1992b) hypothesized that speakers of English would habitually attend to the number of various objects more than Yucatec speakers. Lucy (1992b) presented participants with picture-sets depicting various scenes of rural life. Each picture-set contained different types of target objects corresponding to the different types of noun phrases that Lucy (1992b) described in his linguistic analysis. Thus, there were three types of target objects:

(a) Animals, corresponding to [+ animate] noun phrases present in both English and Yucatec.
(b) Implements, corresponding to [− animate, + discrete] noun phrases present in English but not in Yucatec.
(c) Substances, corresponding to [− animate, − discrete] noun phrases present in both English and Yucatec.

Each picture-set consisted of six pictures. Picture 1 was the original picture and the rest of the pictures were the alternate pictures. Each alternate picture contained a difference in a type of target object from the original. Thus, alternate 2 (Animals) contained a change in the number of Animals (e.g. two dogs versus one dog), alternates 3 and 4 contained a change in the number of Implements (e.g. two buckets versus one bucket, two shovels versus one shovel, etc.) and alternates 5 and 6 contained a change in the number or amount of Substances (e.g. two puddles of mud versus one puddle of mud, bigger versus smaller piece of meat, etc.). Lucy (1992b) asked 12 monolingual English and 12 monolingual Yucatec speakers to decide which alternate picture was 'most like' the original picture. As expected, Yucatec speakers treated the changes in the number of Animals as most significant, thus choosing alternates 3 and 4, and 5 and 6 equally often, but not alternate 2. English speakers treated the changes in the number of Animals and Implements as most significant, thus choosing alternates 5 and 6 most often, but not alternates 2, 3 and 4.

Athanasopoulos (2006) asked how bilingual speakers, whose languages instantiate the features of animacy and discreteness differently, might behave in Lucy's (1992b) picture-matching task. For this purpose, Lucy's (1992b) picture-matching task was given to intermediate and advanced Japanese speakers of English as an L2 and to monolingual speakers of English and Japanese. Recall that Japanese is a classifier language like Yucatec. Athanasopoulos (2006) hypothesized that monolingual speakers will behave similarly to participants in Lucy's (1992b) study: (a) English monolinguals will regard alternates containing changes in the number or amount of Substances to be more similar to the original picture, thus treating changes in the number of Animals and Implements as significant; (b) Japanese monolinguals should regard alternates containing changes either in the number of Implements or the number/amount of Substances to be more similar to the original picture, thus treating changes only in the number of Animals as significant. The non-linguistic behavior of these bilinguals would determine whether knowledge of [− animate, − discrete] noun phrases continues to influence their similarity judgments (and thus they would attend only to changes in the number of Animals), or whether L2 acquisition of grammatical number marking on [− animate, + discrete] noun phrases changed those similarity judgments, directing their attention toward changes in the number of Implements as well as Animals.

Because Japanese children are exposed to English from the age of 12 in their national curriculum, it is nearly impossible to find Japanese speakers who are both completely monolingual and also educated at a university level. The term 'Japanese monolingual' is used by convention here and in the subsequent studies by Athanasopoulos and colleagues to refer essentially to individuals who might best be described as functional monolinguals with minimal English proficiency. On the other hand, it is very easy to find participants who are monolingual in English even when they are educated at a university level. Thus, all English monolinguals in this and subsequent studies by Athanasopoulos were selected on the basis of self-reports stating that they considered themselves to be completely monolingual in English.

Fourteen English monolinguals, 28 Japanese monolinguals and 38 Japanese speakers of L2 English took part in the study. All were of comparable age (early to mid twenties) and socio-economic background (all university students, either in Japan or the UK). The L2 speakers were subsequently separated into two groups, depending on how they scored on a general proficiency test of English (the Quick Placement Test (QPT), 2001) and on a grammaticality judgment task, specifically assessing L2 knowledge of number marking and articles, both properties associated with [− animate, + discrete] noun phrases in English. These tasks yielded an 'advanced' group ($n = 21$) and an 'intermediate' group ($n = 17$). The majority ($n = 30$) of the L2 speakers had been living in the UK at the time of testing, with length of residence ranging between 3 and 24 months. They had started learning English at the age of 12, and they were given instructions in English.

Responses were scored as the number of times that each participant selected a type of alternate (Animals, Implements or Substances) as most like the original picture. Scores were then converted into percentages and the mean was calculated for each group of participants. Figure 2.2 shows the distribution of participants' responses for each alternate type.

Since the proportion of Animals, Implements or Substances responses is 100 minus the sum of the remaining two categories, e.g. Animals = 100 – (Implements + Substances), for the statistical analysis each category was treated as a separate dependent variable, the independent variable being groups. Figure 2.2 shows that all groups make a clear distinction between Animals on the one hand and Implements and Substances on the other. Paired-samples *t*-tests for Animals versus combined Implements and Substances confirmed this tendency as statistically significant, $t\,(27) = -18.445$, $p < 0.05$ for the Japanese monolinguals, $t\,(16) = -13.924$ for the intermediate L2 speakers, $t\,(20) = -26.303$ for the advanced L2 speakers and $t\,(13) = -24.287$ for the English monolinguals. Since both Japanese and English instantiate grammatical number marking in [+ animate] nouns, this finding is not surprising.

We now turn to the crucial distinction between Implements and Substances, present in English but absent in Japanese with regard to grammatical number marking. Paired samples *t*-tests showed that the English monolinguals and the L2 advanced speakers made a significant

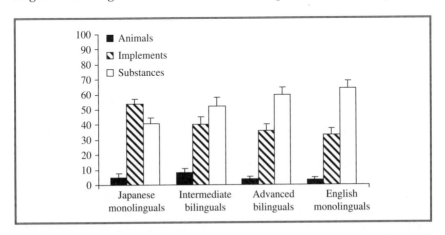

Figure 2.2 Proportion of preferences, expressed as percentages, for each alternate type

distinction between Implements and Substances, tending to select the latter most of the time: t (13) = 3.465, $p < 0.05$ for the English monolinguals; t (20) = 2.741, $p < 0.05$ for the advanced L2 speakers. On the other hand, the intermediate L2 speakers and the Japanese monolinguals did not make a significant distinction between Implements and Substances, treating both more or less similarly: t (27) = 1.814, $p > 0.05$ for the Japanese mono-linguals; t (16) = 1.098, $p > 0.05$ for the intermediate L2 speakers.

The results from the monolingual groups supported the initial hypotheses: English and Japanese monolinguals matched the pictures according to the grammatical distinctions in their respective language. The results also showed a remarkable contrast between intermediate and advanced L2 speakers. The intermediate L2 speakers showed sensitivity only to changes in the number of Animals, and regarded changes in the number of Implements or in the number or amount of Substances as less significant. The advanced L2 speakers, on the other hand, regarded changes in the number of Animals and Implements as more significant than changes in the number or amount of Substances. Their cognitive disposition toward Implements seems to have changed from the L1-based preference to the preference displayed by native speakers of the L2. The evidence seems to suggest that L2 acquisition of grammatical number marking on [− animate, + discrete] noun phrases has influenced their cognitive disposition toward referents of that type of noun phrase.

The results of this study suggest that knowing and using an L2 with contrasting grammatical distinctions from the L1 may have profound consequences for non-linguistic cognition. But interestingly, the study also shows that such effects are heavily modulated by linguistic proficiency, thus supporting Pavlenko's (2005) argument that bilingual cognition is highly variable. In this particular study, it seems that intermediate L2 speakers' similarity judgments are largely guided by the L1, demonstrating L1-based cognitive processing. However, in the case of advanced speakers, results demonstrate a shift toward the L2-based cognitive pattern, probably motivated by the internalization of a novel grammatical distinction, which is non-existent in the L1.

Nevertheless, as the study was exploratory in nature, it raised many more questions than it answered. For example, the bilinguals were given instructions in English by a non-Japanese administrator, leaving open the possibility that they functioned in an English-language mode (Grosjean, 1998), and this enhanced their cognitive disposition toward referents of [− animate, + discrete] noun phrases. A related confound is that the bilinguals were living and tested in the UK, therefore it could be argued that the L2 cognitive shift had nothing to do with the language but with the English culture instead. Although the majority of bilinguals had lived in the UK for more or less the same amount of time, which was in any case relatively short, we cannot dismiss the possibility that even minimal exposure to the L2-speaking environment may affect cognition. Thus, Athanasopoulos' (2006) findings may suggest that the mind of advanced bilinguals may resemble that of monolingual speakers of their L2 because they are 'thinking' in their L2, and/or because they are 'immersed' in the L2 sociocultural milieu. Indeed, Cook *et al.* (2006) showed effects of length of stay in the L2-speaking country on the way Japanese-English bilinguals extended the novel name for a target object or substance to a shape or material alternate. Those bilinguals who had stayed in the UK for more than three years shifted their name-extension preferences toward those of monolingual speakers of English. On the other hand, those bilinguals who had stayed in the UK for less than three years displayed a pattern that was more similar to that displayed by Japanese monolinguals. It may also be the case that bilinguals maintain two distinct ways of processing reality, and may alternate between different preferences when using their different languages or in different experimental settings (cf. Grosjean, 1998, 2001).

2.5 The Role of Proficiency, Cultural Immersion and Language of Instructions

To address the issues raised by the previous study, Athanasopoulos (2007) conducted a triads matching task where equal numbers of objects, corresponding to singular count and mass nouns in English, were presented to English and Japanese monolinguals, as well as Japanese-English bilinguals. Previous research discussed earlier in this chapter (e.g. Lucy & Gaskins, 2003) had already established that there is an interaction between language type and preference type in similarity judgment tasks, such as the triads matching task, which requires participants to make decisions about the similarity between objects based on their shape or material characteristics. Speakers of grammatical number marking languages, like English, habitually attend to the shape of objects because it distinguishes between discrete objects and non-discrete substances. This cognitive disposition reflects the grammatical count/mass distinction in their language. Contrarily, speakers of classifier languages, like Yucatec and Japanese, tend to make material-based choices, as their languages do not grammatically mark the distinction between count and mass nouns, and treat all common nouns as mass.

To disentangle the effects of the language of instructions, there were two experimental settings: some bilinguals were tested in English by a non-Japanese administrator, while others were tested in Japanese by a Japanese administrator. To address the relative impact of proficiency and cultural immersion, bilinguals were selected to have variable levels of English proficiency (their native language was Japanese), and variable length of stay in the L2 country. Rigorous measures of L2 proficiency were implemented by means of a general proficiency test (QPT, 2001) and a grammaticality judgment task, measuring specific knowledge of grammatical number marking on count nouns, i.e. the crucial grammatical construction where Japanese and English differ. Selecting a wide range of bilinguals, with varying proficiency levels, varying amounts of time spent in the UK and different languages of instructions would ultimately allow for a multiple regression analysis, a technique used to assess the relative impact of a range of variables on behavior, and to determine which of the variables in question can best account for this behavior.

The participants were 25 monolingual English-speaking adults, 25 monolingual Japanese-speaking adults, 26 Japanese-English bilinguals instructed in English by a non-Japanese-speaking administrator and 18 Japanese-English bilinguals instructed in Japanese by a native speaker of Japanese. The vast majority of participants in all groups fell within the same age-range (early to mid twenties) and all were university students in Japan or the UK. The two groups of bilinguals had comparable ranges of English proficiency, length of stay in the UK and age of L2 acquisition. Specifically, the group that received task instructions in English had lived in the UK for an average of nine months (range 3–24 months). Their mean score on the QPT was 74% (SD = 10%, range 60–90%) and on the grammaticality judgment task 81% (SD = 17%, range 36–100%). The group that received task instructions in Japanese had lived in the UK for an average of 10 months (range 3–24 months). Their mean score on the QPT was 71% (SD = 9%, range 60–93%) and on the grammaticality judgment task 75% (SD = 17%, range 46–100%). Independent samples t-tests showed that the two bilingual groups did not differ significantly in their QPT and grammaticality judgment scores, t (42) = 0.914, $p > 0.05$, and t (42) = 1.190, $p > 0.05$, respectively. The vast majority of bilinguals in both groups had started learning English at the age of 12.

All groups were given a triads matching task requiring participants to match a standard object with a shape or material alternate, with two experimental conditions: a count condition, where the standard object was a solid entity that can be labeled in English as a count noun, and a mass condition where the standard object was a substance that can be labeled in English as a mass noun. There were six trials for each condition, thus 12 trials in total. In each trial, the participant was presented with a triad of a standard and two alternates, shape or material. All entities were presented on white paper plates and were covered with a piece of paper. During each trial, the standard was uncovered first, and the participant was prompted to pay attention to it. Then, the two alternates were uncovered and the participant was prompted to point to the entity that was the 'same' as the standard.

Responses were scored as the number of times each participant selected a shape or material alternate in each condition. Scores were then converted into percentages and the mean was calculated for each group. Since proportion of material responding is 1 minus the proportion of shape responding, for the statistical analysis the frequency of shape responses in each condition was the dependent variable. Figure 2.3 shows the proportion of shape responses that each group made in each of the two conditions.

A 4 (group) × 2 (condition) mixed ANOVA (with group as a between-subjects factor and condition as a within-subjects factor) yielded a significant main effect of condition, $F(1, 90) = 81$, $p < 0.05$, such that all groups selected shape more in the count than in the mass condition. The main effect of group was also significant, $F(3, 90) = 4.35$, $p < 0.05$, indicating that there are differences between groups in the proportion of shape responses. Crucially, the group × condition interaction was also significant, $F(3, 90) = 2.94$, $p < 0.05$. This indicates that the *way* participants made their shape preferences in the two conditions differed across the four groups.

In order to examine more closely the proportion of shape responses in each condition across the four groups, separate one-way ANOVAs were conducted. These showed a significant main effect of group in the count condition, $F(3, 90) = 7.66$, $p < 0.05$. *Post-hoc* tests showed that the English monolinguals and the bilinguals who were instructed in the L2 English selected the shape alternate significantly more frequently than the Japanese monolinguals, $p < 0.05$, while the bilinguals instructed in the

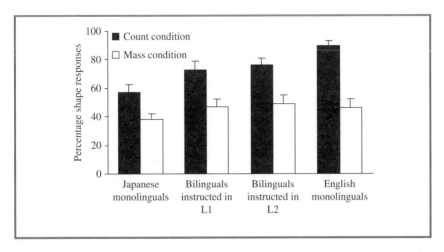

Figure 2.3 Proportion of shape responses, expressed as percentages, in the count and mass condition across the four groups

L1 Japanese did not differ significantly from any of the other groups, $p >$ 0.05. There was no significant main effect of group in the mass condition, $F(3, 90) = 0.82$, $p > 0.05$.

For the multiple regression analysis, the two bilingual groups were pooled together ($n = 44$), since the previous analyses showed no significant differences between them. A Pearson's correlation analysis showed that there was a highly significant correlation between grammaticality judgment scores and QPT scores ($r = 0.47$, $p = 0.001$). Therefore, the mean of the two scores was calculated for each participant, and a new variable was created, simply called 'proficiency'. Thus, the independent variables entered into the multiple regression analysis were proficiency (averaged from grammaticality judgment scores and QPT scores), length of stay in the L2 country and language of instructions, with shape scores in the count condition of the object classification task as the dependent variable. The overall regression was statistically significant, $F(3, 40) =$ 7.87, $p < 0.05$ ($R^2 = 0.37$). Proficiency was the only significant independent predictor of shape responses ($\beta = 0.55$, $t = 4.29$, $p < 0.05$). Although significantly correlated with shape responses in a Pearson's correlation analysis ($r = 0.27$, $p < 0.05$), the length of stay in the L2 country was not a statistically significant independent predictor, nor was the language of instructions.

This analysis suggests that although the Japanese-English bilinguals' cognitive behavior appears to be between those of the monolingual groups, the best predictor of their performance was L2 proficiency, but not the length of stay in the L2 country or the language of instructions. Thus, it seems that when controlling for L2 proficiency (measured rigorously by means of both a specific grammaticality judgment task and a general test), extra-linguistic variables, such as the length of stay in the L2 country and the language of instructions, are not significant predictors of restructuring in bilingual cognition in the domain of grammatical number. However, the role of these extra-linguistic variables may be apparent in other ways, and this is readily observable in the data: the bilingual cognitive behavior correlated with length of stay in Pearson correlation analyses, and the *post-hoc* tests showed that the group that was instructed in the L1 did not differ significantly from any of the other groups.

It may be the case then that more rigorous measures are required in order to disentangle the effects of cultural immersion and language of instructions on bilingual cognition. For example, all bilinguals in Athanasopoulos' (2007) study were living and studying in the UK. Perhaps simply varying the experimenter and the language of instructions is not sufficient to induce the relevant language mode. Thus, it would be highly desirable, although practically extremely difficult, in addition to the above measures, to test bilingual speakers of comparable proficiency levels in both the L1 and L2 countries, and include bilinguals who have never lived in the L2 country before. Another issue certainly worth investigating is age of L2 acquisition. In both of Athanasopoulos' studies, the majority of bilinguals had started learning the L2 at the age of 12 because that is the age when English is introduced in the Japanese educational system. While the cut-off point between early and late bilingualism is by no means set in stone, the effects of linguistic structure on cognition may vary as a function of age of acquisition.

Another crucially important issue concerns the very nature of the crosslinguistic cognitive effects and the bilingual restructuring observed. While Lucy and Gaskins (2003) have argued that similarity judgment tasks, such as the triads matching task, reflect habitual patterns of non-linguistic thought, other researchers have argued that the effects of language on such tasks may result from implicit verbal coding strategies, i.e. the effects are the result of the participants implicitly verbalizing the stimuli and reveal nothing about non-linguistic thought (Munnich & Landau, 2003; Pilling *et al.*, 2003). In the case of the object similarity studies described earlier, many of the stimuli used were recognizable objects and substances that could be labeled with count or mass nouns. Thus, it is not possible to know to what degree the patterns observed reflect genuine cognitive tendencies or whether they are simply the result of implicit verbal descriptions of the stimuli.

2.6 How 'Non-Linguistic' is Object Categorization?

As discussed in the introduction to this volume, a popular misconception of Whorf's principle of linguistic relativity is to assume that there are two versions of a hypothesis, a strong and a weak one. The historical roots of this division are not a primary concern of this chapter, however it is important to stress once again that such a division was never put forward by Whorf. In fact, Whorf himself largely avoided making claims about non-linguistic thought, and when he did, he assumed that language is not a necessary prerequisite of thinking:

> Moreover, the tremendous importance of language cannot, in my opinion, be taken to mean necessarily that nothing is back of it of the nature of what has traditionally been called "mind." My own studies suggest, to me, that language, for all its kingly role, is in some sense a superficial embroidery upon deeper processes of consciousness, which are necessary before any communication, signalling, or symbolism whatsoever can occur, and which also can, at a pinch, effect communication (though not true AGREEMENT) without language's and without symbolism's aid…The statement that "thinking is a matter of LANGUAGE" is an incorrect generalization

of the more nearly correct idea that "thinking is a matter of different tongues". (Whorf, 1956: 239; emphases in original)

In other words, according to Whorf, non-linguistic thought is very much possible. Thus, thinking is not constrained by language, but different languages highlight different patterns of thinking.

In this light, the question of whether cognitive processes are non-linguistic or not becomes pointless. The question might be more usefully rephrased as 'what is the *extent* of the influence of linguistic structure on cognitive processes, such as similarity judgments and categorization?' Studies to date have shown that when stimuli consist of real objects with a readily available name, then similarity judgments are highly suscep-tible to influence from linguistic structure, not only in monolingual populations, but, crucially, in bilingual populations as well, where the degree of cognitive shift toward the L2 patterns depends primarily on language proficiency, and to a lesser extent on language of instructions and cultural immersion.

Athanasopoulos and Kasai (2008) wanted to identify the extent to which grammatical representation of number could influence similarity judgments of novel objects. To this end, they utilized a series of artificial two-dimensional objects as stimulus materials (for an example see Athanasopoulos & Kasai, 2008). Thus, a possible verbal coding bias on the basis of the object's name and its status as a count or mass noun is significantly reduced. The task in question required participants to match these novel objects with a shape or color alternate. Implementing a color alternate instead of a material one does not mean that color and material have equal perceptual attributes. But it does afford the advantage that the stimuli cannot be lexically labeled with a count or mass noun, i.e. the crucial grammatical properties where English and Japanese differ. Thus, it cannot be argued that participants made their choice because they were influenced by a readily available name (e.g. 'the spoon' or 'the pile of sand'). Obviously, participants could still label using a simple noun phrase like 'the red one' (count) or 'the red stuff' (mass), however in that case the color name is used as an adjective and as such it is inherently neutral with regard to any semantic or grammatical content denoting count or mass status.

In addition, Athanasopoulos and Kasai (2008) aimed to address the issue of whether the patterns observed in previous studies reflect the bilinguals' general cognitive outlook, or whether they are due to the experi-mental context, which may have facilitated the L2 pattern. To this end, they implemented a triads matching task, comparing similarity judg-ments in Japanese and English monolinguals, and Japanese-English bilinguals of different proficiency levels and in different experimental contexts, i.e. intermediate and advanced speakers who lived and studied in the UK, and intermediate and advanced speakers who lived and studied in Japan, and had never lived in an English-speaking country before. Furthermore, Athanasopoulos and Kasai (2008) measured bilinguals' use of grammatical number marking in English during speech production. This would allow for straightforward comparisons between non-verbal cognitive tendencies and spontaneous linguistic performance on the grammatical feature claimed to be influencing object classification. The aim was to gain a more complete picture of the relationship between cognition and language in the bilingual mind than in previous studies.

Sixteen monolingual English-speaking adults and 16 monolingual Japanese-speaking adults participated in the study. In addition, two groups of bilingual speakers took part: one group consisted of 32 advanced Japanese L2 speakers of English divided into two subgroups: (1) 16 were tested in the UK and instructed in English by a non-Japanese speaker (mean age of L2 acquisition: 10 years old, range 5–13; mean length of stay in the UK: 7 months, range 3–20 months), (2) 16 were tested in Japan and instructed in Japanese by a native speaker of Japanese (mean age of L2 acquisition: 11 years old, range 6–13; had never lived in an English-speaking country before). The second group consisted of 32 intermediate Japanese L2 speakers of English, also divided into two subgroups: (1) 16 were tested in the UK in English by a non-Japanese speaker (all started acquiring the L2 at 12, mean length of stay in the UK: 6 months, range 3–24 months), (2) 16 were tested in Japan and instructed in Japanese by a native speaker of Japanese (mean age of L2 acquisition: 11 years old, range 5–12; had never lived in an English-speaking country before).

All participants were university students either in the UK or in Japan. The vast majority of them were in their early to mid twenties. Proficiency in English was once again measured with the QPT (2001). In addition to the QPT, the bilinguals were also given a picture description task, where they were asked to describe orally a picture depicting a scene from a typical town center in England. The specific grammatical property measured in the bilinguals' oral descriptions was obligatory grammatical number marking on count nouns. The responses for each bilingual were scored by calculating the ratio of correctly supplying plural marking to the number of required contexts (these were established on the basis of how previously tested native speakers referred to the same objects/people in the picture, and not on the basis of what the picture showed). The mean percentage ratio of producing correct plural morphology was 77% (SD = 29) for advanced bilinguals and 63% (SD = 32) for intermediate bilinguals. Although not hugely different, these scores were nonetheless statistically significantly different, independent samples t-test, $t(62) = 1.830$, $p < 0.05$.

Thirty color illustrations of novel objects were used as stimuli. They were then organized into 10 different triads. Each triad was composed of a standard object and two alternates, a shape alternate, which had the same shape as the standard but different color, and a color alternate, which had the same color as the standard but different shape. All stimuli were drawn and edited on the same scale, thus eliminating a potential size variable. Additionally, the colors used within each triad were carefully selected so that the shape alternate was not similar in color to the standard. Conversely, care was taken so that the color alternate was not similar in shape to the standard. Finally, the shapes used were arbitrary novel shapes as opposed to highly recognizable shapes, like squares, triangles and circles.

An interactive computer program was created as a test instrument. The software used to create the program was Flash 5 by Macromedia. The participants had to use the computer mouse in order to interact with the program. There were a total of 10 trials. Each trial consisted of two stages. In the first stage, the standard novel object appeared at the top of the screen and participants were asked to click on it. In the second stage, once the participants had clicked on the standard, the two alternates appeared side by side underneath the standard and at an equal distance from it, and participants were instructed to click on the alternate that they thought was 'the same' as the standard. The position of the alternates relative to the standard was counterbalanced across trials, such that the shape alternate appeared in five out of ten trials on the left side of the screen, and in five out of ten trials on the right side of the screen, and vice versa for the color alternate. The order in which each trial was presented was randomized for each participant, utilizing Flash's Actionscript for this purpose. The procedure was repeated for the remaining nine trials. Each participant's response was recorded for each trial and was saved as a data file that appeared at the end of the experiment.

Responses were scored as the number of times each participant selected a shape or color alternate. Scores were then converted into percentages and the mean was calculated for each group of participants. Because the proportion of color responses is 1 minus the proportion of shape responses, the frequency of shape responses was used as the dependent variable. Figure 2.4 shows the proportion of shape responses for the two monolingual groups and the advanced and intermediate bilingual groups.

Because the English monolinguals and many of the bilinguals selected the shape alternate almost at ceiling, the data were not normally distributed, and this prevented the use of parametric statistical tests like ANOVA. Therefore, results were analyzed by means of a Logit, with frequency of shape responses as the dependent variable. Overall, this showed a significant main effect of group, $x^2 = 51.279$, $p < 0.01$. Separate

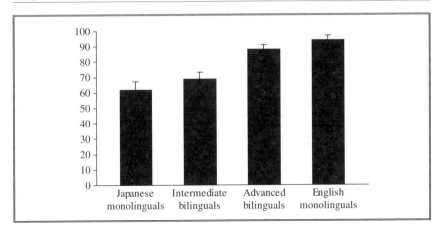

Figure 2.4 Proportion of shape responses, expressed as percentages, across the four groups

Logit analyses showed a significant difference between the English and Japanese monolinguals, $x^2 = 23.309$, $p < 0.01$; between English monolinguals and intermediate bilinguals, $x^2 = 19.781$, $p < 0.01$; between advanced and intermediate bilinguals, $x^2 = 21.737$, $p < 0.01$; and between advanced bilinguals and Japanese monolinguals, $x^2 = 23.729$, $p < 0.01$. There were no significant differences between English monolinguals and advanced bilinguals, $x^2 = 4.535$, $p > 0.05$; and between Japanese monolinguals and intermediate bilinguals, $x^2 = 10.136$, $p > 0.05$. To sum up, the results show that English monolinguals and advanced L2 speakers selected the shape alternate significantly more frequently than intermediate L2 speakers and Japanese monolinguals. Furthermore, a comparison of those bilinguals tested in the L1 with those tested in the L2 showed no significant difference between them, $x^2 = 9.436$, $p > 0.05$.

Although the analysis above demonstrates robust differences between groups, Figure 2.4 shows that Japanese monolinguals and intermediate L2 speakers did show a shape bias, albeit significantly smaller than the other two groups. Tests against chance level (50%) showed that the groups in question did select shape significantly above chance: t (15) = 2.162, $p < 0.05$ for Japanese monolinguals; t (31) = 4.433, $p < 0.01$ for intermediate L2 speakers. English monolinguals and advanced L2 speakers showed a strong reliable bias toward shape: t (15) = 16.232, $p < 0.01$ and t (31) = 12.889, $p < 0.01$, respectively. This pattern of results provides a very informative answer to the question 'to what extent does linguistic structure influence similarity judgments?' It appears that when stimuli are selected to eliminate a possible verbal coding bias on the basis of count or mass status (the crucial crosslinguistic difference between Japanese and English), individuals tend to prefer shape as a basis for similarity, regardless of language background, thus reverting to the initial cognitive bias shown in prelinguistic Japanese children (cf. Imai & Gentner, 1997). However, the current results also show that the degree to which this shape bias manifests itself is different for speakers of different languages and appears to conform to language-specific patterns of individuation.

In order to directly compare bilinguals' cognitive tendencies with their production of number marking in English, the two groups of advanced and intermediate bilinguals were pooled together into one group ($n = 64$). Each bilingual's shape score in the triads matching task and plural marking score in the picture description task was entered into a Pearson's correlation analysis, partialling out age of L2 acquisition. Results showed that the correlation was weak but statistically significant, $r = 0.338$, $p < 0.05$. The correlation between age of L2 acquisition and shape preferences was also significant ($r = -0.275$, $p < 0.05$), but when plural marking scores were partialled out, the correlation became non-significant, $r = -0.190$, $p > 0.05$. An additional correlation between shape preference and plural marking scores was performed on those bilinguals who had lived in the UK ($n = 32$), partialling out both length of stay in the UK and age of L2 acquisition. Results showed that the correlation was moderate and statistically significant, $r = 0.385$, $p < 0.05$. There was no significant correlation between shape preference and length of stay in the UK, $r = 0.095$, $p > 0.05$. These results mean that even when controlling for extra-linguistic variables, such as length of stay in the L2 country and age of acquisition, there is a significant relationship between the shift in cognitive preferences and specific linguistic competence, i.e. the better the bilinguals are at producing correct number marking in the oral production task, the more they select the shape alternate in the triads matching task.

The pattern of results from the bilingual participants is interesting for a multitude of reasons. Firstly, despite the fact that using artificial stimuli yielded a language-independent global pattern of similarity judgments, the effects of language can readily be seen, not only in the degree to which monolinguals differ in their similarity judgments, but crucially in the finding that a weak but persistent direct link between specific linguistic competence and similarity judgments can be found in the bilingual participants. Secondly, these findings showed that non-linguistic socio-cultural variables, such as length of stay in the L2-speaking country, do not play a role in bilingual cognitive restructuring in the domain of grammatical number. The results also suggest that learning the L2 earlier in life may facilitate the redirection of attention to new perceptual attributes of reality, but it is ultimately specific linguistic competence that is most tightly linked with the bilingual cognitive shift. Thirdly, the findings from the current study showed that it is unlikely that bilinguals maintain two separate cognitive representations of language-specific concepts, and they alternate between the two mental views of the world according to the language or setting they are tested in. The current findings suggest that learning specific grammatical categories might alter the individual's cognitive representations in a more permanent way, leading to genuine cognitive reorganization.

2.7 Discussion of the Grammatical Number Studies

The findings from the studies on grammatical number marking and object classification preferences have provided direct empirical evidence that bears on the relationship between linguistic categories and non-linguistic cognition in the bilingual mind (Pavlenko, 2005). The data show that, in some cases, cognitive processing in bilinguals is influenced primarily by the L1. But this is more evident in intermediate bilinguals. On the other hand, advanced bilinguals seem to shift their cognition toward the L2 as a function of internalization of novel grammatical categories. This interpretation of the results should be followed by an important qualification. While averaged group patterns may suggest a complete shift toward the L2 pattern, there exists a considerable amount of variation within advanced bilinguals, which suggests only partial or incomplete restructuring in certain individuals, even when a very advanced level of proficiency in the L2 has been reached. In addition, the studies provide very little evidence to suggest that bilinguals behave in two distinct ways depending on the experimental setting they are engaged in. That is, bilingual cognition in the domain of grammatical number is not moderated in any significant way by the setting the individuals find themselves in; whether bilinguals were given task instructions in the L1 or L2, whether they were in the L1-speaking or L2-speaking country, whether they interacted with a native L1 speaker or not, there was little difference in their behavior.

In addition, it appears that age of L2 acquisition and length of cultural immersion in the L2-speaking country exert some influence on cognitive restructuring in the domain of number, albeit minimal, and ultimately, when proficiency is controlled for, non-significant. It could be argued, however, that while the aforementioned studies rigorously measured L2 proficiency, both by means of general proficiency tests and specific tests in different modalities, such as oral production or grammaticality judgments, they did not include a wide enough margin for either length of cultural immersion or age of L2 acquisition. For example, across studies, bilinguals had lived in the L2-speaking country for a maximum of two years, which may not be quite enough to show any potential influence of cultural immersion. Cook et al. (2006) showed that Japanese-English bilinguals' behavior on a task similar to the one in Imai and Gentner (1997) and Athanasopoulos (2007) shifted toward the L2 only after participants had spent a minimum of three years in the L2-speaking country. Moreover, the range of age of L2 acquisition used in Athanasopoulos and Kasai (2008) is quite short (5–12 years old), and it is remarkable that any effect of that variable is apparent at all. The age of five years is considered by many scholars in the field of bilingualism as the point at which any additional language learning is seen as 'second' language learning (Carroll, 2008). Other studies claim that seven or 12 years old is the 'cut-off' point or 'critical period' for 'successful' language acquisition (Johnson & Newport, 1989). Thus, wider age ranges need to be used in further research, which include bilinguals who have learned both languages from birth, as well as those who have learned them sequentially.

A further issue to address in future research is the relationship between L1 knowledge and cognition. The studies by Athanasopoulos and colleagues were the first to show a direct link between acquired L2 knowledge and cognitive processing of objects, but did not measure their participants' knowledge of the relevant constructions in the L1, which, in the case of Japanese, would be numeral classifier constructions. Recent studies have shown that acquisition of an L2 may affect pre-existing L1 knowledge of a range of linguistic domains, such as semantics, syntax and phonology (see e.g. Cook, 2003). Thus, further studies need to take into account the changing L1 knowledge and its relationship with the changing cognitive state of the bi- or multilingual speaker.

Obviously, it is very difficult for a single empirical study to single-handedly address all of the above issues. However, discussion of those issues is important as it puts the findings and conclusions of Athanaso-poulos and colleagues' preliminary studies into perspective, and paves the way for further research, both in the fields of bilingualism and cross-cultural cognition. Considering the multitude of factors that may affect bilingual cognition is especially important when attempting to investi-gate whether crosslinguistic effects of bilingualism on cognition are empirically observable in other domains.

An additional research question that needs to be addressed in the future is whether there will be differential effects on bilingual cognition as a function of the nature of the particular linguistic domain (Green, 1998). Specifically, a grammatical domain, such as number marking, makes certain obligatory distinctions, crucial for grammaticality. Speak-ers of English use grammatical number marking when quantifying countable nouns, not because they choose to do so, but because their language leaves them with no other choice: if they do not apply plural marking, the resulting phrase will be ungrammatical. The reverse is also true, i.e. applying plural marking and quantifying mass nouns directly will also result in ungrammaticality. Speakers of Japanese and Yucatec, on the other hand, are not forced to distinguish between countable and non-countable nouns, as there is no obligatory plural marking in their nominal systems. But modifying nouns directly with a numeral will result in ungrammaticality, hence they must also attend to some specific structure for the purposes of grammaticality.

In contrast, a lexical domain (e.g. color terms) does not impose obligatory distinctions on speakers, but instead provides the speaker with ready labels for the description of reality. In most cases, speakers adhere to those labels as conventionally applied devices for the exchange of meaning. If a speaker does not adhere to those conventions, the resulting phrase will not necessarily be ungrammatical; rather it will violate this aforementioned tacit agreement and result in erroneous communication. In addition, naming patterns are more susceptible to change than grammatical patterns, as evidenced by the frequent invention of new words to describe new aspects of reality, or the semantic shift of previously existing words to describe new concepts and ideas, as in cases of political spin or political correctness. Crosslinguistic differences in this domain need not concern obligatory distinctions, but rather different ways of describing and parsing reality. From a categorization viewpoint, the crucial crosslinguistic difference here is demarcation of boundaries. For example, it is a relatively well-established finding that if one language has one term to describe both the blue and green areas of color space, speakers of that language will not attend to that distinction cognitively as readily as speakers of a language that has separate terms for those colors (Davidoff *et al.*, 1999; Kay & Kempton, 1984). How are contrasting ways of categorizing reality in language reconciled in the cognition of bilingual individuals? Athanasopoulos' (2009) study of cognitive representation of color in Greek-English bilinguals provides tentative answers to these questions.

2.8 Bilingual Blues

Cognitive processing of color has traditionally been at the forefront of the language and thought debate, and has been used both as a prime example of linguistic effects on cognition (Brown & Lenneberg, 1954) as well as a primary example of universality (Berlin & Kay, 1969; Heider-Rosch, 1972). Subsequent studies have acknowledged physiological and perceptual constraints on color vision common to all humans, but empirically demonstrated that the way individuals judge the similarity or the difference between color stimuli may depend on how their language carves the world into nameable parts (Davidoff *et al.*, 1999; Roberson *et al.*, 2000). For example, a study by Roberson *et al.* (2005) found that speakers of languages that mark the boundaries of color categories on color space differently showed categorical perception (judging two stimuli to be more similar if they fall within a category boundary than if they cut across the boundary) for the specific color areas encoded in their respective languages.

Bilingualism has been central to the color debates from a very early stage. Early studies showed profound shifts in bilinguals' color categories and foci (best examples) toward those of monolingual speakers of their L2 (Caskey-Sirmons & Hickerson, 1977; Ervin, 1961; Lenneberg & Roberts, 1956). Yet, as discussed in the introduction to this chapter, many scholars have paid little attention to bilingualism when investigating representation of color categories across languages and cultures. Some studies have interpreted the English-like behavior of speakers of other languages (who happened be L2 speakers of English) as evidence for universality (e.g. Berlin & Kay, 1969). Taking into account the studies by Caskey-Sirmons and Hickerson (1977) and others that showed a semantic shift of color boundaries and foci toward the L2, it is likely that the bilingual participants in Berlin and Kay's (1969) study were influenced by their knowledge of English. In other cases, bilingualism is not controlled properly or not taken into account at all, resulting in conflicting results (e.g. the studies on Russian blues by Laws *et al.*, 1995 and Winawer *et al.*, 2007).

Like Russian, Greek divides the blue region of color space into two distinct regions, a darker shade called *ble*, and a lighter shade called *ghalazio* (Androulaki *et al.*, 2006). Athanasopoulos (2009) wanted to find out whether the *ble/ghalazio* distinction would become less salient in the cognition of Greek-English bilinguals as a result of using an L2 that does not mark the contrast between these categories. He did this by asking Greek-English bilingual and English monolingual participants to rate the perceptual similarity between dark blue and light blue color squares.

Because the teaching of English as an L2 is implemented in the Greek educational system from very early on, it is very difficult to find participants who are college-educated and yet completely monolingual in Greek. Thus, Athanasopoulos (2009) selected a group of 30 Greek native speakers with a wide range of proficiency levels in English, ranging from 61 to 90 on the Nation vocabulary test (Nation, 1990), which measures vocabulary in English and can be used as an indication of general proficiency (see e.g. Cook *et al.*, 2006). These participants were students at a UK university at the time of testing, with a mean length of stay in the UK of 33 months, ranging from two to 96 months. The age at which they started to learn English ranged from one to 13 years old, with a mean age of seven. The participants reported that they used English for nine hours per day on average, ranging from three to 17 hours. Selecting participants with a wide range of L2 proficiency, length of stay in the L2-speaking country, age of L2 acquisition and amount of L2 use would allow the author to correlate these variables with the participants' similarity judgments of light and dark blue colors.

In addition to the above variables, Athanasopoulos (2009) also sought to investigate the impact of specific language proficiency on bilingual color cognition. Therefore, he asked participants to list all the color terms they could think of, first in one language (English or Greek), then in the other (counterbalanced throughout the sample). Elicitation of color lists was used here to measure the saliency of *blue*, *ble* and *ghalazio* in semantic memory (the higher up the list a term appears, the more available it is in semantic memory). This would allow for correlations between the semantic saliency of each term (i.e. how high it appears on the list) with participants' similarity judgments. On average, *ble* was placed sixth on the list (SD = 4, range 1–17), *ghalazio* was placed 12th (SD = 7, range 2–28) and *blue* was placed fifth (SD = 3, range 1–13). The similarity judgment task was also given to a group of 22 English monolingual university students whose age, socio-economic and educational backgrounds were comparable to those of the Greek-English bilinguals.

The stimuli were individual 10×20 mm glossy Munsell chips, mounted on 40 mm square pieces of white cardboard. Munsell color chips are defined in terms of three dimensions: Hue, Value (lightness) and Chroma (saturation) (Munsell Color Company website: http://www.xrite.com/top_munsell.aspx). Twenty native Greek speakers who did not take part in the similarity judgment experiment were asked to name dark and light blue Munsell chips. Based on the naming patterns of these participants, five pairs of within-category stimuli and three pairs of cross-category stimuli were created. That is, five pairs where both members of the pair were consistently (within-group agreement over 80%) called *ble* or *ghalazio*, and three pairs where one member was consistently called *ble* and the other was consistently called *ghalazio*. The Munsell designations of the stimuli used are expressed in the form Hue/Value/Chroma. The within-category pairs were 10B/2/6-10B/4/10, 5PB/2/8-5PB/4/12, 5B/6/8-5B/8/4, 10B/6/10-10B/8/6 and 5PB/6/10-5PB/8/6. The cross-category pairs were 5B/4/10-5B/6/8, 10B/4/10-10B/6/10 and 5PB/4/12-5PB/6/10. All stimuli were perceptually equidistant, meaning that the perceptual distance between each stimulus was maintained at two Value levels (since lightness is the critical dimension for the purposes of this particular task).

Each participant was asked to judge 'how different or similar these two colors are' using a 10-point scale, where 10 represents maximum dissimilarity and 1 represents maximum similarity. Each pair was shown twice, counterbalancing the position of each individual chip in the pair. The order of presentation of pairs was randomized across the whole sample. On completion of the similarity judgment task, participants were asked to complete a biographical questionnaire, then list the color terms in one language, then complete the Nation vocabulary test, and finally list the color terms in the other language. Instructions were given to all participants in their native language by a Greek-English bilingual speaker. Figure 2.5 shows the mean similarity judgments of within and cross-category pairs for the two groups of participants.

A 2 (Group: English versus Greek) × 2 (Pair type: within versus cross) mixed ANOVA showed that the main effects of Group and Pair type were not significant, $F(1, 50) = 0.513$, $p > 0.05$, and $F(1, 50) = 0.448$, $p > 0.05$, respectively. The Group × Pair type interaction approached significance, $F(1, 50) = 3.247$, $p = 0.08$. The next step in the analysis focused on examining whether the cognitive behavior of Greek speakers is modulated by any of the variables that were measured and which previous research has shown may affect the way bilinguals perform in non-linguistic similarity judgment tasks. For this purpose, a new variable was calculated, hereafter called the Categorical Perception Index (CPI), by subtracting each participant's mean similarity judgment score for within-category pairs from their mean similarity judgment score for cross-category pairs. Obviously, the greater the remaining score, the more distinction is made between within and cross-category pairs. The CPI was then partially correlated with general L2 proficiency as measured by the Nation test, length of stay in the L2 country, age of L2 acquisition, amount of L2 use and semantic saliency of *ble, blue* and *ghalazio*, as

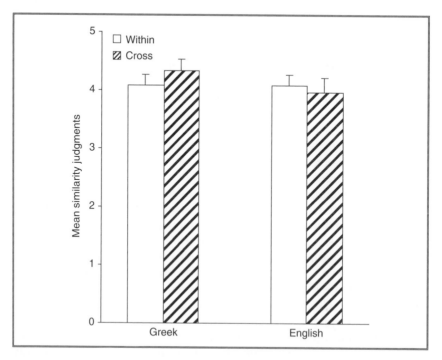

Figure 2.5 Mean similarity judgments of within and cross-category pairs

measured by the position of each term on each participant's list of color terms. Using partial correlations here is crucial, as they reveal the relationship between the CPI and each variable, taking into account the potential impact of all the other variables. So, any significant correlation obtained reveals a true relationship between two variables, eliminating all other potentially confounding or mediating variables.

The strongest significant correlation was obtained for the semantic saliency of *ble* ($r = -0.53$, $p < 0.01$). This means that the further down *ble* appears on the color list (and thus the greater its number on the list), the less bilinguals distinguish between within and cross-category pairs. There was also a moderate correlation with the semantic saliency of *blue* ($r = 0.41$, $p < 0.05$), such that the higher *blue* appears in each participant's color list (and thus the smaller its number on the list), the less distinction is made between within and cross-category pairs. Finally, the weakest significant correlation was obtained for the length of stay in the UK ($r = -0.39$), such that the longer bilinguals have stayed in the L2 country, the less they distinguish between within and cross-category pairs. None of the remaining variables correlated significantly with the CPI. These results show that when controlling for a range of variables that may influence bilingual cognition, semantic saliency of specific color terms and length of stay in the L2 country significantly influence bilingual cognition in the domain of color.

Since memory for specific color terms and length of stay in the L2 country were significantly correlated with the CPI, further analyses were carried out in order to examine whether there is a discernible threshold in memory and/or length of stay at which participants abruptly shift their similarity judgment patterns, or whether these shift progressively. To this end, a median split was performed in the Greek-English bilinguals based on their memory for the relevant color terms and their length of stay in the UK. Using CPI as the dependent variable, their behavior was compared against each other and against that of the English monolingual group in separate one-way ANOVAs.

For memory for *ble* and *blue*, bilinguals were split into a High group and a Low group. The High group placed the relevant term between first and fourth place on the color term list, while the Low group placed the relevant term below fourth place on the list. For length of stay in the L2 country, the two groups that were formed were a Long-stay group who had been living in the UK between 24 and 96 months, and a Short-stay group who had been living in the UK between 2 and 22 months. Figure 2.6 shows the mean CPI scores for each bilingual group, alongside that of the English monolingual group.

For *ble*, a one-way ANOVA showed a significant main effect of Group, $F(2, 49) = 4.212$, $p < 0.05$. *Post-hoc* Bonferroni tests showed that the only significant difference was between the High group and the English

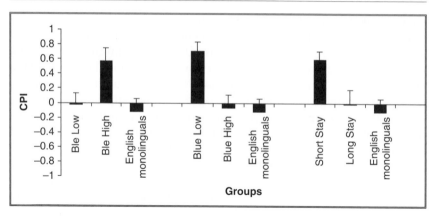

Figure 2.6 CPI for bilinguals split by semantic memory for *ble*, semantic memory for *blue*, and length of stay in the UK, and English monolinguals. The higher the CPI, the more distinction is made between within and cross-category stimulus pairs

monolinguals ($p < 0.05$). This means that those bilinguals who tended to place *ble* in the first four places on their list distinguished significantly more between within and cross-category pairs than the English monolinguals. Thus, cognitive behavior begins to shift toward the L2 pattern once *ble* is placed consistently below fourth place on the list.

For *blue*, a one-way ANOVA showed a significant main effect of Group, $F(2, 49) = 6.221$, $p < 0.01$. *Post-hoc* Bonferroni tests showed that the Low group differed significantly both from the High group ($p < 0.05$) and the English monolingual group ($p < 0.01$), while there was no significant difference between the High group and the English monolingual group ($p > 0.05$). This means that those bilinguals who tended to place *blue* below fourth place on the list distinguished significantly more between within and cross-category pairs than the High group and the English monolinguals. Thus, cognitive behavior shifts completely toward the L2 pattern once *blue* is placed consistently above fifth place on the list.

For length of stay in the L2 country, a one-way ANOVA showed a significant main effect of Group, $F(2, 49) = 4.269$, $p < 0.05$. *Post-hoc* Bonferroni tests showed that the only significant difference was between the Short-stay group and the English monolinguals ($p < 0.05$). This means that once individuals have spent 24 months in the L2-speaking country, their color cognition begins to shift toward the L2 pattern.

The findings from Athanasopoulos' (2009) color study add two important new dimensions to investigations of bilingual cognition. Firstly, the link between the weakening of an L1 color term in semantic memory and similarity judgments of dark blue and light blue squares shows that it may not just be acquisition of novel linguistic categories that may influence the way bilinguals behave in cognitive tasks, but also attrition of the original L1 term. Secondly, the finding of a persistent effect of length of stay in the L2 country but not of general L2 proficiency, suggests that sociocultural factors may exert a stronger influence on the relationship between color terms and color cognition, than on the relationship between grammatical number and object cognition, where the majority of studies show significant effects of language proficiency. This conclusion is corroborated by a new study of categorical color perception in Japanese-English bilinguals (Japanese, like Greek, also distinguishes between two shades of blue). Athanasopoulos *et al.* (in press) found that the way their bilingual participants judged the distinction between light and dark blue stimuli primarily depended on the amount of L2 use in their daily activities: those that tended to use English more, also tended to distinguish less between different shades of blue, resembling English monolinguals in this respect.

While it is certainly too early to draw firm conclusions on the issue of which specific factors may affect bilingual cognition, the currently available data suggest that focusing the enquiry on linguistic *or* cultural influence may obscure an interestingly complex situation. It appears that *both* culture and language may influence the way bilinguals perceive categorical divisions, but to different degrees and in different ways. This is precisely the reason why linguistic and sociocultural variables are best conceptualized as points on a continuum rather than discrete and mutually exclusive categories (see Section 2.3).

2.9 Conclusion

The relationship between linguistic categories and higher cognitive processes, such as reasoning and categorization, is an ongoing concern in a variety of disciplines. This chapter provided a detailed overview of recent studies that have attempted to extend that investigation to the domain of bilingualism. It was argued that such an investigation carries significant ecological validity because the majority of the world's population uses more than one language in order to communicate. Results from these studies showed that bilingual cognition in the domain of grammatical number may resemble either monolingual norm, primarily as a function of language proficiency, while factors such as acculturation, experimental setting and age of acquisition may play a significant but secondary role. In the domain of color, it was demonstrated that the way bilinguals judge color distinctions lexicalized in one language but not the other, depends on the availability of the relevant terms in semantic memory, on the amount of time they have spent in the L2 country and on the amount of time they use the L2 in their daily activities. By considering the methodological advantages that the study of bilingualism affords, in that we are able to directly correlate linguistic and sociocultural variables with cognition, it becomes apparent that this is indeed a fertile and ultimately much more revealing way of examining the precise role of linguistic and extra-linguistic variables on cognitive processing. The examination of bilingual cognitive processing of reality has the potential to reveal fundamental processes of human cognition, and elucidate aspects of the language and thought debate that have hitherto remained unexplored.

References

Androulaki, A., Gomez-Pestana, N., Mitsakis, C., Jover, J., Coventry, K. and Davies, I. (2006) Basic color terms in Modern Greek: Twelve terms including two blues. *Journal of Greek Linguistics* 7, 3–45.

Athanasopoulos, P. (2006) Effects of the grammatical representation of number on cognition in bilinguals. *Bilingualism: Language and Cognition* 9, 89–96.

Athanasopoulos, P. (2007) Interaction between grammatical categories and cognition in bilinguals: The role of proficiency, cultural immersion, and language of instruction. *Language and Cognitive Processes* 22, 689–699.

Athanasopoulos, P. (2009) Cognitive representation of color in bilinguals: The case of Greek blues. *Bilingualism: Language and Cognition* 12, 83–95.

Athanasopoulos, P., Damjanovic, L., Krajciova, A. and Sasaki, M. (in press). Representation of color concepts in bilingual cognition: The case of Japanese blues. *Bilingualism: Language and Cognition* 14.

Athanasopoulos, P. and Kasai, Ch. (2008) Language and thought in bilinguals: The case of grammatical number and nonverbal classification preferences. *Applied Psycholinguistics* 29, 105–121.

Berlin, B. and Kay, P. (1969) *Basic Color Terms: Their Universality and Evolution.* Berkeley, CA: University of California Press.

Bowerman, M. and Choi, S. (2001) Shaping meanings for language: Universal and language-specific in the acquisition of spatial semantic categories. In M. Bowerman and S. Levinson (eds) *Language Acquisition and Conceptual Development* (pp. 475–511). Cambridge: Cambridge University Press.

Bowerman, M. and Levinson, S. (eds) (2001) *Language Acquisition and Conceptual Development.* Cambridge: Cambridge University Press.

Brown, R. and Lenneberg, E. (1954) A study in language and cognition. *Journal of Abnormal and Social Psychology* 49, 454–462.

Carroll, D. (2008) *Psychology of Language* (5th edn). Belmont, CA: Thomson Wadsworth.

Caskey-Sirmons, L. and Hickerson, N. (1977) Semantic shift and bilingualism: Variation in the color terms of five languages. *Anthropological Linguistics* 19, 358–367.

Cook, V. (1991) The poverty-of-the-stimulus argument and multi-competence. *Second Language Research* 7, 103–117.

Cook, V. (1992) Evidence for multicompetence. *Language Learning* 42, 557–591.

Cook, V. (1997) The consequences of bilingualism for cognitive processing. In A. De Groot and J. Kroll (eds) *Tutorials in Bilingualism: Psycholinguistic Perspectives* (pp. 279–300). Hillsdale, NJ: Lawrence Erlbaum.

Cook, V. (1999) Going beyond the native speaker in language teaching. *TESOL Quarterly* 33, 185–209.

Cook, V. (2002) Background to the L2 user. In V. Cook (ed.) *Portraits of the L2 User* (pp. 1–31). Clevedon: Multilingual Matters.

Cook, V. (2003) The changing L1 in the L2 user's mind. In V. Cook (ed.) *Effects of the Second Language on the First* (pp. 1–18). Clevedon: Multilingual Matters.

Cook, V., Bassetti, B., Kasai, Ch., Sasaki, M. and Takahashi, J. (2006) Do bilinguals have different concepts? The case of shape and material in Japanese L2 users of English. *International Journal of Bilingualism* 10, 137–152.

Davidoff, J., Davies, I. and Roberson, D. (1999) Color categories in a stone-age tribe. *Nature* 398, 203–204.

Ervin, S. (1961) Semantic shift in bilingualism. *American Journal of Psychology* 74, 233–241.

Gentner, D. and Goldin-Meadow, S. (eds) (2003) *Language in Mind: Advances in the Study of Language and Thought*. Cambridge, MA: MIT Press.

Gopnik, A. (2001) Theories, language, and culture: Whorf without wincing. In M. Bowerman and S. Levinson (eds) *Language Acquisition and Conceptual Development* (pp. 44–69). Cambridge: Cambridge University Press.

Gopnik, A. and Choi, S. (1995) Names, relational words, and cognitive development in English and Korean speakers: Nouns are not always learned before verbs. In M. Tomasello and W. Merriman (eds) *Beyond Names for Things: Young Children's Acquisition of Verbs* (pp. 63–80). Hillsdale, NJ: Erlbaum.

Gopnik, A., Choi, S. and Baumberger, T. (1996) Crosslinguistic differences in early semantic and cognitive development. *Cognitive Development* 11, 197–227.

Gopnik, A. and Meltzoff, A. (1987) The development of categorization in the second year and its relation to other cognitive and linguistic developments. *Child Development* 58, 1523–1531.

Gopnik, A. and Meltzoff, A. (1992) Categorization and naming: Basic-level sorting in eighteen-month-olds and its relation to language. *Child Development* 63, 1091–1103.

Green, D. (1998) Bilingualism and thought. *Psychologica Belgica* 38, 253–278.

Grosjean, F. (1982) *Life with Two Languages: An Introduction to Bilingualism*. Cambridge: Cambridge University Press.

Grosjean, F. (1989) Neurolinguists, beware! The bilingual is not two monolinguals in one person. *Brain and Language* 36, 3–15.

Grosjean, F. (1992) Another view of bilingualism. In R. Harris (ed.) *Cognitive Processing in Bilinguals* (pp. 51–62). Amsterdam: North Holland.

Grosjean, F. (1998) Studying bilinguals: Methodological and conceptual issues. *Bilingualism: Language and Cognition* 1, 131–149.

Grosjean, F. (2001) The bilingual's language modes. In J. Nicol (ed.) *One Mind, Two languages* (pp. 1–22). Oxford: Blackwell.

Gumperz, J. and Levinson, S. (eds) (1996) *Rethinking Linguistic Relativity*. Cambridge: Cambridge University Press.

Heider-Rosch, E. (1972) Universals in color naming and memory. *Journal of Experimental Psychology* 93, 10–20.

Heider, E. and Olivier, D. (1972) The structure of the color space in naming and memory for two languages. *Cognitive Psychology* 3, 337–354.

Hespos, S. and Spelke, E. (2004) Conceptual precursors to language. *Nature* 430, 453–456.

Imai, M. and Gentner, D. (1997) A crosslinguistic study of early word meaning: Universal ontology and linguistic influence. *Cognition* 62, 169–200.

Imai, M. and Mazuka, R. (2003) Re-evaluating linguistic relativity: Language-specific categories and the role of universal ontological knowledge in the construal of individuation. In D. Gentner and S. Goldin-Meadow (eds) *Language in Mind: Advances in the Study of Language and Thought* (pp. 429–464). Cambridge, MA: MIT Press.

Jarvis, S. and Pavlenko, A. (2008) *Crosslinguistic Influence in Language and Cognition.* New York/London: Routledge.

Johnson, J. and Newport, E. (1989) Critical period effects in second language learning: The influence of maturational state on the acquisition of English as a second language. *Cognitive Psychology* 21, 60–99.

Kay, P. and Kempton, W. (1984) What is the Sapir-Whorf hypothesis? *American Anthropologist* 86, 65–79.

Laws, G., Davies, I. and Andrews, C. (1995) Linguistic structure and non-linguistic cognition: English and Russian blues compared. *Language and Cognitive Processes* 10, 59–94.

Lenneberg, E. and Roberts, J. (1956) The language of experience: A study in methodology. Memoir 13: supplement to *International Journal of American Linguistics* 22, 13.

Levinson, S. (2001) Covariation between spatial language and cognition, and its implications for language learning. In M. Bowerman and S. Levinson (eds) *Language Acquisition and Conceptual Development* (pp. 566–588). Cambridge: Cambridge University Press.

Lucy, J. (1992a) *Language Diversity and Thought: A Reformulation of the Linguistic Relativity Hypothesis.* Cambridge: Cambridge University Press.

Lucy, J. (1992b) *Grammatical Categories and Cognition. A Case Study of the Linguistic Relativity Hypothesis.* Cambridge: Cambridge University Press.

Lucy, J. and Gaskins, S. (2001) Grammatical categories and the development of classification preferences: A comparative approach. In M. Bowerman and S. Levinson (eds) *Language Acquisition and Conceptual Development* (pp. 257–283). Cambridge: Cambridge University Press.

Lucy, J. and Gaskins, S. (2003) Interaction of language type and referent type in the development of nonverbal classification preferences. In D. Gentner and S. Goldin-Meadow (eds) *Language in Mind: Advances in the Study of Language and Thought* (pp. 465–492). Cambridge, MA: MIT Press.

Mandler, J. (1997) Development of categorization: Perceptual and conceptual categories. In G. Bremner, A. Slater and G. Butterworth (eds) *Infant Development: Recent Advances* (pp. 163–190). Hove: Psychology Press.

Martinez, I. and Shatz, M. (1996) Linguistic influences on categorization in preschool children: A crosslinguistic study. *Journal of Child Language* 23, 529–545.

Munnich, E. and Landau, B. (2003) The effects of spatial language on spatial representation: Setting some boundaries. In D. Gentner and S. Goldin-Meadow (eds) *Language in Mind: Advances in the Study of Language and Thought* (pp. 112–155). Cambridge, MA: MIT Press.

Munnich, E., Landau, B. and Dosher, B. (2001) Spatial language and spatial representation: A crosslinguistic comparison. *Cognition* 81, 171–207.

Nation, P. (1990) *Teaching and Learning Vocabulary.* New York: Newbury House/Harper Row.

Oates, J. and Grayson, A. (2004) *Cognitive and Language Development in Children.* Oxford: Blackwell.

Pavlenko, A. (1999) New approaches to concepts in bilingual memory. *Bilingualism: Language and Cognition* 2, 209–230.

Pavlenko, A. (2005) Bilingualism and thought. In A. De Groot and J. Kroll (eds) *Handbook of Bilingualism: Psycholinguistic Approaches* (pp. 433–453). Oxford: Oxford University Press.

Pilling, M., Wiggett, A., Özgen, E. and Davies, I. (2003) Is color categorical perception really perceptual? *Memory & Cognition* 31, 538–551.

Quick Placement Test (2001) Oxford: Oxford University Press.

Quinn, P. (1994) The categorization of above and below spatial relations by young infants. *Child Development* 65, 58–69.

Quinn, P., Cummins, M. and Kase, J. (1996) Development of categorical representations for above and below spatial relations in 3- to 7-month-old infants. *Developmental Psychology* 32, 942–950.

Roberson, D. (2005) Color categories are culturally diverse in cognition as well as in language. *Cross-Cultural Research* 39, 56–71.

Roberson, D., Davidoff, J., Davies, I. and Shapiro, L. (2004) The development of color categories in two languages: A longitudinal study. *Journal of Experimental Psychology: General* 133, 554–571.

Roberson, D., Davidoff, J., Davies, I. and Shapiro, L. (2005) Color categories: Evidence for the cultural relativity hypothesis. *Cognitive Psychology* 50, 378–411.

Roberson, D., Davies, I. and Davidoff, J. (2000) Color categories are not universal: Replications and new evidence from a Stone-age culture. *Journal of Experimental Psychology: General* 129, 369–398.

Sera, M., Berge, C. and del Castillo Pintado, J. (1994) Grammatical and conceptual forces in the attribution of gender by English and Spanish speakers. *Cognitive Development* 9, 261–292.

Soja, N., Carey, S. and Spelke, E. (1991) Ontological categories guide young children's inductions of word meaning: Objects names and substance terms. *Cognition* 38, 179–211.

Vygotsky, L. (1934/1962) *Thought and Language*. Cambridge, MA: MIT Press.

Whorf, B.L. (1956) *Language, Thought, and Reality: Selected Writings of Benjamin Lee Whorf*. Edited by J.B. Carroll. Cambridge, MA: MIT Press.

Winawer, J., Witthoft, N., Frank, M., Wu, L., Wade, A. and Boroditsky, L. (2007) Russian blues reveal effects of language on color discrimination. *Proceedings of the National Academy of Sciences* 104, 7780–7785.

Chapter 3

Language-specific Patterns in Event Construal of Advanced Second Language Speakers

BARBARA SCHMIEDTOVÁ, CHRISTIANE VON STUTTERHEIM
and MARY CARROLL

3.1 Introduction

People communicating with second language (L2) users[1] of their native language often have the feeling that their interlocutors sound non-native even if they do not make obvious lexical and grammatical errors. In fact, Carroll and colleagues (Carroll & Lambert, 2003, 2006; Carroll & v. Stutterheim, 2003) have demonstrated that very advanced L2 speakers rarely display formal inaccuracies: their L2 grammar is nearly perfect. And yet the perception of 'non-nativeness' persists and it is not necessarily limited to pronunciation. This phenomenon is particularly evident in the production of complex stretches of discourse. In what follows, we will review a series of studies suggesting that the problem may lie in insufficient knowledge about language-specific principles of information organization, i.e. selecting and structuring information for expression. This issue will be examined with the focus on event[2] construal.

Previous studies of event construal in typologically different languages (Carroll *et al.*, 2004; Carroll & v. Stutterheim, in press; v. Stutterheim & Nüse, 2003; v. Stutterheim *et al.*, 2002) have demonstrated that the way speakers select and organize information depends on specific features of the grammatical system of a given language, in particular tense and aspect.[3] The findings show that categories that are deeply anchored in the linguistic system (i.e. grammaticalized) give rise to highly automatized preferences when selecting and structuring information for expression. The use of these preferences results in language-specific principles of information organization that speakers implement when solving complex verbal tasks (cf. Nüse, 2003; v. Stutterheim & Nüse, 2003). This view is in line with Slobin's (1996a) Thinking for Speaking hypothesis: the preparation of content for verbalization in the mind of a speaker is shaped by specific linguistic categories available in the speaker's language system.

The novelty of the work presented here is in showing that linguistic categories are not only relevant in the organization of information for verbalization, but that they also focus speakers' attention on certain aspects of a given situation. This is the so-called Seeing for Speaking hypothesis, as proposed by Carroll *et al.* (2004): when language A codes a certain meaning grammatically and language B codes the same meaning lexically or by phrasal means, then speakers of language A should attend to the relevant feature of a given visual scene, when the associated concept is relevant for the context in question, while speakers of language B may not do so, or at least not to the same extent. In what follows, we will discuss a number of studies conducted to test both the Thinking for Speaking and Seeing for Speaking hypotheses.

The structure of the chapter is as follows: Section 3.2 provides a brief overview of the theoretical framework; Sections 3.3 and 3.4 summarize findings of previous studies of event construal by native speakers of different languages and by L2 users; Section 3.5 introduces the methodology used in the three studies discussed here; Section 3.6 presents the findings of these studies and, in some cases, reanalyses or additional analyses of the data; and Section 3.7 is dedicated to a discussion of the findings. We end with some preliminary conclusions.

3.2 Theoretical Framework

3.2.1 Organizing information for verbalization: Conceptualization

In the model of language production proposed in Levelt (1989, 1999), the process of conceptualization takes place in the *conceptualizer*, where the so-called 'preverbal message' is constructed before it is mapped onto the linguistic form by accessing lexical, syntactic and phonological resources (the formulator) and is prepared for articulation (the articulator). In modeling processes involved in event conceptualization, however, we need a more detailed theory of the different processes that take place in the conceptualizer. According to v. Stutterheim and Nüse (2003), these processes involve segmentation, selection, structuring and linearization of the information to be expressed (cf. also Habel & Tappe, 1999).

In the first step, *segmentation*, particular components (or units) have to be selected from a knowledge base that is not organized hierarchically with respect to a given subject. Complex dynamic situations, for example, may be decomposed into smaller events, states or processes. In the process of information *selection*, the speaker has to choose those units that will be verbalized as well as the components by which these units can be represented. These components include entities, spaces, times and actions/states that can be described in terms of propositional units.

The next step is *structuring*. The units chosen must be structured in accordance with the requirements related to the type of predicate and argument roles (e.g. 'give' versus 'receive') and how they are anchored within a particular referential frame (e.g. spatial and temporal anchoring), as well as information status (i.e. allocation of topic and focus). In this process, the speaker has to choose the point of view from which the situation will be reported, which, in the case of event construal, for example, refers to whether the event is described as ongoing or as completed (v. Stutterheim & Nüse, 2003: 865). The next step in the planning process is *linearization*. Here, words are ordered in such a way that they can be expressed in a linguistic sequence (Levelt, 1982).

3.2.2 Grammaticalization and grammaticalized concepts

So, what role does grammar, and more specifically aspect, play in these four processes when talking about events? In the present approach, grammar is seen as a system of meanings that has gained prominence in a given language through the process of grammaticalization (cf. Bybee *et al.*, 1994; Talmy, 1988). Speakers have to attend to grammaticalized conceptual categories when planning expression for speaking. The assumption is that when a fully grammaticalized linguistic category is obligatory, it has a high level of automatization in use in the relevant contexts.

Aspectual concepts, such as 'ongoingness' or 'perfectivity', are prime examples of grammaticalized conceptual categories. As the cross-linguistic findings discussed below show, speakers of languages in which an aspectual viewpoint is expressed obligatorily by means of verbal morphology (e.g. Modern Standard (MS) Arabic, English, Russian or Spanish), are led to conceptualize and convey corresponding aspects of a dynamic situation. Speakers of languages that offer only lexical means to convey the same kind of information (e.g. German, Norwegian), do so to a lesser extent. In this sense, preferences in structuring information emerge given the presence of particular grammaticalized forms that encode a particular concept in a given language.

3.2.3 The theory of event construal

Undoubtedly, speakers do not put into words everything they perceive. Consequently, what is selected for verbalization does not completely reflect all that the speaker has perceived with respect to a given situation. When speakers process input for verbalization, they select and interpret information on the basis of a particular perspective. Carroll *et al.* (2004) have proposed that possible preferences in event construal are driven, in part, by what is considered in a particular language as a *reportable event* when grounding events in context.

In the past decade, numerous studies have examined how language-specific structures influence event representation and conceptualization. These studies examined how relevant concepts are mapped linguistically in motion events (Bohnemeyer *et al.*, 2007; Gumperz & Levinson, 1996; Kopecka, 2008; Slobin, 1991, 2000; Talmy, 1988, 2000), in separation events, such as to cut or break something (Majid *et al.*, 2007, 2008), in event serialization (Talmy, 2000) and in sequencing sets of events in larger pieces of discourse (Carroll *et al.*, 2008; Carroll & v. Stutterheim, in press; v. Stutterheim *et al.*, 2003; v. Stutterheim & Nüse, 2003).

The specific focus of the work presented in this chapter is on the construal of goal-oriented motion events. Characteristic of this event type is the continuing motion of entities (animate or inanimate objects) toward an endpoint. In situations of this type, speakers may refer to the motion event in holistic terms, thereby including the goal, or they may select a beginning, intermediate or final phase of the motion event. As the studies show, the choice of one of these views is not random, but is dependent on the presence or absence of grammatical aspectual markers expressing the concept of ongoingness in the linguistic system of a given language.

3.3 Language-specific Patterns in the Encoding of Motion Events by Native Speakers

Empirical research on general motion events has mainly focused on the typological theory of lexicalization patterns as described by Talmy (1988, 1991, 2000). Talmy differentiates between *satellite-framed languages* (S-languages), such as English, and *verb-framed languages* (V-languages), such as Spanish. In S-languages, the path information is typically expressed in the satellite whereas the manner of motion and the co-event are coded in the verb root, e.g. in English 'the rock rolled down the hill'. V-languages, in contrast, typically code path in the verb together with the fact of motion and the coding of manner is not obligatory, e.g. in Spanish '*la botella entró a la cueva (flotando)*' [the bottle moved into the cave (floating)].[4] Research based on Talmy's framework was undertaken by Slobin and colleagues (Berman & Slobin, 1994; Slobin, 1996a, 1996b, 1997, 2000, 2003, 2006). They found that English and Spanish speakers differ in their attention to specific aspects of motion events in both linguistic and conceptual tasks. English speakers used more verbs of motion encoding manner and provided richer descriptions of path trajectories in separate constituents. They also attended more to the manner of movement along a path, whereas Spanish speakers paid more attention to scene setting and static descriptions. Slobin (2004, 2006) also refined Talmy's original proposal by introducing a third type of language – the *equipollent* type in which attention to path and manner are equally balanced. Slobin's general thesis, however, has remained unchanged: the salience and type of manner encoding can influence attention to details of experienced motion events as well as the imagery formed on the basis of motion event descriptions in speech or writing (Slobin, 2006: 59).

While earlier research on native speakers has been concerned with the question of whether linguistic categories affect conceptualization or verbalization, more recent research is also concerned with the scope of these effects. The latter is examined by including carefully designed non-linguistic tasks (e.g. categorization, memory, recognition, similarity judgments) into the experimental design. Some studies have shown systematic linguistic preferences in linguistic tasks (e.g. narrations, picture description); these effects, however, disappeared in non-linguistic tasks (e.g. Papafragou *et al.*, 2002, 2006). Several other studies have found language-specific differences in non-linguistic tasks that were performed without or after verbal encoding (e.g. categorization/matching: Athanasopoulos & Kasai, 2008; Levinson *et al.*, 2002; Lucy, 1992; Naigles & Terrazas, 1998; memory and/or similarity judgments: Gennari *et al.*, 2002; v. Stutterheim *et al.*, in press; recognition: Billman & Krych, 1998; Billman *et al.*, 2000). For example, Gennari *et al.* (2002) examined the influence of language-specific lexicalization patterns on similarity judgments after linguistic encoding. They found that Spanish speakers were more likely to select the same-path alternate, while English speakers showed no preference. This was consistent with the pattern of descriptions observed in the same study for each language (Gennari *et al.*, 2002: 74).

Recent eye-tracking studies provided further evidence that speakers pay attention to language-specific aspects of motion events (Flecken, in press; Papafragou *et al.*, 2008; v. Stutterheim *et al.*, in press; v. Stutterheim & Carroll, 2006). Papafragou *et al.* (2008) investigated the allocation of attention to path and manner components in English and Greek speakers. It was found that Greek speakers were more likely than English speakers to focus on the path-endpoint region, and English speakers were more likely than Greek speakers to focus first on the manner region. The authors argued that attention allocation at the earliest stages of event apprehension is affected by linguistic encoding preferences, but only when language is needed for the given task (Papafragou *et al.*, 2008: 174).

Another line of research has focused on the role of aspect in conceptualization of events (cf. Carroll & v. Stutterheim, 2003; Schmiedtová *et al.*, 2007; v. Stutterheim & Nüse, 2003). It was found that the presence or absence of aspect in the language system affects the way in which events are construed. Several recent studies found evidence for aspect affecting the encoding of goal-oriented motion (cf. for Swedish and Spanish: Bylund, 2008, 2009, this volume; for Italian: Natale, 2008; for Dutch and German: Flecken, in press). Hart and Albarracín (2009) argue that aspect plays a central role in conceptualization. Their study investigated the influence of aspect on memory and re-enactment in English. It was found that the use of the imperfective aspect denoting ongoingness enhanced memory for action-relevant knowledge and increased tendencies to reproduce an action at a later time (Hart & Albarracín, 2009: 6).

To sum up, more than a decade of research on the encoding and conceptualization of motion events demonstrated that language-specific linguistic categories play a central role in event construal. There is no consensus, however, regarding the scope of these effects. Some researchers limit these effects to linguistic tasks (e.g. Papafragou *et al.*, 2002), while others also find effects in non-linguistic tasks[5] (e.g. Gennari *et al.*, 2002; Naigles & Terrazas, 1998). Eye-tracking studies of motion events corroborate the view that language-specific categories focus speakers' attention on specific components of the presented event (e.g. Papafragou *et al.*, 2008). The differences in the results may be due to differences in the experimental design, choice of stimulus type and, in some cases, to relatively small numbers of participants. In any case, since only a limited number of studies so far have tackled this issue experimentally, more studies are needed to understand the size of the effect language-specific categories have on event construal.

3.4 Language-specific Patterns in the Encoding of Motion Events by Second Language Speakers

In view of the differences found between speakers of typologically different languages, the next question to address is how these differences play out in second language acquisition (SLA). SLA research on motion events has also centered on Talmy's (1985, 1991, 2000) framework, mainly investigating the realization of manner and path information in L2 learning and use. The leading questions here are: how do L2 speakers master the mapping between linguistic form and conceptual representation for motion events in the L2, and to what degree can L2 speakers adapt their first language (L1)-specific thinking for speaking patterns to those of the L2? An important variable for this line of research is the degree of typological similarity between the L1 and the L2 in question.

As Cadierno (2008) notes, to date only a few SLA studies have addressed the L2 expression of motion events. Cadierno (2004) studied the acquisition of L2 Spanish by intermediate and advanced learners with Danish as the L1. The study focused on the semantic components 'path' and 'ground'. The researcher found that L1 patterns influenced the elaboration of path and the degree of complexity in the L2. However, the learners did not produce any event conflation constructions. In other words, the L2 learners in this study construed – at least to some degree – motion events in a target-like fashion. In a follow-up study, Cadierno and Ruiz (2006) compared two groups of advanced L1 Danish learners of L2

Spanish, focusing on their expression of path and manner. The study found only traces of the L1 patterns in the L2. The main conclusion was that L1-specific thinking for speaking patterns plays only a limited role in advanced learners and a more prominent role in initial and intermediate learners. Navarro and Nicoladis (2005) examined whether L1 English advanced speakers of L2 Spanish can learn to map path of motion onto the main verb. The authors came to a conclusion similar to Cadierno and Ruiz (2006): despite some traces of English patterns in the target language, the learners came close to mastering the L2 Spanish patterns, but still displayed some traces of the L1 English pattern. Yet another view on the role of L1-specific patterns in SLA is represented by Hendriks *et al.* (2008), who studied the acquisition of caused motion by intermediate and advanced L1 English speakers of L2 French. Their findings show that even advanced learners rely on L1 patterns when construing causal motion in the L2.

Another line of research focuses on the interplay between language and gestures in the description of motion events in L2 learners (Kellerman & van Hoof, 2003; Negueruela *et al.*, 2004). The findings suggest that some learners can adapt to the L2 pattern, while others, including some advanced learners, make systematic use of L1-specific gestures. Kellerman and van Hoof (2003) coined the term 'manual accents' to refer to advanced learners whose spoken language is nearly perfect but whose gestures nevertheless follow an L1-specific pattern.

To sum up, the findings of empirical studies of event construal are mixed. Some studies claim that restructuring of L1 concepts in favor of L2 concepts is possible (e.g. Cadierno, 2004), depending on L2 learners' proficiency in the target language as well as perceived typological distance between the L1 and the L2. In turn, Hendriks *et al.* (2008) argue that such restructuring either does not happen at all, or happens only for a few learners. Evidence from SLA studies investigating restructuring of conceptual knowledge in other domains also varies. A conceptual shift toward the L2 has been found for classification preferences in object naming and categorization (Athanasopoulos, 2006; Athanasopoulos & Kasai, 2008; see also Athanasopoulos, this volume) but not for time and space (Carroll, 1993, 1997; Carroll & v. Stutterheim, 2003; Schmiedtová, 2003, 2004, 2010).

The purpose of this chapter is to add to this body of evidence by discussing three related studies of construal of goal-oriented events. The studies reviewed here focus on the role of grammatical aspect, providing a new angle on the construal of events. Furthermore, in addition to linguistic production, other data, such as speech onset times and eye tracking, are presented. These data provide indispensable insights into the conceptualization process. The present review of this research might thus shed more light on the complex relationship between linguistic form, associated meaning and the underlying concepts used when events are construed. Finally, it can also contribute to the current debate on conceptual restructuring in L2 speakers. We will begin with the research question posited in the studies, then outline typological differences between the languages examined, and provide information about participants, materials and procedure used.

3.5 Method

3.5.1 Research question

Although each of the three studies reviewed below has its own particular focus, it is possible to formulate a general research question that unites all of them, namely, what are the similarities and differences between L1 and L2 speakers in conceptualizing motion events for verbalization? Based on the work reviewed earlier, we posit that the absence or presence of grammaticalized concepts, such as aspect, in a given L1 plays a decisive role in learning to structure information in an L2. Grammaticalized concepts are pertinent in any type of language production since they constitute highly automatized preferences that L1 or L2 speakers must recruit when selecting and organizing information for expression. The acquisition of grammaticalized concepts and of principles of use related to these categories pose a formidable task for the learner. We begin our overview by discussing how different languages construe goal-oriented motion events, i.e. in what respects they differ and what grammaticalized structures are responsible for these differences.

3.5.2 Languages studied

Two groups of languages are examined in the studies discussed below: the aspect group, which comprises MS Arabic, Czech, Russian, English, Spanish, and the non-aspect group, which includes German and Norwegian. The interaction between grammatical aspect and attention paid to a possible endpoint will be discussed in depth for German, English, Czech and Russian. The results for MS Arabic, Norwegian and Spanish will be provided for additional support.

Table 3.1 provides an overview of the languages investigated in terms of the relevant aspectual categories, based on Dahl's (1985) crosslinguistic study. The aspectual categories, *imperfective, progressive* and *secondary imperfective*, refer to an ongoing action or event, although they do not denote this viewpoint in the same way. In contrast, *perfective* is used to refer to a *completed* action. (For a more detailed discussion of the difference between imperfective, progressive and secondary imperfective, see Schmiedtová & Flecken, 2008; Schmiedtová & Sahonenko, 2008; v. Stutterheim *et al.*, 2009.)

Table 3.1 Aspect systems

	German	Norwegian	English	Spanish	MS Arabic	Czech	Russian
Imperfective	No	No	No	Yes	Yes	Yes	Yes
Progressive	No	No	Yes	Yes	Yes	No	No
Secondary imperfective	No	No	No	No	No	Yes	Yes
Perfective	No	No	No	Yes (in the past tense)	Yes	Yes	Yes

In German, no grammatical device is available for expressing ongoingness: speakers construe goal-oriented events as bounded with the inclusion of a possible endpoint, applying a holistic view. It should be kept in mind that in some dialects German speakers can express ongoingness using the constructions *bei/am* (at the) + verbal noun, e.g. *Eine Frau ist am Stricken* [a woman is knitting (at-the knit)] or *dabei* (there-at) + *sein* (to be) + INF, e.g. *Jemand ist dabei das Brot zu schneiden* [someone is cutting bread]. The crucial difference between German and English, however, is in the fact that the English progressive is a highly automatized, obligatory linguistic marker that speakers must consider when construing events, whereas for German speakers this construction represents a highly marked option constrained to particular types of situations and contexts.

Norwegian is similar to German in that Norwegian, too, does not have grammatical aspect. Speakers of Norwegian must resort to lexical means when they want to express ongoingness. Usually, serial posture verbs are used for this purpose, such as *sitter/ligger/står* (to sit/to lie/to stand) + *og* (and) + FIN, e.g. *En dame sitter og strikker* [a lady is sitting and knitting].

Spanish conveys aspect through verb stem inflection and verbal periphrasis. A distinction is made in the present tense between the simple form and the progressive, which is created through *estar* (to be) + present participle, e.g. *Una señora está tejiendo* [a woman is knitting]. The present participle thus conveys imperfectivity and its basic function is to present the unfolding phase of a situation without attention to its temporal confines (cf. Bylund, 2008, this volume).

In English, the grammaticalized opposition between the simple form and the progressive *be* + *ing* requires the selection of a temporal perspective. Events can be decomposed into phases (e.g. a person is leaving the supermarket and heading across the parking lot). Two factors are relevant in this context: (a) any phase can be selected, in principle, as a reportable event; (b) the progressive allows the speaker to anchor the event in the domain of discourse (i.e. specify the time interval or time of assertion, cf. Klein, 1994), as in 'a man is fishing'; 'a chef is cooking'; 'a duck is waddling'. Consequently, the progressive delivers information on a specific time of assertion, in contrast to the use of the simple present verb form (e.g. a man fishes, a chef cooks, a duck waddles), where a generic reading is suggested. If the simple present verb form is used, generic readings can be avoided, where necessary, by adding adjuncts, as in 'the duck waddles into the barn'. The necessity of supplying anchorings in clarifying the status of the event with respect to specificity and time of assertion may lead speakers to take a more holistic view of the event (Carroll *et al.*, 2004).

Turning to Czech and Russian, it should be stressed that, unlike in English, two aspects can be marked in these languages: the imperfective aspect conveying ongoingness expressed by two forms (either the simplex imperfective or the secondary imperfective),[6] and the perfective aspect denoting completion.[7] The use of the perfective aspect may lead to a preference for endpoints when construing goal-oriented motion events (holistic perspective). Consider the following examples from Czech (1) and Russian (2). The event described in the examples is a goal-oriented motion in which a person is walking toward a building with a prominent door:

(1) *Někdo*   *ve-jde*   *do dveří*
     Somebody (Nom)   enter (Perf.Prs.3.SG)   in door (Gen)
     Somebody   will be entering/enters   through the door
(2) *Kto-to*   *vo-jdet*   *v dveri*
     Somebody (Nom)   will enter (Fut.3.SG)   in door (Acc[8])
     Somebody   will enter/come in   through the door

Crucially, a verb marked for perfectivity requires an additional argument referring to a possible endpoint. Here the prefixed Czech verb *ve-jít* (to enter, to come in) is marked for the perfective and used in combination with the locative adjunct specifying the reaching of the endpoint. An utterance with a perfectively marked verb and no additional arguments is not commonly used in isolation to refer to a single event in the present tense, as in Example (3).[9] The same holds true for Russian (4).

(3) *Někdo*   *ve-jde (?)*
     Somebody (Nom)   enter-in (Perf.Prs.3.SG)
     Somebody   will be entering/enters
(4) *Kto-to*   *vo-jdet (?)*
     Somebody (Nom)   will enter-in (Fut.3.SG)
     Somebody   will enter/come in

The utterances in Examples (1) and (2) can also appear in the past tense, as in Example (5) for Czech and Example (6) for Russian. The attendance to the endpoint and the argument structure remain the same.

(5) *Někdo*   *ve-še-l*   *do dveří.*
     Somebody (Nom)   walk-in (Perf.Past.3.SG) in door (Gen)
     Somebody   walked in   through the door
(6) *Kto-to*   *vo-she-l*   *v dveri*
     Somebody (Nom)   walk-in (Perf.Past.3.SG) in door (Acc)
     Somebody   walked in   through the door

Overall, when the perfective aspect is used, the endpoint must be included in the verbalization. To complete the picture, we will also go through the other two aspectual categories, the simplex imperfective and the secondary imperfective, which are available in the Czech and Russian aspectual systems and focus speakers' view on the ongoingness of the event presented.

The use of the simplex imperfective[10] – a morphologically unmarked form that is inherently imperfective – and the mentioning of a possible endpoint seem to work differently in Czech and Russian. In Russian, as seen in Example (7), the simplex imperfective can be used as a bare phrase without any other arguments, while in Czech, as seen in Example (8), the use of the simplex imperfective requires some kind of anchoring that does not need to relate to endpoint specification.

(7) *Mašina*   *jed'et*
     Car (Nom) ride (Impf.Prs.3.SG)
     A car   is riding
(8) *Auto*   *jede*   *rychle / po silnici / do vesnice*
     Car (Nom) ride (Impf.Prs.3.SG) fast /on road.LOC /in village.LOC
     A car   is riding   fast /on the road / into the village

A counterpart of the Russian utterance in Example (7) would not be grammatical in Czech. In addition, in both languages the encoding of manner, path and endpoint presented in Example (8) as three alternatives for anchoring the simplex imperfective can occur together in one utterance.

By means of suffixation (Czech suffixes -*a*-, -(*o*)*va*; Russian suffixes: -*iva*-/-*yva*-, -*va*-, -*a*-/-*ja*-) perfective verbal stems can be imperfectivized. This aspectual form is called the secondary imperfective.[11] Like the perfectively marked verbs, verbs in the secondary imperfective require the use of additional arguments. Since the secondary imperfective is not combinable with verbs of motion, we will not discuss this form any further here.[12]

Czech and Russian share an aspectual system that provides aspectual means for speakers to view goal-oriented motion events under two perspectives: (1) under the holistic perspective by using the perfective aspect, thereby including a possible endpoint; or (2) focusing on the ongoingness of the event by using the simplex imperfective. The two languages differ insofar as in Russian the simplex imperfective can be used alone without any other arguments, while in Czech the simplex imperfective has to be combined with another argument, but this argument does not have to express the endpoint in question.

MS Arabic, like Czech and Russian, is an aspect-dominant language. It too disposes of grammatical means to express completion (perfective aspect) and ongoingness (imperfective and progressive aspect). Hence, MS Arabic can, in principle, view goal-oriented events under two perspectives, depending on what aspect is used: perfective ⇒ focus on completion; imperfective/progressive ⇒ focus on ongoingness.

To sum up, based on the assumption that grammaticalization of aspect plays a crucial role in structuring information, we investigated two groups of languages: the aspect group (MS Arabic, Czech, Russian, English, Spanish) and the non-aspect group (German, Norwegian). We posited that when the aspect category is absent, as in German, speakers may tend to take a holistic perspective on goal-oriented motion events, with endpoints a part of the conceptualization and verbalization of these events. Other languages, such as English, have only one grammaticalized aspect. There, the progressive aspect is fully grammaticalized and when used, there is a high likelihood that goal-oriented motion events are conceptualized as ongoing. In this case, the perspective taken is the phasal decomposition. There are also languages, such as Russian or MS Arabic, which have more than one grammaticalized aspect: usually, a grammaticalized opposition between the perfective and the imperfective (or progressive) aspect. Speakers of these languages must choose an aspect when construing goal-oriented motion. In other words, they have to choose either the holistic perspective or the phasal decomposition.

Importantly, while the absence or presence of aspect guides the selection of a particular perspective for conceptualization of goal-oriented events, it does not exclude the use of other perspectives. One could say that in terms of information structure, speakers are guided by the available aspectual devices to choose a particular perspective that enables them to select and highlight some pieces of information and suspend others.

3.5.3 Participants

All the L1 and L2 speakers who participated in the three studies discussed below were undergraduate or graduate students, or, in the case of some L2 speakers, professionals (e.g. German translators, teachers of German as a foreign language). All participants were raised with a single language spoken by both parents and in that environment at least until schooling age (usually at age five or six). At the time of the experiment, all had knowledge of other languages.

L1 speakers of languages other than German were typically recruited from the beginner courses in the annual 'International summer school of German culture and language' at the University of Heidelberg (for a discussion of participants interviewed elsewhere, see descriptions of studies 2 and 3). These L1 speakers had no or very rudimentary knowledge of German. To control as much as possible for the potential influence of German on the native speakers' L1 system, the recordings in their mother tongue were restricted to the first week of their stay in Heidelberg. Overall, all L1 speakers, except for native speakers of German, had either no knowledge of German or showed lower levels of proficiency in the L2 than any L2 speaker. Participants in all studies were financially rewarded for their participation (between €5–10).

The L2 speaker data were also collected in Heidelberg, except for Czech learners of German (for more details, see study 3 by Schmiedtová & Sahonenko, 2008). In the studies reviewed in this chapter, proficiency in L2 German was not tested by means of a language proficiency test, but was assessed on the basis of several criteria linked to linguistic and extra-linguistic parameters.[13] (a) Formal accuracy was considered with respect to nominal and verbal morphology, syntax and lexical repertoire. All measures were assessed in relation to linguistic means used by native speakers in the same task. For example, if errors in declination and/or verbal inflection were found in the L2 speaker's production, this participant was excluded from the L2 speaker group. (b) All L2 speakers spoke German on a daily basis. According to the self-assessment questionnaires,[14] 87% of these speakers perceived German as their dominant language. (c) Only participants whose length of exposure to German – defined as a combination of the length of residence in the L2 environment and the length of L2 instruction – was longer than seven years (on average 8.15 years, SD = 2.59) were selected. L1 English and Russian speakers of L2 German lived in Germany for an average of 10.1 years (SD = 2.4). L1 Czech learners of L2 German and L1 German learners of L2 English spent at least one year in the respective target language country.

Study 1: v. Stutterheim (2003)

One hundred and ten participants took part in the study. Eighty L1 speakers included 20 L1 speakers of MS Arabic, 20 L1 speakers of English, 20 L1 speakers of German and 20 L1 speakers of Spanish. The average age of the participants was 25.6 years (age range 19–28 years). Each group consisted of 10 females and 10 males, except for MS Arabic, where there were 17 females and 3 males. Thirty L2 speakers included 15 L1 German speakers of L2 English (10 females, 5 males) and 15 L1 English speakers of L2 German (8 females, 7 males). The average age of these participants was 28.9 years (age range 26–34). All participants were interviewed in Heidelberg.

Study 2: v. Stutterheim and Carroll (2006)

One hundred and twenty participants took part in the study. Eighty L1 speakers included 20 L1 speakers of MS Arabic (15 females, 5 males), 20 L1 speakers of English (10 females, 10 males), 20 L1 speakers of German (10 females, 10 males) and 20 L1 speakers of Norwegian (10 females, 10 males). The L1 English and L1 German participants were the same as in the previous study. The average age of these participants was 26.5 years (age range 20–29 years). Forty L2 speakers included 20 L1 English speakers of L2 German (12 females, 8 males) and 20 L1 German speakers of L2 English (13 females, 7 males). Their average age was 29.7 years (age range 26–37). All participants were interviewed in Heidelberg, with the exception of L1 Norwegian speakers who were interviewed at the University of Oslo, Norway.

Study 3: Schmiedtová and Sahonenko (2008)

One hundred and twenty participants took part in the study. Ninety L1 speakers included 30 L1 speakers of Czech, 30 L1 speakers of German and 30 L1 speakers of Russian. Each group consisted of 15 females and 15 males. The average age of the participants was 24.6 years (age range 18–28 years). Thirty L2 speakers included 15 L1 Russian speakers of L2 German (11 females, 4 males) and 15 L1 Czech speakers of L2 German (9 females, 6 males). The first group was composed of Russian students and postgraduates at the University of Heidelberg. By the time of the study, all had lived in Germany for a minimum of five years and used German daily. The average age of the participants was 28.7 years (age range 26–34 years). In the second group, there were advanced students of German at the Charles University in Prague.[15] The average age of the participants was 23.7 years (age range 18–24). The participants were interviewed in Heidelberg, with the exception of L1 Czech speakers (interviewed in Prague, Czech Republic) and L1 Russian speakers (interviewed in St. Petersburg, Russia).

3.5.4 Materials

The three studies used the same materials, a set of short video clips showing everyday situations depicting goal-oriented motion that were filmed by the members of the project. There were three types of clips:

(1) *Critical* test items showed locomotions in which a possible endpoint was not reached. For instance, the clip 'two women walking toward

a house' depicted the initial or intermediate phases of the event – the endpoint was not shown, but could be inferred. It was hypothesized that on these items speakers of different languages would display differences in the inclusion of the possible endpoint.

(2) *Control* test items showed locomotions in which the movement reached the endpoint. It was hypothesized that on these items speakers of different languages would select the same components for verbalization. For instance, describing the clip 'somebody walking into a house', all speakers were expected to mention the endpoint, which is the house.

(3) *Fillers* (distractors) showed activities with no inferable endpoint (e.g. 'a washing machine working') or static scenes with no observable change (e.g. 'a boat on the river', 'a candle burning').

The critical and control test items were mixed with fillers (distractors) with an approximate ratio of 20% critical and 20% control items to 60% fillers. Presentations were carried out on the basis of several randomized testing lists that were distributed equally across all participants tested with a given set. Fillers were inserted semi-randomly in-between critical and control items to ensure that participants did not easily deduce the structure of the experiment. Study 1 (v. Stutterheim, 2003) employed 36 clips (8 critical, 8 control, 20 fillers); study 2 (v. Stutterheim & Carroll, 2006) employed 80 clips (18 critical, 18 control, 44 fillers); and study 3 (Schmiedtová & Sahonenko, 2008) employed 40 clips (8 critical, 8 control, 24 fillers). The 8 critical and 8 control items were identical for all three studies; 10 additional items for each set were used in study 2. There was also an overlap in the use of fillers: 10 fillers used in study 1 were also used in studies 2 and 3; all fillers used in study 3 were also used in study 2.

3.5.5 Experimental procedure

Video clips were presented to the participants on a computer screen. The instructions were first presented in written form and then explained orally to the participants. The language of instructions was the language under investigation and the person giving the instructions was a native speaker of that language. In this manner, the influence of language mode on the experimental design was kept under control. The text of the instructions was kept constant across all investigated languages. Participants were asked to say what was happening in the scenes as soon as they recognized the situation. The question posed to them in the respective language was *What is happening*?[16] In addition, it was stressed that the participant should not concentrate on other features of the scene, but focus on the events taking place.

The length of the clips within each set was kept constant; depending on the set, it was between 6 and 12 seconds. Five training clips were first presented to each participant. The five clips included the critical feature tested in the experiment (the reaching or not reaching of the endpoint) and were used only in the training phase and not in the experiment itself. In the experiment, the clips were presented one by one, with an 8 second pause in between. The participants provided their verbalizations on-line and it was acceptable to talk during the pauses, but the verbalization was not supposed to interfere with the presentation of the next scene. All participants practiced this aspect in the training phase. In the real experiment, all verbalizations were produced within the time window given by the length of the movie and the length of the pause (approximately 14 seconds). The production was recorded automatically by the same computer that presented the stimuli. All participants were recorded individually. Afterward, the participants were asked to fill out a questionnaire regarding their age, gender, schooling, education and knowledge of languages. Altogether, the study took approximately 25 minutes.

Apart from audio data, which were collected in all three studies, v. Stutterheim (2003) also recorded speech onset times (SOT) and v. Stutterheim and Carroll (2006) eye-tracking data. Both data types were recorded automatically and simultaneously with audio recordings. The apparatus used in recording SOT and eye movement was the remote system, *Eye Follower*™, developed by Interactive Minds, Dresden, Germany, on the basis of an *LC-Technologies* system. The cameras were attached to the monitor for binocular eye tracking and the eye-gaze system accommodated all natural head movements during normal computer operation. The gaze point sampling rate was 120 Hz, with a highly accurate $0.45°$ gaze-point tracking accuracy throughout the operational head range. The TFT monitor was 20″ and participants were seated approximately 50–80 cm from the screen. Calibration was carried out once for each participant before the experiment (tracking eye gaze on yellow dots on a black screen that appeared in identical order at specific positions on the screen).

3.5.6 Data analysis

Data elicited on the basis of the control and critical items were transcribed and analyzed in the original language. Responses to filler items were not considered for data analysis. The verbs were coded using Klein's (1994) differentiation between zero-state, one-state and two-state verb types. In addition, aspect was also coded for aspect languages (MS Arabic, Czech, English, Russian). Here, a distinction was made between the progressive/imperfective and the perfective form. The final coding variable was the expression of endpoint, encoded either lexically by a locative adjunct (e.g. 'to a house', 'in the direction of a house') or by a combination of morphological and lexical marking, as outlined for Czech and Russian in Section 3.5.2 above (e.g. *v-jíždět do dvora* [to be riding into a backyard] (prefixed verb + local adjunct)). The transcription and all linguistic analyses were carried out by native speakers of the respective languages.

Inferential statistics were not applied consistently in the original studies. Study 1 and 2 reported statistics for SOTs and eye-tracking data, study 3 for some linguistic data. For the purposes of the chapter, whenever possible, we have reanalyzed the raw data to provide statistical results. For the analyses of linguistic data, non-parametric statistics were used, in particular the chi-square test for comparing proportions within one sample (we are, however, aware of the limitations of the multiple chi-square tests).

3.6 Results

We will first present production data results from L1 speakers, considering the three studies in chronological order. Then, we will proceed to the findings from L2 speakers and present them in the same manner.

3.6.1 First Language speakers

Study 1 (v. Stutterheim, 2003) showed that no crosslinguistic differences occurred for the control items. In other words, there were no differences between MS Arabic, English, German and Spanish speakers with respect to the construal of goal-oriented motion in scenes that depicted the reaching of an endpoint (χ^2 (3) = 6.91, n.s.). However, the study revealed differences for critical items, in which the endpoint was not reached but could be inferred (χ^2 (3) = 22.87, $p < 0.05$). L1 German speakers showed a preference to construe a possible endpoint, while speakers of MS Arabic, English and Spanish were unlikely to do so. Figure 3.1 provides an overview of endpoints mentioned in descriptions of the critical items.

Findings showed that speakers of German mentioned an endpoint three times as frequently as speakers of MS Arabic, English and Spanish. The differences between speakers of German and speakers of the other three languages were significant (German-MS Arabic: χ^2 (1) = 88.2, $p < 0.001$; German-English: χ^2 (1) = 84.06, $p < 0.001$; German-Spanish: $\chi^2(1) = 86.1$, $p < 0.001$). No significant effects were found comparing MS Arabic, English and Spanish (MS Arabic-Spanish: χ^2 (1) = 0.02, n.s.; MS Arabic-English: χ^2 (1) = 0.07, n.s.; English-Spanish: χ^2 (1) = 0.02, n.s.).

The following examples illustrate these preferences in descriptions of a single critical item depicting two women walking toward a house.

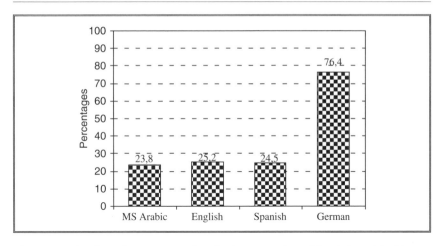

Figure 3.1 Study 1: Percentage of endpoints mentioned in eight critical items ($n = 20$ participants per group; MS Arabic: SD = 5.4; English: SD = 4.8; Spanish: SD = 4.2; German: SD = 5.8)

(9) Two women   are walking   down the road   L1 English
(10) '*Imra'atāni*   *tasīrāni*   *fi š-šāri'*   L1 MS Arabic
     woman (dual)   walk (Imperf.dual)   on the-road
     Two women   are walking   on the road
(11) *Dos mujeres*   *están caminando*   *por la calle*   L1 Spanish
     two women   walk (Prog.Prs.3.PL)   on the road
     Two women   are walking   on the road
(12) *Zwei*   *Frauen*   *laufen*   *auf einemFeldwegRichtung*
     two   women   walk (Prs.3.PL)   on a (DAT) path   direction
     Two   women   are walking   down on a path   towards
     einesHauses   L1 German
     a (GEN) house (GEN)
     a house.

Then, comparative analysis of SOTs was conducted based on the assumption that speakers of languages that require an endpoint for the construal of a reportable event will wait for the event to become evident as a whole before starting to speak, whereas speakers of languages that can depict any phase of the event in its own right will not have to wait for the unfolding of the endpoint (v. Stutterheim, 2003: 193). The SOT findings for native speakers of English and German are presented in Figure 3.2.[17]

The results showed that, on average, English native speakers started to speak 3.6 seconds after the stimulus onset (i.e. after the beginning of the video clip), while German native speakers started to speak 4.3 seconds after the stimulus onset, i.e. 0.7 seconds later (*t*1 (24) = 3.13, *p* = 0.04; *t*2

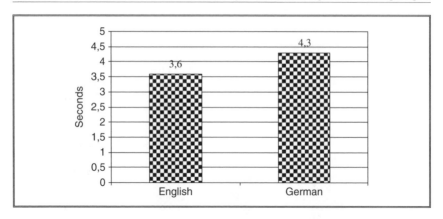

Figure 3.2 Study 1: Average SOTs in English and German for eight critical items ($n = 20$ participants per group; English: SD = 0.4; German: SD = 0.5)

(27) = 10.71, p < 0.001). It appears then that German speakers waited for the goal-oriented motion event to unfold.

Study 2 (v. Stutterheim & Carroll, 2006) investigated the encoding of endpoints in four different languages: MS Arabic, English, German and Norwegian. In addition to audio data, eye-tracking data were collected.

The analysis revealed that there were no differences for the control items (χ^2 (3) = 4.85, n.s.). In critical scenes, speakers of German and Norwegian mentioned the endpoint more frequently than speakers of English and MS Arabic, in which phasal decomposition is grammaticalized (Figure 3.3). No differences existed in terms of the number of endpoints mentioned between speakers of German and Norwegian (χ^2 (1) = 0.48, n.s.) or between speakers of English and MS Arabic (χ^2 (1) = 0.12, n.s.). Differences were found between speakers of Norwegian and MS Arabic (χ^2 (1) = 151.1, $p < 0.001$), Norwegian and English (χ^2 (1) = 144.4, $p < 0.001$), German and MS Arabic (χ^2 (1) = 198.45, $p < 0.001$) and German and English (χ^2 (1) = 190.18, $p < 0.001$).

Study 2 also examined eye tracking based on the assumption that speakers of non-aspect languages, such as German, will scan more and dwell longer in the critical region (the possible endpoint) than speakers of aspect languages, such as English, who are less likely to mention endpoints in goal-oriented motion events. In order to determine whether speakers looked at the critical region before they started speaking or while they were already speaking, the authors distinguished between fixations[18] before and after speech onset (SO). The findings for English and German are summarized in Figure 3.4.

A paired samples *t*-test revealed that native speakers of German focused on the critical region longer than native speakers of English

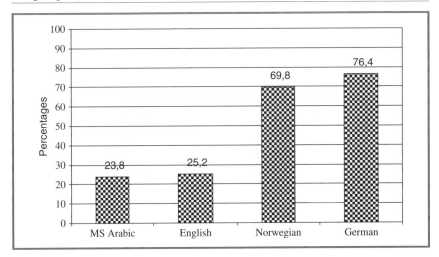

Figure 3.3 Study 2: Percentage of endpoints mentioned in 18 critical items (*n* = 20 participants per group; MS Arabic: SD = 5.4; English: SD = 4.8; Norwegian: SD = 4.0; German: SD = 5.8)

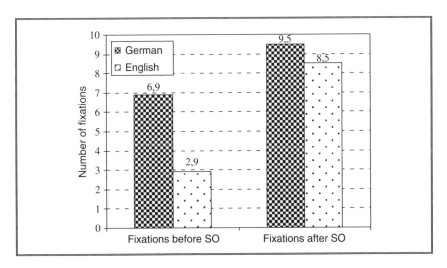

Figure 3.4 Study 2: Number of fixations before and after SO on 18 critical items (*n* = 20 participants per group; before SO: German: SD = 1.3; English: SD = 1.2; after SO: German: SD = 1.5; English: SD = 1.5)

both before (t (17) $=5.45$, $p < 0.001$) and after speaking onset (t (17) $= 4.55$, $p < 0.001$).

Study 3 (Schmiedtová & Sahonenko, 2008) examined the endpoint encoding in Czech, German and Russian. There were no differences between the groups for the control items (χ^2 (2) $= 3.72$, n.s.). In descriptions of critical items, Czech speakers provided more endpoints than Russian speakers (χ^2 (1) $= 11.59$, $p < 0.001$). Significant differences were also identified in endpoint mentioning between speakers of German and speakers of Czech (χ^2 (1) $= 13.45$, $p < 0.001$), as well as between speakers of German and speakers of Russian (χ^2 (1) $= 4.8$, $p < 0.05$). Figure 3.5 sums up the findings for Czech, German and Russian.

The following examples illustrate a typical description of a goal-oriented motion event by Czech and Russian speakers (for a typical German description, see Example (12).

(13) *Dvě ženy*   *jdou*   *po cestě k nějakému stavení*
     two women walk (Impf.prs.3.PL) on road (LOC) to some (DAT)
     building.DAT
     Two women   are walking   down the road to a building
(14) *Dve ženščiny*   *idut*   *po*   *doroge*
     two women   walk (Impf.prs.3.PL) on   road (LOC)
     Two women   are walking   on   the road

In the Russian example (14), the event is presented as unbounded and in progress, without mentioning the endpoint. In contrast, the

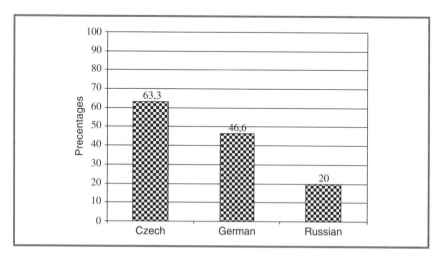

Figure 3.5 Study 3: Percentage of endpoints mentioned for eight critical items ($n = 30$ participants per group; Czech: SD $= 4.0$; German: SD $= 5.2$; Russian: SD $= 4.9$)

Czech example (13) illustrates the use of the local adjunct, *k nějakému stavení*, which makes the event bounded. Although Czech and Russian speakers employ two different perspectives to encode an identical event, they both use the same aspect and the same verb: the simplex imperfective of the verb *to walk* (Czech: *jít*, Russian: *idti*). To understand how differences in endpoint mentioning between Czech and Russian are related to aspectual differences, we have to briefly review some findings on events other than motion, i.e. situations with a qualified resultant state, e.g. 'somebody throwing away garbage', 'somebody cutting down a tree'. In these situations, an activity leads to a result that is depicted in the scene presented to the participants. That is, one can see in the scene 'somebody throwing away garbage' that the garbage gets thrown away. Schmiedtová and Sahonenko (2008) found that native speakers of Czech and Russian used different aspects when construing this type of events despite having the same morphological means at their disposal in the respective aspectual systems. The results are shown in Figure 3.6.

We can see that for events with a qualified resultant state, native speakers of Czech favored the prefixed perfective over any other

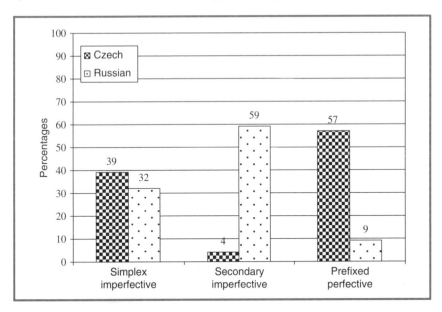

Figure 3.6 Study 3: Aspectual preferences for events with a qualified resultant state in eight critical items (*n* = 30 participants per group; simplex imperfective: Czech: SD = 3.5; Russian: SD = 4.4; secondary imperfective: Czech: SD = 2.3; Russian: SD = 4.7; prefixed perfective: Czech: SD = 4.3; Russian: SD = 3.7)

aspectual form (χ^2 (2) = 13.4, $p < 0.001$). In contrast, native speakers of Russian showed a preference for the secondary imperfective (χ^2 (2) = 11.4, $p = 0.003$). No differences occurred in the use of the simplex imperfective between the two language groups (χ^2 (2) = 0.29, n.s.).

Differences in the use of aspect and the underlying semantic shift in the perfective form lead to differences in event construal and hence to different perspectives on the event: while Czech native speakers view situations with a qualified resultant state as completed, under the holistic perspective, Russian native speakers view such situations as ongoing (for more discussion, see below).

(15) *Někdo*	*vy-sypa-l*	*smetí*	*do koše*
somebody	throw	garbage (ACC)	into bucket
	(Perf.past.3.SG)		(GEN)
Somebody	threw	garbage	into a bucket
(16) *Kto-to*	*vy-brasy-va-et*	*musor*	*v jaščik*
somebody	throw	garbage (ACC)	into crate
	(2[nd]Impf.prs.3.SG)		(ACC)
Somebody	is throwing	garbage	into a dustbin

About one third of all prefixed forms used for this event type in the Czech data are present perfectives, as shown in Example 17.

(17) *Někdo*	*vy-syp-e*	*smetí*	*do koše*
somebody	throw (Perf.prs.3.SG)	garbage (ACC)	into bucket
			(GEN)
Somebody	throws	garbage	into a bucket

According to standard Czech grammars (e.g. Petr, 1987), the present perfective is supposed to refer to completion of a situation in the future, thus denoting future reading. However, the present perfective in Example (17) is anchored in the here-and-now, denoting a present reading. In other words, the perfective aspect in Czech can also have a here-and-now reading. This is not the case in Russian where the present perfective in the here-and-now reading is not grammatical and, additionally, is never used by native speakers (Schmiedtová & Sahonenko, 2008: 66). In other words, the two perfectives are no longer equivalent. This finding strongly suggests a shift and a broadening of the semantic features of the perfective in Czech (cf. Schmiedtová, 2010).

The findings on situation with qualified resultant state are related to the findings on goal-oriented motion in the following way. Verbs of motion form a special group of verbs that do not form the secondary imperfective either in Czech or in Russian. Also, for dynamic situations in which a potential goal is depicted as not reached, speakers of both languages do not use the perfective aspect. Because of these constraints on motion, speakers of Czech and Russian cannot differ in their choice of aspect – they are both restricted to the use of the simplex imperfective. But they differ in the perspective taken on the motion event: Czech native speakers prefer to construe the goal-oriented motion holistically, using a local adjunct. Russian native speakers show a preference for construing the event as ongoing, using the simplex imperfective, which does not require any additional arguments; it can be complemented by mentioning information other than references to endpoints. These differences in perspective are driven by differences in the underlying aspectual operations, which become visible in other types of events than motion.

3.6.2 Summary of the first language results

All three studies provided evidence for the influence of L1-specific structures on the construal of goal-oriented motion events. MS Arabic, English and Spanish share the same grammatical feature – the progressive and/or the imperfective aspect, which provides the formal means for selecting a subinterval of an event conceptualized for language production, a perspective that we label phasal decomposition. That means that speakers of these languages follow similar principles in structuring information for verbalization, viewing goal-oriented events as ongoing. In contrast, in German and Norwegian, where grammaticalized aspect encoding imperfectivity is absent, speakers follow a different set of principles for structuring information: they view goal-oriented events under a holistic perspective and hence include possible endpoints in their verbalizations.

The findings from the verbal production were corroborated by results from SOT (study 1) and eye-tracking data (study 2). German speakers showed a preference for the holistic perspective, which required them to wait before speaking until the scene as a whole had unfolded. On the other hand, for English and Spanish speakers any phase of a motion event constitutes a reportable event; consequently, they do not have to wait for a possible closure. The eye-tracking results demonstrated that native speakers of German focused on the endpoint before and after starting to speak, while native speakers of English started speaking before looking at the critical region. This finding was interpreted as an indication that in conceptualizing content in order to form a verbal representation of the scene depicted, German speakers direct more attention to specific components of the visual input compared to English speakers (v. Stutterheim & Carroll, 2006).

A special case was presented for Czech and Russian (Schmiedtová & Sahonenko, 2008). It was shown that speakers of Czech encode goal-oriented motion differently from speakers of Russian, although superficially they seem to share the same set of aspectual markers. The Russian group preferred the verbalization of goal-oriented motion events as ongoing, excluding the endpoint from the event description, while the Czech group typically described these events holistically, including the endpoint in the event description. At first glance, the different perspectives on motion events seem not to be related to aspect since speakers of both languages use the simplex imperfective to encode motion. This choice, however, is caused by the constraints on the combinatorial possibilities of verbs of motion and the perfective and the secondary imperfective aspects. To investigate the role of aspect in event construal, events with a qualified resultant state were examined. This event type can be described through all aspects available in the linguistic system of the two languages. It was found that speakers of Czech preferred the perfective aspect and it was used in the past as well as in the present tense. This preference goes hand in hand with the use of the holistic perspective. Speakers of Russian, on the other hand, favored the secondary imperfective and viewed the same type of event as ongoing. What we can see from these results is that speakers from closely related languages that share a similar aspectual system, may show different preferences when it comes to aspect use. But importantly, the differences in aspect use are caused by the change of the semantics of the perfective: unlike the Russian, the Czech perfective is no longer bound to the deictic now, as shown in the present task. Additionally, different event types can also be expected to trigger the use of different verb types. An example of such an interplay are motion events in which Czech speakers had to make use of lexical means in order to view these events from a holistic perspective.

3.6.3 Second language speakers

Given the crosslinguistic differences established in the studies discussed above, we can now ask whether L2 speakers construe goal-oriented motion in accordance with the principles of information organization in the L2.

Study 1 (v. Stutterheim, 2003) investigated two groups of L2 speakers: L1 English speakers of L2 German and L1 German speakers of L2 English. Since the baseline study revealed no crosslinguistic differences for the control items, the analyses focused only on critical items.

The analysis, which also included data from L1 speakers of German and English discussed earlier, revealed significant differences in the number of mentioned endpoints between L1 German and L1 English speakers (χ^2 (1) = 84.06, $p < 0.001$) and between L1 German and L2 German speakers (χ^2 (1) = 57.64, $p < 0.001$). There were no significant differences between L1 English and L2 English speakers (χ^2 (1) = 0.44, n.s.). Moreover, both learner groups were compared to their monolingual countrymen. There was no significant difference between English speakers of German and native speakers of English (χ^2 (1) = 1.52, n.s.). However, a difference was found between German speakers of English and native speakers of German (χ^2 (1) = 44.5, $p < 0.001$). These findings suggest that L1 German speakers of L2 English have at least partially acquired the target language perspective on goal-oriented motion, whereas L1 English speakers of L2 German still rely on the L1 perspective when talking about events in the L2. These results are illustrated in Figure 3.7.

The analysis of SOT data, illustrated in Figure 3.8, showed that after the beginning of the video clip, L1 German speakers started to speak much later than L1 English speakers ($t1$ (24) = 3.13, $p = 0.04$; $t2$ (27) = 10.71, $p < 0.001$). L2 German speakers displayed the L1-like SOT pattern in the target language by keeping their speech onset time at around 3.8 seconds (F (1, 122) = 0.69, n.s.), while L2 English speakers shortened their speech onset times to 3.4 seconds (F (1, 131) = 13.46, $p < 0.001$). As in the mentioning of endpoints, L2 English speakers seem to have moved toward the target language (v. Stutterheim, 2003: 201). These results support the general pattern found in the linguistic data.[19]

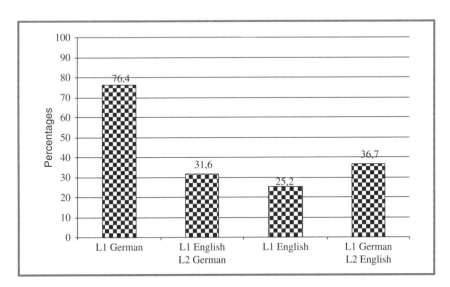

Figure 3.7 Study 1: Percentage of endpoints mentioned in eight critical items by L2 speakers ($n = 20$ participants per group; L1 English: SD = 4.8; L1 German: SD = 5.8; $n = 15$ participants per group; L1 English L2 German: SD = 3.6; L1 German L2 English: SD = 4.1)

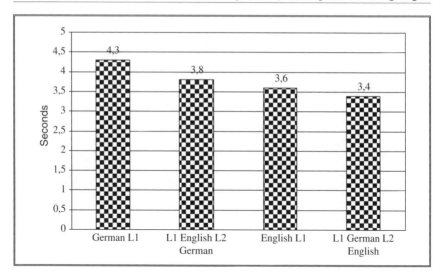

Figure 3.8 Study 1: Speech onset times of L2 speakers in eight critical items
($n = 20$ participants per group – English L1: SD = 0.4; German L1: SD = 0.5;
$n = 15$ participants per group – L1 English L2 German: SD = 0.3; L1 German
L2 English: SD = 0.5)

Study 2 (v. Stutterheim & Carroll, 2006) investigated two L2 speaker
groups.[20] These were L1 German speakers of L2 English and L1 English
speakers of L2 German. The analysis revealed that, in this study, speakers
of L2 English and L2 German did not construe goal-oriented events in a
target-like fashion. Rather significant differences in the number of
endpoints mentioned for critical items were found between L1 and L2
English speakers (χ^2 (1) = 14.06, $p < 0.001$) and between L1 and L2
German speakers (χ^2 (1) = 76.16, $p < 0.001$). In addition, both L2 groups
were compared with their own L1 groups. The comparison between
native speakers of English and L1 English speakers of L2 German was
not significant (χ^2 (1) = 0, 26, n.s.). The comparison between native
speakers of German and L1 German speakers of L2 English revealed
significant differences (χ^2 (1) = 32.72, $p < 0.001$). These results are in line
with those reported in study 1. Here, too, L1 German speakers of L2
English encoded significantly fewer endpoints than German monolinguals. Although L1 German speakers of L2 English are still far from
construing goal-oriented motion in the pattern typical for the target
language, they show divergence from their L1 pattern. This finding could
be interpreted as a beginning of restructuring. Figure 3.9 summarizes the
results of the study.

In study 3 (Schmiedtová & Sahonenko, 2008), Czech and Russian
learners of L2 German were examined. Since the baseline study did not

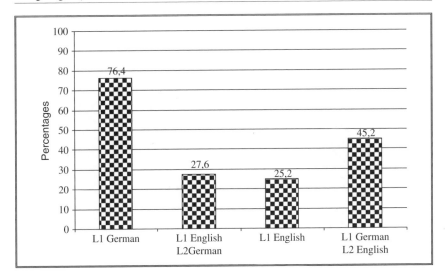

Figure 3.9 Study 2: Percentage of endpoints mentioned in eight critical items by L2 speakers ($n = 20$ participants per group; L1 English: SD = 4.8; L1 German: SD = 5.8; L1 English L2 German: SD = 3.5; L1 German L2 English: SD = 3.5)

reveal any effects for control items, the analyses focused on the endpoint mentioning in the critical items. Figure 3.10 displays the results for critical items, L1 results are repeated for comparison.

The analysis revealed that L1 Czech speakers of L2 German mentioned a significantly higher number of endpoints than L1 German speakers (χ^2 (1) = 18.18, $p < 0.001$), while L1 Russian speakers of L2 German mentioned significantly fewer endpoints than L1 German speakers (χ^2 (1) = 8.74, $p < 0.01$). No difference was found in the comparison between monolingual speakers of Czech and Czech speakers of German (χ^2 (1) = 1.57, n.s.). Similarly, the comparison between monolingual speakers of Russian and L1 Russian speakers of L2 German did not reveal any significant differences (χ^2 (1) = 3.78, n.s.). These results show that L1 Czech and L1 Russian speakers of L2 German both used L1-rooted principles for construing goal-oriented motion in the target language: The Russian group focused on the ongoingness of the situation, whereas the Czech group construed goal-oriented motion events under the holistic perspective. These results are in line with the patterns found for L1 Czech, L1 German and L1 Russian (Schmiedtová & Sahonenko, 2008: 62–63). The following are examples of the L2 speakers' description of the scene discussed previously.

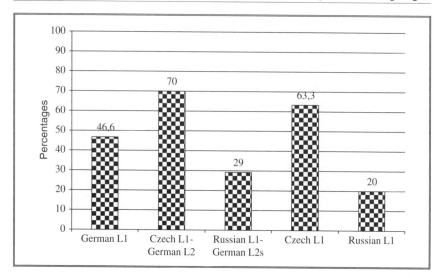

Figure 3.10 Study 3: Percentage of endpoints mentioned in eight critical items by L2 speakers ($n = 30$ participants per group; Czech: SD = 4.0; German: SD = 5.2; Russian: SD = 4.9; $n = 15$ participants per group – L1 Czech L2 German: SD = 3.1; L1 Russian L2 German: SD = 3.7)

(18) *Zwei Frauen*	*gehen*		*zu einem*	*Kloster*	L1 Czech-
					L2 German
two women	go (prs.3.PL)		to a (DAT)	monastery	
Two women	are going		towards a	monastery	
(19) *Frauen*	*gehen*		*einen Weg*	*entlang*	L1 Russian-
					L2 German
women	go (prs.3.PL)		a (ACC) path	along	
Women	are going		along	a path	

As in the L1-baseline data, members of both groups use the same verb *gehen* (to go), but differ systematically in their focus on a possible endpoint in the target language.

3.6.4 Summary of the second language results

To sum up, the evidence provided by the three studies for the linguistic encoding of endpoints by advanced L2 speakers is mixed. Studies 1 and 2 showed that one advanced learner group – L2 German speakers – retained L1-rooted principles in the construal of events, while the other learner group – L2 English speakers – displayed the pattern favored in the target language. Our explanation for these differences involves the transparency of encoding of the new conceptual category: the English progressive is formally encoded and perceptually prominent, the holistic perspective in German is not. Overall, however, all three studies point to the effects of the L1 system on the conceptualization in the L2.

3.7 General discussion

This chapter reviewed findings from three empirical studies that examined similarities and differences between L1 and L2 speakers in the construction of goal-oriented motion events. The reviewed studies share the assumption that the absence or presence of aspect in a given L1-system plays a decisive role in learning to structure information in an L2. All studies provide substantial crosslinguistic evidence on the extent to which aspect guides the selection of a particular perspective on goal-oriented motion events in L1 production. Study 1 also presented SOT results, which supported the findings from the production data. Study 3 provided new insights on the use of aspect in L1 Czech and L1 Russian. Even though Czech, like Russian, is an aspect-dominant language, Czech speakers behaved differently when construing goal-oriented motion events: they used the holistic perspective and clustered with the speakers of the endpoint-oriented languages. This finding links in with results from other analyses which had shown that the Czech aspectual system has been affected by language contact with German (Schmiedtová, 2010). In particular, a reanalysis of the perfective has led to a verbal form that allows for the integration of endpoints under the perspective of the deictic *now* that is expressed in the combination of a perfective and present tense, under a present tense reading (see Example (17)).

The findings of the three studies are consistent with results of the previous studies on language-specific patterns in event encoding (e.g. Gennari *et al.*, 2002; Papafragou *et al.*, 2002). They also show that effects of language arise when linguistic forms are recruited for conceptualization. The SOT and eye-tracking results from studies 1 and 2, however, challenge Papafragou *et al.*'s (2002) view that allocation of attention during event perception is not affected by the native language of the speaker. The results of studies 1 and 2 provide further support for Slobin's (1996a) Thinking for Speaking hypothesis, expanding its scope to aspect. The results of study 3 show that verbalization is affected not only by the availability of a particular feature, but also by preferences in usage.

Eye-tracking data offer unique evidence of the linkage between aspect, the perspective taken on goal-oriented events and eye fixation (study 2; v. Stutterheim & Carroll, 2006). The researchers found that speakers who adopt a holistic perspective on events fixate on the possible endpoint both before and after speech onset markedly longer than speakers who adopt an ongoing perspective. This finding shows that visual attention prior to and during verbal encoding is influenced by language-specific categories, such as aspect. This suggests, in turn, that the influence of linguistic categories goes beyond organization of content for verbalization – it also affects the speaker's attention to certain aspects of a given situation. In light of these findings, the proposal was made to extend the Thinking for Speaking hypothesis to the Seeing for Speaking hypothesis (Carroll *et al.*, 2004; v. Stutterheim, 2007; Schmiedtová *et al.*, 2008). As discussed earlier, the Seeing for Speaking hypothesis assumes that when language A codes a certain meaning grammatically and language B codes the same meaning lexically or phrasally, then speakers of language A should attend to the relevant feature of a given visual scene, while speakers of language B may not do so, or at least not to the same extent.

As for L2 speakers, the findings reported in the three studies varied. Study 1 (v. Stutterheim, 2003) showed a conceptual shift from L1 preferences to L2 preferences for one group of L2 speakers: advanced L1 German speakers of L2 English have partially acquired the English-like perspective for the verbalization of goal-oriented motion, visible both in their verbal performance and in their SOTs. The fact that L1 English speakers of L2 German did not demonstrate the same approximation of the L2 patterns could be linked to the lack of transparency in German, i.e. the fact that in German the relevant perspective is not marked grammatically.[21] Thus, results from study 1 are in line with other studies claiming that restructuring in L2 speakers is possible (cf. Athanasopoulos, 2006; Cadierno 2004). In contrast, studies 2 and 3, as well as study 1 for the second group of L2 speakers, found the opposite: the L2 speakers investigated in these studies continued to rely on L1-specific patterns when construing goal-oriented motion in the L2. These results are consistent with those of other studies that found only partial or no evidence of conceptual restructuring in L2 speakers (cf. Carroll & Lambert, 2003; Carroll, 1997; Carroll & v. Stutterheim, 2003; Hendriks *et al.*, 2008; Kellerman & van Hoof, 2003; Schmiedtová, 2004). Consequently, more studies and more triangulated evidence are necessary to have a full picture of the factors that lead to conceptual restructuring in different L2 domains.

3.8 Conclusions

The studies discussed here have relevance both for crosslinguistic research and for research on bilingualism and SLA. With regard to cross-linguistic differences, these studies show that L1 perspectives taken on events are grammatically driven. Such perspectives, in turn, can become the source of further processes of grammaticalization. These findings suggest that languages can be clustered on the basis of preferred patterns of information organization, an approach outlined in Carroll and v. Stutterheim (2003: 395). With regard to bilingualism and SLA, the studies discussed in this chapter demonstrated that L1-specific patterns of selecting and structuring information in conceptualizing motion events pose a long-lasting challenge for L2 learners and only a few L2 speakers can overcome these challenges. When it comes to goal-oriented motion, the majority of L2 speakers think in the L1 when speaking in the L2.

Acknowledgments

The research discussed here was partly supported by DFG grant STU-131/6-2 to Christiane v. Stutterheim. We would like to thank three anonymous reviewers for their helpful comments on earlier versions of this chapter. The authors wish to express their gratitude to Aneta Pavlenko who read and commented critically on many drafts of this chapter and who provided invaluable support at the beginning of this enterprise. All remaining errors in fact or interpretation are, however, ours.

Notes

1. The term *L2 user* (Cook, 1999) is used synonymously with the terms *L2 learner* and *L2 speaker* in this chapter.
2. The terms *event* and *situation* are used interchangeably in this chapter.
3. To avoid confusion, we use the term *aspect* to refer to grammatical aspect (for more discussion on this topic, see Klein, 1994; Schmiedtová & Flecken, 2008; v. Stutterheim *et al.*, 2009).
4. Both examples are originally from Talmy (2000: 49–50).
5. This, however, only applies when linguistic knowledge is recruited for the given non-linguistic task.
6. These two forms do not denote the same aspectual concept; however, since this otherwise very relevant difference is not vital for the argument of the present chapter, we will not explain this in detail.
7. Importantly, whenever a verb is used, the speaker must decide whether to use the perfective or the imperfective, i.e. every verb has a particular aspect.
8. The reason Russian and Czech use the locative adjunct *through a door* with different cases – the genitive in Czech and the accusative in Russian – is due to the use of different prepositions: in Russian the preposition *v* (in) and in Czech the preposition *do* (in).
9. It is conceivable to use present perfective with no additional arguments in a sequence of a set of events, e.g. *Někdo vejde, vezme si kabát a zase odejde* [Somebody comes in, takes the coat and leaves again]. The same is true for Russian.
10. For more detailed discussion on the function and status of this form in Czech, see Schmiedtová (2004); for the comparison between Czech and Russian, see Schmiedtová and Sahonenko (2008).
11. For an overview and discussion of these forms, see Schmiedtová and Sahonenko (2008).
12. The secondary imperfective is often used in Russian but rarely in Czech for events depicting change of state with a possible resultant state (cf. Schmiedtová & Sahonenko, 2008).
13. To enroll at a German university, all foreign students have to pass the so-called 'Deutsche Sprachprüfung für den Hochschulzugang ausländischer

Studienbewerber (DSH)', a standardized language test that combines an extensive written test with a spoken language test.

14. All participants were asked to fill out a general questionnaire providing information about their age, educational background, other foreign languages spoken, daily use of L2 German, motivation to learn L2 German, length of residence and length of instruction in the L2. The question asked about their dominant language was: *Welche Sprache sprechen Sie am häufigsten im Alltag?* [What language do you speak on a daily basis most frequently?]

15. The language of instruction for all courses in the German department at the Charles University in Prague is German.

16. The questions were as follows: in MS Arabic *Mādā yağri?*; in Czech *Co se děje?*; in German *Was passiert?*; in Russian *Čto proischodit?*; in Norwegian, *Hva som skjer?*; and in Spanish *¿Que está pasando?*.

17. SOTs for speakers of MS Arabic were not available at the time of writing this chapter. Because of technical difficulties during the data collection, insufficient Spanish SOT data were recorded, therefore no statistics could be applied to Spanish SOTs. For results on MS Arabic and Spanish SOT data see v. Stutterheim *et al.* (in press).

18. Fixations within the area of interest were calculated using an area-based algorithm where a set of fixations with a maximum deviation of 25 screen pixels (corresponding to a gaze movement of less than roughly $0.5°$ and approximately 68 cm distance from eye to screen), and a minimum sample count of 6, is recognized as a fixation.

19. Statistical analyses for the SOT data in L2 speakers were taken from v. Stutterheim (2003: 201).

20. No eye-tracking data were available for L2 speakers at the time of writing this study. For eye tracking in Dutch-German bilinguals, see Flecken (in press).

21. For more discussion of the role perceptual saliency may play in achieving native-like proficiency in the L2, see Schmiedtová (2004).

References

Athanasopoulos, P. (2006) Effects of the grammatical representation of number on cognition in bilinguals. *Bilingualism: Language and Cognition* 9, 89–96.

Athanasopoulos, P. and Kasai, C. (2008) Language and thought in bilinguals: The case of grammatical number and nonverbal classification preferences. *Applied Psycholinguistics* 29, 105–121.

Berman, R. and Slobin, D. (1994) *Relating Events in Narrative: A Crosslinguistic Developmental Study.* Hillsdale, NJ: Lawrence Erlbaum.

Billman, D. and Krych, M. (1998) Path and manner verbs in action: Effects of "skipping" and "exiting" on event memory. *Proceedings of the 20th Annual Conference of the Cognitive Science Society* (pp. 156–161). Hillsdale, NJ: Lawrence Erlbaum.

Billman, D., Swilley, A. and Krych, M. (2000) Path and manner priming: Verb production and event recognition. *Proceedings of the 22nd Annual Conference of the Cognitive Science Society* (pp. 615–620). Mahwah, NJ: Lawrence Erlbaum.

Bohnemeyer, J., Enfield, N., Essegbey, J., Ibarretxe-Antunano, I., Kita, S., Lüpke, F. and Ameka, F. (2007) Principles of event segmentation: The case of motion events. *Language* 83, 495–532.

Bybee, J., Perkins, R. and Pagliuca, W. (1994) *The Evolution of Grammar*. Chicago, IL: Chicago University Press.

Bylund, E. (2008) Procesos de conceptualización de eventos en español y en sueco: Diferencias translingüísticas [Event conceptualization processes in Spanish and Swedish: Crosslinguistic differences]. *Revue Romane* 43, 1–24.

Bylund, E. (2009) Effects of age of L2 acquisition on L1 event conceptualization patterns. *Bilingualism: Language and Cognition* 12, 305–322.

Cadierno, T. (2004) Expressing motion events in a second language: A cognitive typological perspective. In M. Achard and S. Niemeier (eds) *Cognitive Linguistics, Second Language Acquisition, and Foreign Language Teaching* (pp. 13–49). Berlin: Mouton de Gruyter.

Cadierno, T. (2008) Learning to talk about motion in a foreign language. In P. Robinson and N. Ellis (eds) *Handbook of Cognitive Linguistics and Second Language Acquisition* (pp. 239–275). New York/London: Routledge.

Cadierno, T. and Ruiz, L. (2006) Motion events in Spanish L2 acquisition. *Annual Review of Cognitive Linguistics* 4, 183–216.

Carroll, M. (1993) Deictic and intrinsic orientation in spatial descriptions: A comparison between English and German. In J. Altarriba (ed.) *Cognition and Culture: A Cross-cultural Approach to Cognitive Psychology* (pp. 23–44). Amsterdam: North-Holland.

Carroll, M. (1997) Changing place in English and German: Language specific preferences in the conceptualization of spatial relations. In J. Nuyts and E. Pederson (eds) *Language and Conceptualization* (pp. 137–161). Cambridge: Cambridge University Press.

Carroll, M. and Lambert, M. (2003) Information structure in narratives and the role of grammaticized knowledge: A study of adult French and German learners of English. In Ch. Dimroth and M. Starren (eds) *Information Structure and the Dynamics of Language Acquisition* (pp. 267–287). Amsterdam: John Benjamins.

Carroll, M. and Lambert, M. (2006) Reorganizing principles of information structure in advanced L2s: French and German learners of English. In H. Byrnes, H. Weger-Guntharp and K. Sprang (eds) *Educating for Advanced Foreign Language Capacities* (pp. 54–73). Washington, DC: Georgetown University Press.

Carroll, M., Roßdeutscher, A., Lambert, M. and Stutterheim, Ch. v. (2008) Subordination in narratives and macrostructural planning: A comparative point of view. In C. Fabricius-Hansen and W. Ramm (eds) *Subordination versus Coordination in Sentence and Text* (pp. 161–184). Amsterdam: John Benjamins.

Carroll, M. and Stutterheim, Ch. v. (2003) Typology and information organization: Perspective taking and language-specific effects in the construction of events. In A. Ramat (ed.) *Typology and Second Language Acquisition* (pp. 365–402). Berlin: Mouton de Gruyter.

Carroll, M. and Stutterheim, Ch. v. (in press) Event representation, event-time relations and clause structure: A crosslinguistic study of English and German. In J. Bohnemeyer and E. Pederson (eds) *Event Representation in Language: Encoding Events at the Language-Cognition Interface*. Cambridge: Cambridge University Press.

Carroll, M., Stutterheim, Ch. v. and Nüse, R. (2004) The language and thought debate: A psycholinguistic approach. In C. Habel and T. Pechmann (eds) *Approaches to Language Production* (pp. 183–218). Berlin: Mouton de Gruyter.

Cook, V. (1999) Going beyond the native speaker in language teaching. *TESOL Quarterly* 33, 185–209.

Dahl, O. (1985) *Tense and Aspect Systems*. Oxford: Blackwell.

Flecken, M. (in press) The role of grammaticalizing structures in tasks of event construal for early bilinguals: Insights from linguistic as well as eye-tracking data. *Bilingualism: Language and Cognition*.

Gennari, S., Sloman, S., Malt, B. and Fitch, T. (2002) Motion events in language and cognition. *Cognition* 83, 49–79.

Gumperz, J. and Levinson, S. (eds) (1996) *Rethinking Linguistic Relativity*. Cambridge: Cambridge University Press.

Habel, C. and Tappe, H. (1999) Processes of segmentation and linearization in describing events. In R. Klabunde and Ch. v. Stutterheim (eds) *Processes in Language Production* (pp. 117–153). Wiesbaden: Deutscher Universitätsverlag.

Hart, W. and Albarracín, D. (2009) What I Was Doing Versus What I Did: Verb aspect influences memory and future actions. *Psychological Science* 20, 238–244.

Hendriks, H., Hickmann, M. and Demagny, A. (2008) How English native speakers learn to express caused motion in English and French. *Acquisition et Interaction en Langue Étrangère* 27, 15–41.

Kellerman, E. and Hoof, A-M. v. (2003) Manual accents. *International Review of Applied Linguistics* 41, 251–269.

Klein, W. (1994) *Time in Language*. London: Routledge.

Kopecka, A. (2008) Continuity and change in the representation of motion events in French. In J. Guo, E. Lieven, N. Budwig, S. Ervin-Tripp, K. Nakamura and S. Ozcaliskan (eds) *Crosslinguistic Approaches to the Study of Language: Research in the Tradition of Dan Isaac Slobin* (pp. 415–426). Mahwah, NJ: Lawrence Erlbaum.

Levelt, W. (1982) Linearization in describing spatial networks. In S. Peters and E. Saarinen (eds) *Processes, Beliefs and Questions* (pp. 199–220). Dordrecht: Reidel.

Levelt, W. (1989) *Speaking*. Cambridge, MA: MIT Press.

Levelt, W. (1999) Producing spoken language: A blueprint of the speaker. In C. Brown and P. Hagoort (eds) *The Neurocognition of Language* (pp. 83–122). Oxford: Oxford University Press.

Levinson, S., Kita, S., Haun, D. and Rasch, B. (2002) Returning the tables: Language affects spatial reasoning. *Cognition* 84, 155–188.

Lucy, J. (1992) *Grammatical Categories and Cognition. A Case Study of the Linguistic Relativity Hypothesis*. Cambridge: Cambridge University Press.

Majid, A., Boster, J. and Bowerman, M. (2008) The crosslinguistic categorization of everyday events: A study of cutting and breaking. *Cognition* 109, 235–250.

Majid, A., Gullberg, M., van Staden, M. and Bowerman, M. (2007) How similar are semantic categories in closely related languages? A comparison of cutting and breaking in four Germanic languages. *Cognitive Linguistics* 18, 179–194.

Naigles, L. and Terrazas, P. (1998) Motion-verb generalizations in English and Spanish: Influences of language and syntax. *Psychological Science* 9, 363–369.

Natale, S. (2008) Semantische Gebrauchdeterminanten der progressiven Verbal-periphrase stare + gerundio. Ein datenbasierte Studie [Semantic determinants in the use of the verbal periphrase *stare +gerundio* denoting the progressive in Italian: An empirical study]. Doctoral dissertation, University of Heidelberg.

Navarro, S. and Nicoladis, E. (2005) Describing motion events in adult L2 Spanish narratives. In D. Eddington (ed.) *Selected Proceedings of the 6th Conference on the Acquisition of Spanish and Portuguese as First and Second Languages* (pp. 102–107). Somerville, MA: Cascadilla Press.

Negueruela, E., Lantolf, J., Jordan, S. and Gelabert, J. (2004) The "private function" of gesture in second language speaking activity: A study of motion verbs and gesturing in English and Spanish. *International Journal of Applied Linguistics* 14, 113–147.

Nüse, R. (2003) Segmenting event sequences for speaking. In H. Härtl and H. Tappe (eds) *Mediating between Concepts and Grammar* (pp. 255–276). Berlin: Mouton de Gruyter.

Papafragou, A., Hulbert, J. and Trueswell, J. (2008) Does language guide event perception? Evidence from eye movements. *Cognition* 108, 155–184.

Papafragou, A., Massey, C. and Gleitman, L. (2002) Shake, rattle,'n' roll: The representation of motion in language and cognition. *Cognition* 84, 189–219.

Papafragou, A., Massey, C. and Gleitman, L. (2006) When English proposes what Greek presupposes: The crosslinguistic encoding of motion events. *Cognition* 98, B75–87.

Petr, J. (1987) *Mluvnice češtiny. Skladba* [*Grammar of Czech. Syntax*]. Praha: Academia.

Schmiedtová, B. (2003) The use of aspect in Czech L2. In D. Bittner and N. Gagarina (eds) *ZAS Papers in Linguistics* (Vol. 29) (pp. 177–194). Berlin: ZAS.

Schmiedtová, B. (2004) *At the Same Time: The Expression of Simultaneity in Learner Varieties*. Berlin: Mouton de Gruyter.

Schmiedtová, B. (2010) Einflüsse des Deutschen auf das Tschechische: ein Sprachvergleich aus der Lernerperspektive [The influence of German on Czech: A crosslinguistic comparison from the learner's perspective]. In S. Höhne and L. Udolph (eds) *Prozesse kultureller Integration und Desintegration. Deutsche, Tschechen, Böhmen im 20. Jahrhundert* [Processes of Cultural Integration and Disintegration: Germans, Czechs, and Bohemians in the 20th Century] (pp. 91–117). München: Oldenbourg.

Schmiedtová, B., Carroll, M. and Stutterheim, C. v. (2007) Implications of language-specific L1 patterns in event construal of advanced second language learners. Paper presented at the annual conference of the American Association for Applied Linguistics, Costa Mesa, CA, April 24, 2007.

Schmiedtová, B. and Flecken, M. (2008) The role of aspectual distinctions in event encoding: Implications for second language acquisition. In S. de Knop and T. de Rycker (eds) *Cognitive Approaches to Pedagogical Grammar* (pp. 357–384). Berlin: Mouton de Gruyter.

Schmiedtová, B. and Sahonenko, N. (2008) Die Rolle des grammatischen Aspekts in Ereignis-Enkodierung: Ein Vergleich zwischen Tschecnischen und Russischen Lernern des Deutschen [The role of grammatical aspects in the encoding of events: A comparison between Czech and Russian learners of German]. In P. Grommes and M. Walter (eds) *Fortgeschrittene Lernervarietäten: Korpuslinguistik und Zweitspracherwerbs-forschung* [Advanced learner varieties: Corpus linguistics and second language research] (pp. 45–71). Linguistiche Arbeiten. Tübingen: Niemeyer.

Schmiedtová, B., Stutterheim, C. v. and Carroll, M. (2008) Seeing for speaking. Paper presented at the Hengstberger Symposium "Seeing for Speaking", Heidelberg, Germany.

Slobin, D. (1991) Learning to think for speaking: Native language, cognition and rhetorical style. *Pragmatics* 1, 7–26.

Slobin, D. (1996a) From "thought to language" to "thinking for speaking". In J. Gumperz and S. Levinson (eds) *Rethinking Linguistic Relativity* (pp. 70–96). Cambridge: Cambridge University Press.

Slobin, D. (1996b) Two ways of travel: Verbs of motion in English and Spanish. In M. Shibatani and S. Thompson (eds) *Grammatical Constructions: Their Form and Meaning* (pp. 195–219). Oxford: Clarendon Press.

Slobin, D. (1997) Mind, code, and text. In J. Bybee, J. Haiman and S. Thompson (eds) *Essays on Language Function and Language Type: Dedicated to T. Givón* (pp. 437–467). Amsterdam: John Benjamins.

Slobin, D. (2000) Verbalized events: A dynamic approach to linguistic relativity and determinism. In S. Niemeier and R. Dirven (eds) *Evidence for Linguistic Relativity* (pp. 107–138). Amsterdam: John Benjamins.

Slobin, D. (2003) Language and thought online: Cognitive consequences of linguistic relativity. In S. Gentner and S. Goldin-Meadow (eds) *Language in Mind: Advances in the Study of Language and Thought* (pp. 157–192). Cambridge, MA: MIT Press.

Slobin, D. (2004) The many ways to search for a frog: Linguistic typology and the expression of motion events. In S. Strömqvist and L. Verhoeven (eds) *Relating Events in Narrative. Typological and Contextual Perspectives* (pp. 219–257). Mahwah, NJ: Lawrence Erlbaum.

Slobin, D. (2006) What makes manner of motion salient? Explorations in linguistic typology, discourse, and cognition. In M. Hickmann and S. Robert (eds) *Space across Languages: Linguistic Systems and Cognitive Categories* (pp. 59–81). Amsterdam: John Benjamins.

Stutterheim, Ch. v. (2003) Linguistic structure and information organisation. The case of very advanced learners. In S. Foster-Cohen and S. Pekarek-Doehler (eds) *EUROSLA Yearbook 3* (pp. 183–206). Amsterdam: John Benjamins.

Stutterheim, Ch. v. (2007) *Sprachspezifische Prinzipien der Informationsverarbeitung* [Language-specific principles of information processing]. Paper presented at the Sprache & Denken Symposium Humboldt University, Berlin.

Stutterheim, Ch. v., Bastin, D., Carroll, M., Flecken, M. and Schmiedtová, B. (in press) How grammaticized concepts shape event conceptualization in the early phases of language production: Insights from linguistic analysis, eye tracking data and memory performance. *Linguistics*.

Stutterheim, Ch. v. and Carroll, M. (2006) The impact of grammatical temporal categories on ultimate attainment in L2 learning. In H. Byrnes, H. Weger-Guntharp and K. Sprang (eds) *Educating for Advanced Foreign Language Capacities* (pp. 40–53). Washington, DC: Georgetown University Press.

Stutterheim, Ch. v., Carroll, M. and Klein, W. (2003) Two ways of construing complex temporal structures. In F. Lenz (ed.) *Deictic Conceptualization of Space, Time and Person* (pp. 97–133). Berlin: Mouton de Gruyter.

Stutterheim, Ch. v., Carroll, M. and Klein, W. (2009) New perspectives in analyzing aspectual distinctions across languages. In W. Klein and P. Li (eds) *The Expression of Time* (pp. 195–216). Berlin: Mouton de Gruyter.

Stutterheim, Ch. v. and Nüse, R. (2003) Processes of conceptualization in language production: Language-specific perspectives and event construal. *Linguistics* 41, 851–881.

Stutterheim, Ch. v., Nüse, R. and Murcia Serra, J. (2002) Crosslinguistic differences in the conceptualization of events. In H. Hasselgård, S. Johansson, C. Fabricius-Hansen and B. Behrens (eds) *Information Structure in a Cross-linguistic Perspective* (pp. 179–198). Amsterdam: Rodopi.

Talmy, L. (1985) Lexicalization patterns: Semantic structure in lexical forms. In T. Shopen (ed.) *Language Typology and Syntactic Description, Vol. 3: Grammatical Categories and the Lexicon* (pp. 36–149). Cambridge: Cambridge University Press.

Talmy, L. (1988) The relation of grammar to cognition. In B. Rudzka-Ostyn (ed.) *Topics in Cognitive Linguistics* (pp. 165–205). Amsterdam: John Benjamins.
Talmy, L. (1991) Path to realization: A typology of event conflation. *Proceedings of the 17th Annual Meeting of the Berkeley Linguistics Society* (pp. 480–519). Berkeley, CA: Berkeley Linguistics Society.
Talmy, L. (2000) *Toward a Cognitive Semantics*. Cambridge, MA: Bradford Book.

Appendix

Here are examples of three control and three critical items used in the studies reviewed in the present chapter. Because of possible printing problems, the pictures are presented in black and white; the original clips were in color. Below each picture is a description of what it depicts. Additionally, for critical items, examples of verbalizations are provided that were frequently produced by speakers of the four focus languages discussed in this chapter – English, German, Czech and Russian.

Critical Item 1. A car is riding on a country road; in the background one can see the first houses of a village; the car does not reach the village entrance in the clip.

English native speaker: A car driving down the road
German native speaker: *Ein Auto fährt die Strasse entlang in einen Ort*
                           [A car is riding along a road to a place]
Czech native speaker: *Auto vjíždí do vesnice*
                           [A car is riding into a village]
Russian native speaker: *Mašina jedet po doroge*
                           [A car is riding on a road]

Critical Item 2. A man is climbing up a ladder toward a balcony; the man does not reach the balcony in the clip.

English native speaker: A man is climbing a ladder
German native speaker: *Ein Mann steigt die Leiter hinauf zu einem Balkon*
                           [A men is climbing up a ladder onto a balcony]
Czech native speaker: *Muž leze po žebříku na balkón do prvního patra*
                           [A man is climbing up a ladder to a balcony on
                             the second floor]
Russian native speaker: *Mužčina lezet po lestnitse*
                           [A man is climbing up a ladder]

Critical Item 3. Two women are walking down the road; at the end of the road there is a big house; the women do not reach the house in the clip.

English native speaker:	Two women are walking down a path
German native speaker:	*Zwei Frauen laufen zu einem Haus*
	[Two women are walking to a house]
Czech native speaker:	*Dvě ženy jdou po cestě k domu*
	[Two women are walking on a road to a house]
Russian native speaker:	*Dve devushki idut po doroge*
	[Two girls are walking on a road]

Control Item 1. A car riding into a courtyard of a farm; the car reaches the courtyard in the clip.

Control Item 2. A woman is cycling into a forest; the woman enters the forest in the clip.

Control Item 3. A dog is running into a house; the dog disappears in the house in the clip.

Chapter 4

Language-specific Patterns in Event Conceptualization: Insights from Bilingualism

EMANUEL BYLUND

4.1 Introduction

In its most generic conception, an event may be characterized as 'something that happens'. Needless to say, things that happen are central to human experience, and language offers a range of means to which we may resort to talk about events. Nevertheless, languages around the world also vary considerably with regard to the relative prominence they give to specific event features. For instance, to talk about a man painting a picture, a speaker of Algerian Arabic would provide information about whether the painting was completed or not, a speaker of Bulgarian would indicate whether the event was witnessed or hearsay, and a speaker of Peninsular Spanish would convey information about whether the event occurred during the moment of speech, the same day or before that day.

Linking this crosslinguistic variation to the idea that linguistic structure may influence the way we think when we prepare content for speech (i.e. when 'thinking for speaking', see Slobin, 1991), the question arises whether differences in event encoding lead speakers of different languages to select and structure event features differently. As seen also in Chapter 3, the issue of whether there are crosslinguistic differences in the information selection and organization, or *conceptualization*, of events is increasingly becoming a concern of empirical research. To date, the majority of the studies in this area of inquiry have focused either on the segmentation and packaging of path and manner of motion (e.g. Allen *et al.*, 2007; Berman & Slobin, 1994; Papafragou *et al.*, 2006, 2008; Strömqvist & Verhoeven, 2004; Talmy, 1985) or on the expression of separation in material integrity, that is, events of 'cutting' and 'breaking' (e.g. Bohnemeyer, 2007; Goddard & Wierzbicka, 2009; Levinson, 2007; Majid *et al.*, 2007, 2008). A commonality of these approaches is that they investigate crosslinguistic differences in event conceptualization through *lexicalized* concepts, i.e. concepts expressed by words.

However, in view of the work of Lucy (1992a, 1992b), Slobin (1997) and Talmy (1988), which emphasizes the role of grammar in conceptual organization, there is also a need to examine the role of grammaticized concepts (i.e. concepts expressed by grammar) in event conceptualization. This approach has been undertaken by a number of recent studies concerned with examining the influence that the grammatical category of aspect exerts on event conceptualization patterns (e.g. Bylund, 2008; Carroll *et al.*, 2004; Schmiedtová & Flecken, 2008; v. Stutterheim *et al.*, 2003; v. Stutterheim & Nüse, 2003; see also Schmiedtová, this volume). The focus on the role of grammatical aspect in event conceptualization is motivated by the fact that the function of this category is to define one of the fundamental characteristics of an event, namely, its temporal distribution (see, e.g. Casati, 2008; Davidson, 1980; Lewis, 1986). The findings provided by the studies within this 'grammatical aspect approach' to event conceptualization show, first, that speakers of languages with grammatical aspect tend to focus more on ongoingness when selecting and structuring event information as compared to speakers of non-aspect languages (e.g. v. Stutterheim & Nüse, 2003), and second, that learners whose second language (L2) differs from their first language (L1) with respect to grammatical aspect are prone to resort to event conceptualization patterns characteristic of their L1, even at advanced stages of acquisition (v. Stutterheim, 2003; Schmiedtová, in press, this volume).

The present chapter, framed within the grammatical aspect approach, aims at illustrating how the study of bilinguals may enhance our understanding of different facets of language specificity in event conceptualization. In doing so, the chapter will review a series of recent investigations of bilingual event conceptualization (Bylund, 2009a, in press; Bylund & Jarvis, in press). These studies approached the question of language-specific event conceptualization from different angles: Bylund and Jarvis (in press) addressed the interconnectedness between grammatical aspect and event conceptualization. This question is clearly central to the grammatical aspect approach, and the findings reported by Bylund and Jarvis illustrate how the study of bilinguals may further this hypothesis. The study by Bylund (2009a) investigated the susceptibility of L1-specific patterns to restructuring under the influence of an L2, and Bylund (in press) addressed language specificity in event conceptualization in bilingual speakers. The two latter studies consequently relate to the area within the grammatical aspect approach concerned with language-specific patterns of event conceptualization in speakers of more than one language.

Throughout the chapter, the notions of *event* and *situation* will be used following v. Stutterheim and Nüse's (2003) account of event conceptualization in language production. Accordingly, the term 'situation' will refer to what takes place in the external world, whereas the term 'event' will refer to a 'self-contained segment in a conceptual representation of a network of interrelated situations, conceptualized as a time-substance relation' (v. Stutterheim & Nüse, 2003: 855).

The chapter is organized in the following way: in Section 4.2, an overview is given of the grammatical aspect approach to the investigation of event conceptualization and its major findings on conceptualization patterns in monolinguals and L2 learners. The function of this overview is to lay out the background to the subsequent sections (4.3–4.5), in which the questions outlined above relating to grammatical aspect and language specificity in (bilingual) event conceptualization are addressed. The chapter closes with some general remarks and suggestions for future studies on language and event conceptualization.

4.2 Event Conceptualization: Previous Studies on Native Speakers and Second Language Learners

4.2.1 Processes of event conceptualization

The preparation of content for speech implies transforming information units into a format that is expressible in a given language (Carroll *et al.*, 2004: 4). In this chapter, Levelt's (1989) model of human language production, as well as the additional work on this topic done by Habel and Tappe (1999) and v. Stutterheim and associates (e.g. v. Stutterheim & Nüse, 2003) will be used to frame the processes involved in this transformation. According to Levelt, three levels of representation constitute the language production system: the conceptual level (the conceptualizer), the lemma level (the formulator) and the phonological level (the articulator). In a communicative situation, the function of the conceptualizer consists of transforming the encyclopedic knowledge relevant to the communicative intention into a temporary conceptual structure (Carroll & v. Stutterheim, 1993), which then triggers access to the linguistic structures necessary to convey the conceptual structure (i.e. the formulator level). In modeling the conceptualization of events, Habel and Tappe (1999) suggest four different planning processes: segmentation, selection, structuring and linearization (see also v. Stutterheim & Nüse, 2003). In what follows, I will illustrate the four planning processes using as an example the situation 'riding a bike'. This situation will be depicted as a woman on a bicycle, riding along a country road at the end of which there is a small village.

Segmentation involves extracting units from a knowledge base. This means that complex situations are broken down in accordance with their features of temporal boundedness (see also Croft, 2007): complex static situations are divided into states or property predications, whereas complex dynamic situations are broken down into smaller events (v. Stutterheim, 2003: 185). In the case of the bike ride depicted above, the speaker could choose to segment the situation in the following way: *a woman is riding a bike*. The speaker could, however, also give a more fine-grained resolution of the situation: *a woman sits on a bike, she pedals and holds the handlebars with both of her hands*. In this way, the situation is broken down into static ('sitting', 'holding') and dynamic ('pedalling') entities.

Selection entails choosing the units of every individual situation that the speaker wishes to verbalize as well as the components that represent the units. Here, components encompass entities, times, spaces and properties. Consequently, in selecting event components of a goal-oriented motion event, the speaker could opt for mentioning an endpoint: *a woman rides **to a village***. The processes of segmentation and selection involve deciding 'what to say' and may therefore be classified as *macroplanning* (Levelt, 1996, 1999). The current chapter will be concerned primarily with discussing crosslinguistic differences in the selection of event components.

Structuring entails a perspectivation of the event components according to spatial and temporal reference frames. As for temporal structuring, v. Stutterheim and Nüse (2003) distinguish three conceptual components: *the event, the timeline* and *the observer/speaker*. The event is represented by a predicate (dynamic in nature) and a corresponding argument. The substance of the event may be decomposed into a beginning, a course and an end. The timeline consists of an abstract sequence of temporal intervals. The observer/speaker is the conceptualizer of the situation (Langacker, 2000). Consequently, in temporally structuring events, the conceptualizer has to select an anchor point for the event substance; the speaker also has to decide how the events should be related to each other (v. Stutterheim & Nüse, 2003: 865). In depicting the bike ride situation in the present tense, the speaker may resort to both aspectual forms and temporal adverbials to establish temporal perspectives, e.g. *a woman is riding a bike, she is looking at the landscape and then she slams on the brakes*. Here, the events 'riding a bike' and 'looking at the landscape' occur within the same temporal interval, whereas 'slamming on the brakes' takes place in a subsequent interval, as signaled by the anaphoric temporal adverbial *then* (it should be noted that the same devices could be used in the past tense as well).

In *linearization*, which is the final step of the planning process, the units selected for verbal representation have to be ordered to be transformed into the one-dimensional medium of language (Carroll *et al.*, 2004; Levelt, 1982). The linearization process thus involves the ordering of words and grammatical constituents (e.g. *the woman passes by at dawn* versus *at dawn the woman passes by*). Whereas the processes of segmentation and selection involve deciding the content of speech, structuring and linearization concern a perspective taking of that content.

As such, these latter two processes relate to the stage of *microplanning* (Levelt, 1996, 1999).

4.2.2 Event conceptualization in first language speakers

Using as a point of departure the framework outlined above, cross-linguistic differences in event conceptualization have been investigated across languages such as Arabic, Czech, Dutch, English, German, Norwegian, Russian, Spanish and Swedish (e.g. Bylund, 2008; Carroll *et al.*, 2004; Schmiedtová & Flecken, 2008; v. Stutterheim & Nüse, 2003; v. Stutterheim *et al.*, 2002; see also Schmiedtová, this volume). The overall findings suggest language-specific patterns in the segmentation, selection and temporal perspectivation of events.[1] In what follows, these findings and their interpretations will be reviewed in more detail.

Patterns of *event segmentation* were investigated in Arabic, English and German by v. Stutterheim and Nüse (2003) and in Spanish and Swedish by Bylund (2008). In both studies, the participants were shown a silent film and were instructed to retell what was happening in the film while watching it. The retellings were divided into propositional units corresponding either to states or events. References to states were not included in the analysis, nor were events that were presented as being components of another event (e.g. *he is looking for a way to try and shut down the machine*, in this sentence the underlined material constitutes an integrated event). The results showed that the speakers of German and Swedish encoded significantly fewer events than did the speakers of Arabic, English and Spanish. Specifically, speakers of Arabic, English and Spanish were prone to verbalize 'smaller', unbounded events such as 'scratching his head' or 'looking around'. These types of events were either omitted in the German and Swedish retellings or implicitly referred to by macroevents, such as 'trying to find a way'.

Crosslinguistic differences in the *selection* of event components have been investigated in a number of studies examining online descriptions of scenes depicting goal-oriented motion events (i.e. an object moving along a trajectory at the end of which there is a possible goal, such as a man riding a horse-drawn carriage toward a village) (Bylund, 2008; Carroll *et al.*, 2004; Schmiedtová *et al.*, 2007; v. Stutterheim *et al.*, 2002; v. Stutterheim & Nüse, 2003). The findings reported in these studies suggest that there are crosslinguistic differences with respect to the encoding of the endpoint of the motion: when asked to describe what is happening in the scenes, speakers of Czech, Dutch, German, Norwegian and Swedish are prone to include in their descriptions an event component representing the endpoint of the motion, e.g. 'a man is riding to a village'; speakers of Arabic, English, Russian and Spanish, on the other hand, when confronted with the same task, to a significantly higher degree tend to omit such endpoint components and instead describe the ongoing phase of the event, e.g. 'a man is riding'.

Additional, non-linguistic evidence on crosslinguistic differences in endpoint encoding is provided by v. Stutterheim and Carroll (2006) and Schmiedtová *et al.* (2007). Using eye-tracking techniques, these studies have demonstrated that while describing motion events, speakers of different languages attend to different entities in the target scenes: speakers of Arabic, English and Spanish were prone to fixate on the object in motion – both before and while speaking – and paid little or no attention to the possible goal. The opposite held for speakers of Dutch, German and Czech. These groups were shown to spend significantly more time looking at the possible goal of the motion. These results thus complement previous findings on language-specific patterns of endpoint encoding, showing that the omission of endpoints in the scene descriptions by some language groups may not be interpreted simply as a result of these speakers not deeming it worthy to mention endpoints; rather it seems as if these speakers, in fact, often do not look toward endpoints.

As for crosslinguistic differences in *temporal structuring*, two general patterns have been attested across speakers of Arabic, Dutch, English, German, Norwegian, Spanish and Swedish (e.g. Bylund, 2008; Carroll & v. Stutterheim, 2003; Carroll *et al.*, 2004; v. Stutterheim & Nüse, 2003). When asked to retell (either while watching or afterwards) the content of a silent film excerpt, speakers of Dutch, German, Norwegian and Swedish were found to resort to what may be called an *anaphoric linking strategy*. According to this strategy, the assertion time of a given event is established in relation to the time of the preceding event by means of anaphoric temporal adverbials (see Klein, 1994). Example 1 illustrates this pattern:

Example 1. Anaphoric shift

(a) *the man gets up from the ground*
(b) *and then he looks around*
(c) *and then a stone falls down*

As seen in Example 1, the events are explicitly presented as occurring in a sequence. Moreover, the event that functions as an anchor for the subsequent event is usually bounded (in the sense that its right temporal boundary is reached). In short, the anaphoric linkage pattern may be characterized as 'event x then event y'.

Such a pattern of temporal perspectivation was not found among the speakers of Arabic, English and Spanish. As a matter of fact, in these language groups the temporal sequence of the events was seldom made explicit. Example 2 illustrates how the scene described above was typically related by speakers of these languages:

Example 2. Deictic point of reference

(a)   *he's slowly waking up*
(b)   *he looks in front of him*
(c)   *and there is a big rock coming down*

In Example 2, a temporal relation of *inclusion* is found: the time interval of event 2(b) is included in that of 2(a) and 2(c). Carroll and associates (2004) suggest that in this pattern of perspectivation, the reference point is made up by a *deictic 'now'*, which may be paraphrased as 'what is happening now?': *he's waking up* (and while doing so) *he looks in front of him* (and while doing so) *a big rock is coming down* (for further discussion, see Carroll & v. Stutterheim, 2003; v. Stutterheim & Nüse, 2003). Within this pattern of temporal perspectivation, verb forms marked for imperfective/progressive play a role in identifying a time span during which certain events are taking place. In short, the pattern of deictic point of reference may be characterized as '(now) event x (now) event y'.

To summarize, the findings reviewed above indicate that when confronted with the same visual input, speakers of Arabic, English, Russian and Spanish segment the flow of events in a more fine-grained way, pay little attention to endpoints both verbally and visually, and resort to deictic linking strategies when sequencing events; in contrast, speakers of Czech, Dutch, German, Norwegian and Swedish refer to and attend to event endpoints, link event sequences anaphorically and are more oriented toward holistic event perspectives.

Two important observations can be made on the basis of these findings. First, and most centrally, the clusters of event construal patterns found across the languages investigated match the clusters given on the basis of grammatical aspect in these languages.[2] Although the aspectual systems of Arabic, English, Russian and Spanish differ to some extent, they have in common the marking of the verb for imperfective (or progressive) aspect on a productive and obligatory scale. The same does not hold for Dutch, German, Norwegian and Swedish, in which aspect does not constitute a grammatical category.[3] This, of course, does not mean that in these languages aspectual contrasts cannot be expressed: there are lexical constructions to which the speaker may resort in order to express, for example, ongoingness, but the use of these constructions is not compulsory. It is thus important to bear in mind that the central difference between the language clusters at hand resides in the codability (i.e. the ease and frequency of expression) of the concept of ongoingness, rather than in the mere possibility to express this concept (for further discussion, see Slobin, 2003; see also Jakobson, 1959).

Consistent with the view that grammar is not just a formal system, but a set of general notions that constitutes a schematic framework for conceptual organization (e.g. Slobin, 1991; Talmy, 1988; Traugott & Heine, 1991), v. Stutterheim and associates suggest that the fact that a language has grammatical aspect implies that the internal temporal constituency of events is treated as prominent in the conceptualization of states of affairs (e.g. Carroll *et al.*, 2004; v. Stutterheim & Nüse, 2003). As a consequence, a speaker of an aspect language is sensitized toward ongoingness and phasal event decomposition. In a task of verbalizing a flow of events, this sensitivity is manifested in the encoding of the ongoing phase of events and the presence of a deictic 'now' to which event times are anchored.

Speakers of non-aspect languages, in contrast, do not exhibit the same degree of sensitivity to event structure in their conceptualizations. This is, allegedly, because these speakers are not pointed by their grammars to pay attention to the internal temporal constituency of events. Instead, these speakers seem to be more oriented toward holistic perspectives according to which events are presented as having a point of completion, and the post time of an event (i.e. the time span subsequent to event completion) may serve as a temporal reference point for the subsequent event. Apart from the absence of grammatical aspect in Dutch, German, Norwegian and Swedish, there is another feature of these languages that could furnish the endpoint orientation patterns: verb particles. In Dutch, German, Norwegian and Swedish, particles are applied on a productive basis to the verb stem and can be used to convey a resultative interpretation of an event (e.g. *eat up*, etc.). Although the role of verb particles within the present context requires further research, it is not inconceivable that the holistic endpoint-oriented pattern found among the speakers of non-aspect languages may be further pronounced in the presence of these forms.

The second observation to be made on the basis of the findings reviewed above concerns language specificity in the conceptualizer. The differences found in segmentation, selection and temporal structuring suggest that the speakers of the two language clusters not only differ in *how* they say things (i.e. when temporally linking events), but also in *what* they choose to say (i.e. when verbalizing events or event components). Consequently, if macroplanning is deciding what to say, then these results are at variance with the suggestion that in language production, there is language specificity only at the level of microplanning (the 'how-to-say-it'), but not at the level of macroplanning (Levelt, 1996, 1999).[4] Along this line of argumentation, the idea has been put forth within the grammatical aspect approach that that the processes in the conceptualizer are language-specific, both at the levels of macro- and microplanning (e.g. Carroll *et al.*, 2004; Schmiedtová, this volume; v. Stutterheim & Nüse, 2003).

4.2.3 Event conceptualization in late second language learners

The findings of crosslinguistic differences in event construal reviewed in the preceding section have implications for L2 learning. For example, a native speaker of German who is in the process of learning English will have to overcome his/her habitual patterns of L1 perspectivation in order to learn to select and organize event information according to the target language. This could constitute a challenging task for the learner, partially because the differences between the L1 and the L2 conceptualization patterns may be subtle and difficult to notice, and partially because these patterns reflect preferences rather than absolute principles, meaning that there is no grammatical rule in, for example, English, preventing speakers from mentioning event endpoints.

The empirical studies carried out on this topic indeed suggest that the patterns of event conceptualization by L2 learners are seldom target-like. Instead, L1 conceptualization patterns have been shown to spill over to the L2, even in highly proficient learners (Schmiedtová, in press, this volume; v. Stutterheim, 2003; v. Stutterheim & Carroll, 2006). An example of this is provided by v. Stutterheim's study (2003) on endpoint encodings in goal-oriented motion events. The L2 learners examined in this study were advanced German learners of English and advanced English learners of German, all of whom had an excellent morphosyntactic command of the target language ('no formal errors'; v. Stutterheim, 2003: 202). The results showed that the learners' scene descriptions contained endpoint frequencies that were either identical or close to those of monolingual speakers of their respective L1s and, consequently, fairly distant from the target language patterns.[5] In view of these findings, it was concluded that even at high levels of L2 proficiency, learners still retain L1 patterns of event construal.

The research reviewed above makes certain claims regarding language specificity in event conceptualization. First, it was suggested that crosslinguistic differences in grammatical aspect are among the clearest linguistic manifestations of underlying crosslinguistic differences in event conceptualization, and second, it was put forth that there is a persistence of L1-specific event conceptualization patterns even at advanced stages of L2 learning. In what follows, the studies by Bylund (2009a, in press) and Bylund and Jarvis (in press) will be reviewed in detail with the intention to address these claims.

4.3 The Interconnectedness between Grammatical Aspect and Event Conceptualization Patterns: Evidence from Bilingual Speakers

A question that may arise in light of the findings reviewed above is whether crosslinguistic differences in event conceptualization reflect the influence of grammar on conceptualization, or whether they are a result of culturally different discursive practices, independent of the grammatical properties of the languages in question (e.g. Smith, 2004; also Montaño-Harmon, 1991). In other words, do these findings provide evidence for some version of the *linguistic relativity principle* (Whorf, 1956; for further discussion, see the introduction to this volume; Athanasopoulos, this volume), that is, the idea that language directs our attention to certain aspects of reality? Or are they better classified as *discursive relativity* (for further discussion, see Lucy, 1996)? One way to approach this question is to study different language systems that supposedly share the same cultural background (e.g. Pederson, 1995). Another way to go about this, as done within the grammatical aspect approach, is to collect data from different languages *and* different cultural groups, keeping constant one grammatical feature.

In addition to these procedures, the study of bilinguals may offer a third way to examine the relationship between grammatical aspect and language-specific event conceptualization: by extending the line of research on grammatical categories and conceptualization to the domain of bilingualism, we gain a unique opportunity to correlate a specific conceptualization pattern with the knowledge of the specific linguistic feature that is hypothesized to be related to this pattern. This type of analysis has only limited usefulness when applied to monolingual speakers, e.g. children who are still in the process of acquiring the L1 (see Choi & Bowerman, 1991; Lucy & Gaskins, 2001). However, by applying this method to adult bilingual speakers, we are able study the relationship between language and conceptualization in cognitively mature individuals, which may allow for a higher generalizability of the findings (see also Athanasopoulos, 2007, 2009, this volume).

Following this line of reasoning, Bylund and Jarvis (in press) set out to investigate both event conceptualization patterns and knowledge of linguistic structures in L1 Spanish–L2 Swedish bilinguals. As described above, Spanish and Swedish differ on the category of aspect, and speakers of Spanish and Swedish concomitantly exhibit different patterns of conceptualizing events. The specific aim of this study was to examine whether there was a relationship between endpoint encoding in the L1 and the ability to identify L1 aspectual errors. In view of previous studies arguing for a connection between grammatical aspect and endpoint encoding patterns (see Section 4.2.2), Bylund and Jarvis hypothesized that the frequency with which the bilingual participants mentioned event endpoints would be related to their grammatical intuitions regarding aspectual contrasts.

The participants were 40 L1 Spanish–L2 Swedish bilinguals residing in Sweden. The age of onset of bilingualism (AOB) of the participants ranged from 1 to 23 years (mean = 9.6 years), and their average length of residence (LoR) in Sweden was 22.7 years (range = 12–34 years). About 70% of the bilinguals were of Chilean origin, while the remainder was born in other Latin American countries (Bolivia, Colombia, Mexico and Peru).[6] Prior to participation in this study, the bilinguals had taken part in a screening experiment for L2 proficiency, in which they had been judged as native speakers of Swedish by at least 3 of 10 native listener judges (for details, see Abrahamsson & Hyltenstam, 2009). The bilinguals' common denominator was consequently that they had attained a proficiency level in Swedish that to a certain extent allowed them to pass for native speakers in everyday oral communication. As for L1 proficiency, the bilinguals claimed to be functional speakers of Spanish and reported regular use of this language (in contrast to L2 proficiency, L1 Spanish proficiency was not assessed prior to participation). The bilinguals were compared with a control group consisting of 15 monolingual native speakers of Spanish. The control participants were either recently arrived immigrants in Sweden or exchange students at Swedish universities. Proficiency in Swedish among the controls ranged from non-existing to very basic (e.g. greeting phrases), according to their own estimations. As in the case of the bilingual participants, 70% of the monolingual participants came from Chile, whereas the rest came from other Latin American countries with no specific concentration (one participant was from Spain). All participants in both the bilingual and the monolingual groups had completed upper secondary school, and the majority also had college-level degrees.

Both groups were given an online event description task. A set of single event scenes was shown on a computer monitor and the participant was instructed by a native speaker of Spanish to describe what was happening in each scene as soon as they recognized the situation.[7] The set of video clips consisted of 41 scenes, divided into goal-oriented motion events ($n = 27$) and distractor items ($n = 14$). The distractor items depicted activities such as a person milking a cow, and their function was to divert the participants' focus away from goal-oriented motion. Because they were not relevant to the study's research questions, the distractors were excluded from analysis. Between each scene the screen turned purple for approximately six seconds and then a star was introduced indicating that a new scene would start. The participants' scene descriptions were transcribed and analyzed with respect to endpoint encoding. Descriptions containing a locative phrase with reference to the moving entity's arrival at or intention to arrive at a goal were classified as endpoint encodings. Examples of such phrases are *to go to a shop*, *to walk towards a castle*, *to land on a field* and *to enter ø a house*.

In addition to the event description task, the bilingual participants took an auditory grammaticality judgment test (GJT) in Spanish. This test was used as a measure of the bilinguals' language knowledge and included a total of 100 sentences. These sentences were presented through headphones and the participants were instructed to judge the grammaticality of each sentence by pushing a green button for 'correct' and a red button for 'incorrect'. Fifty out of the 100 sentences were grammatically incorrect (incorrect sentences contained one error only). The maximum score possible was 100 points. One point was given every time the participant's judgment corresponded to the grammaticality of the sentence. The software used to present the sentences and register responses was E-Prime (Schneider *et al.*, 2002a, 2002b). The linguistic structures included in the test were verb agreement, gender agreement, verbal clitics and preterite/imperfect (i.e. aspectual distinctions). Although the primary interest of the study was the bilinguals' sensitivity to distinctions involving grammatical aspect, the inclusion of other linguistic structures in the GJT served as a method to assess the possibility that endpoint encoding patterns could be related not only to grammatical aspect, but to other linguistic categories or language knowledge in general.

The results regarding the descriptions of goal-oriented motion events revealed that the bilinguals encoded endpoints to a significantly higher degree than did the Spanish-speaking controls. For example, a scene depicting two persons walking on a country road toward a house was described by the bilinguals as *dos personas están caminando hacia una casa* ('two people walking towards a house'), whereas the controls referred to this scene simply as *dos personas están caminando* ('two people are walking'). On average, the bilinguals included an endpoint in 30.9% (SD = 11.4) of their scene retellings. The controls, on the other hand, encoded endpoints when describing 22.9% (SD = 8.8) of the scenes. The difference between the groups' endpoint frequencies was statistically significant, t (53) = 2.44, $p < 0.02$. These results are laid out in Figure 4.1.

It turned out that the bilinguals' scene descriptions differed from those of the monolingual controls not only in terms of endpoint frequencies, but also with regard to the use of the simple present tense (as opposed to the progressive). On average, the bilinguals used the simple present in 36.1% (SD = 23.6) of the endpoint scenes, whereas the controls did so in 13.6% (SD = 7.1) of the scenes. This difference was statistically significant, t (53) = 3.62, $p = 0.0007$.

Having established that the bilinguals' endpoint encoding was significantly higher than that of the monolinguals, the next step in the analysis consisted of assessing the possible relationship between bilingual

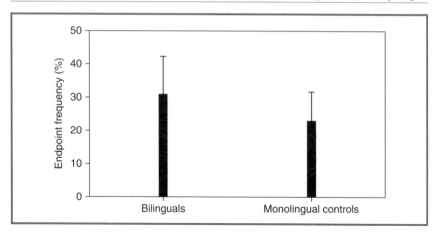

Figure 4.1 Endpoint encoding frequencies, bilinguals and monolinguals

endpoint encoding and proficiency with aspectual contrasts. However, informed by previous research, Bylund and Jarvis aimed at investigating the correlation between endpoint encoding and proficiency with aspectual contrasts in relation to other variables, such as AOB and LoR in the L2 environment, which have been shown to exert an effect on conceptual competence in bilinguals (e.g. Athanasopoulos & Kasai, 2008; Boroditsky, 2001; Boroditsky *et al.*, 2003; Bylund, 2009a). Originally, the relative impact of these variables on endpoint encoding was to be investigated by means of a multiple regression analysis, with AOB, LoR in the L2 environment, total score on the GJT, and the scores on each of the four GJT categories (i.e. aspectual contrasts; verbal agreement; gender agreement; verbal clitics) as independent variables, and endpoint encoding frequencies as the dependent variable. This procedure was, however, not recommendable as the independent variables turned out to be significantly inter-correlated (Field, 2009). Instead, endpoint frequencies were correlated with each of the independent variables, while the confounding effects of the other independent variables were factored out by means of partial correlations. Table 4.1 shows the result of these correlations.

As can be seen in Table 4.1, two of the independent variables were significantly correlated with endpoint encoding frequencies. The first of these was the score obtained on the GJT area concerning aspectual contrasts. The negative correlation found between these measures means that the less sensitive a participant was to errors involving an incompatibility between grammatical aspect (i.e. the use of preterite versus imperfect) and the aspectual meaning inferable from the context of the sentence, the greater his/her predilection was for mentioning endpoints. None of the remaining grammatical areas tested, nor the total score on the GJT, seemed to have an impact on the endpoint encoding.

Table 4.1 Pearson's *r* for partial correlations between EP and each variable, controlling for all the other variables

	Asp score	*VA score*	*GA score*	*Clitc score*	*SP freq*	*AO L2 acq*	*LoR in L2 env*	*GJT score*
EP freq	−0.44**	−0.01	−0.13	−0.05	0.04	−0.39*	−0.15	−0.15

*p < 0.05, **p < 0.01
Asp: aspectual contrasts; VA: verbal agreement; GA: gender agreement; Clitc: Clitical pronouns; SP: simple present; EP: endpoint

The second independent variable correlated with endpoint frequencies was AOB or the onset of L2 acquisition. The negative correlation found here suggests that the younger the participant was when he/she started acquiring L2 Swedish, the greater his/her predilection for encoding endpoints in the L1. As such, this finding is consistent with previous research on age effects on conceptual competence (e.g. Athanasopoulos & Kasai, 2008; Boroditsky, 2001; see Section 4.4 for further discussion of this topic). LoR in the L2 environment, on the other hand, did not seem to exert an effect on endpoint encoding patterns. The absence of LoR effects could, in this case, be attributed to the fact that all the bilinguals had been living in Sweden for at least 12 years: previous research on L2 effects on the L1 suggests that LoR is expected to exert a major influence on L1 development during the first 10 years of residence in the L2 environment (Ammerlaan, 1996; De Bot & Clyne, 1994; Gürel, 2004). The finding that the predilection for encoding endpoints was significantly correlated with the ability to detect aspectual errors thus corroborated the hypothesis set out by Bylund and Jarvis.

The correlation between endpoint encoding preferences and the capacity to detect aspectual errors was interpreted as a manifestation of the bilinguals' general sensitivity to features of ongoingness. More specifically, it was suggested that this correlation reflects a continuum of different degrees of sensitivity to ongoingness in which at the one end there are those participants who tended to overlook morphology referring to ongoingness, and de-emphasized ongoingness in their motion event descriptions by mentioning endpoints. At the other end of the continuum, there are those participants with a high degree of sensitivity toward ongoingness who, first, detected errors in the use of grammatical morphology used to express ongoingness, and second, construed goal-oriented motion events as ongoing, leaving out references to endpoints.

The findings reported in Bylund and Jarvis' (in press) study illustrate the methodological advantages of investigating language and conceptualization in bilingual speakers. In previous crosslinguistic studies of event conceptualization (e.g. Bylund, 2008; Carroll *et al.*, 2004), the influence of grammatical aspect on language specificity has been inferred on the basis of matching specific language constellations with specific conceptualization patterns. Therefore, the correlation between the participants' knowledge of aspectual contrasts and their endpoint encoding patterns reported by Bylund and Jarvis (in press) constitutes a new type of evidence of a direct link between event conceptualization and grammatical aspect. As such, this finding strongly supports the assumptions underlying the grammatical aspect approach to event conceptualization.

The finding also lends support to the view that bilingualism, instead of being overlooked (e.g. Berlin & Kay, 1969; Munnich *et al.*, 2001) or taken as evidence that *contradicts* the linguistic relativity principle (Macnamara, 1970), may constitute a fruitful avenue for research on the relationship between language and thought (see Green, 1998; Pavlenko, 2005). The method of correlating conceptualization patterns with sensitivity to aspectual contrasts affords certain advantages for the grammatical aspect approach. An important task for future studies within this line of inquiry will be to probe the interconnectedness between knowledge of grammatical aspect and other processes of event conceptualization, such as segmentation and temporal structuring. Apart from serving as a validation of the correlation method employed by Bylund and Jarvis (in press), these investigations would have the potential to further corroborate the claim that language-specific patterns of event segmentation and temporal structuring are also connected to the category of aspect.

4.4 The Stability of First Language Patterns of Event Conceptualization: Reverse Transfer

Apart from providing evidence of the interconnectedness between grammatical aspect and endpoint encoding preferences, Bylund and Jarvis (in press) also reported that the age by which the participants' bilingualism began exerted an effect on the degree of conformity with Spanish monolingual patterns of endpoint encoding. That is to say, the earlier they had become bilingual, the more their L1 endpoint encoding patterns seemed to be influenced by the L2. This finding bears on our understanding of the stability of the L1 patterns, and relates to the studies conducted so far on L2 learners. As mentioned in Section 4.2, a consistent result in these studies is that L1-based patterns dominate even at advanced stages of acquisition (e.g. Carroll & v. Stutterheim, 2003; v. Stutterheim, 2003; also Schmiedtová, this volume). However, the finding of Bylund and Jarvis suggested that transfer may also occur in the reverse direction, that is, L2 patterns may influence the L1.

Against this background, Bylund (2009a) set out to study in more detail the susceptibility of L1 conceptualization patterns to L2 influence. The specific aims of the study were to examine, first, the frequency with which endpoints were encoded in the L1, and second, whether these patterns varied as a function of AOB. Informed by previous research on age effects on L1 retention (e.g. Bylund, 2009b; Silva-Corvalán, 1994; Yeni-Komshian *et al.*, 2000), it was hypothesized that speakers with an AOB lower than 12 would exhibit a higher degree of L2 influence in their L1 event conceptualization than speakers whose AOB was higher than 12.

Thirty one L1 Spanish–L2 Swedish bilinguals with residence in Sweden participated in the study. The AOB of the participants ranged from 1 to 19 years of age (mean = 8.9) and their LoR was between 12 and 42 years (mean = 24.8). These participants were functional speakers of Spanish and about 70% of them were of Chilean origin. Their L2 proficiency had been controlled for by means of a screening experiment, in which they had been judged as nativelike by at least 6 of the 10 judges (for details, see Abrahamsson & Hyltenstam, 2009).[8] The bilinguals' event conceptualization patterns were compared with those of a monolingual Spanish-speaking control group (same as described in Section 4.3). This group was matched with the bilinguals with regard to chronological age and educational background.

A set of videoclips showing goal-oriented motion events was used to elicit L1 Spanish data on endpoint encoding. This set of clips, as well as the collection procedure, was the same as described above (Section 4.3). Likewise, the same principles were used to classify endpoint encodings.

Results showed that the bilinguals' patterns of endpoint encoding in goal-oriented events were intimately connected to AOB. The overall tendency was that bilinguals with early AOBs were more prone to encoding endpoints than those with late AOBs. As a consequence, there was a statistically significant negative correlation between endpoint encoding frequencies and AOB, $r = -0.49$, $p < 0.01$. The relationship between the bilinguals' patterns of endpoint encoding and their AOB is depicted in Figure 4.2.

As seen in Figure 4.2, AOB of 12 years turned out to be a divide for convergence with Spanish monolingual behavior in the sense that there was an elevated, non-convergent encoding of endpoints up until AOB of 12 (hereinafter the participants with AOB < 12 years will be referred to as 'early bilinguals', and those with AOB > 12 years as 'late bilinguals'). The mean number of events encoded by the early bilinguals was 9.4 (SD = 3.2), whereas for the late bilinguals and the Spanish-speaking controls it was 6.4 (SD = 1.9) and 6.2 (SD = 2.4), respectively.

A one-way analysis of variance (ANOVA) was run to determine whether the early bilinguals' endpoint frequencies differed from the late

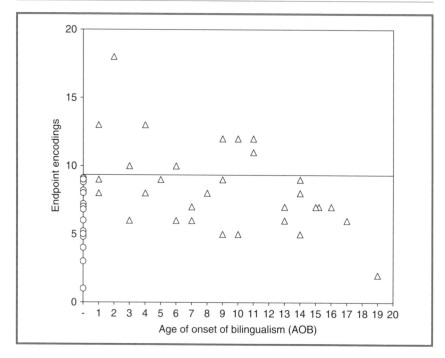

Figure 4.2 Endpoint encodings and age of onset bilingualism. ○ = monolingual controls; Δ = bilinguals; horizontal line = upper monolingual range

bilinguals and the Spanish monolinguals. The results indicated a general difference between groups, F (2, 43) = 7.395, $p < 0.01$. A *post-hoc* test (Tukey-HSD) showed that the participants with early AOB differed significantly from those with late AOB and the Spanish controls, $p < 0.01$ and $p < 0.01$, respectively. There was, however, no difference between the latter two groups, $p > 0.05$. The effects of LoR in the L2 environment were also assessed. Similar to the findings in Bylund and Jarvis' (in press) study, this variable did not exert an effect on endpoint encoding, $r = 0.13$, $p > 0.05$.

The elevated use of endpoints found among early bilinguals was interpreted as restructuring of L1 patterns under the influence of the L2. The possibility that these conceptualization patterns, instead of being evidence of L2 influence, would reflect a stagnation at or a regression to an earlier acquisitional stage was discounted given that endpoint frequencies are low at all stages of L1 Spanish acquisition (i.e. 3–9 years; Sebastián & Slobin, 1994). The interpretation pursued in Bylund (2009a) was consequently that AOB had an impact on the degree of susceptibility to L1 restructuring. However, given that the deviant patterns were L2-induced, the role of L2 proficiency in this age trend required further explanation: an alternative interpretation could be that AOB does not have an effect on age-related differences in restructuring susceptibility; rather, it could simply be a result of the bilinguals with early AOBs having acquired the L2 patterns – and consequently having transferred them to the L1 – whereas the bilinguals with late AOBs have not acquired these L2 patterns, let alone transferred them to the L1.

There are two reasons why such an interpretation of the findings is problematic. First, claiming that the subjects' L2 proficiency alone had produced the attested non-convergences would not be adequate, since L2 knowledge per se can hardly be claimed to bring about transfer automatically. The idea that there is an inverted relationship between L1 and L2 proficiency is not a given in the field (e.g. Bylund *et al.*, in press; Hyltenstam *et al.*, 2009) and research on interacting L1 and L2 proficiency levels has so far mainly concerned pronunciation (for an overview, see Flege, 1999).

A second reason for not attributing a great deal of importance to the role of L2 proficiency when interpreting the age trend was the fact that the participants in the study had been carefully selected on the basis of their near-native proficiency in Swedish. This means that the variable of L2 proficiency was held as high and as constant as possible across the AOB span. Given this characteristic of the participants, L2 proficiency alone was unlikely to be responsible for the varying levels of conformity to Spanish monolingual patterns of endpoint encoding. Instead, it was suggested that in order to account for the age trend, it was necessary to invoke a factor that affected early and late AOBs differently and still allowed for proficiency variability in the first group.

Informed by research findings on immigrant children (Hakuta & D'Andrea, 1992; Yeni-Komshian *et al.*, 2000) and international adoptees (e.g. Isurin, 2000), indicating that L1 retention in early AOBs is highly dependent on a high frequency of use, it was suggested that the bilinguals' degree of *L1 contact* may be just such a factor. Following this line of reasoning, the varying degrees of conformity found in the early AOB group were suggested to be the result of an interaction between individual variation in L1 contact and heightened restructuring susceptibility. Varying levels of L1 contact may very well be found in late AOBs, but since L1 maintenance in this group is allegedly less dependent on these factors (Bylund, 2009b; Schmid, 2007), individual variation should play a minor role in the restructuring outcome. Although this interpretation is consistent with the Critical Period Hypothesis, future investigations would ideally examine data on diachronic and synchronic patterns of language use and L2 proficiency data in order to provide a complete picture of the hypothesized age effects.

To summarize, the results reported in Bylund's (2009a) study seem to suggest that there is a point around puberty when there is a change in the

susceptibility to L1 restructuring. Past this point, L1 event conceptualization patterns seem to become stabilized and are less restructurable.[9]
Apart from confirming von Stutterheim's (2003) suggestion about the
stability of L1 patterns in late bilinguals, this finding also connects to
the general issue of age effects on conceptual competence. So far, the
discussions of this issue have revolved around age of acquisition
influence on the degree to which L2 conceptual patterns are acquired
(e.g. Athanasopoulos & Kasai, 2008; Boroditsky, 2001; but see Chen,
2007). Similarly, researchers have also discussed how age of L2 acquisition may influence the *L1* patterns in the sense that it constrains the
amount of L2 knowledge that can be acquired and, consequently,
transferred to the L1. An example of this is found in Munnich *et al.*'s
(2001) study on crosslinguistic differences in spatial language and spatial
memory. Here, the authors argue that the fact that the participants
were exposed to English only after the age of 12 guaranteed non-native
proficiency in this language, which in turn would prevent L2 influence
on L1 performance.[10] However, in light of the findings reported in
Bylund (2009a), I would suggest that instead of discussing age effects on
L1 conceptual competence exclusively from an L2 point of view, it may
be preferable to consider age effects from the perspective of bilingualism.
That is to say, if it is the case that the L1 system's susceptibility to
restructuring changes over time, as shown in Bylund's (2009a) study,
then this characteristic should be incorporated into the notion of age
effects. Accordingly, age effects on L1 restructuring can be seen as two-
fold: on the one hand, AOB may affect the size of the pool of L2 material
that may be transferred to the L1 (in the sense that AOB presumably
correlates with L2 attainment), and on the other, it modulates the L1
system's degree of susceptibility to L2 influence.

Two observations should, however, be made in relation to this
discussion on age-related restructuring susceptibility; first, age should
be conceived of as a factor that modulates the L1's *degree* of susceptibility
to restructuring. In other words, categorical assumptions about the L1
system being impermeable to L2 influence past a certain age are best
avoided. Second, age effects may be selective with regard to conceptual
domain and modality. That is to say, some conceptual domains may
become more resistant over time to restructuring than others. Consider,
for example, that while Bylund (2009a) documented no L2 influence on
L1 endpoint encoding for motion events in *late fluent bilinguals*, Brown
and Gullberg (2008) found L2 effects on L1 gesturing about manner of
motion in a group of Japanese *adult intermediate learners* of English.
Hence, in discussing age effects, caution should be advised with respect
to strong generalizations from one conceptual domain or modality to
another.

4.5 Language-specific Patterns in Bilingual Event Conceptualization

Having discussed the relationship between knowledge of aspectual distinctions and endpoint encoding in bilinguals, and the effects of age on L1 restructuring susceptibility, the last part of this chapter will focus on how event construal patterns are organized in the bilingual mind. A common denominator of the studies reviewed so far is that they have been concerned with examining event conceptualization in only one of the two languages of a bilingual. While these findings offer valuable insights into L1- and L2-based conceptual transfer and the factors at stake in these processes, they provide little information about how L1 and L2 systems may interact in bilinguals. Undoubtedly, inasmuch as we are interested in understanding the degrees of language specificity and interconnectedness of two conceptual systems in one mind, it is necessary to investigate event conceptualization in both of the bilingual's languages.

In view of this reasoning, Bylund (in press) set out to explore patterns of event conceptualization in the L1 and L2 of Spanish-Swedish bilinguals. In particular, the study examined segmentation and temporal structuring. As seen in Section 4.3, Spanish and Swedish patterns differ in this respect: whereas speakers of Swedish seem to prefer a coarse level of event granularity and an explicit marking of the temporal sequence of events, speakers of Spanish exhibit more fine-grained event segmentation patterns and leave the order of occurrence to be inferred. The questions asked in this study concerned the extent to which the bilinguals' patterns of event segmentation and temporal structuring were similar to monolingual patterns, and whether the bilinguals operated with differentiated or amalgamated strategies when construing events.

The participant group consisted of 25 L1 Spanish–L2 Swedish early bilinguals residing in Sweden.[11] These participants were born in Latin American countries (the majority were Chileans, whereas the rest came from Peru, Colombia and Mexico) and had been living in Sweden for 24.6 years on average (range = 12–34). AOB (which in most cases coincided with the participant's relocation to Sweden) ranged from 1 to 11 years (mean = 5.7), and mean age at the time of testing was 30.2 (range = 20–41). Two control groups consisting of monolingual native speakers of Spanish ($n = 15$) and Swedish ($n = 15$) also participated in the study. These groups had been matched with the bilingual speakers with regard to educational level and chronological age (the Spanish-speaking controls were also matched with regard to country of origin). Participants in the control groups were born and raised in a monolingual Spanish- or Swedish-speaking setting. Strict monolingualism was, however, not a requirement, and basic skills in foreign languages (as reported by the participants themselves) were accepted. None of the controls had, however, spent a considerable amount of time in a foreign country where such foreign language skills could be practiced.

The bilingual speakers participated twice in the study, producing narratives elicited by the same stimulus both in the L1 and the L2. They were tested by a native speaker of (Chilean) Spanish in the Spanish test sessions and by a native speaker of Swedish in the Swedish test sessions. On average, 1.8 years elapsed between the bilingual participants' L1 and L2 sessions. The monolingual controls participated once in the study, producing narratives in their L1.

The data were elicited by means of a film retelling task that required the participants to produce an online oral description of an excerpt of Charlie Chaplin's silent film *Modern Times*. The excerpt used for analysis was the sequence where a feeding machine is feeding Chaplin. This excerpt is 4 minutes and 15 seconds long and contains a non-stop, complex flow of events. The participants' retellings were transcribed and analyzed with regard to segmentation and temporal perspectivation. For segmentation, the number of propositional units referring to events was tabulated for each participant and used as an index of the degree of event granularity in that person's task performance. Units referring to states and events that were presented as components of other events were not taken into consideration (this was the same procedure as described in Section 4.2). Temporal structuring, in turn, was examined in relation to which events were linked to each other by means of anaphoric, sequential temporal adverbials. Examples of anaphoric temporal adverbials in Swedish are *sedan* (or '*sen*') and *så* (see, e.g. Noyeau *et al.*, 2005; Viberg, 2001), all of which may be translated into English with the word *then*. Examples of Spanish anaphoric adverbials are *luego* and *después*, which, as in the case of the Swedish anaphorics, can be translated into English as *then*.[12]

Regarding the relationship between bilinguals' event segmentation in L1 Spanish and the event segmentation patterns found in the Spanish and Swedish L1 control groups, the results showed that there was a significant difference between the three groups, $F(2, 54) = 12.822$, $p < 0.001$ (one-way ANOVA). The average number of events encoded was 61.7 (SD = 8.9) for the monolingual Spanish speakers, 49.1 (SD = 14.5) for the bilingual Spanish speakers and 39.1 (SD = 10.7) for the monolingual Swedish speakers. The results are laid out in Figure 4.3.

Post-hoc procedures (Tukey-HSD) showed that the differences in numbers of events encoded by these groups were statistically significant (Spanish monolinguals versus Swedish monolinguals, $p < 0.001$; bilinguals versus monolingual Spanish, $p < 0.01$; bilinguals versus Swedish monolinguals, $p < 0.05$). Although the bilinguals as a group differed from

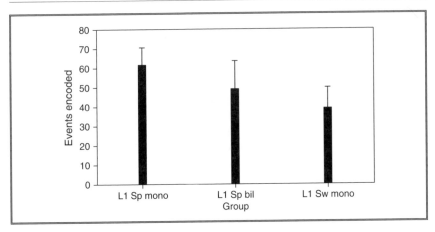

Figure 4.3 Number of events encoded

the Spanish-speaking controls, there was a fair amount of individual variation in their segmentation patterns. This suggested that some of the bilinguals were closer to the Spanish segmentation frequencies than others. In order to see whether the independent variables AOB, LoR in the L2 environment and daily L1 use, exerted an effect on this behavior, Pearson correlations were carried out. The results showed no statistically significant correlations between any of these variables and the number of segmented events (AOB, $r = 0.11$, $p = 0.60$; LoR, $r = -0.06$, $p = 78$; L1 use, $r = -0.10$, $p = 63$).

As for temporal structuring in Spanish, the bilinguals were found to use anaphoric connectors to link on average 4.3% (SD = 4.3) of the events encoded, and the Spanish-speaking controls did so for 2.1% (SD = 2.9). The Swedish speakers, on the other hand, used anaphoric connectors in 26.0% (SD = 12.2) of the cases. A Kruskal–Wallis test indicated significant differences between the groups, KW = 32.564, $p < 0.0001$. A *post-hoc* test (Dunn) indicated no significant difference between the Spanish monolinguals and the bilinguals ($p > 0.05$). There were, however, significant differences between the Spanish-speaking groups and the Swedish monolinguals: both the Spanish-speaking monolinguals and bilinguals differed significantly from the Swedish monolinguals, $p < 0.001$ and $p < 0.001$, respectively. The results of the groups' use of anaphoric connectors are presented in Figure 4.4.

The results relating to the bilinguals' event segmentation in L2 Swedish showed a similar pattern to that found in their L1 segmentation. The mean number of events encoded by the bilinguals was 52.4 (SD = 13.5), whereas it was 61.7 (SD = 8.9) for the Spanish-speaking monolinguals and 39.1 (SD = 10.7) for Swedish-speaking monolinguals. An ANOVA showed significant differences among groups, $F_{(2, 54)} = 14.150$,

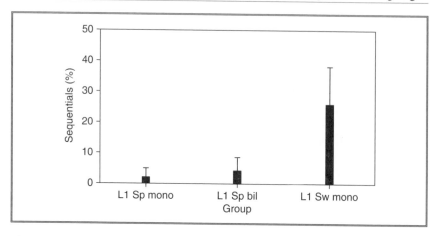

Figure 4.4 Percentage of events linked by means of anaphoric (sequential) connectors

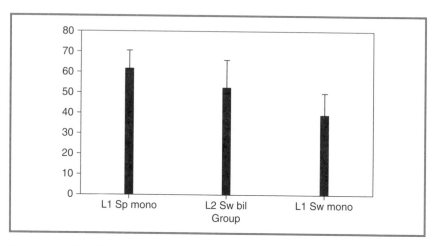

Figure 4.5 Number of events encoded

$p < 0.001$. *Post-hoc* procedures (Tukey-HSD) indicated significant differences between all groups (bilinguals versus Swedish-speaking monolinguals, $p < 01$; bilinguals versus Spanish-speaking monolinguals, $p < 0.01$; Swedish-speaking monolinguals versus Spanish-speaking monolinguals, $p < 0.001$). These results are presented in Figure 4.5.

As in the case of the segmentation patterns in Spanish, there was a certain amount of variation in the bilinguals' segmentation patterns in Swedish. Thus, even though the bilinguals as a group differed from the Swedish controls, some of them were closer to the monolingual segmentation frequencies than others. Separate Pearson correlations were run to examine whether the independent variables AOB, LoR in the L2 environment and daily L1 use were connected to this behavior. Again, no significant correlations were found between any of these variables and the number of encoded events: AOB, $r = 0.11$, $p = 0.60$; LoR, $r = -0.06$, $p = 78$; L1 use, $r = -0.10$, $p = 63$.

With regard to temporal structuring in Swedish, it was found that the bilinguals used the anaphoric connectors *sen* and *så* to connect 18.5% (SD = 14.2) of the encoded events. The Swedish-speaking monolinguals and Spanish-speaking monolinguals did so for 26% (SD = 12.2) and 2.1% (SD = 2.9), respectively. A Kruskal–Wallis test indicated significant differences between groups, KW = 25.669, $p < 0.0001$. A *post-hoc* test (Dunn) showed no differences between the Swedish-speaking mono-linguals and the bilinguals, $p > 0.05$. However, these two groups differed significantly from the Spanish-speaking monolinguals, $p < 0.001$ and $p < 0.001$, respectively. These results are laid out in Figure 4.6.

Turning to the within-group comparisons of the bilinguals' L1 and L2 patterns, a paired-samples *t*-test showed no significant difference between the number of events encoded in the L1 (mean = 49.1) and L2 (mean = 52.4), t (24) = 1.24, $p > 0.05$. There was, on the other hand, a highly significant difference between the frequency of use of sequential markers in the L1 (mean = 2.1%) and L2 (mean = 18.5%), W = 256.00, $p < 0.0001$ (Wilcoxon). These findings show that the bilinguals resorted to different strategies when linking events temporally in each of their languages.

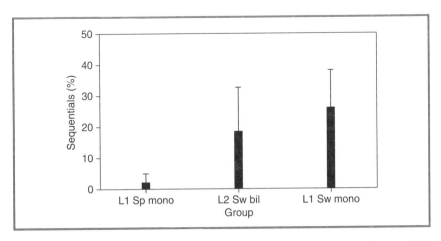

Figure 4.6 Percentage of events linked by means of anaphoric (sequential) connectors

To summarize, the findings reported in Bylund's (in press) study suggest that, first, when segmenting events the bilinguals differed from monolingual speakers in each of their languages: they had a lower degree of granularity in their L1 Spanish than did the Spanish-speaking monolinguals, whereas they exhibited a higher degree of granularity in their L2 Swedish than did the Swedish monolinguals. The degree of event granularity was the same in both the L1 and the L2. This behavior may be labeled *convergence*, which implies a merged conceptualization pattern distinct from both the L1- and L2-based patterns (Pavlenko, 2005; for a recent study, see Ameel *et al.*, 2009). Second, the bilinguals behaved in a nativelike way in both their languages with respect to temporal structuring, exhibiting a deictic frame in their L1 and anaphoric linkage in their L2. Accordingly, the bilinguals can be assumed to have differentiated the L1- and L2-specific ways of linking events temporally. The differentiation of two sets of language-specific conceptual patterns can be classified as *conceptual co-existence* (for further discussion on the notions of convergence and co-existence, see Jarvis & Pavlenko, 2008; Pavlenko, 1999, 2005, 2009).

As was seen in the analysis, none of the factors – be it AOB, LoR in the L2 environment or daily L1 use – could predict the bilinguals' patterns of event segmentation that deviate from those of the monolinguals. At first sight, this may seem surprising. There are, however, certain characteristics of the bilingual participant group that may explain this result. First, the participants had acquired both languages before puberty (AOB < 12 years). Since research findings to date suggest that age effects on language proficiency in general are more salient between early and late bilinguals rather than within either of these groups (Abrahamson & Hyltenstam, 2008; Bylund, 2009b; DeKeyser, 2000; Montrul, 2008; Yeni-Komshian *et al.*, 2000), the absence of AOB effects in Bylund's (in press) study is not completely unexpected. Second, LoR in the L2 environment of the participants ranged between 11 and 31 years. As mentioned above, several studies on L1 maintenance and L2 acquisition suggest that LoR no longer plays a significant role past the first 10 years of LoR (e.g. Ammerlaan, 1996; Bylund, 2009b; De Bot & Clyne, 1994; DeKeyser, 2000; Gürel, 2004; Oyama, 1976). Hence, the lack of LoR effects among the participants in Bylund's (in press) study seems to be consistent with previous studies.

However, there is no obvious reason why an effect was not found for the amount of contact the bilinguals have with the L1 on the patterns of event segmentation they produce in both languages (cf. Hakuta & D'Andrea, 1992; Yeni-Komshian *et al.*, 2000; De Leeuw *et al.*, 2010). Possibly, this result may be explained by taking into account the research method rather than the participant characteristics. Bylund (in press) relied on self estimates of global L1 use (expressed as a percentage) as an index of L1 use. Even though self estimates are employed in other studies (e.g. Flege, 1999), it cannot be ruled out that these may not be sensitive enough to capture possible effects of L1 contact on event segmentation. Hence, in order to elucidate the possible impact of language use on L1 and L2 event segmentation patterns, future studies may find it useful to work with more varied measures of this factor (e.g. taking into account the type of domains in which the L1 and L2 are spoken, see De Leeuw *et al.*, 2010).

Why, then, did the bilinguals differentiate the languages when linking events temporally but not when segmenting them? Although Bylund (in press) by and large left this question open to further research, some useful observations can be made regarding the properties of the segmentation and temporal structuring processes. These processes pertain to two different levels of conceptualization: as mentioned in Section 4.2.1, event segmentation relates to the process by which the speaker decides 'what to say', so-called *macroplanning* (Levelt, 1999). Temporal structuring, in contrast, is related to the process by which the speaker decides 'how to say it' (i.e. *microplanning*). Along this line of reasoning, the finding of convergence at the level of macroplanning, and co-existence at the level of microplanning, is consistent with De Bot's (1992) adaptation of Levelt's (1989) model of bilingual speech produc-tion, according to which in bilinguals the processes of microplanning are language-specific, whereas the processes of macroplanning are not. Although De Bot (1992: 8) does not discuss this suggestion in detail, he contends that it is 'a more economic solution' having language specificity only at the level of microplanning.

Following De Bot's suggestion, Bylund (in press) noted that since event segmentation is essentially about dividing a continuous flow of experience into verbalizable units (Chafe, 1994; Croft, 2007), it may entail a higher cognitive load than framing that content discursively (i.e. in this case, structuring the events along a timeline). From this processing point of view, it could be more economical for the bilingual speaker to resort to a single strategy when parsing experience. However, given the scarcity of empirical research on the processes underlying the speech production of monolingual speakers (see Croft, 2007; Levelt, 1999) – let alone bilingual speakers – an explanation of Bylund's findings based on the assumption that macroplanning requires more processing capacity than microplan-ning should be seen as tentative. Consequently, further research is needed to address the question of language specificity and processing load in bilingual conceptualization.

4.6 Conclusions

The principal aim of this chapter has been to review some recent studies on event conceptualization in bilinguals and illustrate their bearing on our understanding of language specificity in event conceptualization. Using as a point of departure the grammatical aspect approach to event conceptualization, the chapter has focused on, first, how correlations between bilinguals' predilection for encoding endpoints and their sensitivity to aspectual contrasts may strengthen the hypothesis that patterns for event conceptualization are intimately connected to the category of grammatical aspect; second, how the susceptibility to L1 restructuring may vary as a function of age; and third, how language specificity in bilingual event conceptualization may vary as a function of conceptual level. Because the studies reviewed in this chapter were all exploratory in nature, the answers they provide may be surpassed by the new questions they raise. In light of these questions, future investigations may find it useful to work with correlational tests in order (a) to ferret out the relationship between different processes of event conceptualization and the category of aspect; (b) to explore more sensitive measures of L1 contact in order to elucidate its interaction with age-related susceptibility to L1 restructuring; and (c) to develop sophisticated theoretical accounts of processing economy that would explain the mechanisms underlying differentiation and amalgamation of conceptual patterns.

One final point in closing concerns the epistemological status of the reviewed findings. To date, the studies carried out within the grammatical aspect approach have dealt with the effects of language on conceptualization in verbal tasks. Thus, these studies can be framed within the thinking-for-speaking paradigm, and the evidence provided by them shows that grammatical aspect may direct a person's selective attention, when speaking, to certain event features. Whereas this finding offers an important piece of information about the influence of grammatical aspect on the thought processes involved in the verbalization of experience, it says little about the effects of aspect on higher-order cognitive processes, such as reasoning, similarity judgments or remembering. The fact that the grammatical aspect approach thus far has employed verbal tasks puts limits on our knowledge about the *degree* to which grammatical aspect influences event cognition. Previous research has shown that certain crosslinguistic differences of event conceptualization (such as encoding of manner and path of motion) are found only in verbal tasks (i.e. scene descriptions), but to a lesser extent – or not at all – in non-verbal tasks (e.g. categorization or memorization, Bohnemeyer *et al.*, 2006; Gennari *et al.*, 2002; Papafragou *et al.*, 2002). Following Lucy's (1992b, 1996) contention that research into language and thought should ideally combine verbal and non-verbal tasks, one may anticipate that the next step to be taken within the grammatical aspect approach will consist of extending the research methodology to experiments based on non-verbal tasks. Such a development would have the potential of providing a more complete picture of the degree of impact of grammatical aspect on event cognition.

Acknowledgments

The work discussed in this chapter was supported by the Swedish National Graduate School in Romance Languages (FoRom) and the Swedish Research Council (grant no. 421-2004-1975 'First Language Attrition in Advanced Second Language Speakers' awarded to N. Abrahamsson, K. Hyltenstam, E. Bylund and K. Stölten). The author wishes to express his gratitude to Panos Athanasopoulos, Johan Falk, Scott Jarvis, Aneta Pavlenko and two anonymous reviewers for insightful comments on an earlier draft of this chapter. Needless to say, none of these persons is responsible for any remaining error of fact or interpretation.

Notes

1. The process of linearization was not addressed in these studies, nor were other aspects of the structuring process such as assignment of thematic roles (see Carroll & Lambert, 2003).
2. Czech seems to constitute an exception to this pattern. Schmiedtová (2009, this volume) explains this divergence by suggesting that the Czech aspectual system has been reanalyzed through extensive and prolonged contact with German. The case of Czech will not be further treated in this chapter; instead the reader is referred to Schmiedtová (2010, this volume) and Schmiedtová and Sahonenko (2008) for further discussion.
3. In Dutch, however, a grammaticalization of the periphrastic progressive construction *aan het* seems to be taking place (Flecken, submitted).
4. In fact, in most models of language production the processes at the conceptual level are assumed to be language-independent (e.g. Francis, 2004; Jackendoff, 1994). However, these assumptions rarely emerge in the context of empirical crosslinguistic analyses.
5. There was, however, a certain difference between the two learner groups in the sense that the German learners seemed to be less far away from the English patterns of endpoint encoding than vice versa. For further discussion of this finding, see v. Stutterheim (2003).
6. Whereas the compound perfect tense has been shown to vary across Spanish varieties (e.g. Berschin, 1976), the key features relevant to the present study (i.e. aspectual oppositions in simple forms) are not reported to vary significantly across varieties of Spanish.
7. These video clips were provided by B. Schmiedtová and C. v. Stutterheim and are discussed in v. Stutterheim (2003) and Carroll *et al.* (2004). The scenes were either taken from television/films or shot by the research staff themselves. For further discussion, see Schmiedtová (this volume).
8. This participant group was a subset of those bilinguals studied by Bylund and Jarvis (in press). However, in Bylund (2009a), it was important to keep L2 proficiency as high as possible, in order to be able to rule out the possibility that variation in L2 proficiency alone could be responsible for the L2-induced deviations (see the discussion ahead). Therefore, originally, the aim was to only include participants who had been judged as native

speakers by *all* listener judges. Unfortunately, this criterion turned out to seriously reduce the number of participants, thus the decision was taken to include those participants that had passed as native speakers by the *majority* of the listener judges.

9. Although the evidence accumulated thus far within the field of L1 attrition seems to suggest that there is indeed a sensitivity decline at around puberty (Hakuta & D'Andrea, 1992; Montrul, 2008; Silva-Corvalán, 1994; Yeni-Komshian *et al.*, 2000; for an overview, see Bylund, 2009b), further research is still necessary to determine with greater certainty the geometric and temporal properties of this decline.

10. It may, however, as Athanasopoulos (this volume) points out, be less relevant whether the participants of Munnich *et al.* (2001) were completely nativelike in English; rather, the critical point is whether they had attained sufficient L2 knowledge that could be transferred to the L1. See also Pavlenko and Malt (in press) for counterevidence to Munnich *et al.*'s (2001) assumption about L1 conceptual competence being resistant to L2 influence post-pubertally.

11. The specific aim of Bylund (in press) was to investigate presumably stabilized event conceptualization patterns in early adult bilinguals who had acquired both languages before puberty. The reason for this is that previous research has focused either on child bilinguals who are still in the process of acquiring conceptual patterns (e.g. Verhoeven & Strömqvist, 2001) or on L2 learners who learned the L2 in adulthood (for an overview, see Schmiedtová, this volume). Following Lenneberg (1967), Flege (1999) and Abrahamsson and Hyltenstam (2008), age 12 was taken as an index of puberty onset. The participants in Bylund (2009a) were a subset of those studied in Bylund and Jarvis (in press).

12. Bylund (in press) also investigated the use of the Spanish *entonces* ('then') and the Swedish *då* ('then'), which are anaphoric connectors denoting simultaneity. The results concerning these connectors indicated no significant differences between any of the groups, and will not be reviewed in this chapter due to limitations of space.

References

Abrahamsson, N. and Hyltenstam, K. (2008) The robustness of aptitude effects in near-native second language acquisition. *Studies in Second Language Acquisition* 30, 481–509.

Abrahamsson, N. and Hyltenstam, K. (2009) Age of acquisition and nativelikeness in a second language: Listener perception vs. linguistic scrutiny. *Language Learning* 59, 249–306.

Allen, S., Özyürek, A., Kita, S., Brown, A., Furman, R., Ishizuka, T. and Fujii, M. (2007) Language-specific and universal influences in children's syntactic packaging of manner and path: A comparison of English, Japanese, and Turkish. *Cognition* 102, 16–48.

Ameel, E., Malt, B., Storms, G. and van Assche, F. (2009) Semantic convergence in the bilingual lexicon. *Journal of Memory and Language* 60, 270–290.

Ammerlaan, T. (1996) 'You get a bit wobbly...' – Exploring bilingual lexical retrieval processes in the context of first language attrition. Doctoral dissertation, Katholieke Universiteit, Nijmegen.

Athanasopoulos, P. (2007) Interaction between grammatical categories and cognition in bilinguals: The role of proficiency, cultural immersion, and language of instruction. *Language and Cognitive Processes* 22, 689–699.

Athanasopoulos, P. (2009) Cognitive representation of color in bilinguals: The case of Greek blues. *Bilingualism: Language and Cognition* 12, 83–95.

Athanasopoulos, P. and Kasai, C. (2008) Language and thought in bilinguals: The case of grammatical number and nonverbal classification preferences. *Applied Psycholinguistics* 29, 105–123.

Berlin, B. and Kay, P. (1969) *Basic Color Terms: Their Universality and Evolution.* Berkeley, CA: University of California Press.

Berman, R. and Slobin, D. (1994) *Relating Events in Narrative: A Crosslinguistic Developmental Study.* Hillsdale, NJ: Lawrence Erlbaum.

Berschin, H. (1976) *Präteritum- und Perfektgebrauch im heutigen Spanisch* [*The Use of Preterite and Imperfect in Modern Spanish*]. Tübingen: Max Niemeyer.

Bohnemeyer, J. (2007) Morpholexical transparency and the argument structure of verbs of cutting and breaking. *Cognitive Linguistics* 18 (2), 153–177.

Bohnemeyer, J., Eisenbeiss, S. and Narasimhan, B. (2006) Ways to go: Methodological considerations in Whorfian studies on motion events. *Essex Research Reports in Linguistics* 50.

Boroditsky, L. (2001) Does language shape thought? Mandarin and English speakers' conceptions of time. *Cognitive Psychology* 43, 1–22.

Boroditsky, L., Schmidt, L. and Phillips, W. (2003) Sex, syntax, and semantics. In D. Gentner and S. Goldin-Meadow (eds) *Language in Mind. Advances in the Study of Language and Thought* (pp. 61–79). Cambridge, MA: MIT Press.

Brown, A. and Gullberg, M. (2008) Bidirectional crosslinguistic influence in L1-L2 encoding of manner in speech and gesture: A study of Japanese speakers of English. *Studies in Second Language Acquisition* 30, 225–251.

Bylund, E. (2008) Procesos de conceptualización de eventos en español y en sueco: Diferencias translingüísticas [Event conceptualization processes in Spanish and Swedish: Crosslinguistic differences]. *Revue Romane* 43, 1–24.

Bylund, E. (2009a) Effects of age of L2 acquisition on L1 event conceptualization patterns. *Bilingualism: Language and Cognition* 12, 305–322.

Bylund, E. (2009b) Maturational constraints and first language attrition. *Language Learning*, 59 (3), 687–715.

Bylund, E. (in press) Segmentation and temporal structuring of events in early Spanish-Swedish bilinguals. *International Journal of Bilingualism.*

Bylund, E., Abrahamsson, N. and Hyltenstam, K. (in press) The role of language aptitude in first language attrition: The case of prepubescent attriters. *Applied Linguistics.*

Bylund, E. and Jarvis, S. (in press) L2 effects on L1 event conceptualization. *Bilingualism: Language and Cognition.*

Carroll, M. and Lambert, M. (2003) Information structure in narratives and the role of grammaticized knowledge. A study of adult French and German learners of English. In Ch. Dimroth and M. Starren (eds) *Information Structure and the Dynamics of Language Acquisition* (pp. 267–287). Amsterdam: John Benjamins.

Carroll, M. and v. Stutterheim, C. (1993) The representation of spatial configurations in English and German and the grammatical structure of locative and anaphoric expressions. *Linguistics* 31, 1011–1044.

Carroll, M. and v. Stutterheim, C. (2003) Typology and information organization: Perspective taking and language-specific effects in the construal of events. In A. Ramat (ed.) *Typology and Second Language Acquisition* (pp. 365–402). Berlin: De Gruyter.

Carroll, M., v. Stutterheim, Ch. and Nüse, R. (2004) The language and thought debate: A psycholinguistic approach. In C. Habel and T. Pechmann (eds) *Multidisciplinary Approaches to Language Production* (pp. 183–218). Berlin: De Gruyter.

Casati, R. (2008) Event concepts. In T. Shipley and J. Zacks (eds) *Understanding Events* (pp. 31–55). Oxford. Oxford University Press.

Chafe, W. (1994) *Discourse, Consciousness and Time. The Flow and Displacement of Conscious Experience in Speaking and Writing*. Chicago, IL: University Chicago Press.

Chen, J-Y. (2007) Do Chinese and English speakers think about time differently? Failure of replicating Boroditsky (2001). *Cognition* 104 (2), 427–436.

Choi, S. and Bowerman, M. (1991) Learning to express motion events in English and Korean: The influence of language-specific lexicalization patterns. *Cognition* 41, 83–121.

Croft, W. (2007) The origins of grammar in the verbalization of experience. *Cognitive Linguistics* 18, 339–382.

Davidson, D. (1980) *Essays on Actions and Events*. New York: Oxford University Press.

De Bot, K. (1992) A bilingual production model: Levelt's speaking model adapted. *Applied Linguistics* 13, 1–24.

De Bot, K. and Clyne, M. (1994) A 16-year longitudinal study of language attrition in Dutch immigrants in Australia. *Journal of Multilingual and Multicultural Development* 15, 17–28.

DeKeyser, R. (2000) The robustness of critical period effects in second language acquisition. *Studies in Second Language Acquisition* 22, 499–533.

De Leeuw, E., Schmid, M. and Mennen, I. (2010) The effects of contact on native language pronunciation in an L2 migrant setting. *Bilingualism: Language and Cognition* 13 (1), 33–40.

Field, A. (2009) *Discovering Statistics Using SPSS*. London: Sage.

Flecken, M. (submitted) The Dutch language in progression: Native speaker judgements as an insight into grammaticalization.

Flege, J. (1999) Age of learning and second language speech. In D. Birdsong (ed.) *Second Language Acquisition and the Critical Period Hypothesis* (pp. 101–132). Mahwah, NJ: Erlbaum.

Francis, N. (2004) The components of bilingual proficiency. *International Journal of Bilingualism* 8, 167–189.

Gennari, S., Sloman, S., Malt, B. and Fitch, W.T. (2002) Motion events in language and cognition. *Cognition* 83, 49–79.

Goddard, C. and Wierzbicka, A. (2009) Contrastive semantics of physical activity verbs: 'Cutting' and 'chopping' in English, Polish, and Japanese. *Language Sciences* 31, 60–96.

Green, D. (1998) Bilingualism and thought. *Psychologica Belgica* 38, 253–278.

Gürel, A. (2004) Selectivity in L2-induced L1 attrition: A psycholinguistic account. *Journal of Neurolinguistics* 17, 53–78.

Habel, C. and Tappe, H. (1999) Processes of segmentation and linearization in describing events. In R. Klabunde and Ch. v. Stutterheim (eds) *Processes in Language Production* (pp. 117–153). Wiesbaden: Deutscher Universitätsverlag.

Hakuta, K. and D'Andrea, D. (1992) Some properties of bilingual maintenance and loss in Mexican background high-school students. *Applied Linguistics* 13, 72–99.

Hyltenstam, K., Bylund, E., Abrahamsson, N. and Park, H-S. (2009) Dominant language replacement: The case of international adoptees. *Bilingualism: Language and Cognition* 12, 121–140.

Isurin, L. (2000) Deserted islands or a child's first language forgetting. *Bilingualism: Language and Cognition* 3, 151–166.

Jackendoff, R. (1994) *Patterns in the Mind: Language and Human Nature.* New York: Basic Books.

Jakobson, R. (1959) Boas' view of grammatical meaning. In W. Goldschmidt (ed.) *The Anthropology of Franz Boas: Essays on the Centennial of his Birth* (pp. 139–145). San Francisco, CA: Chandler.

Jarvis, S. and Pavlenko, A. (2008) *Crosslinguistic Influence in Language and Cognition.* New York: Routledge.

Klein, W. (1994) *Time in Language.* London: Routledge.

Langacker, R. (2000) *Grammar and Conceptualization.* Berlin: De Gruyter.

Lenneberg, E. (1967) *Biological Foundations of Language.* New York: Wiley & Sons.

Levelt, W. (1982) Linearization in describing spatial networks. In S. Peters and E. Saarinen (eds) *Processes, Beliefs and Outcomes* (pp. 199–220). Dordrecht: Reidel.

Levelt, W. (1989) *Speaking: From Intention to Articulation.* Cambridge, MA: MIT Press.

Levelt, W. (1996) Perspective-taking and ellipsis in spatial descriptions. In P. Bloom, M. Peterson, L. Nadel and M. Garrett (eds) *Language and Space* (pp. 77–107). Cambridge, MA: MIT Press.

Levelt, W. (1999) Producing spoken language: A blueprint of the speaker. In C. Brown and P. Hagoort (eds) *The Neurocognition of Language* (pp. 83–120). Oxford: Oxford University Press.

Levinson, S. (2007) Cut and break verbs in Yélî Dnye, the Papuan language of Rossel Island. *Cognitive Linguistics* 18, 207–218.

Lewis, D. (1986) *On the Plurality of Worlds.* Oxford: Blackwell.

Lucy, J. (1992a) *Language Diversity and Thought. A Reformulation of the Linguistic Relativity Hypothesis.* Cambridge: Cambridge University Press.

Lucy, J. (1992b) *Grammatical Categories and Cognition. A Case Study of the Linguistic Relativity Hypothesis.* Cambridge: Cambridge University Press.

Lucy, J. (1996) The scope of linguistic relativity: An analysis and review of empirical research. In J. Gumperz and S. Levinson (eds) *Rethinking Linguistic Relativity* (pp. 177–202). Cambridge: Cambridge University Press.

Lucy, J. and Gaskins, S. (2001) Grammatical categories and the development of classification preferences: A comparative approach. In M. Bowerman and S. Levinson (eds) *Language Acquisition and Conceptual Development* (pp. 257–283). Cambridge: Cambridge University Press.

Macnamara, J. (1970) Bilingualism and thought. *Georgetown University 21st Annual Round Table* 23, 25–40.

Majid, A., Boster, J. and Bowerman, M. (2008) The crosslinguistic categorization of everyday events: A study of cutting and breaking. *Cognition* 109, 235–250.

Majid, A., Gullberg, M., van Staden, M. and Bowerman, M. (2007) How similar are semantic categories in closely related languages? A comparison of cutting and breaking in four Germanic languages. *Cognitive Linguistics* 18, 179–194.

Montaño-Harmon, M. (1991) Discourse features of written Mexican Spanish: Current research in contrastive rhetoric and its implications. *Hispania* 74, 417–425.

Montrul, S. (2008) *Incomplete Acquisition in Bilingualism. Re-examining the Age Factor.* Amsterdam: John Benjamins.

Munnich, E., Landau, B. and Dosher, B. (2001) Spatial language and spatial representation. A crosslinguistic comparison. *Cognition* 81, 171–201.

Noyeau, C., de Lorenzo, C., Kihlstedt, M., Paprocka, U., Sanz Espinar, G. and Schneider, R. (2005) Two dimensions of the representation of complex event structures: Granularity and condensation. Towards a typology of textual production in L1 and L2. In H. Hendriks (ed.) *The Structure of Learner Varieties* (pp. 157–202). Berlin: De Gruyter.

Oyama, S. (1976) A sensitive period for the acquisition of a non-native phonological system. *Psycholinguistic Research* 5, 261–285.

Papafragou, A., Hulbert, J. and Trueswell, J. (2008) Does language guide event perception? Evidence from eye movements. *Cognition* 108, 155–184.

Papafragou, A., Massey C. and Gleitman, L. (2002) Shake, rattle, 'n' roll: The representation of motion in language and cognition. *Cognition* 84, 189–219.

Papafragou, A., Massey, C. and Gleitman, L. (2006) When English proposes what Greek presupposes: The crosslinguistic encoding of motion events. *Cognition* 98, B75–87.

Pavlenko, A. (1999) New approaches to concepts in bilingual memory. *Bilingualism: Language and Cognition* 2, 209–230.

Pavlenko, A. (2005) Bilingualism and thought. In A. De Groot and J. Kroll (eds) *Handbook of Bilingualism: Psycholinguistic Approaches* (pp. 433–453). Oxford: Oxford University Press.

Pavlenko, A. (2009) Conceptual representation in the bilingual lexicon and second language vocabulary learning. In A. Pavlenko (ed.) *The Bilingual Mental Lexicon: Interdisciplinary Approaches* (pp. 125–160). Bristol: Multilingual Matters.

Pavlenko, A. and Malt, B. (in press) Kitchen Russian: crosslinguistic differences and first-language object naming by Russian-English bilinguals. *Bilingualism: Language and Cognition*.

Pederson, E. (1995) Language as context, language as means: Spatial cognition and habitual language use. *Cognitive Linguistics* 6, 33–62.

Schmid, M. (2007) The role of L1 use for L1 attrition. In B. Köpke, M. Schmid, M. Keijzer and S. Dostert (eds) *Language Attrition. Theoretical Perspectives* (pp. 135–154). Amsterdam: Benjamins.

Schmiedtová, B. (2010) Einflüsse des Deutschen auf das Tschechische: ein Sprachvergleich aus der Lernerperspektive [The influence of German on Czech: A language comparison from a learner perspective]. In S. Höhne and L. Udolph (eds) *Prozesse kultureller Integration und Desintegration. Deutsche, Tschechen, Böhmen im 20. Jahrhundert [Processes of Cultural Integration and Disintegration. Germans, Czechs, Bohemians in the 20th Century]* (pp. 91–117). München: Oldenburg.

Schmiedtová, B. (in press) The development of the expression of simultaneity in L2 Czech: A special focus on (very) advanced learners. In S. Haberzettl (ed.) *The End State in SLA*. Amsterdam: John Benjamins.

Schmiedtová, B., Carroll, M. and Stutterheim, Ch. v. (2007) Implications of language-specific L1 patterns in event construal of advanced second language learners. Paper presented at the annual conference of the American Association for Applied Linguistics, Costa Mesa, CA, April 24, 2007.

Schmiedtová, B. and Flecken, M. (2008) The role of aspectual distinctions in event encoding: Implications for second language acquisition. In S. de Knop and T. de Rycker (eds) *Cognitive Approaches to Pedagogical Grammar* (pp. 357–384). Berlin: De Gruyter.

Schmiedtová, B. and Sahonenko, N. (2008) Die Rolle des grammatischen Aspekts in Ereignis-Enkodierung: Ein Vergleich zwischen Tschechischen und Russischen Lernern des Deutschen [The role of grammatical aspect in event encoding: A comparison between Czech and Russian learners of German]. In P. Gommes and M. Walter (eds) *Fortgeschrittene Lernervarietäten: Korpuslinguistik und Zweitspracherwerbforschung* [*Advanced Learner Varieties: Corpus Linguistics and Bilingualism Research*] (pp. 45–71). Tübingen: Max Niemeyer Verlag.

Schneider, W., Eschman, A. and Zuccolotto, A. (2002a) *E-Prime User's Guide.* Pittsburgh, PA: Psychology Software Tools.

Schneider, W., Eschman, A. and Zuccolotto, A. (2002b) *E-Prime Reference Guide.* Pittsburgh, PA: Psychology Software Tools.

Sebastián, E. and Slobin, D. (1994) The development of linguistic forms: Spanish. In R. Berman and D. Slobin (eds) *Relating Events in Narrative: A Crosslinguistic Developmental Study* (pp. 239–284). Hillsdale, NJ: Lawrence Erlbaum.

Silva-Corvalán, C. (1994) *Language Contact and Change. Spanish in Los Angeles.* Oxford: Clarendon Press.

Slobin, D. (1991) Learning to think for speaking: Native language, cognition, and rhetorical style. *Pragmatics* 1, 7–25.

Slobin, D. (1997) The origins of grammaticizable notions. Beyond the individual mind. In D. Slobin (ed.) *The Crosslinguistic Study of Language Acquisition* (Vol. 5) (pp. 265–323). Mahwah, NJ: Lawrence Erlbaum.

Slobin, D. (2003) Language and thought online: Cognitive consequences of linguistic relativity. In D. Gentner and S. Goldin-Meadow (eds) *Language in Mind. Advances in the Study of Language and Thought* (pp. 157–191). Cambridge, MA: MIT Press.

Smith, C. (2004) The domain of tense. In J. Guéron and J. Lecarme (eds) *The Syntax of Time* (pp. 597–619). Cambridge, MA: MIT Press.

Strömqvist, S. and Verhoeven, L. (eds) (2004) *Relating Events in Narrative. Vol II. Typological and Contextual Perspectives.* Mahwah, NJ: Erlbaum.

Stutterheim, Ch. v. (2003) Linguistic structure and information organisation: The case of very advanced learners. In S. Foster-Cohen and S. Pekarek Doehler (eds) *EuroSLA Yearbook* (pp. 183–206). Amsterdam: John Benjamins.

Stutterheim, Ch. v. and Carroll, M. (2006) The impact of grammaticalized temporal categories on ultimate attainment in advanced L2 acquisition. In H. Byrnes, H. Weger-Guntharp and K. Sprang (eds) *Educating for Advanced Foreign Language Capacities* (pp. 40–53). Washington, DC: Georgetown University Press.

Talmy, L. (1985) Lexicalization patterns: Semantic structures in lexical forms. In T. Shopen (ed.) *Language Typology and Syntactic Description* (pp. 55–149). Cambridge: Cambridge University Press.

Talmy, L. (1988) The relation of grammar to cognition. In B. Rudzka-Ostyn (ed.) *Topics in Cognitive Linguistics* (pp. 165–205). Amsterdam: John Benjamins.

Traugott, E. and Heine, B. (1991) *Approaches to Grammaticalization* (Vol. 2). Amsterdam: John Benjamins.

v. Stutterheim, Ch., Carroll, M. and Klein, W. (2003) Two ways of construing complex temporal structures. In F. Lenz (ed.) *Deictic Conceptualization of Space, Time and Person* (pp. 97–133). Berlin: De Gruyter.

v. Stutterheim, Ch. and Nüse, R. (2003) Processes of conceptualization in language production: Language specific perspectives and event construal. *Linguistics* 41, 851–881.

v. Stutterheim, Ch., Nüse, R. and Murcia-Serra, J. (2002) Crosslinguistic differences in the conceptualization of events. In H. Hasselgård, S. Johansson, B. Behrens and C. Fabricius-Hansen (eds) *Information Structure in a crosslinguistic Perspective* (pp. 179–198). Amsterdam: Rodopi.

Verhoeven, L. and Strömqvist, S. (eds) (2001) *Narrative Development in a Multilingual Context.* Amsterdam: John Benjamins.

Viberg, Å. (2001) Age-related and L2-related features in bilingual narrative development in Sweden. In L. Verhoeven and S. Strömqvist (eds) *Narrative Development in a Multilingual Context* (pp. 87–128). Amsterdam: John Benjamins.

Whorf, B. (1956) *Language, Thought, and Reality. Selected Writings of Benjamin Lee Whorf.* Edited by John Carroll. Cambridge, MA: MIT Press.

Yeni-Komshian, G., Flege, J. and Liu, S. (2000) Pronunciation proficiency in the first and second languages of Korean-English bilinguals. *Bilingualism: Language and Cognition* 3, 131–149.

Chapter 5
Thinking, Speaking and Gesturing about Motion in more than One Language

MARIANNE GULLBERG

5.1 Introduction

Languages differ considerably in the meanings they express. For instance, the verb *tz'apal* in Tzeltal means 'standing of stick-shaped object vertically erect with base buried in support' (Brown, 2006). English has no single word for this meaning and typically does not include such detail in descriptions of placement. A long-standing question is to what extent differences in what is encoded in linguistic categories cause crosslinguistic differences in 'thinking', that is, differences in the mental operations involved in selecting and organizing information, which speakers engage in as they prepare to talk about the world. Slobin (1996) has suggested that the linguistic categories afforded by a language guide speakers' choices concerning what to talk about and how to say it, a notion captured by the term *thinking for speaking*. A growing body of work suggests that monolingual native speakers of different languages typically talk about different aspects of events, exemplified, for instance, by motion events, a fundamental aspect of human spatial experience (e.g. Aurnague *et al.*, 2007; Levinson & Wilkins, 2006; Strömqvist & Verhoeven, 2004).

Crosslinguistic differences in *linguistic conceptualization* or *event construal* – that is, in what meanings are selected for expression and how they are linguistically packaged – raise important questions in second language acquisition (SLA) and bilingualism studies regarding how speakers who know more than one language 'think' about or construe events as they set out to talk about them, and regarding the role of 'the other language'. For instance, a Spanish speaker would normally say the equivalent of *she exited the house* (*salió de la casa*). What happens when such a speaker learns English where the equivalent native description may be *she tiptoed out of the house*?

A general question is how the mental representations of words and grammatical structures of different languages influence each other as they are brought together in linguistic conceptualizations of events. For second language (L2) speakers, a key question is to what extent they continue to rely on conceptualizations from the first language (L1) when speaking the second ('conceptual transfer'[1]), and to what extent they reorganize their conceptualizations and shift attention to information typically selected and expressed in the target language. A second question is what the properties and nature of such speakers' linguistic conceptualizations are. Although transfer and crosslinguistic influence are 'traditional' areas of inquiry in the study of L2 acquisition and multilingual processing, it remains a challenging problem to probe how speakers conceptualize events. Specifically, it remains a vexing issue to gauge what types of information speakers consider as relevant when they talk about motion. Differences in speech alone may not be informative in this regard. For instance, the fact that the Spanish speaker in the example above does not overtly mention the manner of motion (*tiptoe*) does not necessarily mean that she does not consider the manner information. This chapter will outline what can be gained by considering all vehicles of language-specific linguistic conceptualization, namely, speech and gestures in conjunction. It reviews what speech-gesture analyses reveal about whether L2 speakers conceptualize motion differently from monolingual native speakers, and what the nature of their conceptualizations is.

To clarify the focus and use of terminology at the outset, this chapter discusses the thinking involved in event construal or linguistic con-ceptualization as defined above. This, in turn, means that it targets the effects of language on speaking (linguistic conceptualization), rather than the effects of language on general cognition (*linguistic relativity*) (e.g. Gumperz & Levinson, 1996). Further, the terms 'event construal' and 'linguistic conceptualization' will be used interchangeably, and the term 'conceptualization' will be used to refer both to the process and to the representation that results from conceptualizing. Finally, the term 'L2 speaker' (cf. Cook, 2002) is adopted throughout to refer to a participant whose acquisition history, proficiency or fluency in a foreign or second language is under scrutiny. Although the same speakers are sometimes referred to as 'bilinguals' in the psychological literature, the usage chosen here reflects the theoretical framework of the majority of the studies cited, situated in the field of SLA research.

The chapter first outlines some key questions about linguistic conceptualization and L2 production, and then discusses how gestures can be informative in this regard. Subsequently, the domain of motion and the methodology involved in speech-gesture analysis are introduced. The next section reviews studies in the domain of (voluntary and caused) motion, first discussing speech and gesture evidence for different conceptualizations in native monolingual discourse, then reviewing analyses of L2 speakers showing evidence of persistent L1 construals, shifts to L2 construals and also of bidirectional influence. The chapter closes with a discussion of some theoretical implications for theories of L2 acquisition and a methodological reflection.

5.2 Linguistic Conceptualization in the Second Language

To talk about the world, speakers must break down the continuous stream of experience into units that can be verbalized, and select what to say and how to say it (cf. macro- and micro-planning; Levelt, 1989). Traditionally, the selection of what to say, or the formation of the so-called preverbal message, has been assumed to be a language-neutral process, that is, not to be influenced by language-specific linguistic categories (for discussions and critiques, see Francis, 2005; Malt & Sloman, 2003; Pavlenko, 2005).

An alternative view holds that the linguistic categories afforded by a language 'filter' experience, promoting language-specific choices concerning both what to say and how to say it (Berman & Slobin, 1994a), a phenomenon alternatively known in the literature as linguistic conceptualization, event construal or thinking for speaking (e.g. Slobin, 1996; v. Stutterheim & Nüse, 2003). This view also suggests that conceptual domains are structured and organized differently cross-linguistically (cf. Slobin, 1997). For instance, to express placement, English focuses on containment and support (e.g. *put in, put on*), whereas Korean targets the type of surface contact between two objects, expressed as tight or loose fit relationships (*kkita* versus various verbs) (Choi & Bowerman, 1991). Such differences are further boosted when elements are combined and 'deployed in the construction of connected discourse' (Berman & Slobin, 1994b: 611), giving rise to language-specific rhetorical styles (e.g. Slobin, 2004a).

These two views make different assumptions about what it means to move from one language to another, and about the learning task for an adult L2 speaker. The first view is compatible with an often held assumption that early lexical L2 acquisition consists of a quest for translation equivalents, linking new L2 forms to old L1 meanings (e.g. Jiang, 2000; Kroll & Sunderman, 2003). Although a useful starting point, it is also clear that L2 acquisition must proceed beyond such a strategy if it is to lead to targetlike language use. The second view holds that because languages select and express different meanings, L2 acquisition must involve some reorganization of lexico-semantic and conceptual representations, and also of the (language-specific) preverbal message, that is, a potential shift of attention to other types of information in conceptualizing what to talk about.

A core question in L2 acquisition and bilingualism studies is whether L2 speakers can overcome the constraints imposed by categories and representations in their L1, and acquire and use targetlike structures in the L2. The enormous literature on transfer or crosslinguistic influence from the L1 indicates that even advanced L2 speakers continue to be influenced by their L1 in a range of domains (for overviews, see Jarvis & Pavlenko, 2008; Kellerman & Sharwood Smith, 1986; Odlin, 2003; Ringbom, 2007). A number of studies show that L2 speakers may categorize objects and events differently (e.g. Graham & Belnap, 1986; Malt & Sloman, 2003), and use and comprehend lexical and grammatical categories differently from monolingual native speakers (e.g. Coppieters, 1987; Jarvis, 1998; Kellerman, 1979; Pavlenko & Jarvis, 2002). Further studies suggest that L2 speakers may exhibit different linguistic conceptualizations from monolingual native speakers, selecting different types of information for expression (e.g. Carroll *et al.*, 2000). That is, even though they use 'correct' L2 forms, they express information typical of the L1 rather than the L2, giving them a 'discourse accent'. This is reminiscent of Kellerman's notion of 'transfer to nowhere', whereby L2 speakers 'seek the *linguistic* tools which will permit them to maintain their L1 perspective' based on the assumption that 'the way we talk or write about experience is not something that is subject to between-language variation' (1995: 141; italics in the original).

This substantial literature notwithstanding, we know surprisingly little about whether L2 speakers reorganize conceptual representations toward a target, and what the reconceptualization process looks like. That is, it remains unclear whether L2 speakers redirect their attention to different types of information and shift preferences in both *what* to talk about and *how* to do it, and whether shifts and adjustments are gradual or wholesale. Furthermore, we know little about the precise nature of L2 speakers' conceptual representations (as indeed we do about L1 speakers' representations) at a given point in time and how the languages involved influence each other. A lot of attention has been given to the influence of the L1 on the L2, but less is known about the possible effects of the L2 on the L1 (but see Cook, 2003; Jarvis & Pavlenko, 2008; Pavlenko & Jarvis, 2002). It also remains unclear whether the properties of the linguistic categories matter for these processes. Notions like similarity, contrast and comparability have played a key role in the theorizing about positive and negative transfer regardless of directionality (e.g. Ringbom, 2007; Pavlenko, 2009), but the cognitive and semantic complexity of linguistic categories may also play a role, although these issues remain largely unexplored.

All these issues raise a methodological challenge, namely, how to examine L2 speakers' conceptualizations. There are multiple answers to this question, but one option is to consider gestures, the movements we perform when we speak, recognized by onlookers as conveying communicatively relevant, language-related meaning (Kendon, 2004; McNeill, 1992).

5.3 Gestures and Linguistic Conceptualization

Gestures, speech and language are increasingly seen as forming an integrated whole that is planned and processed together in comprehension, production and development (e.g. Kendon, 2004; McNeill, 2005). For instance, gestures affect speech comprehension both in ambiguous and unambiguous contexts (e.g. Cassell *et al.*, 1999; Rogers, 1978). They are also integral to speech production, as seen in the mutual influence of the modalities whereby the content and fluency of speech is affected by the presence or absence of gestures (e.g. Graham & Argyle, 1975; Rauscher *et al.*, 1996). The modalities further develop in parallel in childhood (e.g. Capirci *et al.*, 2005; Iverson & Goldin-Meadow, 2005; Nicoladis *et al.*, 1999) and, conversely, break down together in stuttering and disfluency (e.g. Mayberry & Jaques, 2000; Seyfeddinipur, 2006). The speech-gesture integration has neural underpinnings as they share common neural substrates. For example, Broca's area, implicated in language processing, is also activated when we observe the gestures of others (e.g. Decety *et al.*, 1997), and the brain integrates speech and gesture as one signal (Özyürek & Kelly, 2007).

Although gestures serve multiple functions both for addressees and speakers (Kendon, 1994), they are also vehicles of language-related meaning. The modalities are semantically and temporally coordinated and express closely related meaning at the same time (e.g. Kendon, 1983; McNeill, 1992). The co-expressivity is not a simple one-word-one-gesture mapping, however. Because gestures are synthetic and imagistic and express spatial information in a different format, they typically do not align with individual words, but rather with 'conceptual affiliates' (De Ruiter, 2000). They can also express information not readily encoded in speech (e.g. velocity, size and shape; Beattie & Shovelton, 2007). Gestures can therefore reveal more about what types of spatial information speakers consider for expression than speech alone. The semantic-temporal coordination further means that gestures are influenced by information structure. They reflect the selection of *what* to say and typically align with newsworthy and focal information in speech (e.g. Levy & McNeill, 1992). They also seem to reflect *how* information is structurally expressed. If meaning is distributed over two spoken clauses, that same meaning is likely to be expressed in two gestures, each expressing similar meaning as the spoken clause (Kita *et al.*, 2007).

Contemporary theories concerning the speech-gesture relationship generally assume that co-expressivity arises because speech and gestures are conceptually linked, although the nature and the locus of the connection are hotly debated (for overviews, see De Ruiter, 2007; Kendon, 2004). Discussions focus on the precise role of imagery, linguistic influences, communicative intentions and how late in the encoding process speech and gesture still interact (De Ruiter, 2007; Kita & Özyürek, 2003; Kita *et al.*, 2007; McNeill, 1992, 2005). These differences notwithstanding, the link itself remains undisputed.

One consequence of a conceptual link between co-expressive speech and gesture is crosslinguistic variation. Insofar as languages differ in what meaning they express and how it is linguistically encoded, so the form and temporal alignment of gestures relative to speech differs crosslinguistically (Duncan, 2005; Kita & Özyürek, 2003; McNeill & Duncan, 2000). That is, gestures are vehicles of *language-specific* meaning and conceptualization. For instance, English speakers saying *the ball rolls down the hill* in one clause may perform a single gesture expressing the rolling and downward motion simultaneously. Turkish speakers, in contrast, may express similar meaning in two clauses (*'descend while rolling'*) and accompany each clause with a single gesture expressing downward movement and the rolling motion, respectively (Kita & Özyürek, 2003). Again, both the selection of meaning and its morpho-syntactic packaging in a given language are reflected in the language-specific gestural forms, the timing of gestures relative to speech and in the distribution of information across modalities. Put differently, gestures reflect information considered relevant for expression (what to say) as well as its linguistic encoding (how to say it), with crosslinguistic consequences. Gestures thus reflect linguistic conceptualization and crosslinguistic differences in such conceptualizations.

5.4 The Test Domain and the Methodology

5.4.1 Voluntary and caused motion

Speakers of different languages talk about motion quite differently. The expression of motion consists of a set of core components: the *motion* itself, the moving entity or the *figure*, the *ground* relative to which the figure moves and the *path* or the trajectory of the motion. In addition, the *manner* in which the figure moves and the *cause* of the movement are also mentioned (Talmy, 1985, 1991). Languages vary considerably in how these components are organized and realized. Talmy (1985, 1991) has suggested a typological divide between languages that typically express and frame the path of the movement in the verb root, as in French *sortir* 'exit' (verb framed), or outside the verb root in so-called satellites (particles, affixes or adverbial elements), as in English *out* (Satellite-framed). The two language types also differ in how they treat manner. Verb-framed or V-languages, exemplified in Example (1), typically express path in the (finite) verb (*sort* 'exits') and only optionally express the manner of motion in an adjunct (*en boitant* 'limping'). Conversely, Satellite-framed or S-languages typically express the manner of motion in the verb root (*limp*) and the path of motion in a satellite (*out*), as in Example (2).

(1) *Oscar sort de la cuisine (en boitant)*
'Oscar exits the kitchen (limping)'

(2) *Oscar limps out of the kitchen*

The typology reflects preferential encoding patterns rather than absolute grammaticization. Put differently, languages often have alternative expressions available, but one is clearly preferred (e.g. English *limp out* versus *exit*). Although the typology has been refined to account for mixed patterns ('equipollently-framed languages', Slobin, 2004b), the basic typological distinction is found across both spoken and signed languages (Hickmann & Robert, 2006; Slobin & Hoiting, 1994; Strömqvist & Verhoeven, 2004; Tang & Yang, 2007).

Examples (1) and (2) are concerned with 'voluntary' motion where the figure moves of its own accord, but expressions of caused motion belong to the same family. These are events where an agent causes a figure object to move to an end location (the goal ground) to which it will relate in a resulting spatial relationship, as in placement events exemplified in Example (3).

(3) *Oscar put the cup on the table*

Placement also displays considerable crosslinguistic variation. Placement verbs vary in semantic granularity ranging from general verbs (e.g. *put*) via posture verbs (e.g. *set, stand, lay*), to classificatory verbs like the Tzeltal example above (Ameka & Levinson, 2007; Kopecka & Narasimhan, in press). In relation to the motion typology, V-languages generally focus on the location or state of the figure (location-focus) and S-languages focus on the manner of being located (posture-focus) (Berthele, 2004; Lemmens, 2002).

Both motion domains thus display crosslinguistic differences in what elements are considered relevant for expression and how they are grouped and realized in sustained discourse. The monolingual literature has examined whether these differences affect what information speakers attend to and select for expression, that is, whether they differ in linguistic conceptualization or thinking for speaking. In the following, I will exemplify research in both domains, first in L1, then in L2 contexts, and illustrate how gesture analysis provides more information than speech alone on how speakers conceptualize motion events.

5.4.2 Methodology: Speech and gesture analysis

Crosslinguistic studies of gestures show that there are systematic crosslinguistic differences in the gesture patterns that accompany speech. Gesture production, whether in the L1 or L2, is subject to as much individual variation as speech is. Generally, however, individuals vary in the propensity to gesture (gesture rate or frequency), but speakers from a given linguistic community display remarkable consistency with regard to *when* and *how* they gesture when performing the same task (cf. Gullberg, 2006). It is important to stress, however, that gesture production is never subject to categorical behavior. Language-specific gesture patterns always refer to preferences, and comparisons between native and L2 production are always made between preferential patterns in the L1 and the L2. Put differently, to be targetlike, L2 speakers are expected to vary to the same extent as or show similar preferences to native speakers.

The logic underlying gesture studies of linguistic conceptualization is that if language X and Y (select and) express different meanings, then the speech-gesture ensembles of each language will differ. In L2 contexts, a targetlike conceptualization should yield targetlike speech *and* targetlike gestures (meaning targetlike preferences). That is, if L2 speakers conceptualize an event like (monolingual) native speakers, their speech and gestures should express similar content with similar timing to native speakers' speech and gestures. If, on the other hand, they operate with a different (L1- or learner-typical) conceptualization, their gestures will look different from those of native speakers. The same logic applies to bilinguals. Separate conceptualizations in each language should yield two separate speech-gesture patterns, one for each language (again, assuming that the languages differ in conceptualization). If the speech-gesture ensembles are similar in both languages but different from those of monolinguals, this suggests converged conceptualizations (e.g. Bullock & Toribio, 2004). Under this logic, then, the forms and timing of gestures offer unique opportunities to study what information L2/bilingual speakers actually consider for speaking.

To elicit motion descriptions while keeping the content and contextual variables constant, and speakers' awareness of their gesture production at a minimum, story retellings, video descriptions or referential communication tasks are often used (Yule, 1997). To promote gesture production, participants view some stimuli and then describe them (1) from memory; (2) to a confederate or naïve interlocutor; and (3) in a dialogic, face-to-face situation (Bavelas *et al.*, 2002). Participants are video- and audio taped for later transcription and coding.

Speech is transcribed and divided into relevant units (e.g. clauses, first spontaneous descriptions). It is generally coded for (1) the meaning conveyed (e.g. path, manner, conflated path and manner, ground, etc.); (2) the lexical category (motion verbs, satellites, etc.); and (3) the construction used (e.g. single versus multiple clauses).

Although no standardized scheme for gesture transcription exists, most studies use one of two influential systems (Kendon, 2004; McNeill, 1992, 2005). All gesture transcription and coding relies on frame-by-frame analysis of the video material. The unit of analysis is often the gesture stroke, which is structurally defined as the most forceful part of the movement in terms of muscular tension, velocity, etc., relative to the surrounding phases (Kendon, 1980; Kita *et al.*, 1998; Seyfeddinipur, 2006). Gestures are coded for (1) the meaning conveyed (e.g. path, manner, conflated path and manner, object information) operationalized as gestural form; (2) the timing of gestures relative to some unit in speech (e.g. the entire clause, parts of speech); and (3) the degree of co-expressivity or meaning overlap between speech and gesture (e.g. match-mismatch, overlapping-complementary-contradictory, etc.). Occasionally, the distribution of meaning elements across speech and gesture (*what is expressed where?*) is also considered.

As an aside, in studies of event conceptualization, it is important to consider speech and gestures in (a) fluent segments of (b) first spontaneous descriptions. The reason for this is that disfluencies, questions and prompts may result in strategic use of gestures for problem solving or deliberate demonstration. Such gestures may have different properties from those performed with low awareness and may be generated by other mechanisms (for more extended methodological discussions, see Gullberg, 1998; 2010).

5.5 The Conceptualization of Motion in Speech and Gesture

5.5.1 Voluntary motion in native discourse

Speech-gesture analyses of monolingual native speakers of typologically different languages show that they typically target different information when talking about voluntary motion following the lexicalization patterns of their languages. In other words, speakers of V-languages, such as Japanese, Turkish and French, overall target the path of motion both in speech (in the main verb root, e.g. French *sortir* 'exit') and in gesture. They also conceptualize the path together with the agent's action (expressed in the verb) as seen in the temporal alignment of path gestures with path verbs in speech, as in Example (4) where the gesture stroke is marked with square brackets (Choi & Lantolf, 2008; Gullberg *et al.*, 2008; Kellerman & Van Hoof, 2003; Kita & Özyürek, 2003; Kita *et al.*, 2007; Stam, 2006).

(4)   il [traverse cette riv]ière
      'he [crosses this ri]ver'   (Gullberg *et al.*, 2008: 222)

Conversely, speakers of S-languages, like English or Mandarin Chinese, focus more on manner but, importantly, they target *both* manner and path (Brown & Gullberg, 2008; Duncan, 2005; Slobin, 2006). They package both elements into one clause in speech (a manner verb, *limp*, and a path satellite, *out*) and may express both in a single gesture conflating path and manner (Kita & Özyürek, 2003; Kita *et al.*, 2007). Furthermore, they can also add multiple path elements (source, goal and medium of path) in the same clause (*out of the kitchen across the floor to the stairs*). Path gestures in S-languages align with satellites, verbs and satellites, ground expressions, etc. (Choi & Lantolf, 2008; Kellerman & Van Hoof, 2003; Stam, 2006), reflecting these broader and more complex construal options in S-languages.

The expression of manner in speech and gesture raises interesting issues. In V-languages, manner is typically optional, and not always overtly expressed in speech, due to smaller manner verb lexicons, or to structural complexities of subordination, or both.[2] It has been hypothesized that speakers of V-languages (a) do not attend to manner as much as speakers of S-languages (Slobin, 2006), but also (b) that they may express manner in gesture rather than in speech (McNeill, 2000; Negueruela *et al.*, 2004), although the evidence for compensatory manner gestures in V-languages is somewhat contradictory. Speakers of Spanish (V-language) do gesture about manner and as frequently as, for instance, speakers of English and Mandarin Chinese (S-languages) (Duncan, 2005). Interestingly, however, they systematically align manner gestures with expressions of ground rather than with spoken manner expressions. Duncan (2005) interprets this systematic alignment pattern as an indication that manner is conceptualized with ground in Spanish, linking a figure's motion to the setting or ground. This, she argues, is not very different from cases such as *slide* in English, where the nature of the ground (e.g. ice) is also relevant to the manner of the figure's motion. The difference is that this is the predominant link in a V-language such as Spanish, whereas in S-languages, such as English or Chinese, manner is predominantly associated with figures and their activities, and manner gestures align with manner verbs or adverbials. Speakers of S-languages also have options regarding manner: for instance, they may choose to background manner in speech by gesturing about path rather than manner (McNeill, 2000). Overall, the gesture evidence provides a somewhat different and more fine-grained picture of linguistic conceptualizations of motion than speech alone, showing that different meaning elements can be conceptualized as belonging together in different ways, and also how structural constraints can be by-passed by using gesture to manipulate the prominence of certain information.

5.5.2 Voluntary motion in L2 discourse

The typological differences outlined above, particularly regarding manner, raise important questions about how L2 speakers conceptualize motion, and about potential loci of transfer and 'stabilization' or 'fossilization', that is, instances where L2 learners stop developing despite continued exposure to target structures (e.g. Han & Odlin, 2006; Selinker, 1972). Moving from a path-focused V-language (e.g. French) into a manner-intense S-language (e.g. English) requires L2 learners to attend to manner as well as to path, and to conceptualize manner as linked to action expressed in verbs. Conversely, moving from a manner-intense S-language (e.g. English) into a manner-indifferent V-language (e.g. French) requires a shift away from manner and a reconceptualization of action as linked to path.

Most studies have focused on the transition from V- to S-languages, that is, on shifts toward new (manner) information and accumulation of path elements. Not unexpectedly, the findings are mixed (cf. Cadierno, 2008). Some studies find that L2 speakers have difficulties expressing manner in the L2 when it is not frequently expressed in the L1 (e.g. Choi & Lantolf, 2008; Negueruela *et al.*, 2004; Wieselman Schulman, 2004). The difficulty does not seem to reside in the manner vocabulary *per se* (cf. Brown & Gullberg, 2008), but rather in the relative prominence of manner and its tight conceptual link to path, reflected in the expression of manner *and* path in a single clause and single conflated gesture in English. In a study of 18 Turkish learners of English at three proficiency levels (beginner, intermediate and advanced), only half of the most advanced L2 speakers with 10 years of immersion in the target culture ($n = 3$) showed a tendency to achieve this packaging in speech *and* gesture (Özyürek, 2002). Some L2 speakers produced formally accurate structures in speech, but accompanied these by gestures expressing only path or only manner. Although Özyürek (2002) refrains from interpreting the data in terms of acquisition, the less proficient groups seem to continue to operate with an L1 conceptualization of path and manner, treating them as separate, unrelated pieces of information. The advanced speakers, who produced targetlike speech but sometimes accompanied it with L1-like gestures, appear to have started restructuring their conceptualization of path and manner, linking the two more often. Unfortunately, it is not clear whether the speech-gesture discrepancies observed in the study occurred between or within individuals, leaving it open as to what exactly the nature of the individual representations might be.

Turning to the transition from S- to V-languages, L2 speakers seem to have similar problems shifting attention *away* from manner when it is not part of the target L2 (e.g. Choi & Lantolf, 2008; Negueruela *et al.*, 2004). English learners of L2 Spanish, for instance, continue to seek ways to express manner. When L2 speech offers no easy solution, they may express manner in gesture (Negueruela *et al.*, 2004). Other studies report that Danish and English learners of L2 Spanish have no difficulties suppressing manner, but instead show a tendency to add path particles and adverbials in Spanish ('satellization'; Cadierno, 2004; Cadierno & Ruiz, 2006). However, these studies provide only speech data, and it is unknown whether manner was expressed in gesture instead.

Together, these studies suggest that L2 speakers have difficulties reconceptualizing motion regardless of the direction of typological transition, with conceptual transfer of L1-typical event conceptualization to the L2. L2 speakers select L1-typical information and express it in L1-typical categories wherever possible.

5.5.3 Evidence of reconceptualization of voluntary motion

Despite the evidence just reviewed, linguistic conceptualization may not be impervious to change. The evidence comes from a line of research looking at bidirectional influence (Brown & Gullberg, 2008, 2010a, 2010b). In this project, we examined the motion descriptions of Japanese speakers with intermediate knowledge of English, resident either in Japan ($n = 15$) or in the USA ($n = 13$), but matched on formal L2 proficiency measured by the Oxford Placement test and the Cambridge First Certificate oral proficiency test criteria. Their L1 production was compared to that of functionally monolingual Japanese speakers ($n = 16$) and their L2 production to that of monolingual English speakers ($n = 13$). All participants retold the animated cartoon 'Canary Row' (Freleng, 1950) to an interlocutor. The monolingual groups retold the story only once, and the Japanese speakers with knowledge of English retold it once in the L1 and once in the L2 to native speakers of Japanese and English, respectively, in counter-balanced order. Not unexpectedly, in L2 English these speakers differed significantly from native English speakers in their continued preference for expressing path in verbs rather than in adverbials (Brown & Gullberg, 2010a). However, strikingly, they also differed significantly from monolingual Japanese speakers in their L1 Japanese. They expressed significantly more path elements per clause than monolingual Japanese speakers through the stacking of path verbs, typical of V-languages, and the addition of significantly more goal expressions (Brown & Gullberg, 2010a, 2010b).

(5) *chiyou-kara Tweety-no tokoro-made nobotte itta*
ground-from Tweety-GEN place-to climb.ascend.Con went
'(He) went climbing from the ground to Tweety's place' (Brown &
Gullberg, 2010b: Example (10)).

Example (5), produced by a Japanese speaker with knowledge of
English, contains four expressions of path in the same clause: two
postpositions, *kara* 'from' and *made* 'to', and a complex motion predicate
consisting of two verbs, *noboru* 'climb.ascend' and *iku* 'go'. Although the
structure in Example (5) is fully grammatical in Japanese, the stacking of
multiple path elements within a single clause is not the preferred pattern
in monolingual production, but is rather typical of S-languages. The
Japanese speakers with knowledge of English produced significantly
more of these structures than the monolingual speakers.

Similarly for manner, although the Japanese speakers with knowledge
of English did not mention more spoken manner than monolingual
Japanese speakers, when they did mention it, they behaved differently
from monolingual Japanese speakers. When Japanese speakers mention
manner in speech, they are most likely to also gesture about manner. In
contrast, when English speakers mention manner in speech, they often
gesture only about path, a phenomenon known as manner modulation.
The Japanese speakers with knowledge of English were significantly
more likely to talk about manner and gesture about path in their L1
Japanese than were monolingual Japanese speakers, thus producing a
pattern typical of S-languages (Brown & Gullberg, 2008). Overall, the
non-monolingual Japanese production resembles English conceptualization with accumulated mention of path and a modulation of manner
when mentioned. This suggests a possible influence of the L2 on L1
conceptualization.

Two things are noteworthy. First, the L2 groups resident in Japan and
the USA did not differ on any of these measures. Both groups showed
shifts in L1 preferences. Second, the shifts did not lead to ungrammaticality. These observations together indicate that cultural immersion is not
responsible for the shifts since they also occur in the group in Japan; the
shifts are also not a matter of L1 attrition, since there is no sign of
ungrammaticality and the group resident in Japan has clearly not lost
any aspect of their L1 used daily. Finally, it is striking that a shift in L1
conceptualization is evident at such modest levels of L2 proficiency.

To summarize, the crosslinguistic differences in how native speakers
conceptualize voluntary motion have consequences for L2 acquisition.
The combined speech-gesture analyses provide details on the conceptualizations, on what is conceptually transferred and what may be
reconceptualized.

5.5.4 Caused motion in native discourse

The crosslinguistic differences in the expression of voluntary motion encompass lexical, syntactic and information structural differences simultaneously. In contrast, in the domain of caused motion, the linguistic conceptualization of placement can be examined while keeping structures relatively constant. For instance, French, Dutch and German speakers speak and gesture differently about placement (Gullberg, 2010a, submitted a). All three languages use similar simple transitive sentence frames, but the meanings of the placement verbs differ. French has a general placement verb (*mettre* 'put') that encodes the caused motion and is applicable to almost any placement event (e.g. Hickmann & Hendriks, 2006; Tesnière, 1959). Dutch and German have (semi-)obligatory specific placement verbs encoding the caused motion *and* the physical and spatial properties of the figure object (e.g. *zetten/ leggen* 'set/lay' in Dutch, *stellen/legen* 'stand/lay' in German; e.g. Kutscher & Schultze-Berndt, 2007; Lemmens, 2006). The verb choice for a given event hinges on the object properties. There is no general superordinate verb that is equivalent to 'put'. The gestural patterns in these three languages differ crosslinguistically both in form and timing (Gullberg, 2010a, submitted a). When describing short video clips of simple placement events (e.g. bottle placed on shelf, bowl placed on table, etc.), French (Figure 5.1a) and German speakers (Figure 5.1b) gesture only about path, as seen in general deictic gestures expressing only the direction through relaxed hands with palm up or down displaying no particular handshapes or pointing. Dutch speakers (Figure 5.1c) instead typically incorporate the object with the path in gestures in which handshapes reflecting the shape of the figure object are super-imposed on the movement. Moreover, French and Dutch speakers predominantly align their gestures with verbs (*met* 'puts', *zet* 'sets'), whereas German speakers chiefly align their gestures with some part of the locational goal phrase (*recht auf den Schreibtisch* 'right on the desk').

The speech-gesture patterns suggest three conceptualizations. Native French speakers conceptualize placement simply as the action of moving, ignoring the figure object. Dutch speakers conceptualize it as the action of moving a specific object. German speakers, finally, conceptualize placement as movement toward a goal ground or end-point (cf. Schmiedtová, this volume), ignoring both the agentive action and the object.

5.5.5 Caused motion in second language discourse

The different conceptualizations of placement raise similar issues for L2 acquisition as voluntary motion. Although both the vocabulary and the structures are considered 'simple', transitions from one pattern to another will require reconceptualization involving either splitting an L1

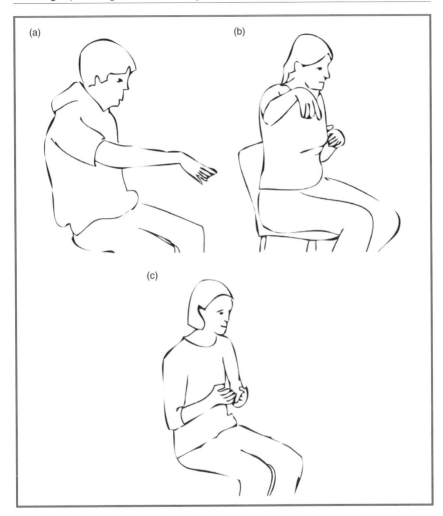

Figure 5.1 (a) Native French speaker producing a gesture expressing path information aligned with the verb and figure object while saying *elle [met elle met le tout] sur le dans le coin* 'she [puts she puts all of it] on the in the corner' (gesture stroke in square brackets). (b) Native German speaker producing a gesture expressing path information aligned with a locative expression while saying *die kommt hinten [recht] auf die Schreibtisch* 'that comes at the back [to the right] on the desk' (gesture stroke in square brackets). (c) Native Dutch speaker producing a gesture expressing object information in the handshape while saying *[dat zet ze] helemaal rechts achter op haar buro* '[that sets she] all the way at the back on her desk' (gesture stroke in square brackets).

verb category into two L2 categories (e.g. from French to German) or 'collapsing' several L1 verb categories into one L2 category (e.g. Dutch to French). Studies have mainly focused on the transition involving the splitting of L1 categories (e.g. Gullberg, 2009; Viberg, 1998). Very little is known about transitions involving the 'collapsing' of two L1 categories, often assumed to be 'easy' since overt speech looks formally accurate. However, with different conceptualizations, all transitions should involve reorganization.

In a recent line of study, I investigated placement descriptions in the speech and gestures of intermediate Dutch ($n = 12$) and German ($n = 12$) foreign language learners of L2 French (Gullberg, 2009). At the time of testing, they were all in their ninth to eleventh year of study of French as a foreign language at the university level in their respective home countries. No participant had spent more than three consecutive weeks in a French-speaking country. All had had very limited contact with native French speakers. They were shown short video clips of everyday placement events (e.g. a woman putting a bowl on a table). When the screen went blank, they had to describe from memory to a native interlocutor what the woman did, yielding descriptions like Example (6).

(6) *et ce bol avec les bananes elle le met sur le bureau à droite* (F2_12)
     'and this bowl of bananas she puts it on the desk to the right'

The results showed that both L2 groups produced targetlike spoken L2 French in terms of the range and frequency of verbs (*mettre* 'put', *placer* 'place', *accrocher* 'stick', etc.) and adverbial modification phrases used (e.g. *debout* 'standing'). L2 speech suggested a targetlike linguistic conceptualization. However, the L2 gesture patterns revealed differences. L1 Dutch learners incorporated more objects in gestures when speaking L2 French than native French speakers, but also fewer than monolingual Dutch speakers. Similarly, the L1 German learners aligned significantly more gestures with goal phrases when speaking L2 French than French speakers, but they also aligned significantly more gestures with verbs than monolingual German speakers. That is to say, both L2 groups showed evidence of conceptual transfer from the L1 (a Dutch focus on objects, a German focus on goals in contrast to the French focus on action), but also of beginning restructuring (a reduced Dutch focus on objects and an increased German focus on action). In fact, the L2 speakers patterned in three different ways as individuals: they displayed a more targetlike, a more L1-like or – most interestingly – an in-between pattern. The in-between group often displayed both L1 and L2 gesture patterns within the same utterance, suggesting ongoing reconceptualization with attention to multiple elements. One might speculate that the restructuring involves a different weighting of these.

Interestingly, there were no significant differences in the biographical data concerning acquisition history that correlated with a particular gesture pattern. Overall, the groups also looked similar with regard to formal accuracy when considered in terms of verb choice and adverbial constructions. However, *post-hoc* analyses revealed that the in-between group was potentially less fluent than the other L2 speakers, meaning that they produced more filled pauses in their utterances (e.g. *uh, uhm,* etc.), but without producing false starts, repetitions, hedges and the like. If L2 speakers are struggling with what information to select, this could lead to formulation difficulties in speech, but difficulties that are not necessarily reflected in issues of formal accuracy. Recall that in contrast to the domain of voluntary motion, the target constructions here are 'simple' and do not require very sophisticated vocabulary or syntax. What they do require is a focus on the right type of information.

In sum, speech-gesture analyses reveal crosslinguistically different conceptualization of (caused) motion even when structure is kept constant: different information is targeted for expression and different types of information are conceptualized together. The speech-gesture ensemble thus provides details on what is conceptually transferred in the L2, on restructuring, and on what elements L2 speakers' representations contain at a given point in time even when speech is formally accurate and offers little information about issues of conceptual transfer.

5.6 Thinking, Speaking and Gesturing about Motion in more than one Language

5.6.1 Transfer, shifts and restructuring

The accumulated native speech-gesture evidence indicates considerable crosslinguistic differences in how motion is linguistically conceptualized. These differences have consequences for L2 speakers who must reconceptualize motion, that is, shift attention to different types of information, potentially expressed in different linguistic categories and structures, to be targetlike. The evidence for such reconceptualization in L2 production is mixed in the studies reviewed. Many studies suggest persistent conceptual transfer from the L1 with L2 speakers continuing to select information for expression typical of the L1 (e.g. path rather than manner) encoded in L1-based categories and structures (e.g. Cadierno & Ruiz, 2006; Carroll *et al.*, 2000; Choi & Lantolf, 2008; Neguerela *et al.*, 2004; Stam, 2006). In general, it is not the linguistic forms that cause difficulties, but the conceptualizations they imply (cf. Carroll & Lambert, 2003: 281). A few studies also show evidence of shifts toward L2-typical conceptualization, that is, of reconceptualization to match the target language (Gullberg, 2009; Özyürek, 2002). Finally, there is evidence of bidirectional influence with speakers showing shifts in L1 conceptualization that seem to originate in conceptualization patterns from the L2 (Brown & Gullberg, 2008, 2010a).

A general observation is that all studies suggest that restructuring is possible, even if few studies indicate a fully target- or monolingual-like conceptualization. Most L2 speakers show evidence of *some* shift toward the L2. Whether or not such shifts are recognized as learning or reconceptualization depends on whether the focus in a given study is on what L2 speakers can do or on what they cannot do, which is ultimately a matter of personal and theoretical inclination and taste. Either way, speech-gesture data provide a more gradient view of conceptual transfer in that the gesture data, in particular, reveal that shifts in representations and conceptualizations are gradual and not necessarily an all-or-nothing process even within a single domain. This is to be expected given the complexity of event conceptualizations. Furthermore, if all shifts are considered – in L2 as well as in L1 conceptualizations – the data seem to support views common in the bilingualism literature to the effect that all linguistic elements in an individual speaker's mind interact. In fact, the data showing influence from an emergent and barely fluent L2 on the L1 (Brown & Gullberg, 2008, 2010a, 2010b) suggest a much more fluid and permeable relationship between representations and systems than is typically assumed in the traditional L2 literature.

An interesting consequence of such permeability is that it brings to the fore the importance of treating the monolingual native speaker norm as a benchmark with some caution, especially as applied in L2 studies concerned with near-nativelikeness and so-called ultimate attainment (Birdsong, 2004; Hyltenstam & Abrahamsson, 2003). If knowledge of another language at even modest levels of formal proficiency affects linguistic conceptualization in the L1, then it becomes methodologically vital to specify what the point of comparison is for L2 speakers; a monolingual native speaker or a native speaker with knowledge of various other languages (e.g. Davies, 2003; Grosjean, 1998). More generally, evidence of permeability suggests that it may be time to abandon the monolithic view of conceptualizations as impenetrable, to change and to start seeing conceptualizations as dynamic and changing, depending on situation and usage patterns in the same way as language proficiency and dominance.

5.6.2 Directions for future inquiry

Gesture analysis adds new details to our understanding of the nature of L2 speakers' linguistic conceptualizations, but it also raises new issues to explore. An obvious question is where conceptual transfer is most likely to occur, and conversely, what shifts are possible. There is speech-gesture evidence for conceptual transfer from the L1 to the L2 at all levels of proficiency and all domains examined. Yet, L2 speakers also seem more likely to abandon an L1 category than to add new L2 categories, or than to expand or split L1 categories to bring them in-line with the L2, although the data are somewhat contradictory (cf. the relative targetlikeness of Dutch and German learners' L2 French placement descriptions; Gullberg, submitted b; versus the persistent L1-like properties of Japanese learners' L2 English descriptions of voluntary motion; Brown & Gullberg, 2010a). However, although a useful starting point, this generalization may not capture the subtle differences dependent on the inherent complexity of the categories involved (cf. Gullberg & Narasimhan, 2010; Narasimhan & Gullberg, 2010), the lexical categories that encode them (e.g. manner in verbs versus in adverbials) and the structural or morphosyntactic prominence of the lexical categories (manner central in verb versus peripheral in adjunct), etc. These intricacies must be examined in more detail for a better understanding of reconceptualization both as product and process.

A further issue concerns the nature of representations once a new L2 representation has developed and co-exists with a previous one. If all lexical elements known to a speaker interact bidirectionally even if only one language is contextually relevant, as suggested by the processing literature (e.g. Van Hell & Dijkstra, 2002), a psycholinguistic question arises regarding the nature of the co-existing conceptualizations. Are linguistic conceptualizations 'slimmer' in speakers who know several languages, exploiting the overlap between the L1 and L2, to achieve processing economy, or are they 'richer', incorporating all distinctions available from both languages? Again, both types seem to be evident in the data, but these issues remain largely unexplored.

A related question is why and where L2 speakers stabilize, failing to shift conceptualization patterns toward a target even after extensive usage and exposure, as well as when shifts in the L1 may be observed even after minimal experience with an L2. It seems counter-intuitive that L1 conceptualizations should shift more easily than L2 conceptualizations, at least given the traditional view of the native speaker norm as a stable and monolithic standard (see Davies, 2003, for discussions). Interestingly, shifts in the L1 do not necessarily lead to ungrammaticality, whereas the consequence of L1 conceptual transfer in the L2 ranges from ungrammaticality to a 'discourse accent' with formally accurate but unidiomatic L2 speech targeting different information than native speakers (although studies documenting naïve native speakers' perceptions of such differences are sorely missing). Are some domains more permeable than others? The reverse question is why some L2 speakers do shift their representations toward the target, as well as how and when they do so. All these issues are traditional questions in L2 research, but gesture analysis opens new ways to explore them.

Finally, the focus throughout this chapter has been on linguistic conceptualizations. A few final remarks are in order about whether gestures can help explore issues of linguistic relativity proper whether in monolingual L1, L2 or bilingual contexts (e.g. Gumperz & Levinson, 1996; Lucy, 1996). It is crucial to the study of linguistic relativity to determine what constitutes evidence for an influence of language on general cognition independently of linguistic activity. It has been argued that both verbal and 'non-verbal' behavior must be examined to avoid circularity (cf. Lucy, 1996). Gestures are not good candidates for such non-verbal behavior. In fact, the tight link between gestures, speech and language demonstrated throughout this chapter indicates that gestures are 'verbal' (i.e. 'linguistic') rather than 'non-verbal' (cf. McNeill, 1985). As such, they do not constitute ideal data to examine the effects of language on general cognition, although they have been used to support such arguments (e.g. Haviland, 1996). Although it is possible that some gestures or certain aspects of gesture production, such as directionality, may be influenced by general cognitive differences in how space is construed, gesture data should be treated with caution in this regard given the strong influence of linguistic activity on gestures. Arguably, gestures are more likely to reflect linguistic than general conceptualization and to demonstrate effects of language on language, at least when people speak and gesture simultaneously.

5.7 Concluding Remarks

Although it is uncontroversial that languages express different meanings and that they do not necessarily match one-to-one crosslinguistically, the possible consequences of these differences and the level at which they reside – the interface between language and cognition – remain controversial. Speakers of more than one language raise further challenges. Understanding what linguistic conceptualizations such speakers operate with and how they develop is crucial to our understanding of the human capacity for thinking and talking about experience. It is truly challenging to understand how experience is processed through the filter provided by one language and what happens to that filter when an alternative filter provides different options. The studies reviewed here suggest that multiple perspectives are possible and that their properties are more dynamic than previously assumed. Speech and gesture analysis combined constitute a new lens through which these processes can be observed. Gestures provide rich and multidimensional data, often adding more detail to what is visible in speech. However, gesture analysis is not mind reading. As should be clear by now, speech and gesture illuminate different aspects of the same underlying conceptualization. Gestures constitute another dimension along which L2 conceptualizations can be explored. They shed important new light on how information is selected, processed and expressed in more than one language.

Acknowledgments

I gratefully acknowledge funding from the Max Planck Institute for Psycholinguistics and a grant from the Nederlandse Organisatie voor Wetenschappelijk Onderzoek (NWO; MPI 56-384, *The Dynamics of Multilingual Processing*) to M. Gullberg and P. Indefrey. I also thank the editor and anonymous reviewers for useful comments. All remaining errors are mine and no doubt the result of ignoring good advice.

Notes

1. No distinction will be made between concept and conceptualization transfer (Jarvis, 2007; Odlin, 2005). The term conceptual transfer will be used throughout.
2. Verb-framed languages may express more manner than previously assumed when other elements such adverbials, descriptions, mimetics and other peripheral constructions are considered (e.g. Brown & Gullberg, 2008; Hickmann & Hendriks, 2006; Hohenstein *et al.*, 2006).

References

Ameka, F. and Levinson, S. (2007) Special issue on locative predicates. *Linguistics* 45, 5/6.

Aurnague, M., Hickmann, M. and Vieu, L. (eds) (2007) *The Categorization of Spatial Entities in Language and Cognition*. Amsterdam: John Benjamins.

Bavelas, J., Kenwood, C., Johnson, T. and Phillips, B. (2002) An experimental study of when and how speakers use gestures to communicate. *Gesture* 2, 1–17.

Beattie, G. and Shovelton, H. (2007) The role of iconic gesture in semantic communication and its theoretical and practical implications. In S. Duncan, J. Cassell and E. Levy (eds) *Gesture and the Dynamic Dimension of Language. Essays in Honor of David McNeill* (pp. 221–241). Amsterdam: John Benjamins.

Berman, R. and Slobin, D. (1994a) Filtering and packaging in narrative. In R. Berman and D. Slobin (eds) *Relating Events in Narrative: A Crosslinguistic Developmental Study* (pp. 515–554). Hillsdale, NJ: Lawrence Erlbaum.

Berman, R. and Slobin, D. (1994b) *Relating Events in Narrative: A Crosslinguistic Developmental Study*. Hillsdale, NJ: Lawrence Erlbaum.

Berthele, R. (2004) The typology of motion and posture verbs: A variationist account. In B. Kortmann (ed.) *Dialectology Meets Typology* (pp. 93–126). Berlin: Mouton de Gruyter.

Birdsong, D. (2004) Second language acquisition and ultimate attainment. In A. Davies and C. Elder (eds) *Handbook of Applied Linguistics* (pp. 82–105). London: Blackwell.

Brown, A. and Gullberg, M. (2008) Bidirectional crosslinguistic influence in L1-L2 encoding of manner in speech and gesture: A study of Japanese speakers of English. *Studies in Second Language Acquisition* 30, 225–251.

Brown, A. and Gullberg, M. (2010a) Bidirectional crosslinguistic influence in event conceptualization? The expression of Path among Japanese learners of English. *Bilingualism: Language and Cognition*.

Brown, A. and Gullberg, M. (2010b) Changes in encoding of path of motion after acquisition of a second language. *Cognitive Linguistics* 21 (2), 263–286.

Brown, P. (2006) A sketch of the grammar of space in Tzeltal. In S. Levinson D. Wilkins (eds) *Grammars of Space. Explorations in Cognitive Diversity* (pp. 230–272). Cambridge: Cambridge University Press.

Bullock, B. and Toribio, J. (2004) Introduction: Convergence as an emergent property in bilingual speech. *Bilingualism: Language and Cognition* 7, 91–93.

Cadierno, T. (2004) Expressing motion events in a second language: A cognitive typological perspective. In M. Achard and S. Niemeier (eds) *Cognitive Linguistics, Second Language Acquisition, and Foreign Language Teaching* (pp. 13–49). Berlin: Mouton de Gruyter.

Cadierno, T. (2008) Learning to talk about motion in a foreign language. In P. Robinson and N. Ellis (eds) *Handbook of Cognitive Linguistics and Second Language Acquisition* (pp. 239–275). London: Routledge.

Cadierno, T. and Ruiz, L. (2006) Motion events in Spanish L2 acquisition. *Annual Review of Cognitive Linguistics* 4, 183–216.

Capirci, O., Contaldo, A., Caselli, M. and Volterra, V. (2005) From action to language through gesture: A longitudinal perspective. *Gesture* 5, 155–177.

Carroll, M. and Lambert, M. (2003) Information structure in narratives and the role of grammaticised knowledge. A study of adult French and German learners of English. In Ch. Dimroth and M. Starren (eds) *Information Structure and the Dynamics of Language Acquisition* (pp. 267–287). Amsterdam: John Benjamins.

Carroll, M., Murcia-Serra, J., Watorek, M. and Bendiscoli, A. (2000) The relevance of information organization to second language acquisition studies: The descriptive discourse of advanced adult learners of German. *Studies in Second Language Acquisition* 22, 441–466.

Cassell, J., McNeill, D. and McCullough, K-E. (1999) Speech-gesture mismatches: Evidence for one underlying representation of linguistic and nonlinguistic information. *Pragmatics & Cognition* 7, 1–33.

Choi, S. and Bowerman, M. (1991) Learning to express motion events in English and Korean: The influence of language-specific lexicalization patterns. *Cognition* 41, 83–121.

Choi, S. and Lantolf, J. (2008) Representation and embodiment of meaning in L2 communication. Motion events in the speech and gesture of advanced L2 Korean and L2 English speakers. *Studies in Second Language Acquisition* 30, 191–224.

Cook, V. (2002) Background to the L2 user. In V. Cook (ed.) *Portraits of the L2 User* (pp. 1–28). Clevedon: Multilingual Matters.

Cook, V. (ed.) (2003) *Effects of the Second Language on the First*. Clevedon: Multilingual Matters.

Coppieters, R. (1987) Competence differences between native and near-native speakers. *Language* 63, 544–573.

Davies, A. (2003) *The Native Speaker: Myth and Reality*. Clevedon: Multilingual Matters.

De Ruiter, J-P. (2000) The production of gesture and speech. In D. McNeill (ed.) *Language and Gesture: Window into Thought and Action* (pp. 284–311). Cambridge: Cambridge University Press.

De Ruiter, J-P. (2007) Postcards from the mind: The relationship between speech, gesture and thought. *Gesture* 7, 21–38.

Decety, J., Grèzes, J., Costes, N., Perani, D., Jeannerod, M., Procyk, E., Grassi, F. and Fazio, F. (1997) Brain activity during observation of actions. Influence of action content and subject's strategy. *Brain* 120, 1763–1777.

Duncan, S. (2005) Co-expressivity of speech and gesture: Manner of motion in Spanish, English, and Chinese. In C. Chang, M. Houser, Y. Kim, D. Mortensen, M. Park-Doob and M. Toosarvandani (eds) *Proceedings of the 27th Annual Meeting of the Berkeley Linguistic Society* (Vol. General Session and parasession) (pp. 353–370). Berkeley, CA: Berkeley Linguistics Society.

Francis, W. (2005) Bilingual semantic and conceptual representation. In J. Kroll and A. De Groot (eds) *Handbook of Bilingualism. Psycholinguistic Approaches* (pp. 251–267). Oxford: Oxford University Press.

Freleng, F. (1950) Canary Row [Film, animated cartoon]. New York: Time Warner.

Graham, R. and Belnap, K. (1986) The acquisition of lexical boundaries in English by native speakers of Spanish. *International Review of Applied Linguistics* 24, 275–286.

Graham, J. and Argyle, M. (1975) A cross-cultural study of the communication of extra-verbal meaning by gestures. *International Journal of Psychology* 10, 56–67.

Grosjean, F. (1998) Studying bilinguals: Methodological and conceptual issues. *Bilingualism: Language and Cognition* 1, 131–149.

Gullberg, M. (1998) *Gesture as a Communication Strategy in Second Language Discourse. A Study of Learners of French and Swedish.* Lund: Lund University Press.

Gullberg, M. (2006) Some reasons for studying gesture and second language acquisition (Hommage à Adam Kendon). *International Review of Applied Linguistics* 44, 103–124.

Gullberg, M. (2009) Reconstructing verb meaning in a second language: How English speakers of L2 Dutch talk and gesture about placement. *Annual Review of Cognitive Linguistics* 7, 222–245.

Gullberg, M. (2010a) Language-specific encoding of placement events in gestures. In J. Bohnemeyer and E. Pederson (eds) *Event Representations in Language and Cognition* (pp. 166–188). Cambridge: Cambridge University Press.

Gullberg, M. (2010b) Methodological reflections on gesture analysis in SLA and bilingualism research. *Second Language Research* 26 (1), 75–102.

Gullberg, M. (submitted a) Linguistic representations influence speech-associated gestures in the domain of placement.

Gullberg, M. (submitted b) What learners mean. What gestures reveal about semantic reorganisation of placement verbs in advanced L2.

Gullberg, M. and Burenhult, N. (in press) Probing the linguistic encoding of placement and removal events in Swedish. In A. Kopecka and B. Narasimhan (eds) *Events of "Putting" and "Taking": A Crosslinguistic Perspective.* Amsterdam: John Benjamins.

Gullberg, M., Hendriks, H. and Hickmann, M. (2008) Learning to talk and gesture about motion in French. *First Language* 28, 200–236.

Gullberg, M. and Narasimhan, B. (2010) What gestures reveal about the development of semantic distinctions in Dutch children's placement verbs. *Cognitive Linguistics* 21 (2), 239–262.

Gumperz, J. and Levinson, S. (1996) Introduction: Linguistic relativity re-examined. In J. Gumperz and S. Levinson (eds) *Rethinking Linguistic Relativity* (pp. 1–18). Cambridge: Cambridge University Press.

Han, Z. and Odlin, T. (2006) Introduction. In Z. Han and T. Odlin (eds) *Studies of Fossilization in Second Language Acquisition* (pp. 1–20). Clevedon: Multilingual Matters.

Haviland, J. (1996) Projections, transpositions, and relativity. In J. Gumperz and S. Levinson (eds) *Rethinking Linguistic Relativity* (pp. 271–323). Cambridge: Cambridge University Press.

Hickmann, M. and Hendriks, H. (2006) Static and dynamic location in French and English. *First Language* 26, 103–135.

Hickmann, M. and Robert, S. (eds) (2006) *Space across Languages: Linguistic Systems and Cognitive Categories.* Amsterdam: John Benjamins.

Hohenstein, J., Eisenberg, A. and Naigles, L. (2006) Is he floating across or crossing afloat? Cross-influence of L1 and L2 in Spanish–English bilingual adults. *Bilingualism: Language and Cognition* 9, 249–261.

Hyltenstam, K. and Abrahamsson, N. (2003) Maturational constraints in SLA. In C. Doughty and M. Long (eds) *Handbook of Second Language Acquisition* (pp. 539–588). Oxford: Blackwell.

Iverson, J. and Goldin-Meadow, S. (2005) Gesture paves the way for language development. *Psychological Science* 16, 367–371.

Jarvis, S. (1998) *Conceptual Transfer in the Interlingual Lexicon.* Bloomington, IN: Indiana University Linguistics Club Publications.

Jarvis, S. (2007) Theoretical and methodological issues in the investigation of conceptual transfer. *Vigo International Journal of Applied Linguistics* 4, 43–71.

Jarvis, S. and Pavlenko, A. (2008) *Crosslinguistic Influence in Language and Cognition.* New York/London: Routledge.

Jiang, N. (2000) Lexical representation and development in a second language. *Applied Linguistics* 21, 47–77.

Kellerman, E. (1979) Giving learners a break: Native language intuitions as a source of predictions about transferability. *Working Papers on Bilingualism* 15, 59–92.

Kellerman, E. (1995) Crosslinguistic influence: Transfer to nowhere? *Annual Review of Applied Linguistics* 15, 125–150.

Kellerman, E. and Sharwood Smith, M. (eds) (1986) *Crosslinguistic Influence in Second Language Acquisition.* New York: Pergamon.

Kellerman, E. and Van Hoof, A-M. (2003) Manual accents. *International Review of Applied Linguistics* 41, 251–269.

Kendon, A. (1980) Gesticulation and speech: Two aspects of the process of utterance. In M. Key (ed.) *The Relationship of Verbal and Nonverbal Communication* (pp. 207–227). The Hague: Mouton.

Kendon, A. (1983) Gesture and speech. How they interact. In J. Wiemann and R. Harrison (eds) *Nonverbal Interaction* (pp. 13–45). Beverly Hills, CA: Sage.

Kendon, A. (1994) Do gestures communicate?: A review. *Research on Language and Social Interaction* 27, 175–200.

Kendon, A. (2004) *Gesture. Visible Action as Utterance.* Cambridge: Cambridge University Press.

Kita, S. and Özyürek, A. (2003) What does crosslinguistic variation in semantic coordination of speech and gesture reveal?: Evidence for an interface representation of spatial thinking and speaking. *Journal of Memory and Language* 48, 16–32.

Kita, S., Özyurek, A., Allen, S., Brown, A., Furman, R. and Ishizuka, T. (2007) Relations between syntactic encoding and co-speech gestures: Implications for a model of speech and gesture production. *Language and Cognitive Processes* 22, 1212–1236.

Kita, S., Van Gijn, I. and Van der Hulst, H. (1998) Movement phases in signs and co-speech gestures, and their transcription by human coders. In I. Wachsmuth and M. Fröhlich (eds) *Gesture and Sign Language in Human-Computer Interaction* (pp. 23–35). Berlin: Springer.

Kopecka, A. and Narasimhan, B. (eds) (in press) *Events of "Putting" and "Taking": A Crosslinguistic Perspective*. Amsterdam: John Benjamins.

Kroll, J.F. and Sunderman, G. (2003) Cognitive processes in second language learners and bilinguals: The development of lexical and conceptual representations. In C. Doughty and M. Long (eds) *The Handbook of Second Language Acquisition* (pp. 104–129). Oxford: Blackwell.

Kutscher, S. and Schultze-Berndt, E. (2007) Why a folder lies in the basket although it is not lying: The semantics and use of German positional verbs with inanimate figures. *Linguistics* 45, 983–1028.

Lemmens, M. (2002) Tracing referent location in oral picture descriptions. In A. Wilson, P. Rayson and T. McEnery (eds) *A Rainbow of Corpora. Corpus Linguistics and the Languages of the World* (pp. 73–85). München: Lincom-Europa.

Lemmens, M. (2006) Caused posture: Experiential patterns emerging from corpus research. In A. Stefanowitsch and S. Gries (eds) *Corpora in Cognitive Linguistics. Corpus-based Approaches to Syntax and Lexis* (pp. 263–298). Berlin: Mouton de Gruyter.

Levelt, W. (1989) *Speaking: From Intention to Articulation*. Cambridge, MA: Bradford Books/MIT Press.

Levinson, S. and Wilkins, D. (eds) (2006) *Grammars of Space. Explorations in Cognitive Diversity*. Cambridge: Cambridge University Press.

Levy, E. and McNeill, D. (1992) Speech, gesture, and discourse. *Discourse Processes* 15, 277–301.

Lucy, J. (1996) The scope of linguistic relativity: An analysis and review of empirical research. In J. Gumperz and S. Levinson (eds) *Rethinking Linguistic Relativity* (pp. 37–69). Cambridge: Cambridge University Press.

Malt, B. and Sloman, S. (2003) Linguistic diversity and object naming by non-native speakers of English. *Bilingualism: Language and Cognition* 6, 47–67.

Mayberry, R. and Jaques, J. (2000) Gesture production during stuttered speech: Insights into the nature of gesture-speech integration. In D. McNeill (ed.) *Language and Gesture* (pp. 199–214). Cambridge: Cambridge University Press.

McNeill, D. (1985) So you think gestures are nonverbal? *Psychological Review* 92, 271–295.

McNeill, D. (1992) *Hand and Mind. What the Hands Reveal about Thought*. Chicago, IL: University of Chicago Press.

McNeill, D. (2000) Imagery in motion event descriptions: Gestures as part of thinking-for-speaking in three languages. In M. Juge and J. Moxley (eds) *Proceedings of the 23rd Annual Meeting of the Berkeley Linguistics Society* (Vol. General session and parasession) (pp. 255–267). Berkeley, CA: Berkeley Linguistics Society.

McNeill, D. (2005) *Gesture and Thought*. Chicago, IL: University of Chicago Press.

McNeill, D. and Duncan, S. (2000) Growth points in thinking-for-speaking. In D. McNeill (ed.) *Language and Gesture* (pp. 141–161). Cambridge: Cambridge University Press.

Narasimhan, B. and Gullberg, M. (2010) The role of input frequency and semantic transparency in the acquisition of verb meaning. Evidence from placement verbs in Tamil and Dutch. *Journal of Child Language*.

Negueruela, E., Lantolf, J., Rehn Jordan, S. and Gelabert, J. (2004) The "private function" of gesture in second language speaking activity: A study of motion verbs and gesturing in English and Spanish. *International Journal of Applied Linguistics* 14, 113–147.

Nicoladis, E., Mayberry, R. and Genesee, F. (1999) Gesture and early bilingual development. *Developmental Psychology* 35, 514–526.

Odlin, T. (2003) crosslinguistic influence. In C. Doughty and M. Long (eds) *The Handbook of Second Language Acquisition* (pp. 436–486). Oxford: Blackwell.

Odlin, T. (2005) Crosslinguistic influence and conceptual transfer: What are the concepts? *Annual Review of Applied Linguistics* 25, 3–25.

Özyürek, A. (2002) Speech-language relationship across languages and in second language learners: Implications for spatial thinking and speaking. In B. Skarabela (ed.) *BUCLD Proceedings* (Vol. 26) (pp. 500–509). Somerville, MA: Cascadilla Press.

Özyürek, A. and Kelly, S. (eds) (2007) Special issue: Gesture, brain, and language. *Brain and Language* 101, 181–184.

Pavlenko, A. (2005) Bilingualism and thought. In J. Kroll and A. De Groot (eds) *Handbook of Bilingualism: Psycholinguistic Approaches* (pp. 433–453). Oxford: Oxford University Press.

Pavlenko, A. (2009) Conceptual representation in the bilingual lexicon and second language vocabulary learning. In A. Pavlenko (ed.) *The Bilingual Mental Lexicon: Interdisciplinary Approaches* (pp. 125–160). Bristol: Multilingual Matters.

Pavlenko, A. and Jarvis, S. (2002) Bidirectional transfer. *Applied Linguistics* 23, 190–214.

Rauscher, F.H., Krauss, R.M. and Chen, Y. (1996) Gesture, speech and lexical access: The role of lexical movements in speech production. *Psychological Science* 7, 226–231.

Ringbom, H. (2007) *crosslinguistic Similarity in Foreign Language Learning*. Clevedon: Multilingual Matters.

Rogers, W. (1978) The contribution of kinesic illustrators toward the comprehension of verbal behavior within utterances. *Human Communication Research* 5, 54–62.

Selinker, L. (1972) Interlanguage. *International Review of Applied Linguistics* 10, 209–231.

Seyfeddinipur, M. (2006) Disfluency: Interrupting speech and gesture. PhD dissertation, Radboud University, Nijmegen.

Slobin, D. (1996) From "thought and language" to "thinking for speaking". In J. Gumperz and S. Levinson (eds) *Rethinking Linguistic Relativity* (pp. 70–96). Cambridge: Cambridge University Press.

Slobin, D. (1997) The origins of grammaticizable notions: Beyond the individual mind. In D. Slobin (ed.) *The Crosslinguistic Study of Language Acquisition* (Vol. 5. Expanding the contexts) (pp. 265–323). Mahwah, NJ: Lawrence Erlbaum.

Slobin, D. (2004a) How people move. Discourse effects of linguistic typology. In C. Moder and A. Martinovic-Zic (eds) *Discourse across Languages and Cultures* (pp. 195–210). Amsterdam: John Benjamins.

Slobin, D. (2004b) The many ways to search for a frog. In S. Strömqvist and L. Verhoeven (eds) *Relating Events in Narrative: Typological and Contextual Perspectives* (pp. 219–257). Hillsdale, NJ: Lawrence Erlbaum.

Slobin, D. (2006) What makes manner of motion salient? Explorations in linguistic typology, discourse, and cognition. In M. Hickmann and S. Robert (eds) *Space in*

Languages: Linguistic Systems and Cognitive Categories (pp. 59–81). Amsterdam: John Benjamins.

Slobin, D. and Hoiting, N. (1994) Reference to movement in spoken and signed languages: Typological considerations. In S. Gahl, A. Dolbey and C. Johnson (eds) *Proceedings of the 20th Annual Meeting of the Berkeley Linguistics Society* (Vol. General session dedicated to the contributions of Charles J. Fillmore) (pp. 487–503). Berkeley, CA: Berkeley Linguistics Society.

Stam, G. (2006) Thinking for speaking about motion: L1 and L2 speech and gesture. *International Review of Applied Linguistics* 44, 143–169.

Strömqvist, S. and Verhoeven, L. (eds) (2004) *Relating Events in Narrative: Typological and Contextual Perspectives*. Hillsdale, NJ: Lawrence Erlbaum.

Talmy, L. (1985) Lexicalization patterns: Semantic structure in lexical forms. In T. Shopen (ed.) *Language Typology and Syntactic Description* (Vol. 3) (pp. 57–149). Cambridge: Cambridge University Press.

Talmy, L. (1991) Paths to realization: A typology of event conflation. In L. Sutton, C. Johnson and R. Shields (eds) *Proceedings of the Berkeley Linguistics Society* (Vol. 17) (pp. 480–519). Berkeley, CA: Berkeley Linguistics Society.

Tang, G. and Yang, G. (2007) Events of motion and causation in Hong Kong sign language. *Lingua* 117, 1216–1257.

Tesnière, L. (1959) *Éléments de syntaxe structurale*. Klincksieck: Paris.

v. Stutterheim, Ch. and Nüse, R. (2003) Processes of conceptualization in language production: Language-specific perspectives and event construal. *Linguistics* 41, 851–881.

Van Hell, J. and Dijkstra, T. (2002) Foreign language knowledge can influence native language performance in exclusively native contexts. *Psychonomic Bulletin & Review* 9, 780–789.

Viberg, Å. (1998) Crosslinguistic perspectives on lexical acquisition: The case of language-specific semantic differentiation. In K. Haastrup and Å. Viberg (eds) *Perspectives on Lexical Acquisition in a Second Language* (pp. 175–208). Lund: Lund University Press.

Wieselman Schulman, B. (2004) A crosslinguistic investigation of the speech-gesture relationship in motion event descriptions. PhD dissertation, University of Chicago.

Yule, G. (1997) *Referential Communication Tasks*. Hillsdale, NJ: Lawrence Erlbaum.

Chapter 6

The Art and Science of Bilingual Object Naming

BARBARA C. MALT and EEF AMEEL

6.1 Introduction

Languages of the world differ from each other in many ways – ranging from aspects of phonology and morphology to syntax and semantics. So, second language (L2) learners and children growing up with more than one language face a challenge of some magnitude in sorting out and mastering the different linguistic systems. Bilingualism researchers, in turn, face the challenge of understanding how a single individual manages to acquire and selectively use these different systems to communicate appropriately with speakers of each language.

Learners and researchers alike presumably find some relief when they encounter shared elements of languages – elements that do not need to be disentangled by the learner, nor examined by the researcher. It has often been assumed that the knowledge associated with nouns for concrete objects (such as those naming chairs, sofas, bottles and jars) would be one such shared element, corresponding closely across languages. That is, although the specific words to be learned would differ by language, the associated knowledge would be parallel. Mastery would then be just a matter of paired-associate learning (e.g. learning that *chair* =*silla* and *bottle* =*botella* for English and Spanish), a process easy for the learner to engage in and easy for the researcher to explain. Below, we describe research that shows this assumption to be wrong. We then describe research that evaluates the implications of this finding for how the knowledge associated with concrete nouns develops in L2 learners, and how it develops in those exposed to two languages from infancy.

6.2 Nouns for Human-made Objects do not Correspond Neatly across Languages

It has sometimes been proposed that the world presents itself as an unstructured 'kaleidoscope flux of impressions' (Whorf, 1956) on which the human observer imposes structure (Leach, 1976). But Rosch and Mervis (1975), building on perspectives from Berlin (1978) and others, suggested the opposite: the world presents readily perceived structure to the observer. According to this proposal, properties in the world occur in clusters – i.e. things with wings typically have feathers and beaks, while things without wings do not – and humans appreciate the existence of these property clusters. In this view, information about the world is stored in memory in terms of these clusters, providing the foundation for coherent concepts, such as those concerning birds, dogs, chairs and jars. Common nouns, such as English *bird*, *dog*, *chair* and *jar*, are associated with the resultant representations, providing the means to communicate about them.

The structured-world hypothesis makes a strong prediction about the knowledge associated with nouns across languages. If the content of this knowledge is strongly determined by perceived structure in the world, then it should be similar across languages. The nouns themselves, of course, will differ, but the associated knowledge should be closely comparable. For instance, one would expect to see that the knowledge associated with the English word *chair*, and the set of objects appropriately labeled *chair* by a speaker of English, would be essentially the same as for the Spanish word *silla*. In the literature on bilingualism, this idea has often been implicitly taken as correct. Researchers typically treat common nouns referring to concrete objects as translation equivalents, although they acknowledge more crosslinguistic variation for abstract nouns and other parts of speech (e.g. De Groot, 2002; Kroll, 1993).

In fact, this idea may be accurate or close to it for some domains. The properties that provide the basis for genus-level distinctions among mammals, for instance, may occur in relatively strong clusters, with few or no instances having properties coming from more than one cluster. This idea is endorsed by biologists who work on classification and taxonomy (e.g. Simpson, 1961). Furthermore, ethnobiological research has suggested that readily perceived property clusters result in similar lexical distinctions across many languages. The sets of animals and plants set apart by name tend to correspond well across many languages and cultures (Berlin, 1978; Hunn, 1977; see Malt, 1995, for a review).

But, the situation may be more complicated for human-made objects (artifacts) for several reasons. Correlations among the properties of these objects may be weaker because individuals and manufacturers are constantly finding new ways to combine functional and physical features to make innovative products. If weak or unclear clustering of properties in the world exists in this domain, it is likely to make the contribution of the human observer greater in determining what objects are segregated from others by name. Outcomes may vary across language communities depending on their specific needs and desires. For instance, a group with an elaborate cooking culture may distinguish soup *tureens* (for serving) from soup *bowls* (for eating) and soup *pots* (for cooking), despite the many similarities of tureens to things called *bowl* and *pot*. The potential for referential ambiguity blocks the use of *bowl* or *pot* for the tureen. At the same time, a manufacturer in the culture may have a goal of having consumers think of a reusable child's juice container as a substitute for disposable cardboard juice boxes. Thus, it markets its plastic version as a juice *box* despite shaping it like a bear or lion, thereby creating a naming chain that expands the range of this particular term, *box*. Because artifacts are made by humans, the objects present at any moment in history will vary from culture to culture, and this variation will also influence which objects seem distinctive enough to warrant being distinguished with a novel name. This variation, in turn, will influence the set of names and their referential ranges that get passed on to the next generation of speakers and that form the background against which that generation distinguishes or groups new objects by name.

Furthermore, even when different language communities are associated with similar histories of artifacts, they may differ in their histories of language contact. Incorporation of new words from outside can spawn shifts in meanings to avoid synonymy (e.g. Clark, 2007), expanding or contracting referential ranges. Thus, the potential for languages to display different patterns of dividing objects by name for common artifacts is substantial. Because the naming pattern of a language at any moment of history reflects its past evolutionary history, this will hold true even though modern forces of globalization make the same artifacts familiar across many cultures these days, giving current speakers of diverse languages largely the same stimulus space to communicate about. Many name choices can end up arbitrary even to native speakers of the language; they will be learned simply as conventions of their language rather than as choices transparently motivated by property clusters and the perceived similarity among the objects.

We have found that there is indeed a surprising degree of variation in naming patterns for the sorts of commercial household containers that are familiar nowadays across many cultures (Malt *et al.*, 1999). We asked native (largely monolingual) speakers of American English, Argentinean Spanish and Mandarin Chinese to name a set of 60 pictures of containers for products such as ketchup, aspirin, salsa, toothpaste and shampoo. Roughly equal numbers of the objects were called *bottle, jar* and *container* (16, 19 and 15, respectively) by American English speakers, with a few called *jug, tube* or *box*. Argentinean Spanish speakers called almost half the objects by a single name, *frasco* (and its diminutive, *frasquito*), and divided the remainder among 14 different names. Chinese speakers called 40 of the objects by a single name (*ping*), 10 more by another name (*guan*) and had three additional names for the remaining 10. Ameel *et al.* (2005) found similar discrepancies between Belgian Dutch and Belgian French for such containers. A smaller scale study by Kronenfeld *et al.* (1985) showed similar variations in the naming patterns for cups, glasses and other drinking vessels used by speakers of English, Japanese and Hebrew, and Pavlenko and Malt (in press) found such variation for drinking vessels between speakers of American English and Russian (see also Pavlenko, this volume).

One might wonder whether these variations merely represent a tendency to name at different levels of abstraction. That is, are the lexical categories (the sets of objects called by a single name) in one language a neat subset of the lexical categories of another? For instance, were the 15 Spanish names neatly sub-dividing the smaller number of English names? Malt *et al.* (2003) found that the smaller categories of one language did not necessarily fit neatly into a larger category of another. They were just as likely to include objects that fell into two or more different categories of the other language. Lexical categories of similar size likewise often showed some cross-cutting category members. Several pairs of lexical categories did share similar prototypes (such as English *jar* with Spanish *frasco*), as measured by the typicality ratings of the objects as members of the categories. However, they did not necessarily share boundaries (i.e. *frasco* encompasses a much wider range of objects than *jar*). So, it seems that the differences in lexical categories of the three languages go beyond merely how finely they differentiate within a domain. Instead, the data implicate a more complex set of interacting factors such as the evolutionary processes we suggested above.

This crosslinguistic variation in referential ranges of object names that we have documented, and by implication the knowledge associated with the nouns, poses obvious challenges for people raised with exposure to two or more languages or who speak one language and want to master a second. These people receive input from different languages that give them different ways of lexically dividing the same stimulus space and bear different implications for the meaning they should attach to the words of the domain. How they handle these conflicting inputs is the main focus of the rest of this chapter.

6.3 Patterns of Word Use and their Relation to Non-linguistic Thought

Before we turn to our central issue, we briefly consider an associated issue: if someone learns two languages that provide different ways of *talking* about the domain, must they switch between two ways of *thinking* about the domain? Our answer is 'not necessarily'.

We take this position for several reasons. First, from a theoretical perspective, we note that language evolved to facilitate communication, not thought (Clark, 1996). What people express in language represents only a small fraction of their encoded experiences with the world (Clark, 2003; Gleitman & Papafragou, 2005) and of the stored information they must draw on in acting on the world. Models of language production make clear that it is possible in principle to selectively package elements of non-linguistic representation for linguistic output without feedback from the linguistic representations influencing the earlier layers (Levelt *et al.*, 1999; Vigliocco *et al.*, 2004). Thus, we see no *a priori* reason to assume that language output requirements affect the many non-linguistic processes involved in experiencing and acting on the world – such as taking in and interpreting sensory input, storing results of that interpretation in memory in rich detail beyond that captured in linguistic description, and drawing inferences using the stored interpretation.

Second, from a logical perspective, if one takes as a starting assumption that all lexical differences are indicative of differences in non-linguistic thought, then the Whorfian hypothesis that language influences non-linguistic thought becomes untestable. One has already drawn a conclusion about the answer based only on the linguistic evidence, making the hypothesis impossible to falsify, thereby placing it outside the scope of scientific inquiry. Only evidence from tasks independent of word use can provide a test of the hypothesis by allowing it to be either supported or rejected. And finally, from an empirical perspective, we have found that speakers of English, Spanish and Chinese sort the objects in our stimulus set according to their similarities in much the same say, agreeing with one another in this task to a significantly greater degree than they do in naming (Malt *et al.*, 1999). The same contrast between shared similarity judgments and language-specific naming patterns was found for other language groups by Ameel *et al.* (2005) and by Kronenfeld *et al.* (1985). The shared similarity ratings indicate that, in at least some domains, speakers of different languages perceive object properties in much the same way (implying shared non-linguistic understanding of them) even though they group the objects by name differently. For objects like common household objects, this state of affairs may come about because most knowledge of the objects' proper-ties comes from directly observing and using the objects rather than through language.

Thus, we do not assume that when people name things differently in different languages, they necessarily have different non-linguistic ways of thinking about the domain or the objects. In the discussion of our work that follows, we talk about *lexical* categories and about differences between speakers of different languages in their *lexical* or *semantic* knowledge (the knowledge associated with words), but not about general purpose, non-linguistic categories and concepts. We do not rule out the possibility that there are consequences of lexical differences that affect non-linguistic cognition, but the work presented here contains no data that we believe merit interpretation as evidence for that possibility.

6.4 The Problem of Artifact Nouns for Late Second Language Learners

We began our investigations of how people exposed to two languages deal with the languages' differing naming patterns (their patterns of application of words to objects) by studying a group of 68 people who came to the USA with first languages (L1) other than English (Malt & Sloman, 2003). The native languages varied, with Asian languages most common, but also including Spanish, Turkish and others. All participants were immersed in English at the time of testing, with most being university undergraduate or graduate students. However, the length of immersion ranged from a few weeks to 18 years. For stimuli, we used the set of 60 common household containers that we had studied earlier (Malt *et al.*, 1999) and an additional set of 60 photos of objects mostly used for preparing and serving food (things usually called *bowl*, *dish* or *plate* in English). We asked the participants to name each picture in English. At the end, they gave us their intuitions about how they selected names by choosing from options that ranged from using specific features to going with what 'just felt right'. Each participant also rated each object's typicality with respect to the major English lexical categories for its set (typicality as *bottle*, *jar* and *container* for the first set of objects and as *bowl*, *dish* and *plate* for the other set). Native speakers of English (about 25 for each stimulus set) performed the same naming and typicality tasks for comparison.

Because even native speakers vary among themselves to some degree in the names they produce for most objects and in typicality judgments, we developed a baseline score for each object, for each task, that reflected the average degree of agreement of individual native speakers to the aggregated native speakers. We could then compare their level of agreement with the level for non-native speakers. Our L2 learners had sufficient command of English to carry out everyday activities in English, including university-level studies, and we found that even those with the shortest length of immersion (less than one year) produced most of the same basic vocabulary words in the naming task that native speakers did. Where they fell short was in their application of the words to specific objects. Dividing the learners into four groups of approximately equal size based on their years of immersion in English (combining speakers of different native languages), we found that learners with less than one year of immersion used naming patterns that diverged quite a bit from the aggregated native speakers. Agreement scores across the other groups increased as a function of years of immersion. The same was true for judgments of typicality, demonstrating that those with the fewest years of immersion lacked a good grasp of what a typical bottle or plate is, but this grasp improved over time. Strategy reports also showed a shift across years of immersion from greater reliance on explicit use of specific features or translation equivalents to a more intuitive selection of words. What was most surprising, though, was that even the participant group with the longest length of immersion (10 or more years) still showed significantly less agreement with the aggregated native speakers than individual native speakers did for most of the words, and this was true in both naming patterns and typicality judgments. Despite their lengthy immersion in English, their word use was not fully native-like.

This study demonstrates that mastering the subtleties of the naming patterns of an L2 is a long and difficult process. This lengthy nature of the process could reflect interference from having a different set of patterns already entrenched. That is, the L2 learner must overcome well-established habits of naming that group of objects differently, and it is natural to suppose that doing so will be difficult. This indeed was our original interpretation of the extended learning period we observed. But we found, in a subsequent study, that children learning a single native language took up to age 14 to fully converge on adult naming patterns for similar sets of stimuli (Ameel *et al.*, 2008; see also Andersen, 1975). This outcome suggests that we may need to adjust our interpretation because even when a learner is dealing with only one language, these artifact categories are apparently complex enough that extensive language experience is required to fully master the patterns involved.

However, we have not compared the types of errors made by L2 learners to the types of errors made by children. It is possible that they are governed by different sources of difficulty. If there is a neurologically driven critical period effect (e.g. Birdsong, 1999) that encompasses word learning, early word learning may differ from later word learning regardless of how many languages are involved. It has been argued that word learning draws on domain-general learning mechanisms (e.g. Bloom, 2000; Markson & Bloom, 1997; Smith, 1999) that are not subject to critical period effects. However, age effects could still exist for other reasons. L1 interference may indeed be a major force for L2 learners (e.g. Jiang, 2000), whereas immature understanding of object features (such as function) or other cognitive developmental issues may be an added source of error for children (e.g. Ameel *et al.*, 2008; Mervis, 1987). A comparison of the two learning trajectories would help clarify to what extent L2 word learning for common nouns is distinct from L1 learning.

We also do not yet know what becomes of the noun categories of the L1 in the process of L2 learning. Some evidence from other studies suggests that there may be a backward influence such that learning a new pattern alters the old (Pavlenko, 2003; Wolff & Ventura, 2003). Reaction-time studies have demonstrated that the lexicon of one language can interact with that of another in some fashion. For instance, words of one language can prime words in the other (e.g. Altarriba, 1992; Kroll & Curley, 1988;

Schwanenflugel & Rey, 1986). Given this potential for interaction between the two systems, the L2 learner may not only be acquiring a second naming pattern, but also altering the first in the process. This is a fascinating possibility that requires more research, currently ongoing (Pavlenko & Malt, in press; see also Pavlenko, this volume).

The possibility of interference or cross-talk between the two languages of L2 learners also makes particularly intriguing the question of what language learners do when faced with exposure to two languages from the start. One possibility is that these early learners, acquiring two native languages during the period in which language acquisition proceeds most effortlessly, are able to do something late learners are not, namely, learn and maintain two separate systems of naming that each fully matches that used by monolinguals in each language. The alternative possibility is that despite early exposure, these children are still not able to accomplish this feat (at least with regard to the lexicon) and, in some way, must achieve a compromise between the languages. This may be particularly likely if the arguments against a critical period for word learning hold true, and if word learning processes and the nature of the resultant representations are fundamentally the same regardless of age. The remainder of this chapter will focus on our recent investigations of how simultaneous bilinguals (exposed to two languages from birth) manage the challenge of word learning when faced with the overlapping but distinct patterns of naming in their two languages.

6.5 How Simultaneous Bilinguals Solve the Naming Problem

Our subsequent research investigated how differences between languages in naming patterns affect word knowledge and use for people learning two languages from infancy. In one study, we examined the relation between how simultaneous bilinguals name in one of their languages and how they name in the other, and also the relation of their two language patterns to the naming patterns of monolinguals in each language (Ameel *et al.*, 2005).

We considered two contrasting hypotheses about these relations. The *two-pattern hypothesis* is based on the possibility that there are no interactions, connections or feedback loops between the two languages of simultaneous bilinguals (or that the effects of any such interactions can be overcome). If this is true, simultaneous bilinguals should acquire and maintain two distinct sets of word-object connections, and the bilingual naming pattern for each language separately will parallel that of the corresponding monolinguals. The *one-pattern hypothesis* is based on the possibility that simultaneous bilinguals develop direct inter-connections or indirect feedback loops between the word forms of the two languages that influence the lexical representations. If this is true, their word knowledge in each language may contain elements of the naming patterns of both languages and consequently may deviate from the knowledge of both monolingual groups. Word-object connections in the two languages in this case will be tuned to one another, and the two naming patterns may merge into a single pattern that differs from either monolingual naming pattern. The truth may also be situated somewhere in-between: the two naming patterns of simultaneous bilinguals may converge toward one common naming pattern, but not match perfectly.

Participants were recruited in Belgium, a bilingual country. Belgium's two largest regions are the Dutch-speaking region of Flanders in the north and the French-speaking region of Wallonia in the south. In Belgium, Dutch- and French-speaking monolinguals live alongside bilinguals who have been raised learning Dutch and French simultaneously.

Naming data and similarity judgments were collected for ordinary household objects from Dutch- and French-speaking monolinguals and Dutch-French bilinguals. We asked whether the different naming patterns we previously found for speakers of languages on three different continents, with substantially different modern cultures as well as linguistic histories, could be replicated with monolingual language groups that largely share the same culture. We also asked whether the dissociation between naming and similarity perception found by Malt *et al.* (1999) would be replicated. Given a positive answer to both, the key question we then addressed was how and to what extent the Dutch and French bilingual naming patterns are related to each other and to the corresponding monolingual patterns.

Three language groups of about 25–30 participants each were tested. Monolingual speakers of Dutch were students or research assistants at the Psychology Department of the University of Leuven, and monolingual speakers of French were students at the Psychology Department of the University of Liège. The participants we considered monolingual for this purpose did have some knowledge of the other language through limited formal instruction at school. However, only three used the other language in their daily activities (three native speakers of Dutch sometimes used French at work) and none rated himself/herself proficient in it on a 7-point scale. Belgian students also typically have some secondary school instruction in English, but these monolinguals did not regularly use any language other than their native tongue.

Each of the bilingual participants had one parent who spoke Dutch and another who spoke French and had been raised speaking both languages by virtue of each parent consistently speaking his or her own language to them. These participants were students (and one research assistant) at the universities of Leuven, Brussels and Louvain-la-Neuve. As with the monolinguals, they would have also had some exposure to

English language instruction in school, but they did not regularly use any languages other than Dutch and French.

Two sets of stimuli were used. One consisted of 73 pictures of household storage containers for food, cleaning products, health and beauty aids, etc. (similar to those in Malt *et al.*, 1999). The other consisted of 67 pictures of cups and dishes for preparing and serving food and drink (similar to those in Malt & Sloman, 2003). The objects were all found at home, work or in stores frequented by the researchers. Since the objects are found throughout Belgium, all three participant groups should have comparable levels of familiarity with the stimulus set. To allow a sensitive comparison of naming patterns, we aimed to include objects that represented the full variability within each domain. Figures 6.1 and 6.2 illustrate some stimuli of, respectively, the bottles and dishes set.

Each participant performed the naming task (for both stimulus sets) followed by the sorting task. Bilinguals named the objects twice in succession (once in Dutch and once in French). To provide an appropriate task set, instructions were provided in the language in which the task was performed: Dutch for the Dutch-speaking monolinguals and for the bilinguals in the Dutch naming task, French for the French-speaking monolinguals and for the bilinguals in the French naming task. The order of the two sets and the order of the two languages for bilinguals were counterbalanced. Participants could give whatever name seemed best or most natural to them. In the sorting task, participants sorted the objects into piles according to overall similarity. They could use as many piles as they wanted, but they were required to use at least two and were discouraged from creating piles containing only one object.

6.5.1 Replication of Malt *et al.* (1999): Naming and sorting by monolinguals

We evaluated whether Dutch and French monolinguals show different naming patterns for these sets of objects and whether any differences in naming are matched by differences in similarity judgments. To compare the naming patterns, we tallied for both language groups the frequency of each name produced for each object. Tallies were based on the head noun of the response (e.g. *fles*, *plastieken fles* and *kleine fles* all counted as instances of the category *fles*). For each object, the dominant category name (i.e. the most frequently produced name) was determined. Tables 6.1 and 6.2 show the dominant category names for the bottles and dishes sets, respectively, together with the number of objects in the set for which each name was dominant.

Tables 6.1 and 6.2 reveal some clear resemblances in how the two languages classify the objects. For instance, in the bottles set, most of the objects called *pot* in Dutch are put into one single French category *pot*,

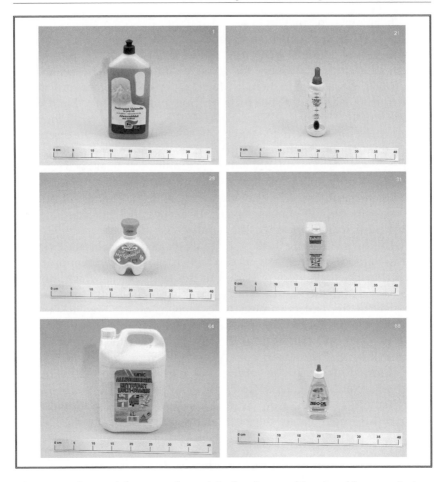

Figure 6.1 Some of the exemplars of the bottles set. (Reprinted by permission, Elsevier Ltd.)

and all the Dutch *tubes* are put together into the French category *tube*. On the other hand, there are also clear differences between the naming patterns of the two languages. For instance, again in the bottles set, the 25 objects called *fles* in Dutch are split into two categories in French: 13 are called *bouteille* and 10 are called *flacon*. The Dutch category *bus* does not have a close correspondence to any French category, with the *bus* objects spread over six French categories (*bouteille, flacon, spray, bidon, brique* and *bombe*).[1]

The dominant names do not capture all the variation in naming produced. For example, only five objects in the bottles set were called by the same name by every Dutch monolingual participant, and the same

Figure 6.2 Some of the exemplars of the dishes set. (Reprinted by permission, Elsevier Ltd.)

was true for the French monolingual participants. To further assess the relation of the naming patterns of the two languages, we used the complete name distribution for each object. For instance, a given object might have been called *bus* 5 times, *fles* 10 times and *pot* 2 times, and *brik*, *doos*, *tube*, etc., 0 times.

Following Malt *et al.* (1999), we first correlated each object's name distribution values with every other object's distribution values within a language group (and stimulus set). This provides a measure, for each pair of objects, of the degree to which the two objects were similarly named by speakers of the language. We then correlated the resultant pair-wise name similarity matrix for one language group with the other

Table 6.1 Linguistic categories for the bottles set for Dutch- and French-speaking monolinguals, and the Dutch composition of each French category

Dutch categories	n	French categories	n	Dutch composition
fles	25	bouteille	16	13 fles, 3 bus
bus	16	flacon	16	10 fles, 3 bus, 2 pot, 1 roller
pot	13	pot	10	9 pot, 1 fles
brik	4	boîte	7	3 doos, 2 brik, 1 blik, 1 pot
doos	4	tube	6	4 tube, 1 pot, 1 stick
tube	4	spray	5	5 bus
blik	2	bidon	3	3 bus
mand	1	brique	2	1 bus, 1 doos
molen	1	berlingo	2	2 brik
roller	1	biberon	1	1 fles
stick	1	bombe	1	1 bus
vat	1	canette	1	1 blik
		pannier	1	1 mand
		poivrier	1	1 molen
		salière	1	1 vat

Source: Reprinted by permission, Elsevier Ltd.

group's matrix. This correlation value indicates the extent to which the two language groups correspond overall in the pairs of objects that have similar name distributions. For the bottles set, the correlation was 0.63; for the dishes set, it was 0.80 ($p < 0.01$ for both). These correlations are substantial, but far from perfect, since only 40% and 64% of the variance, respectively, is accounted for. Thus, both the dominant names and these correlations between the name distribution similarities indicate that the French- and Dutch-speaking monolinguals have differences in their naming, along with the similarities.

To investigate whether the monolingual language groups differed in non-linguistic similarity perception, we derived a measure of non-linguistic similarity for each pair of objects from the sorting data. For each possible pair of objects, we counted how many participants of a language group placed that pair into the same pile. A large number of participants putting a pair of objects in the same pile is evidence for high

Table 6.2 Linguistic categories for the dishes set for Dutch- and French-speaking monolinguals, and the Dutch composition of each French category

Dutch categories	n	French categories	n	Dutch composition
kom	19	plat	19	11 schaal, 7 kom, 1 bord
tas	15	tasse	17	15 tas, 1 beker, 1 pot
schaal	13	bol	12	11 kom, 1 schaal
bord	8	assiette	8	7 bord, 1 schaal
beker	4	chope	3	2 beker, 1 glas
pot	4	pot	3	3 pot
glas	2	bougeoir	1	1 houder
asbak	1	caquelon	1	1 kom
houder	1	cendrier	1	1 asbak
		gobelet	1	1 beker
		verre	1	1 glas

Source: Reprinted by permission, Elsevier Ltd.

perceived similarity and a smaller number is evidence for lower perceived similarity. The matrices of pair-wise non-linguistic similarity judgments of the two language groups were then correlated to determine whether the groups agreed on which pairs were more and less similar. The resultant correlations of 0.87 for the bottles set and 0.88 for the dishes set ($p < 0.01$ for both) indicate that the French- and Dutch-speaking monolinguals agree to a considerable extent on the similarities among the bottles.

Last, following Malt *et al.* (1999), we assessed whether the degree of differences in naming by the two groups was matched by the degree of differences in perceived similarity. We applied the cultural consensus model (CCM) of Romney *et al.* (1986) to both the naming and sorting data. The idea of the CCM is to represent the relations among the responses of all participants regardless of group, using an association measure, and then see if group differences emerge in a principal components analysis (see Ameel *et al.*, 2005, for details). If there are no group differences in a task, the best fitting model would be a model with one factor on which the language groups load equally. If there are differences between groups, then several factors should emerge that distinguish the groups.

For both naming and sorting, two factors emerged that distinguished the Dutch- and French-speaking monolinguals. However, the improvement in fit from the one-factor model to the two-factor model was substantially smaller for the sorting data than for the naming data. This outcome indicates that the monolingual language groups show larger differences in naming than in sorting. So the dissociation between naming and similarity found by Malt *et al.* (1999) for speakers of English, Chinese and Spanish was replicated here with speakers of two languages who live in close contact and largely share a culture. Crosslinguistic differences in naming patterns for common objects do not seem to derive from differences in similarity perception, nor from differences in item familiarity or current cultural differences. Rather, as we discussed earlier, they more likely stem from differences in the histories of the languages and cultures.

6.5.2 Naming in simultaneous bilinguals

Of most central interest is how the Dutch and French naming patterns of bilinguals relate to each other and the naming patterns of the monolinguals. For each stimulus set, we calculated the correlation between the name distribution similarities of the bilinguals speaking Dutch and speaking French. These correlations were compared to the corresponding correlations between the Dutch-speaking and French-speaking monolinguals.

The two contrasting hypotheses concerning bilingual lexical organization make different predictions about these correlations. The two-pattern hypothesis predicts that the correlation between the name distribution similarities of the bilinguals in Dutch and in French will be equal to the correlation between the name distribution similarities of the Dutch- and French-speaking monolinguals. The one-pattern hypothesis – at least the strong version of it – predicts that there will be a perfect match (a correlation of 1) between the two naming patterns of bilinguals. A more moderate version suggests that the bilingual correlation will not be perfect but will be significantly larger than the monolingual correlation.

The correlations between the two naming patterns of the bilinguals for the bottles dishes set were 0.88 and 0.91, respectively. These correlations are significantly larger than the corresponding correlations between the naming patterns of Dutch- and French-speaking monolinguals, which were 0.68 and 0.80. These results are inconsistent with the two-pattern hypothesis, and more consistent with the one-pattern hypothesis. However, they also suggest that the strong version of the one-pattern hypothesis is too strong, since the correlations between the two naming patterns of the bilinguals are not perfect. This outcome points to a moderate version of the one-pattern hypothesis, namely, that the two naming patterns of simultaneous bilinguals shift toward each other, but do not completely converge.

In sum, the results showed that the simultaneous bilinguals agreed better on naming in their two languages than monolinguals of the two languages did. This outcome provides a clear conclusion. Simultaneous bilinguals do not seem to be able to develop and maintain two separate naming patterns for common household artifacts that fully match monolingual patterns in a given language. Rather, the naming patterns of bilinguals in their two languages converge toward each other.

6.6 What Converges in Semantic Convergence?

In a follow-up study (Ameel *et al.*, 2009), we have investigated in more detail which aspects of lexical category structure in simultaneous bilinguals are affected by the convergence our previous study documented. Depending on how much experience with word-object mappings is needed to overcome the cross-language influence and to establish monolingual-like mappings, category centers and boundaries can be affected by convergence to different extents. Convergence may be more pronounced in the category boundaries than in the category centers, since boundary exemplars are less frequently encountered than centrally situated exemplars. Memory traces for low-frequency atypical exemplars may be weaker than those for high-frequency typical exemplars and more susceptible to the influence of input in the other language. However, the possibility of convergence in the category centers cannot be excluded. Thus, we examined both the centers and the boundaries of lexical categories in the two languages of a bilingual to see whether and how semantic convergence was manifested in each.

6.6.1 Category centers

To investigate category centers, we first compared the extent to which bilinguals and monolinguals agree on typicality ratings for corresponding categories. If bilinguals have monolingual-like category centers, the correlation between the Dutch and French typicality ratings of bilinguals for paired categories should not differ from the same correlation for Dutch-speaking and French-speaking monolinguals. If, on the other hand, bilinguals have converging category centers, the correlation between the Dutch and French typicality ratings of bilinguals for paired categories will be significantly higher than the same correlation for Dutch-speaking and French-speaking monolinguals.

We used the same bottles and dishes sets (Ameel *et al.*, 2005) described above. Belgian Dutch-speaking monolinguals, Belgian French-speaking monolinguals and Belgian Dutch-French simultaneous bilinguals (20–30 per group) rated goodness of example for each object on a 7-point scale with respect to a number of category names. To compare the typicality ratings of different language groups, we selected pairs of frequently generated category names that were approximate (but not perfect) translation equivalents in Dutch and French. For the bottles set, the selected pairs of category names were *fles-bouteille* and *pot-pot* (first name in Dutch; second name in French). For the dishes set, four pairs of category names were selected: *kom-bol, tas-tasse, schaal-plat* and *bord-assiette*. Each monolingual participant gave typicality ratings in one language for the categories of both the bottles and dishes set. The bilinguals provided the complete set of typicality ratings for each stimulus set both in Dutch and in French, with order of languages counterbalanced.

Typicality ratings were averaged for each object with respect to each category name across participants of a language group. For each set of paired categories (*fles-bouteille, pot-pot, kom-bol, tas-tasse, schaal-plat, bord-assiette*), we then computed across all objects the correlation between the mean Dutch and French typicality ratings for the bilinguals and for the monolinguals. Table 6.3 shows these correlations.

The correlations for bilinguals were significantly higher than the correlations for monolinguals. This finding suggests that the centers of corresponding categories for bilinguals are more similar to each other than the corresponding category centers for monolinguals.

This shift of corresponding category centers toward each other for bilinguals can be due either to converging boundaries influencing the category centers or to more general, overall convergence of category membership. Our second analysis was aimed at discriminating between these two possible sources of the category center convergence as well as providing further evidence for the shift of bilingual category centers. We represented the same linguistic categories in a multi-dimensional geometrical space (MDS). Each exemplar of a category is represented by its coordinates on the dimensions. According to a prototype view

Table 6.3 Correlations between mean typicality ratings of bilinguals and monolinguals for each pair of categories

Pairs of categories (Dutch – French)	*Bilinguals*	*Monolinguals*
fles – bouteille	0.98	0.91
pot – pot	0.98	0.94
kom – bol	0.88	0.70
tas – tasse	0.99	0.99
schaal – plat	0.95	0.91
bord – assiette	0.99	0.94

Source: Reprinted by permission, Elsevier Ltd.

(Hampton, 1979; Rosch & Mervis, 1975), category centers can be represented by the point in the multi-dimensional space that is located in the middle of the points representing the category exemplars (Smith & Minda, 1998; Smits *et al.*, 2002). We then examined the positions of these centers for monolinguals and bilinguals in the two languages.

Positions of the category centers can be determined both in a boundary-dependent and a boundary-independent way (see below). If boundary-independent category centers for bilinguals are situated closer to each other than boundary-independent category centers for monolinguals, bilingual category centers converge regardless of the influence of the boundary exemplars. If it is only bilingual boundary-dependent category centers that are situated closer to each other than monolingual ones, convergence of category centers arises from convergence at the boundaries.

For this analysis, we wanted to compare the positions of category centers of different language groups in a common underlying representation reflecting the similarities among the objects. Since we had not found substantial differences between the sorting data of the different language groups, we derived pair-wise similarity judgments for the combined participants by counting the number of participants across all three groups who placed an object pair in the same pile. Two- to five-dimensional scaling solutions were computed from these similarity data for the two stimulus sets. For each object set and language group, we then computed the centers for the different categories.

The boundary-*dependent* center for each category was computed across all the stimuli of an object set. Thus, outliers at the boundaries of the categories contribute to the location of the calculated centers in this method, along with all the other exemplars. In the computation, each stimulus of an object set was weighted by its name frequency for the relevant group. For example, to find the category center of *fles* for the Dutch-speaking monolinguals, the coordinates of each object given by the sorting data were multiplied by the frequency with which the object was called *fles* by the Dutch-speaking monolinguals. Next, these weighted coordinates were summed and the coordinates of the category center were calculated as the weighted sum divided by the sum of all the frequencies. This procedure was repeated for two- to five-dimensional MDS representations. To determine the positions of category centers that were *independent* from boundary exemplars, we computed central tendency points defined by the median instead of mean values on each of the coordinate axes in a two-dimensional MDS solution. Since median values are not affected by outliers, this method eliminated the influence of boundary exemplars.

Figures 6.3 and 6.4 contain the two-dimensional MDS representations for the two stimulus sets, with the boundary-dependent centers of the different categories for each language group.

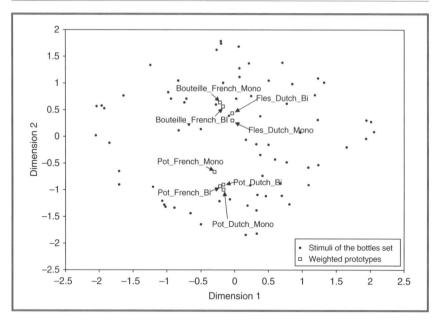

Figure 6.3 Two-dimensional MDS representation of the bottles set. The black dots represent the 73 stimuli of the bottles set, the white diamonds represent the category centers of the four different language groups (suffixes: Dutch_Mono = Dutch-speaking monolinguals, French_Mono = French-speaking monolinguals, Dutch_Bi = bilinguals in Dutch and French_Bi = bilinguals in French). (Reprinted by permission, Elsevier Ltd.)

This observation was supported by calculating the difference in average Euclidean distance between the corresponding category centers for each language group across category pairs (e.g. between *fles* and *bouteille*). Across both stimulus sets, and for all dimensions, the bilingual differences were significantly smaller than the differences for the corresponding monolingual category centers. The same pattern of results was also found for the boundary-independent category centers. This finding indicates that the convergence of bilingual category centers is not just due to convergence of the category boundaries, but to convergence of overall membership.

6.6.2 Category boundaries

The remaining analyses examined the nature of convergence at the boundaries in more detail. Category boundaries for many types of entities, including artifacts, are known to be fuzzy (Rosch & Mervis, 1975). For such categories, there exist borderline cases situated at the boundaries of the category, which are not clearly in or out of the category.

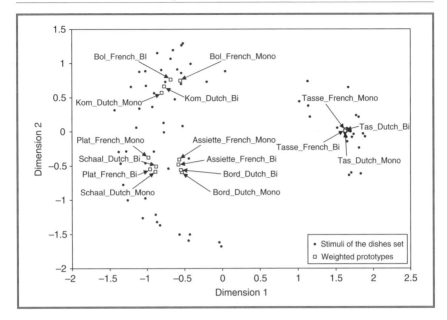

Figure 6.4 Two-dimensional MDS representation of the dishes set. The black dots represent the 67 stimuli of the dishes set, the white diamonds represent the category centers of the four different language groups (suffixes: Dutch_Mono = Dutch-speaking monolinguals, French_Mono = French-speaking monolinguals, Dutch_Bi = bilinguals in Dutch and French_Bi = bilinguals in French). (Reprinted by permission, Elsevier Ltd.)

These boundary exemplars are subject to inter- and even intra-individual naming variability (Hampton, 1979; McCloskey & Glucksberg, 1978). They share fewer features with other category exemplars, they are less typical for the category and they are learned later (Rosch & Mervis, 1975). The learning difficulty presumably comes about because the assigned name is less driven by similarity relations than those for more typical exemplars; instead, their naming is presumably more strongly determined by idiosyncrasies of specific cultural and linguistic histories, discussed above. Since the outcomes of these linguistic and cultural influences are language-specific, languages will differ from each other, and it is the boundary exemplars, whose features less clearly dictate category affiliations, that are more likely to receive different names in two languages.

Convergence of category boundaries could be manifested in either of two ways: the boundaries could be either more complex or simpler than those of monolinguals. *More complex* categories would arise if bilinguals are not able to keep boundary idiosyncrasies separate in the two languages, causing boundary exemplars of a particular category in one language to be incorporated into the corresponding category in the other language as well. Suppose that a particular (boundary) object has come to be called *fles* in Dutch, even though it does not share many features with other *fles* objects. Then this object will also be considered as a member of the corresponding French *bouteille* category, even though this assignment is not monolingual-like in French (since the language-specific event that caused the object to be named *fles* in Dutch did not operate on the French naming pattern).

On the other hand, bilinguals could have *simpler* categories than monolinguals if the idiosyncratic boundary exemplars of each language get only poorly encoded as a member of the relevant category in either language. The poor encoding might come about because of the reduced input compared to monolinguals, which may be particularly acute in the case of atypical exemplars. As a result, their boundary exemplars will be absent from the relevant categories of both languages, resulting in less complex categories for bilinguals compared to monolinguals. Under this scenario, bilinguals may be more likely to assign idiosyncratic boundary exemplars to the category to which they are most similar, rather than following the monolingual category assignment.

In the first analysis, we compared the complexity of bilingual categories to that of monolingual categories. We used a method called LINSEP (Van Assche, 2006), which quantifies the complexity of categories in terms of how many dimensions it takes to separate pairs of categories from each other. The more dimensions needed to separate category pairs linearly, the more complex the categories. A very simple example can illustrate this (see Figure 6.5). The category structure shown in the left panel is relatively simple: category A contains the circles, category B the squares. To separate these categories from each other, only the dimension of form needs to be taken into consideration. The category

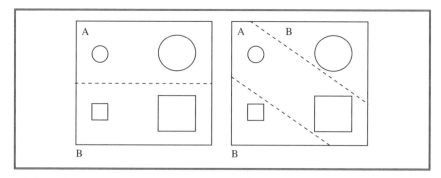

Figure 6.5 An example of a simple category structure (left panel) and a complex category structure (right panel)

structure in the right panel is more complex, since both the dimensions of form and size are needed to distinguish between the categories: category A contains the small circle and the large square; category B contains the large circle and the small square.

LINSEP allows us to compare how many dimensions are needed to separate bilingual versus monolingual categories. For both the bottles and dishes set, we found that the minimum dimensionality at which perfect linear separability could be obtained was significantly lower for bilinguals than for monolinguals. This outcome implies that the categories of bilinguals are less complex than the corresponding monolingual categories, since bilinguals need fewer dimensions to separate their categories linearly.

The lower complexity of bilingual categories suggests that idiosyncratic boundary exemplars are dropped from their monolingual-like categories in both languages for bilinguals and assigned instead to categories according to their similarity. However, the linear separability analyses do not provide direct evidence about this possibility. A more direct way to evaluate whether bilinguals drop boundary exemplars from their monolingual-like categories (and assign them to similarity-based categories) is to compare the proportions of outliers for bilinguals and monolinguals. In our final analysis, we made this comparison.

In geometrical representations, an outlier can be defined as an object that is located closer to the center of another category than to the center of its own category. We computed outliers for bilinguals and monolinguals for the two sets of stimuli in a two-dimensional MDS representation. (We used only a two-dimensional space because increasing the dimensionality of a solution may cause an outlier to become a non-outlier, making differences harder to detect.) Overall, the results showed significantly smaller proportions of outliers for bilinguals than for monolinguals, indicating that bilinguals drop at least some of the boundary exemplars in the monolinguals' categories of both languages. They make fewer violations of similarity-based naming than monolinguals, confirming that they reassign some boundary exemplars that may reflect language-specific idiosyncrasies in monolingual naming patterns.

6.7 Summary and Conclusions

Although it has often been assumed that the meanings associated with nouns for concrete objects correspond closely across languages, we have found that, at least for a range of common household artifacts, this assumption is incorrect. Speakers of different languages have distinctly (though by no means completely) different patterns of dividing the objects by name. Their perception of the objects' properties, as revealed in similarity sorting tasks, is more similar than their naming patterns, suggesting that speakers' naming patterns reflect differing linguistic and cultural histories of their languages, but may not necessarily reflect any deeper differences in understanding of the objects by the individuals or their cultures. The differences in naming patterns we have observed pose challenges for people who learn to speak more than one language. Our studies show that L2 learners take many years to come close to matching the patterns of word use of native speakers, even when they have the appropriate words in their vocabularies, and even when immersed in the L2 environment. Furthermore, we have found that bilinguals raised with two languages do not fully match the separate patterns of monolingual speakers of the two languages. Their patterns of word use reflect a partial compromise between the patterns of the two languages as spoken by monolinguals. This convergence in patterns of word use in the two languages is manifested by bilinguals in both their lexical category centers and their category boundaries.

Several aspects of the L2 learner results are worth further investigation. One is why, exactly, these learners immersed in English are so slow to fully match native naming patterns. As we noted earlier, we originally assumed that it had to do with interference from the L1: once a person has acquired one mapping of names to objects, it is presumably harder to learn a second that requires moving away from the already well-established pattern. But our subsequent finding that monolingual children acquiring their L1 took a very similar period of time to become adult-like in their use of words for similar household objects raises questions about this interpretation. It could be that the L2 learners are just following the same learning trajectory as L1 learners, which happens to be very lengthy. One might find this suggestion implausible on the argument that older learners should be faster learners due to their greater cognitive maturity or their more mature understanding of the objects, which would help them detect the features governing native word uses.

On the other hand, the L2 learners were, for the most part, still using their L1 in some daily contexts (such as at home). Their exposure to input in the target language may therefore be more limited than the exposure for a monolingual child learner, and so a greater ability to learn could be masked by reduced exposure to the necessary information. We did not find a clear correspondence of the patterns of L2 English word use with the L1 patterns in our study (see Malt & Sloman, 2003), but because the L2 learners came from many different language backgrounds, such correspondences may have been hard to detect. A direct comparison of the uses of specific words and the errors that are made by mature L2 learners and child L1 learners for the same objects would be useful. For instance, our child learners used certain words too broadly initially and others too narrowly. Do L2 learners consistently do the same for the same words, or does it vary depending on the L1 background?

A third possible explanation for the lengthy learning trajectory also exists: on-going use of the L1 may exert a continued pull away from the monolingual patterns of the other language even as exposure to that language exerts a pull toward them, thus keeping the L2 user who still uses the L1 from ever completely converging on the L2 pattern (at least for those words for which the L2 pattern is hard to master; Malt and Sloman (2003) did find that performance eventually became equivalent to native monolinguals for some words). A better understanding of the sources of difficulty for the L2 learners would help determine to what extent the same cross-language influences that appear to result in convergence for the more balanced bilinguals in our subsequent studies are operating in the asynchronous learning case.

If there is an influence of the L1 on the L2 in this asynchronous case, one might then also ask whether learning the L2 has any backward effect on the usage patterns of the L1 (a topic on which there is only limited evidence so far, as we noted earlier). It is possible that a mature L1 system is well-enough established in memory to be relatively immune to any backward influence due to L2 immersion in adulthood, but that those who are immersed in the L2 at earlier ages (and who, perhaps, end up with dominance of the L2 over the L1) will show such an influence. Alternatively, it may be that whatever linkages exist between the two lexicons (e.g. through shared conceptual representations; Kroll & Curley, 1988) will result in a backward influence regardless of age of immersion, given sufficient usage of the L1.

From a practical perspective, several questions arise. Given the variability that also exists among native speakers in naming many objects, one might wonder if and when native speakers detect the discrepancies from their own usage, and whether any detectable discrepancies have real consequences to either comprehension by the addressee or to perceived speaker competence. If they do, then it is important to consider whether there are instructional procedures that can speed up the acquisition of monolingual-like patterns for L2 learners. These procedures might include sensitizing them to the existence of the subtle differences from the L1 or providing explicit information about what those differences might consist of. However, a better grasp of the actual sources of difficulty will help inform what corrective actions might be relevant or whether any are likely to be of value. The conditions for acquiring the needed input – through exposure to individual instances in real-world interactions – may be so far removed from the instructional setting that instruction would have little benefit.

Our data showing convergence in word use for bilinguals using two languages from birth raise additional issues to pursue. It seems clear in this case that in some way the performance in one language is influenced by exposure to the other. However, the precise mechanisms that lead to this outcome remain largely unknown. We have talked so far as if the convergence we found must arise entirely through an interaction of representations in the mind of individual bilinguals. But linguistic convergence of various sorts has also been observed at a larger scale, where two language communities dominant in different languages begin to acquire similarities in aspects of phonology, syntax or other language elements through contact with each other (see, e.g. Bullock & Gerfen, 2004 on converging phonology). In such cases, the language systems passed from one generation of speakers to the next have begun to converge. Thus, convergence is not restricted to cases of proficiency in both languages, but may occur with lesser degrees of contact. Indeed, in an unpublished analysis, we compared the correspondence of naming patterns for monolingual French and Dutch speakers in France and Holland, respectively, with the correspondence between monolingual speakers of the two languages in Belgium, and we found that the monolingual Belgians resembled each other in naming our stimuli more than the monolinguals in France and Holland did. The parents of our bilinguals were each dominant in a different language and spoke to the children in different languages, but presumably they were able to communicate with each other through one or both languages. It is possible that they may have begun to converge in their naming patterns through contact with each other, passing on the altered patterns to their children, who further converged them. Thus, fully understanding the origin of the convergence we observed will require examining the naming input such bilingual children are exposed to at home.

In terms of more specific mechanisms that may yield convergence, we have suggested that two key elements may be the reduced exposure to each language that a bilingual receives, and the inter-connectedness, in some way, of representations supporting the use of the two languages. However, we are far from having a clear notion of what a model of bilingual word learning would need to look like that would support the interactions and produce the observed convergence of boundaries and centers. Such a model would have to include a knowledge base that would serve to represent the knowledge of objects in the world, a way of linking this knowledge base to sets of lexical items in two languages (which would, ultimately, need to be part of much larger linguistic representational systems that include the syntax and phonology of each language), and links between elements at one or more levels that allow interactions to occur, yet accommodate the fact that bilinguals most often generate sentences in one and only one language at a time. In addition, it would need to specify the processes that operate over the links such that information about names heard in one language comes to influence the object-name links that are established in the other. For instance, when an object in the world is perceived and is heard labeled *fles* in Dutch, does a link that has already been established between *fles* and *bouteille* in French (without necessarily explicit instruction; perhaps by sharing links to the set of objects that have been heard labeled by both) become activated, resulting in a link being established between the object and *bouteille* (that is, even if no monolingual speaker labels that object *bouteille*)?

The model could be used to test whether our suggestion of weak object-word links in each language for a simultaneous bilingual relative to monolinguals is a relevant component of an explanation of how the boundary convergence comes about, or whether convergence can come about without a reduced link strength relative to some value set for monolinguals. It may also help clarify how category centers come to converge despite the frequent input from typical exemplars. Such a model could then be used to make predictions about how the timing of learning one language relative to the other would influence outcomes, and whether late learning of an L2 would be likely to influence well-established L1 naming patterns (or under what conditions; i.e. when L1 object-word links are rarely activated after L2 learning). Further empirical work on such conditions of learning is needed, though, to test the model against. Our ongoing research aims to make progress on both fronts.

Note

1. American English naming data for the same stimulus sets gathered in another study show that objects from the bottles set named *fles* and *bus* in Dutch, and *bouteille* and *flacon* in French, are mostly called *bottle* in English. Objects called *pot* in Dutch and French are mostly called *container* or *jar* in English. Objects from the dishes set with *kom* as their Dutch dominant name and *bol* as their French dominant name are mostly called *bowl* in English, those called *tas* in Dutch and *tasse* in French are mostly *mug* or *cup*, those called *schaal* in Dutch and *plat* in French are *dish* or *bowl*, and those called *bord* in Dutch and *assiette* in French are mostly *plate* or *bowl* in English.

References

Altarriba, J. (1992) The representation of translation equivalents in bilingual memory. In R. Harris (ed.) *Cognitive Processing in Bilinguals* (pp. 157–174). Amsterdam: Elsevier.

Ameel, E., Malt, B. and Storms, G. (2008) Object naming and later lexical development: From baby bottle to beer bottle. *Journal of Memory and Language* 58, 262–285.

Ameel, E., Malt, B., Storms, G. and Van Assche, F. (2009) Semantic convergence in the bilingual lexicon. *Journal of Memory and Language* 60, 270–290.

Ameel, E., Storms, G., Malt, B. and Sloman, S.A. (2005) How bilinguals solve the naming problem. *Journal of Memory and Language* 53, 60–80.

Andersen, E. (1975) Cups and glasses: Learning that boundaries are vague. *Child Language* 2, 79–103.

Berlin, B. (1978) Ethnobiological classification. In E. Rosch and B. Lloyd (eds) *Cognition and Categorization* (pp. 9–26). Hillsdale, NJ: Lawrence Erlbaum.

Birdsong, D. (1999) *Second Language Acquisition and the Critical Period Hypothesis*. Mahwah, NJ: Lawrence Erlbaum.

Bloom, P. (2000) *How Children Learn the Meanings of Words*. Cambridge, MA: MIT Press.

Bullock, B. and Gerfen, C. (2004) Phonological convergence in a contracting language variety. *Bilingualism: Language and Cognition* 7, 95–104.

Clark, E. (2003) Languages and representations. In D. Gentner and S. Goldin-Meadow (eds) *Language in Mind: Advances in the Study of Language and Thought* (pp. 17–24). Cambridge, MA: MIT Press.

Clark, E. (2007) Conventionality and contrast in language and language acquisition. In M. Sabbagh and C. Kalish (eds) *Right Thinking: The Development of Conventionality. New Directions in Child & Adolescent Development* (Vol. 115) (pp. 11–23). San Francisco, CA: Jossey-Bass.

Clark, H. (1996) Communities, communalities, and communication. In J. Gumperz and S.C. Levinson (eds) *Rethinking Linguistic Relativity* (pp. 324–358). Cambridge: Cambridge University Press.

De Groot, A. (2002) Lexical representation and lexical processing in the L2 user. In V. Cook (ed.) *Portraits of the L2 User* (pp. 32–63). Clevedon: Multilingual Matters.

Gleitman, L. and Papafragou, A. (2005) Language and thought. In R. Morrison and K. Holyoak (eds) *Cambridge Handbook of Thinking and Reasoning* (pp. 633–661). Cambridge: Cambridge University Press.

Hampton, J. (1979) Polymorphous concepts in semantic memory. *Journal of Verbal Learning and Verbal Behavior* 18, 441–461.

Hunn, E. (1977) *Tzetal Folk Zoology: The Classification of Discontinuities in Nature*. New York: Academic Press.

Jiang, N. (2000) Lexical representation and development in a second language. *Applied Linguistics* 21, 47–77.

Kroll, J. (1993) Accessing conceptual representations for words in a second language. In R. Schreuder and B. Weltens (eds) *The Bilingual Lexicon* (pp. 53–81). Amsterdam: John Benjamins.

Kroll, J. and Curley, J. (1988) Lexical memory in novice bilinguals: The role of concepts in retrieving second language words. In M. Gruneberg, P. Morris and R. Sykes (eds) *Practical Aspects of Memory* (Vol. 2) (pp. 389–395). London: Wiley.

Kronenfeld, D., Armstrong, J. and Wilmoth, S. (1985) Exploring the internal structure of linguistic categories: An extensionist semantic view. In J. Dougherty (ed.) *Directions in Cognitive Anthropology* (pp. 91–113). Urbana, IL: University of Illinois Press.

Leach, E. (1976) *Culture and Communication: The Logic by which Symbols are Connected*. Cambridge: Cambridge University Press.

Levelt, W., Roelofs, A. and Meyer, A. (1999) A theory of lexical access in speech production. *Behavioral and Brain Sciences* 22, 1–38.

Malt, B. (1995) Category coherence in cross-cultural perspective. *Cognitive Psychology* 29, 85–148.

Malt, B. and Sloman, S. (2003) Linguistic diversity and object naming by non-native speakers of English. *Bilingualism: Language and Cognition* 6, 47–67.

Malt, B., Sloman, S. and Gennari, S. (2003) Universality and language specificity in object naming. *Journal of Memory and Language* 49, 20–42.

Malt, B., Sloman, S., Gennari, S., Shi, M. and Wang, Y. (1999) Knowing versus naming: Similarity and the linguistic categorization of artifacts. *Journal of Memory and Language* 40, 230–262.

Markson, L. and Bloom, P. (1997) Evidence against a dedicated system for word learning in children. *Nature* 385 (6619), 813–815.

McCloskey, M. and Glucksberg, S. (1978) Natural categories: Well defined or fuzzy sets? *Memory and Cognition* 6, 462–472.

Mervis, C. (1987) Child-basic object categories and early lexical development. In U. Neisser (ed.) *Concepts and Conceptual Development: Ecological and Intellectual Factors in Categorization* (pp. 201–233). Cambridge: Cambridge University Press.

Pavlenko, A. (2003) "I feel clumsy speaking Russian": L2 influence on L1 in narratives of Russian L2 users of English. In V. Cook (ed.) *Effects of the Second Language on the First* (pp. 32–61). Clevedon: Multilingual Matters.

Pavlenko, A. and Malt, B. (in press) Kitchen Russian: Crosslinguistic differences and first-language object naming by Russian-English bilinguals. *Bilingualism: Language and Cognition.*

Romney, A., Weller, S. and Batchelder, W. (1986) Culture as consensus: A theory of culture and informant accuracy. *American Anthropologist* 88, 313–338.

Rosch, E. and Mervis, C. (1975) Family resemblances: Studies in internal structure of categories. *Cognitive Psychology* 7, 573–605.

Schwanenflugel, P. and Rey, M. (1986) Interlingual semantic facilitation: Evidence for a common representational system in the bilingual lexicon. *Journal of Memory and Language* 25, 605–618.

Simpson, G. (1961) *Principles of Animal Taxonomy.* New York: Columbia University Press.

Smith, J. and Minda, J. (1998) Prototypes in the mist: The early epochs of category learning. *Journal of Experimental Psychology: Learning, Memory, and Cognition* 24 (6), 1411–1436.

Smith, L. (1999) How general learning processes make specialized learning mechanisms. In B. MacWhinney (ed.) *The Psychology of Learning and Motivation* (pp. 249–291). San Diego, CA: Academic Press.

Smits, T., Storms, G., Rosseel, Y. and De Boeck, P. (2002) Fruits and vegetables categorized: An application of the generalized context model. *Psychonomic Bulletin and Review* 9, 836–844.

Van Assche, F. (2006) *The Use of LS Solvers in the Determination of Linear Separability of n-Tuple Classes.* Technical report. Leuven: Catholic University of Leuven.

Vigliocco, G., Vinson, D., Lewis, W. and Garrett, M. (2004) Representing the meanings of object and action words: The featural and unitary semantic space hypothesis. *Cognitive Psychology* 48, 422–488.

Whorf, B. (1956) *Language, Thought and Reality: Selected Writings of Benjamin Lee Whorf.* Edited by John Carroll. Cambridge, MA: MIT Press.

Wolff, P. and Ventura, T. (2003) When Russians learn English: How the meaning of causal verbs may change. In B. Beachley, A. Brown and F. Conlin (eds) *Proceedings of the Twenty-Seventh Annual Boston University Conference on Language Development* (pp. 822–833). Boston, MA: Cascadilla Press.

Chapter 7

(Re-)naming the World: Word-to-Referent Mapping in Second Language Speakers

ANETA PAVLENKO

> Les termes prétendus équivalents dans des langues diverses ne le sont que partiellement, puisque chacun d'eux a des significations spéciales que les autres n'ont point. [The terms assumed equivalent in different languages are only partial equivalents, because each has unique meanings that others do not.] (Epstein, 1915: 115)

7.1 Introduction

In Pascal Mercier's (2009) novel, *Night Train to Lisbon*, the protagonist, a multilingual classics teacher, Raimund Gregorius, suddenly experiences a dizzy spell and his memory for languages starts deserting him – first Portuguese words and then Persian ones leave the recesses of his memory. Desperate to retain his linguistic hold on the world, Gregorius begins pacing around the room, 'calling everything by its familiar German name' (Mercier, 2009: 315), and finding reassurance in his ability to map his words onto the world around him. This episode reminds us that, despite being only one constitutive aspect of our linguistic knowledge, it is the ability to name that grounds us and allows us to develop and maintain our relationship with the world at large. But how do we map our words onto the world? And do the words of our second language (L2) follow the mappings established for the first language (L1)?

Traditional investigations of the bilingual lexicon do not provide us with any answers to these questions because they remain 'inside' the mind and focus on the relationship between words in bilinguals' languages or between words and their assumed 'meanings'. External reality, if represented at all, is usually reduced to pictures of 'ducks', 'dogs' or 'bikes'. In theories and models that come out of these studies, picture naming is assumed to be a legitimate stand-in for the naming process as a whole. The only 'glitches' in this process stem from interlingual connections, which may lead to activation of the wrong language or misuse of false cognates, and not from difficulties inherent in mapping words onto the world.

This is not to say that traditional approaches are faulty – over the years, studies with decontextualized words have furnished invaluable information about the building blocks of language processing (e.g. Kroll & De Groot, 2005). In fact, this methodology is also used in one of the studies discussed below. My main concern is with design constraints on psycholinguistic studies: currently, they can tell us a lot about the speed with which people perform word and non-word tasks but very little about the central function of language – the things we do with words in the real world. This issue has been relegated to other areas of linguistics – sociolinguistics, discourse analysis and linguistic anthropology. Elsewhere, I have offered an extended critique of models of the bilingual lexicon grounded in traditional psycholinguistic approaches (Pavlenko, 2009). In what follows, I will illustrate an alternative context-based approach to the study of the bilingual lexicon that incorporates external reality into empirical investigations and makes inter-speaker variation a legitimate focus of the inquiry.

The purpose of the studies discussed here was to examine how different types of translation equivalence and different contexts and ages of acquisition affect the mapping of words onto external referents. The term *word-to-referent mapping* will refer to ways in which speakers deploy their lexical resources to refer to objects, actions, events and phenomena in the outside world, a process also known as *lexical choice* or *naming*. The relationship between words and external referents will be used to examine *linguistic (lexical) categories*, i.e. internal representations that guide the mapping process. I will also consider the sources of *referential indeterminacy*, or the lack of agreement on referent names, and show that even in one's native language the mapping of words to external referents can be a perplexing process of trial and approximation, fraught with difficulties and imperfections. Even the most common objects may be named differently by different speakers (*inter-speaker variation*) or by the same speaker on different occasions (*intra-speaker variation*). Some objects, actions, events or phenomena may have no name at all and others may elicit an array of competing alternatives, none of which seem particularly fitting. The learning of an L2, then, constitutes a process of re-naming the world, and the degree of destabilization created by this process depends on one's learning context, the languages involved and the theory of language held by the speaker in question. Some perceive the process of re-naming as a linking of new forms to pre-existing categories, others as a drastic change in understanding and experiencing the world, and yet others may situate themselves somewhere in between.

I will begin my discussion with a brief overview of what is known to date about word-to-referent mapping in monolingual and bilingual speakers (see also Malt & Ameel, this volume). Then, I will discuss the methodology employed in the studies conducted by myself and my colleagues. Subsequently, I will present three sets of studies that examined word-to-referent mapping in the context of translation non-equivalence and full and partial translation equivalence. The findings of these studies will be used to outline factors that affect word-to-referent mapping by bilingual speakers. I will end by considering the implications of these findings for our understanding of the bilingual mental lexicon and internal representations.

7.2 Word-to-Referent Mapping in Monolingual and Bilingual Speakers

7.2.1 Word-to-Referent mapping out of context

The 1950s' debates about linguistic relativity gave rise to several strands of inquiry, including the study of naming and categorization of experience (e.g. Berlin & Kay, 1969; Brown, 1958). This strand received a new impetus in the 1970s when Eleanor Rosch (1973a, 1973b, 1975, 1977, 1978) developed an experimental paradigm for determining category boundaries through typicality ratings of potential category members (e.g. *robin* as a member of a category *bird* or *stool* as a member of a category *furniture*). Her approach was taken up by other cognitive psychologists (for a summary, see Murphy, 2002) and eventually spread to the fields of language acquisition (e.g. Andersen, 1975; Keil, 1989), linguistic anthropology (e.g. Kempton, 1981; Kronenfeld, 1996) and cognitive linguistics (e.g. Lakoff, 1987), with linguistic categories treated as a kind of cognitive categories (Lakoff, 1987; Murphy, 2002; Taylor, 1995).

Decades of research on linguistic categorization have produced important insights into the process of word-to-referent mapping. To begin with, Rosch (1973b, 1977, 1978) showed that cognitive categories have an internal structure, which includes a core (focal or prototypical members) and a periphery (borderline members). Prototypical category members (e.g. *robin* as a *bird*) were shown to be recognized faster than borderline members (e.g. *penguin* as a *bird*) by native speakers of English. Rosch *et al.* (1976) found that in taxonomies of common objects there is a basic level of abstraction that represents the most inclusive level of categorization (e.g. *dog, chair*) and is situated between the superordinate (e.g. *animal, furniture*) and subordinate (e.g. *retriever, rocker*) levels. Basic level object names were most frequently chosen by the participants to refer to concrete objects. Later studies also revealed the so-called exemplar effect, i.e. speakers' reliance on previously seen category members in judgments about new entities (for a review, see Murphy, 2002).

In sociolinguistics, naming and category membership were examined by Labov (1973), who asked native speakers of English to name pictures of containers that differed from each other in measurements, shape, material and function. His findings illustrated the referential indeterminacy of the most familiar kitchen objects and revealed that inter-speaker naming agreement was affected by the properties of the containers in question, such as shape (e.g. the presence of a handle), material, width and depth, with agreement being lower for borderline category members. Most importantly, the agreement was affected by the perceived function of the container, so that the same container would be named *cup* with high agreement if it contained coffee and with low agreement if it contained food or flowers. Similar findings came from an anthropological study by Kempton (1981), who examined the interaction between typicality, shape and function in the naming of ceramic vessels in rural varieties of Mexican Spanish.

Crosslinguistic studies of linguistic categories revealed that naming patterns differ across languages, with speakers of different languages placing the same objects into different categories. Kronenfeld *et al.* (1985; see also Kronenfeld, 1996) found that speakers of English, Hebrew and Japanese divide drinking containers in different ways due to differences in the salient attributes of the core category members. Thus, in English the overriding determinant for glassness was material (hence, the placement of paper and plastic containers into the category *cups*), while in Hebrew it was shape (hence, placement of paper and styrofoam cups into the category *cos* [glass]). Hebrew and Japanese further differed in the shape associated with prototypical glassness: in Hebrew a prototypical *cos* [glass] had cylindrical shape without handles, while in Japanese *gurasu* [glass] were non-cylindrical stemmed objects made of glass, best exemplified by what English speakers would call a *brandy snifter*. The researchers also pointed to differences in function: English speakers, for instance, saw *cups* mainly as containers for hot drinks and *glasses* as containers for cold drinks. Similar findings came from crosslinguistic studies of household containers conducted by Malt and associates (Ameel *et al.*, 2005; Malt *et al.*, 1999, 2003). These studies have demonstrated that linguistic categories linked to the so-called translation equivalents may be formed around different prototypes and display different structures (see also Malt & Ameel, this volume).

Studies with L2 learners and bilingual speakers showed that beginning and intermediate L2 learners may display the influence of L1 categories in L2 naming (Graham & Belnap, 1986) and that even advanced L2 speakers who had spent 10 or more years in the target language country may exhibit discrepancies from monolingual naming patterns and typicality judgments (Malt & Sloman, 2003). Simultaneous bilinguals were shown to display a converging naming pattern (Ameel *et al.*, 2005).

To sum up, studies of word-to-referent mapping out of context show that the naming of entities commonly takes place at the basic level and is affected by: (a) referent properties that make particular entities more or less typical in terms of a particular category; (b) perceived function of the referents; and (c) crosslinguistic differences in category structure. In bi- and multilingual speakers, the naming is additionally affected by the type of bilingualism (e.g. simultaneous versus sequential), the length of L2 exposure and the level of L2 proficiency. Given the complexity of these factors, it is not surprising that acquisition of target-like naming patterns – even for household containers – requires an extended amount of time, both in first (Andersen, 1975; Ameel *et al.*, 2008) and second language acquisition (Malt & Sloman, 2003).

7.2.2 Word-to-Referent mapping in context

The 1970s also marked the beginning of a related line of inquiry, the study of lexical choice in the context of elicited narratives. Two key studies have shaped the field and defined research agendas for decades to come. The first, known as Pear Stories, was carried out by Wallace Chafe and colleagues (Chafe, 1980) in order to examine 'how a speaker of a Western language and a speaker of a language which differs radically from the Western type would express the same experience' (Du Bois, 1980: 1). To ensure that participants described 'the same experience', the researchers produced their own film, now known as *the pear film*, and collected oral and written retellings of the film from speakers of Chinese, English, German, Greek, Haitian Creole, Japanese, Malay, Persian, Quiché Maya, Sacapultec and Thai. These narratives were collected – sometimes repeatedly – in order to see how verbaliza- tions of the same visual stimulus differ across speakers of different languages, across speakers of the same language and across different retellings by the same speaker. The analyses of the retellings collected in Chafe (1980) produced a range of findings regarding crosslinguistic similarities and differences in the deployment of consciousness, narra- tive strategies and lexical choices.

The key findings of relevance to the present discussion come from Downing's (1980) analysis of the retellings of the pear film by 20 speakers of American English and 20 speakers of Japanese. The researcher examined all nominal references to concrete entities in the two narrative corpora (English $n = 1363$ words; Japanese $n = 786$ words) and identified three types of factors affecting lexical choice in these narratives: cognitive, contextual and textual.

The two cognitive factors identified by Downing (1980) are codability and the presence of a basic level of categorization. The latter factor is based on Rosch's (1978; Rosch *et al.*, 1976) work, which suggested that basic level names (e.g. *chair*) are used more frequently than names at the superordinate (e.g. *furniture*) or subordinate (e.g. *kitchen chair*) levels. Downing's (1980) study validated this conclusion for words in context – in the pear film narratives, basic level names constituted 93% of the nouns in the English corpus and 83% in the Japanese corpus.

The idea of *codability* – the presence or absence of a standardized label for the referent in question and the number of possible lexical alternatives – stems from Brown and Lenneberg's (1954) reformulations of linguistic relativity principles. Highly codable entities, in this view, have one standardized label that will be used consistently and with high agreement by speakers of the language in question. In Downing's (1980) study, such labels included *ladder, moustache, face, leg, hand* and *eye*. Other entities, such as *apron, paddleball* and *basket*, were referred to with a number of different labels, oftentimes accompanied by lengthy pauses, false starts and a high number of modifiers, all of which were seen as indicators of low codability. Downing (1980) also found that codability was not a stable trait and linked variation across speakers to their individual lexicons.

Contextual factors, identified by Downing (1980), included but were not limited to the nature of the speech situation, the speaker's goals, perspective (including the level of specificity in narration), the attitude toward the referent, the identity of the addressee and the stylistic level selected by the speaker. The researcher also identified textual factors, the most important among them being the position of a word within the text, whereby different labels may be selected for the same referent depending on whether the referent is being introduced or followed.

The second paradigm-setting study, known as Frog Stories (Berman & Slobin, 1994), began in the 1980s as an investigation of narratives elicited with a picture book, *Frog, Where are You?* (Mayer, 1969). Pioneered by Michael Bamberg (1987) and adopted by Dan Slobin and Ruth Berman, the Frog Story design has now been used by a large number of researchers studying L1 and L2 development and attrition (e.g. Berman & Slobin, 1994; Strömqvist & Verhoeven, 2004; Verhoeven & Strömqvist, 2001). As in the case of the pear film, the design is very useful for the study of lexical choice in context because speakers cannot avoid mentioning particular key elements of the story. Only a few studies, however, considered lexical choice in bilingual speakers.

Olshtain and Barzilay (1991) collected Frog Story narratives from English-Hebrew bilinguals, all of them Americans who learned their L2 Hebrew as teenagers or adults and had spent between eight and 25 years in Israel. Their L1 English performance was compared to that of monolingual speakers of English living in the USA. The authors found that there was high agreement among the monolinguals on the names for the animate and inanimate entities under investigation: *jar, cliff, pond, gopher* and *deer*. Bilinguals, on the other hand, displayed word-finding difficulties and low levels of agreement in naming these entities, using circumlocution and semantically related alternatives (e.g. *bottle, bowl* or *jug* for *jar; stag, antelope, elk* or *little animal* for *deer*). This performance was interpreted as lexical attrition in the L1.

Similar findings come from Kaufman's (2001) study conducted with Hebrew-English bilingual children (ages 6–14) who were born or had spent between two and 10 years in the USA. She found that the children appealed to a variety of substitutions when dealing with lexical gaps in L1 Hebrew. In the case of basic-level animate entities (e.g. *cvi* [deer], *yanshuf* [owl]), they resorted to superordinate categories (e.g. *xaya* [animal], *gdola* [bird]), extended descriptions or circumlocutions, or requests for help and code-switches to L2 English (e.g. *deer, owl*). In the case of basic-level inanimate entities (e.g. *cincenet* [jar]), they used basic-level approximations (e.g. *bakbuk* [bottle], *kufsa* [box], *keara* [bowl]) or superordinate terms (e.g. *kli* [container]).

A few studies also used other elicitation stimuli. Jarvis (1998, 2000) compared retellings of a segment from the silent film *Modern Times* by Finnish and Swedish learners of L2 English. He found that in references to a collision involving Charlie Chaplin and the female protagonist, L1 Finnish speakers favored the verbs *hit* and *crash* and L1 Swedish speakers favored a hybrid phrasal verb *run on*. The researcher linked these distinct lexical preferences to the L1 influence and, more specifically, to different conceptualizations of collisions in Finnish and Swedish.

Together, the studies discussed above allow us to identify four types of factors that affect inter- and intra-speaker variation in lexical selection: (a) linguistic (i.e. word properties), (b) referent-specific (i.e. referent properties), (c) individual (i.e. speaker properties) and (d) text- and context-specific (i.e. text and context properties). *Linguistic factors* include the overall codability of the referent, the availability of the basic-level word, the structure of the lexical category in question, lexical differentiation in the domain in question and the existence of lexical alternatives. The intra-group agreement appears to be higher for basic-level words with high codability and a low number of alternatives. *Referent-specific factors* include referent properties and perceived function of the referent, both of which contribute to its perceived typicality in terms of a particular linguistic category. Highly typical referents appear to be named with higher inter-group agreement. *Individual factors* include the richness of the individual lexicon, familiarity with the referent (i.e. the ability to rely on previously seen exemplars), as well as speaker's goals, perspective and attitude. Of these, familiarity is likely to lead to higher intra-group agreement. *Text-* and *context-specific factors* include the nature of the speech situation, stylistic level or register, identity of the addressee and the word's position in the text (i.e. referent introduction versus reference continuation). Higher agreement is likely to occur for the initial introduction of the referent. In bilingual speakers, the degree of approximation of target-like naming patterns was additionally influenced by: (a) the type of bilingualism (e.g. simultaneous versus sequential); (b) the level of language proficiency or attrition; and, for sequential bilinguals, (c) the length of exposure to the L2.

In the present chapter, I will focus on ways in which lexical selection is influenced by: (a) codability; (b) crosslinguistic relationship between linguistic categories (translation equivalence); (c) the context of L2 acquisition; and (d) the age of L2 acquisition.

7.3 Methodology

All but one of the studies discussed below rely on the same methodological approach to the study of lexical choice – narrative elicitation with visual stimuli (for an in-depth discussion of narrative collection and analysis, see Pavlenko, 2008a). Participants in a *narrative elicitation task* are asked to retell a story they inferred from a series of pictures or a film clip. As a method that combines aspects of experimental and ethnographic approaches to the study of language use, narrative elicitation enjoys several advantages. Like ethnographic data, elicited oral narratives allow researchers to study spontaneous lexical choices in their linguistic and visual contexts, thus ensuring the ecological validity of the investigation. Like experimental data, elicited narratives involve a measure of control: All participants describe the same visual stimulus, consequently, their lexical choices can be compared across groups. The combination of both approaches allows for a meaningful examination of the relationship between words and their real-world referents, represented in the visual stimulus. Having said this, it is also necessary to acknowledge the weaknesses of the approach. The controlled nature of the visual stimuli limits the scope of the data to third person descriptions, while the narrative nature of the task allows some participants to avoid mentioning particular external referents. Nevertheless, the advantages of this approach outweigh its weaknesses and naming avoidance can be addressed by follow-up questions and increased numbers of participants.

All visual stimuli allow experimenters to hold the visual referents constant. Films, however, have an advantage over other visual stimuli for the purposes of word-to-referent mapping inquiry. Unlike picture books, they recreate an authentic external reality; they also make the story-telling task less artificial and more 'adult-like' and thus, more similar to spontaneous narratives. In the studies described below, six short film clips with a musical soundtrack, but no verbal interactions, were used as elicitation stimuli. Four films – *The Ithaca Story, Kiev Story, The Letter* and *Pis'mo* [The Letter] – were specifically made by this researcher for studies with Russian-English bilinguals. Two films were made in 1995–1996 in the USA (*The Ithaca Story, The Letter*) and the other two, based on the same script, in 1996 in Kiev, Ukraine (*Kiev Story, Pis'mo*). The decision to film two versions of each script, in different visual environments, was made in order to examine the influence of the visual context on interpretation of the films. The decision to make the latter two films in Ukraine, rather than in Russia, was made for production cost reasons. This decision did not reduce the authenticity of the context – in the 1990s, Kiev continued to be a Russian-speaking city and thus constituted an authentic Russian-language environment. The St. Petersburg participants in the study commented that the action in *Kiev Story* was taking place 'somewhere in Russia' and that the apartment in *Pis'mo* looked like a 'typical St. Petersburg communal apartment'.

To ensure that the phenomena identified in the studies were not limited to elicitations with films made by the researcher, later studies also adopted two segments from the British TV series about Mr. Bean, *Mr. Bean in the parking lot* and *Mr. Bean in the swimming pool*.

All participants performed the narrative recall task individually. They were told that they will see a short film clip and, after the end of the film, will be asked to recall it, speaking directly into the tape-recorder. In this way, participants' lexical choices referred not to directly visible referents but to referents previously seen and now remembered (as is common in everyday speech). Throughout, the instructions were provided in the language of the recall. All the recalls were tape-recorded and then transcribed and analyzed in the original language.

In the data analysis, lexical choices were analyzed quantitatively and qualitatively. Throughout, *lemmas* (units of meaning or words) were differentiated from *tokens* (lexical items or lexemes). Quantitative analyses examined similarities and differences across groups in terms of narrative length, lexical richness, the size of emotion vocabulary, the distribution of morphosyntactic categories in emotion word corpora and homogeneity of lexical choices. Qualitative analyses identified instances of dysfluency, crosslinguistic influence, lexical borrowing, loan translation, circumlocution, structural and semantic errors, and avoidance.

In what follows, I will discuss the findings of three sets of studies. The first explores word-to-referent mapping by monolingual and bilingual speakers in reference to events, the second in reference to phenomena, and the third in reference to objects.

7.4 Now You See It, Now You Don't: Word-to-Referent Mapping and Translation Non-equivalence

The first study discussed here examined the effects of codability and the context of L2 acquisition on the performance of speakers of two languages, English (where the event in question was codable) and Russian (where it was not) (Pavlenko, 1997, 2003). In what follows, such a relationship between the two languages will be referred to as *translation non-equivalence* and the terms existent in one language but not the other as *language-specific terms* or *non-equivalents*. The study addressed the following questions: (1) Will native speakers of English and Russian differ in recalls of a situation that can be described with an English word that has no Russian translation equivalent? (2) If they do indeed differ, would recalls by Russian-English bilinguals pattern with the speakers of their L1 or L2? (3) Would bilinguals' performance be affected by the language of recall, the context of L2 acquisition and/or the visual context?

The word under investigation in the study was *privacy*, encoded in English but not in Russian. A frequently used term, *privacy* has multiple instantiations in Anglo-Saxon cultures. In fact, several English-speaking countries, including Australia, Canada, the UK and the USA, have privacy laws, whereby an 'invasion of privacy' may constitute a separate legal charge (Alderman & Kennedy, 1995; Scott, 1995). The study focused on the spatial dimension of privacy, often referred to with a collocation *personal space*. This notion embodies a common Anglo-Saxon perception that the distance of three to four feet constitutes a 'bubble of personal space' and an unwarranted appearance of a stranger within that bubble, in an uncrowded space, may become a source of concern (Fast, 1970; Hall, 1966; Hall & Hall, 1990; Wood, 1994).[1]

In the Russian language, the word *privacy* has no translation equivalent that would separate its meaning from that of *одиночество* (solitude), *тайна* (secrecy) or *интимность* (intimacy), and the collocation *personal space* does not have any translation equivalents. The Constitution of the Russian Federation provides guarantees of *личная неприкосновенность* (personal inviolability, article 22), *неприкосновенность частной жизни* (inviolability of personal life, article 23), *личные и семейные тайны* (personal and family secrets, article 23) and *тайна переписки и телефонных переговоров* (secrecy of correspondence and phone communication, article 23). These terms, however, do not render the key meaning of privacy as a natural and important human right to do things unobserved by others, nor do they refer to the bubble of personal space (Karasik *et al.*, 2005; Pavlenko, 1997; Wierzbicka, 1991). In the past few years, under the influence of English, Russian adopted a lexical borrowing, *privatnost'*, to refer to privacy as a legal and social concept, and a loan translation, *chastnoe prostranstvo* [private/personal space]. These terms were not available in 1995–1997 when the study was conducted and even now their scope of use is limited and their meaning has to be explained.[2]

The lack of the concepts of privacy and personal space, and the difficulty of adequately rendering these notions through the means of the Russian language are frequently mentioned by Russian scholars (e.g. Karasik *et al.*, 2005; Shlapentokh, 1989), by foreigners who visited Russia or the USSR (e.g. Richmond, 1992; Smith, 1983) and by Russian immigrants socialized into English (e.g. Reyn, 2000; Ripp, 1984). Speaking Russian, these immigrants, like the study participant quoted below, resort to code-switching in discussing privacy:

> (1) Или, например, *privacy* ... какая *privacy*?.. по–русски этого нету, я не
> могу сказать по–русски, знаешь, ну я могу сказать "Я хочу побыть одна",
> но это звучит слишком драматично, да?.. когда ты говоришь по–английски
> "*I need my privacy*" это более как ежедневная вещь и никто, никого это не
> волнует...

> [Or take, for instance, *privacy*... what *privacy*?.. in Russian this doesn't exist, I cannot say in Russian, you know, well, I can say "I want to be alone", but this sounds too dramatic, yes?.. when you say in English "*I need my privacy*" this is more like an everyday thing and no one, it doesn't bother anyone...] (Pavlenko, 2003: 275)

In the study in question, I hypothesized that, as a result of these crosslinguistic differences, English speakers may pay more attention than Russian speakers to interpersonal distances and perceived violations of personal space and that bilinguals who settle in an English-speaking context may internalize the concepts of privacy and personal space. To investigate these hypotheses, the study used two films, based on a single script, *The Ithaca Story* and *Kiev Story*. In the films, a young woman strolls through busy city streets. She stops to chat with two friends, but refuses their invitation to stay. She then continues to walk and eventually sits down on an empty bench. Taking a (note)book out of her bag, she starts writing something down (in *The Ithaca Story*) or reading (in *Kiev Story*). A young man comes over and sits down on the bench, within approximately four feet of the woman. He does not look in her direction. The woman starts fidgeting and eventually puts her (note)book in the bag, gets up and leaves.

The decision to portray a male–female interaction was based on two factors. First of all, previous research on violations of privacy and personal space in North American contexts had suggested that men invade women's spaces more frequently than women invade men's spaces and more than men invade other men's spaces (Wood, 1994). At the same time, invasions of women's spaces by men can have a range of alternative interpretations, from an innocent flirtation to a pick-up attempt. Consequently, a male–female interaction in the film offered the participants several possible interpretations. The participants were asked to retell the story, with the expectation that in imposing narrative structure on a sequence of events, they would infer the reasons for the woman's departure.

Altogether, 130 participants took part in the study. The discussion of participants and their performance will rely on Pavlenko (1997) for monolingual data and on Pavlenko (2003) for a reanalysis of the bilingual data, with some 1997 participant data deleted for not conforming to the study requirements (see Table 7.1 for an overview of the research design).

Native speakers of English ($n = 40$, 20 females, 20 males, ages 18–26, mean $= 19.8$) were undergraduate students at Cornell University. Native speakers of Russian ($n = 40$, 20 females, 20 males, ages 18–26, mean $= 22.9$) were undergraduate students at the University of St. Petersburg. All participants had foreign language (FL) instruction in secondary school and at the university, but reported low levels of FL competence and consequently were treated as 'monolinguals' for the purposes of the study. Each group was randomly divided into subgroups of 20 participants who watched and recalled one of the films.

Russian-English bilinguals ($n = 50$) were divided into two groups. Bilingual Group 1 FL users of English ($n = 18$, 8 females, 10 males, age range 18–26, mean $= 22.7$) were undergraduate students at the University of St. Petersburg. They had studied English in middle and high school (for up to six years) and at the university (for up to four years). Unlike participants considered to be 'monolingual', FL users were enrolled in advanced English-language classes at the University of

Table 7.1 Study 1: Experimental conditions and sample sizes

	Language of recall	
Participants	*English*	*Russian*
Native speakers of English	*The Ithaca Story* ($n = 20$) *Kiev Story* ($n = 20$)	
Native speakers of Russian		*The Ithaca Story* ($n = 20$) *Kiev Story* ($n = 20$)
Bilingual Group 1 FL users	*The Ithaca Story* ($n = 10$) *Kiev Story* ($n = 8$)	
Bilingual Group 2 L2 users	*The Ithaca Story* ($n = 10$) *Kiev Story* ($n = 8$)	*The Ithaca Story* ($n = 10$) *Kiev Story* ($n = 4$)

St. Petersburg, where they were recruited. None of the participants ever visited an English-speaking country or had any long-term contact with native speakers of English. The participants were randomly divided into two film conditions.

Bilingual Group 2 L2 users of English ($n = 32$, 18 females, 14 males, age range 18–31, mean = 21.6) were undergraduate and graduate students at Cornell University. These participants arrived in the USA between the ages of 10 and 26.5 (mean age of arrival = 16.0). Twenty-eight participants arrived as immigrants and four as international students. They had limited exposure to English prior to arrival and had learned English in the USA through English as a second language (ESL) classes, public or private school attendance, and naturalistic exposure. By the time of the study, the participants had spent between one and 17 years in the USA (mean length of exposure = 6.0). They used Russian with their families, relatives and Russian-speaking friends, and English with English-speaking friends and for educational and everyday interactional purposes. The participants were randomly divided into two subgroups, Russian and English, and within these subgroups into conditions by film.

All participants performed the recalls individually. They were given a tape-recorder and the following instructions, either in English or in Russian: 'Please, tell what you just saw in the film'/ 'Пожалуйста, расскажите, что вы видели в фильме '. At the end of the recall, the few participants who did not make spontaneous inferences about the girl's departure were asked: 'Why do you think the girl left?'/ 'Как вам кажется, почему девушка ушла?'

Four findings of the study are relevant to the discussion here. First, the analysis revealed the effects of codability on participants' narratives. Native speakers of English and Russian differed in the dominant interpretations of the woman's departure: while English-language interpretations emphasized the woman's loss of comfort, Russian-language ones favored gender-based scenarios, such as 'unsuccessful pick-up' or 'dislike of the guy'. Most importantly, English speakers consistently saw something in *The Ithaca Story*[3] film that Russian speakers did not: the bubble of personal space. In their recalls, 17 out of 20 English speakers (85% agreement) spontaneously referred to the invasion of privacy or personal space (e.g. 'she felt almost invaded, like her privacy was being invaded', 'the girl's privacy was being invaded', 'the guy was invading her space', 'he was in her space kind of'). Several participants also commented on the distance between the two characters (e.g. 'he sat down a little too close for her comfort', 'he was... maybe too close'). Russian speakers did not observe any invasion or intrusion, and did not comment on the spatial proximity of the characters, in either film, although they could have said that the man was sitting *слишком близко* (*slishkom blizko* [too close]) to the woman. These results suggest that crosslinguistic differences in codability of *privacy* and *personal space* (at least in 1995–1997 when the study was conducted) led the speakers of the two languages to partition space differently: English speakers consistently paid more attention to interpersonal distances and perceived violations of personal space.

Secondly, the analysis of the bilingual performance revealed that the context of language acquisition influences internalization and use of translation non-equivalents. FL users performed similarly to monolingual Russian speakers in their recalls: they favored gender-based interpretations and never commented on the spatial proximity of the characters. During the debriefing procedure, five FL users were able to provide some definitions of *privacy*, but stated that they were not sure when and how to use this term. L2 users offered both types of interpretations of the woman's departure: comfort-based ones that were dominant among English speakers and gender-based ones dominant among Russian speakers. Most importantly, like English speakers and unlike Russian speakers, five bilingual participants saw the bubble of personal space being invaded in *The Ithaca Story* film and commented on it, one in an English-language narrative and four in Russian-language narratives. A replication of this study with the films *The Letter* and *Pis'mo* (Pavlenko, 2002b; see the following Section 7.4), which portrayed violation of informational privacy, revealed the same difference between FL and L2 users. FL users did not comment on the privacy of information, while several L2 users referred to the character's need to be alone and not to share personal information. Two of them made direct references to *privacy* and *personal space* in English-language narratives ('her personal space was intruded'; 'she, uhm, obviously gets angry at her roommate about not keeping her privacy') (Pavlenko, 2002b).

This invocation of privacy by seven bilingual individuals undoubtedly lacks the magnitude required by mainstream psycholinguistic research. At the same time, these results, achieved in spontaneous performance, rather than in artificial laboratory tasks, satisfy ecological validity requirements. Showing that these seven bilinguals saw and described something that 80 speakers of their L1 (40 in the first study and 40 in the second study) did not comment on, they reveal a new way of relating words to the world mediated by the newly internalized lexical categories *privacy* and *personal space*. The finding that only L2 users attempted to refer to privacy and personal space suggests that internalization of lexical categories not encoded in the speakers' L1 requires interaction with target language speakers, where the use of the words in question would draw speakers' attention to aspects of external reality that prompted this use. As seen below, in an excerpt from a follow-up interview with one of the study participants, these experiences are not always pleasant and the new categories may not be highly valued; nevertheless, they become new interpretive frames for understanding events:

> (2) Я бы сказал... здесь такое ударение на личное/частное, такое большое... каждый, так, скажем... я бы сказал, американцы, так, они... так... они очень большое внимание уделяют своей личности, *privacy*, даже когда люди знакомятся, они, я бы сравнил бы, здесь они легко знакомятся и дальше дело идет хорошо, а потом уже достигаешь такого барьера, стены, уже эта стена, стена *privacy*, то есть, через нее ты уже не пройдешь...

> [I would say... there is such an emphasis here on personal/private, such big... everyone, so to say... I would say, Americans, so, they... so... they pay a lot of attention to their personality, *privacy*, even when people meet, they, I would compare, here they meet easily and all goes well, and then you reach that barrier, a wall, already this wall, the wall of *privacy*, that is, you can't get through it...] (Pavlenko, 2003: 275–276)

The third finding is that the language of recall does not necessarily constrain the use of translation non-equivalents: while three bilingual speakers in the two sets of studies referred to *privacy* and *personal space* in English-language narratives, four made attempts to refer to these notions in narratives told in Russian. In the absence of Russian translation equivalents, these attempts resulted first in hesitations and pausing, due to unsuccessful lexical searches, and then in references that violated semantic and morphosyntactic constraints of Russian. These references included one lexical borrowing, 'интрузивность' (*intruzivnost'*/intrusiveness), two loan translations, 'он... мм... вторгается в ее одиночество' (he... uhm... is invading her solitude) and 'тот молодой человек, который вторгся в ее... эмоции, чувства' (that young man who invaded her... emotions, feelings), and one self-interrupted clause, 'что он пересек, то есть, что она уже не может быть одна' (that he crossed, so, that she can no longer be alone). These attempts show that in the bilingual mind external referents may trigger internal representations of categories that are not encoded in the language-in-use. This lack of lexicalization, in turn, may lead to dysfluencies, lexical borrowing, loan translation and, in some cases, code-switching. In the follow-up interviews, the participants acknowledged that they looked for translation equivalents of *privacy*, but did not feel comfortable code-switching because the instructions required them to speak Russian. In the interviews, however, they appealed to code-switching to refer to *privacy*, as seen in excerpts (1) through (3).

The study also suggested that cultural context, operationalized here as visual context, may affect the use of translation non-equivalents in monolingual and bilingual participants. As already mentioned earlier, 85% of the native speakers of English referred to *privacy* or *personal space* in recalls of *The Ithaca Story*, filmed in Ithaca, USA, while only 10% ($n = 2$) referred to these notions in recalls of *Kiev Story*, filmed in Kiev, Ukraine. Among bilingual participants, 25% ($n = 5$) referred to *privacy* in recalls of *The Ithaca Story*, and none in *Kiev Story* recalls. This difference may have two alternative interpretations. To begin with, it is possible that the films simply differ in how they portray the encounter between the two characters and the situation in *The Ithaca Story* is perceived as a more prototypical example of an invasion of privacy. Alternatively, it may be the case that speakers of English, monolingual or bilingual, may be more willing to apply language-specific terms, such as *privacy* or *personal space*, to contexts perceived as culturally congruent with the terms (the environment in *Kiev Story* was perceived as 'Russian' by monolingual and bilingual Russian speakers and as 'foreign' by English speakers). This possibility was indirectly confirmed in the follow-up interviews with bilingual participants, several of whom mentioned that Russian speakers may find the notions of *privacy* and *personal space* ridiculous and/or unacceptable. The participant quoted below commented on the lack of association between Russian life and *privacy*:

(3) английское слово *privacy* для меня существовало, но оно никогда у меня не ассоциировалось с жизнью российской, никогда оно у меня не переводилось... оно существовало совершенно отдельно, мм, особым *privacy* миром, каким оно вот и является таковым. То есть, для того, чтобы подумать об этом на русском языке, мне нужно было бы найти очень много специальных отдельных слов, и когда мне хотелось что-то такое вот утвердить свою *privacy*, я именно употребляла слово *privacy* даже по отношению к своему мужу... русскому.

[...the English word *privacy* has existed for me but for me it was never associated with Russian life, it was never translated... it existed complete separately, in its own *privacy* world, just as it is. So, in order to think about it in Russian, I would need to find very many special separate words, so when I wanted to somehow assert my *privacy*, I would use the word *privacy* even when talking to my husband... a Russian.] (Pavlenko, 2003: 274–275)

To sum up, the study provided experimental evidence in support of the argument that crosslinguistic differences in codability lead to differences in perception and verbalization of events involving the referent in question. Native speakers of English used collocations *violation of privacy* and *invasion of personal space* to refer to aspects of external reality that are not encoded in Russian and, as a result, were either imperceptible to monolingual Russian speakers or judged to be unworthy of mentioning. The study also established that the context of language acquisition affects internalization of translation non-equivalents: some L2 users who resided in the L2 environment were able to map *privacy* and *personal space* onto the external reality in the same way as native speakers of English. In contrast, FL users were unable to do so because they only had the definition of the word, but did not know how to map it onto external referents. The language of recall did not preclude the triggering of translation non-equivalents – four out of five references to *privacy* appeared in Russian-language narratives, suggesting that categories of one language are available during verbal performance in another. Last but not least, the congruence between translation non-equivalents and visual (cultural) context was found to favor the use of the non-equivalent or language-specific terms.

7.5　A Rose By Any Other Name: Word-to-Referent Mapping and Translation Equivalence

The next series of studies shifted the inquiry into the domain of emotions and examined the effects of the context of acquisition on the use of translation equivalents and non-equivalents, the non-equivalent this time being a term encoded in Russian but not in English (Pavlenko, 1997, 2002a, 2002b, 2008b; Pavlenko & Driagina, 2007). These studies asked two questions: (1) How do translation equivalence and non-equivalence affect lexical choice in narratives elicited from native speakers of English and Russian? (2) How does the context of acquisition affect the use of translation equivalents and non-equivalents by Russian-English and English-Russian bilinguals? The translation equivalents in question were *upset/расстроенная* (*rasstroennaia*, fem) and *scared/испуганный* (*ispugannyi*, masc). The non-equivalent was the Russian emotion verb *переживать* (*perezhivat'*), which refers to the active process of experiencing emotions keenly or, literally, 'suffering things through', and does not have an English-language counterpart.

The studies were conducted using three films. The first set of studies used two films, *The Letter* and *Pis'mo*, based on the same script and made, respectively, in Ithaca, USA, and Kiev, Ukraine (Pavlenko, 1997, 2002a, 2002b; Pavlenko & Driagina, 2007). In the films, a young woman walks down the street, comes home, gets her mail, walks into her apartment, opens one letter and starts reading. She appears emotional as she reads the letter, then puts it down, then rereads it again. Another young woman walks in, and, in an attempt to understand what is going on, picks up the letter and starts reading it. The first woman notices that the second one is reading her letter, grabs the letter, and leaves the room. In recalls, participants were expected to make inferences regarding the first woman's emotions and her departure from the room.

A follow-up study was conducted with a different elicitation stimulus, a segment from the British *Mr. Bean* TV series, entitled *Mr. Bean in the swimming pool* (Pavlenko, 2008b). In this segment, Mr. Bean arrives at a swimming pool, tries to climb on a children's slide, and is chased by the lifeguard from the children's section. Then he moves to the adult section and notices a diving board. He decides to jump from it, but when he reaches the top and looks down he becomes visibly scared and changes his mind. Yet, he cannot go back the way he came because two boys behind him are waiting for their turn. Eventually, as Mr. Bean is hanging off the diving board still reluctant to jump, one boy stomps on his hand and Mr. Bean falls into the swimming pool. In the process, he loses his swimming trunks and decides to stay in the pool until everyone leaves. Then, he climbs out naked and is spotted by a girls' swimming team. The participants recalling the film were expected to make inferences regarding Mr. Bean's emotions.

Altogether, 241 participants took part in the studies. The following discussion relies on Pavlenko (1997, 2002a) and Pavlenko and Driagina (2007) for monolingual data collected with *The Letter* and *Pis'mo*, on Pavlenko (1997, 2002b, 2008b) and Pavlenko and Driagina (2007) for bilingual data collected with these films, and on Pavlenko (2008b) for monolingual and bilingual data collected with the use of *Mr. Bean in the swimming pool* (see Table 7.2 for an overview of the research design). The discussion is supplemented with new analyses involving frequencies of particular lexical choices.

Native speakers of English ($n = 70$) were recruited at two universities in the USA, one private and one public, to control for possible language variation stemming from geographical and socio-educational factors. Undergraduate students at Cornell University ($n = 40$, 20 females, 20 males, ages 18–26, mean = 19.8) recalled *The Letter* and *Pis'mo*. Because the films were based on the same script, only 20 participants watched and recalled each film. Undergraduate students at the Pennsylvania State University ($n = 30$, 15 females, 15 males, ages 18–22, mean = 20.2) recalled *The Letter* and *Mr. Bean in the swimming pool*. All participants had FL instruction but reported low levels of FL competence.

Native speakers of Russian ($n = 69$) were recruited at two universities in Russia that differed in geographic location and socio-educational characteristics of the student population, and resembled their US counterparts (for a discussion of the universities, see Pavlenko and Driagina, 2007). Undergraduate students at the University of St. Petersburg ($n = 40$, 20 females, 20 males, ages 18–26, mean = 22.9) recalled *The Letter* and *Pis'mo*. Once again, only 20 participants watched and recalled each film. Undergraduate students at Tomsk State University ($n = 29$, 21 females, 8

Table 7.2 Study 2: Experimental conditions and sample sizes

	Language of recall	
Participants	*English*	*Russian*
Native speakers of English	*The Letter* ($n = 50$) Pis'mo ($n = 20$) *Mr. Bean* ($n = 30$)	
Native speakers of Russian		*The Letter* ($n = 49$) Pis'mo ($n = 20$) *Mr. Bean* ($n = 19$)
Bilingual Group 1 FL users of English	*The Letter* ($n = 10$) Pis'mo ($n = 8$)	
Bilingual Group 2 L2 users of English	*The Letter* ($n = 20$) Pis'mo ($n = 4$) *Mr. Bean* ($n = 20$)	*The Letter* ($n = 10$) Pis'mo ($n = 7$)
Bilingual Group 3 FL users of Russian		*The Letter* ($n = 30$) *Mr. Bean* ($n = 30$)

males, ages 18–21, mean $= 19.7$) recalled *The Letter* and 19 of these recalled *Mr. Bean*. All participants reported low levels of FL competence.

Bilinguals ($n = 102$) who participated in the studies were divided into three groups. Bilingual Group 1 FL users of English ($n = 18$, 10 males, 8 females, age range 18–26, mean $= 22.7$) were undergraduate students at the University of St. Petersburg. They were the same participants who took part in the study discussed in Section 7.2 and were randomly divided into two film conditions. Participants who watched *The Ithaca Story* also watched *The Letter*, and those who watched *Kiev Story* also watched Pis'mo.

Bilingual Group 2 L2 users of English ($n = 54$) were recruited at two universities to match the participants considered to be 'monolingual'. Undergraduate and graduate students at Cornell University ($n = 31$, 18 females, 13 males, age range 18–31, mean $= 21.6$) recalled *The Letter* and Pis'mo. These were the same participants who took part in the previously discussed study minus one who only recalled *The Ithaca Story*. Under-graduate and graduate students at the Pennsylvania State University ($n = 23$, ages 18–40, mean $= 25.7$) recalled *The Letter* and *Mr. Bean* in L2 English. *The Letter* narratives were collected from 18 participants (8 females, 10 males) and *Mr. Bean* narratives from 20 participants (10 females, 10 males). The participants' age of arrival in the USA varied between the ages of 9 and 33 (mean $= 21.4$). The length of exposure to English in the USA varied between 1 and 10 years (mean $= 4.2$). Most of the participants had studied English in secondary and higher education establishments in Russia and other post-Soviet countries (e.g. Kazakhstan, Ukraine) between three and 19 years (mean = 8.9) and came to the USA as students.

Bilingual Group 3 American FL users of Russian ($n = 30$, 15 females, 15 males, ages 19–56, mean = 26.9) were undergraduate and graduate students enrolled in advanced-level Russian courses in the intensive immersion program at the Middlebury College Summer Russian School. The students differed in the length of study of the language (range 1–16 years, mean = 5.3), but were ranked similarly by the program, as advanced language learners.

All participants performed the recalls individually. They were given a tape-recorder and the following instructions, either in English or in Russian: 'Please, tell what you just saw in the film'/'Пожалуйста, расскажите, что вы видели в фильме'. Participants who did not make spontaneous inferences about the young woman's departure in *The Letter* and *Pis'mo* were asked: 'Why do you think the girl left?'/'Как вам кажется, почему девушка ушла?'

Two sets of findings are relevant to this discussion. The first set of findings involves the performance of monolingual participants. The analysis of *The Letter* narratives revealed striking homogeneity within the monolingual corpora in descriptions of emotions experienced by the main character while reading the letter. In English speakers' narratives, 90% of the participants used the adjective *upset*, and in Russian speakers' narratives, 73% used translation equivalents of the word *upset*, the verb расстраиваться (*rasstraivat'sia*), the adjective расстроенная (*rasstroennaia*) and the noun расстройство (*rasstroistvo*) (Pavlenko, 2002a; Pavlenko & Driagina, 2007). The high intra-group agreement suggests that emotions portrayed by the actress in the film were perceived as prototypical in terms of the lexical categories in question. The inter-group agreement on translation equivalents suggests that these prototypes may be shared by the speakers of Russian and English. Recalls of *Pis'mo* elicited more variation in lexical choice, possibly due to the performer's acting style. Nevertheless, the character was described as *upset* by 45% of the English-speaking participants and as *rasstroennaia* by 30% of the Russian speakers (Pavlenko, 2002a). Higher agreement was reached in recalls of *Mr. Bean*, where 57% of the English speakers used the adjective *scared* and 68% of the Russian speakers the verb *ispugat'sia* (to get scared) to describe emotions experienced by Mr. Bean on the diving board. The inter-group agreement on these translation equivalents suggests that they, too, are formed around the same prototype, captured in the film.

Translation non-equivalence, on the other hand, resulted in differences in recalls, similar to ones identified in the study of *privacy* and *personal space*. Of the native speakers of Russian, 32% ($n = 22$) used the verb *perezhivat'* to refer to the main protagonist's emotions in *The Letter* and *Pis'mo*, while narratives by English speakers had no similar references to emotions as an active process. Interestingly, most of these references came from *The Letter* narratives (19 participants), only three participants used the term in recalls of *Pis'mo*. This suggests that the performance in *The Letter* was perceived as more prototypical of *perezhivat'* and that in the domain of emotions the use of translation non-equivalents does not require congruence between the cultural context and the language-in-use.

The two monolingual groups also differed in morphosyntactic categories used for emotion description: English speakers consistently favored emotion adjectives in the contexts where Russian speakers favored emotion verbs and, in some cases, adverbs (Pavlenko, 2002a, 2008b; Pavlenko & Driagina, 2007). This finding may have two alternative interpretations. It is possible that structural preferences are just a usage convention and have no implications for perception of emotions. Wierzbicka (1992) argues, however, that these morphosyntactic preferences are indicative of different conceptualizations of emotions: English favors the conceptualization of emotions as states and Russian of emotions as actions and processes, which finds reflection in intransitive verbs, like *perezhivat'*, and a richer set of expressions linking emotions to the body and facial expression. Indirect evidence in favor of the latter argument was found in greater attention to body language and facial expressions paid by Russian speakers in their recalls of *The Letter* and *Pis'mo* (Pavlenko, 2002a).

The second set of findings involves bilinguals' performance. The use of translation equivalents was not affected by the context of acquisition, the language of recall or visual context. Both FL and L2 users approximated dominant lexical choices of the target language speakers. In L2 English narratives elicited by *The Letter*, 79% of the L2 users of English and 50% of the FL users of English described the main character as *upset*. In L2 Russian narratives elicited by *The Letter*, 30% of the FL users of Russian described the main character using the verb *rasstrai-vat'sia* or the corresponding adjective. In recalls of *Mr. Bean*, 60% of Russian L2 users of English described Mr. Bean as *scared* and 37% of American FL users of Russian used the translation equivalent *(is)pugat'sia* (Pavlenko, 2008b). These findings suggest that target-like use of L2 translation equivalents does not require exposure to L2 contexts, most likely because the new forms are mapped onto familiar external referents.

Furthermore, the results revealed that FL Russian, FL English and L2 English users also displayed target-like structural preferences, the adjectival pattern in English and the verbal one in Russian (Pavlenko, 2008b; Pavlenko & Driagina, 2007). These findings suggest that inter-nalization of new structural preferences also does not require exposure to the L2 context. The change in structural mappings is not, however, smooth and immediate: some FL users' narratives also displayed a transfer of the adjectival pattern from the L1 English to the L2 Russian (Pavlenko & Driagina, 2007).

On the other hand, the use of the non-equivalent *perezhivat'* was affected by the context of acquisition. None of the 30 American FL users of Russian used *perezhivat'*, even though the word is salient in Russian-language textbooks. During the debriefing, several FL users recognized the verb and stated that they 'studied it' but were still not sure when to use it. These findings partially replicate those of the privacy study, suggesting that FL instruction is not sufficient for internalization of new lexical categories. I was not, however, able to identify a group of L1 English L2 users of Russian living in Russia that would be comparable to the Russian L2 users of English in terms of language proficiency, to see if they had internalized the notion of *perezhivat'*.

Unexpectedly, it was also found that L2 acquisition in the target language context may have a backward effect on L1 performance. Russian-language narratives of Russian L2 users of English residing in the USA displayed instances of transfer of the L2 English adjectival pattern into L1 Russian (Pavlenko, 2002b). These instances suggest that the process of structural re-mapping that took place during the acquisition of English also affected word-to-referent mapping in Russian. The narratives also revealed a decreased salience of the verb *perezhivat'*: it was used by only 1 out of 17 participants who performed the recalls in Russian.

To sum up, the emotion lexicon studies demonstrated that the context of L2 acquisition affects acquisition of language-specific lexical categories, but not of translation equivalents or structural non-equivalents. Together, the studies discussed here and in the previous section clarified the role of the context of L2 acquisition in the internalization of translation equivalents and non-equivalents and hinted at potential L2 influence on the L1. The next logical step was to examine the L2 influence on the L1 in word-to-referent mapping, and the best way to proceed was by using partial translation equivalents, which until now have remained unexamined.

7.6 What's in a Name?: Word-to-Referent Mapping and Partial Translation Equivalence

To understand how words are mapped onto referents in the context of partial translation equivalence and how these mappings may change in the L1 under the influence of the L2, Pavlenko and Malt (in press) conducted a study in which monolingual and bilingual speakers were asked to name a wide variety of drinking containers. Three research questions were asked in the study: (1) How do native speakers of Russian and English map words onto the same set of referents? (2) In the context of differences between native speakers of Russian and English, how do Russian-English bilinguals name the same referents in their L1 Russian? (3) How does the age of arrival in the L2 context affect the bilinguals' performance?

In comparison with the previous studies, this study shifted the focus of the investigation from the L2 to L1 performance (or, more specifically, to L2 influence on L1), and also from phenomena to objects, and thus from abstract to concrete words. The study also differed from the earlier ones in terms of methodology because it drew on the approach developed by Malt and associates (see Malt & Ameel, this volume), thereby relying on the naming and rating of object pictures rather than on narrative elicitation. The decrease in ecological validity stemming from the focus on decontextualized words was balanced out by the use of a wide array of photographs that allowed us to examine the structure of the linguistic categories in question and the relationship between naming and participants' judgments on familiarity and typicality of the referents with regard to particular lexical categories. The objects under investigation in the study were drinking containers that English speakers commonly name *cups*, *glasses* or *mugs*. Based on previous empirical studies and semantic analyses (e.g. Wierzbicka, 1984), the words *mug* and *кружка* (*kruzhka*) were expected to be full equivalents and the word pairs *cup/чашка* (*chashka*) and *glass/стакан* (*stakan*) partial equivalents, because a porcelain *cup*, for instance, is called *chashka* (cup) in Russian, but a paper or plastic *cup* is called *stakan* (glass).

A total of 69 participants took part in the study. Native speakers of English ($n = 20$) were undergraduate students at Lehigh University and Temple University, USA. Native speakers of Russian ($n = 20$) were undergraduate students at the University of Kazan, Russia. All 40 participants rated themselves at 7 on a 1–7 scale in their native language across four skills: listening, speaking, reading and writing. Only a few, however, were completely monolingual. Most English-speaking participants had some knowledge of another language, in which they rated themselves at lower levels of proficiency. Several of the Russian participants also had knowledge of another language, most commonly English and/or Tatar. Some rated themselves as bilingual in Russian and Tatar, but none rated themselves as proficient in English.

Russian-English bilinguals ($n = 29$) were undergraduate and graduate students and staff members at Temple University. All rated themselves as fluent in Russian and English. To confirm their Russian fluency, two narratives and four picture descriptions were elicited in Russian from each bilingual participant. Based on the age of arrival in the USA, they were divided into three groups: early, childhood and late bilinguals.

Early bilinguals ($n = 9$) were between the ages of 18 and 24 (mean = 19.9). They arrived in the USA between the ages of 1 and 6 (mean = 3.4) as members of Russian-speaking immigrant families from Russia, Ukraine, Uzbekistan and Moldova. All grew up in Russian-speaking families, using Russian at home with family members and relatives and English outside the home (including with Russian-speaking friends). All attended English-speaking schools and had spent between 13 and 18.5 years in the USA (mean = 16.5). They rated themselves at the top of the proficiency scale in English (mean = 7.0) and lower in Russian (mean = 4.5).

Childhood bilinguals ($n = 9$) were between the ages of 18 and 27 (mean = 20.7). They arrived in the USA between the ages of 8 and 15 (mean = 11.7) as members of Russian-speaking immigrant families from Russia, Ukraine and Latvia. All began their education in Russian-language schools and continued in English-speaking secondary schools. Growing up in the USA, they continued to use Russian at home with family members and relatives and English outside the home (including with Russian-speaking friends). By the time of the study, they had spent between six and 12 years in the USA (mean = 9.0). They rated themselves at almost the top of the proficiency scale in English (mean = 6.6) and slightly lower in Russian (mean = 5.9).

Late bilinguals ($n = 11$) were between the ages of 21 and 37 (mean = 28.0). They arrived in the USA between the ages of 19 and 27 (mean = 22.8) as students from Russian-speaking families in Russia, Ukraine, and Armenia. Nine participants had graduated from Russian-language secondary schools, one from a Ukrainian-Russian bilingual school and one from an Armenian-Russian bilingual school. The majority had also received undergraduate education in Russian. By the time of the study, they had spent between six months and 15 years in the USA (mean = 5.2). In the USA, they used Russian with Russian-speaking friends and colleagues and on the telephone with family members and friends at home, and English for work and study and with English-speaking friends. They rated themselves somewhat below the top of the proficiency scale in English (mean = 5.4) and almost at the top in Russian (mean = 6.9).

Data collection was performed on-line but an experimenter helped administer the tasks, offering clarifications, when necessary, in the language of the task. The participants began by filling out an on-line language background questionnaire, which included self-ratings of the four skills in Russian and English. Then, each participant performed five consecutive tasks using photographs of 60 common drinking containers, made specifically for the study (for examples, see Figures 7.1 and 7.2). The set consisted of objects that were likely to be called *cup*, *mug* or *glass* in English and *chashka*, *kruzhka* or *stakan* in Russian.

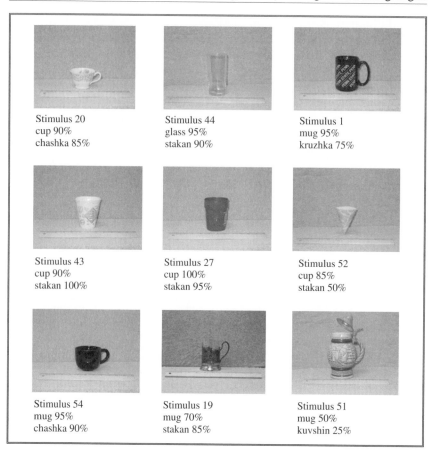

Figure 7.1 Some of the exemplars from the drinking containers set (% refers to the percentage of native speakers of English and Russian who produced the name listed) (Reproduced with permission, Cambridge University Press)

The objects were chosen to represent a wide range of drinking containers and included containers made in the USA (e.g. a beer stein; see Figure 7.1, stimulus 51) and those made in Russia (e.g. a tea glass in a metal glass-holder; see Figure 7.1, stimulus 19). The large size of the stimulus set and the wide range of objects in it allowed for a sensitive comparison of patterns of word use.

The website had two versions, English and Russian. Native speakers of English used the English-language version of the website, and native speakers of Russian and Russian-English bilinguals used the Russian version. In task 1, Naming and Confidence, the 60 photographs were presented one at a time, in randomized order, on the computer screen. The participants were asked to name the objects as they would in

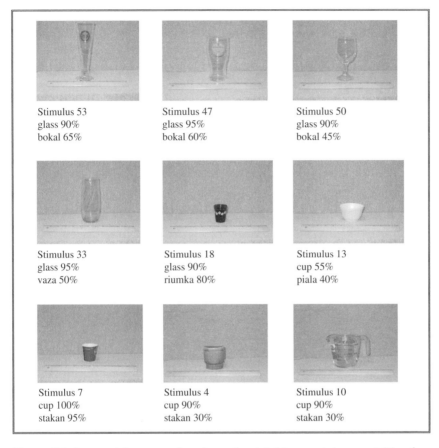

Figure 7.2 Some of the exemplars from the drinking containers set (% refers to the percentage of native speakers of English and Russian who produced the name listed) (Reproduced with permission, Cambridge University Press)

an ordinary conversation and to indicate how confident they were that other native speakers would use the same name to refer to the object, using a Likert scale from 1 (labeled 'not very confident at all') to 7 (labeled 'very confident'). In task 2, Familiarity, the same 60 photographs were presented in a different randomized order and participants were asked to rate the familiarity of each sort of object depicted on a Likert scale from 1 (labeled 'not very familiar at all') to 7 (labeled 'very familiar'). In tasks 3–5, Typicality, the same 60 photographs appeared in a randomized order (different for each task) and participants were asked to rate the typicality of each object with regard to a name using a Likert scale from 1 (labeled 'not very typical at all') to 7 (labeled 'very typical').

As in other studies by Malt and associates (see Malt & Ameel, this volume), the names produced for each object were tallied for each language group, producing a frequency distribution in each language. Confidence, familiarity and typicality ratings were averaged across respondents for each object in each category for which ratings were collected. The native speakers of Russian and English and the early and childhood Russian bilinguals all had a mean confidence in their choices (across the 60 stimuli) of above 5 on the 7-point scale, whereas early bilinguals had a mean confidence of 4.4. This dip for the early bilinguals is consistent with their lower self-reported proficiency in Russian. All groups were reasonably familiar with the stimuli, with the average familiarity rating across the 60 stimuli for the four groups ranging from 5.3 to 6.3. Thus, the stimulus set seems to primarily contain objects quite familiar to all groups studied.

Two sets of findings are relevant for this discussion. The first set of findings concerns the performance of native speakers of Russian and English, and, consequently, the internal structure of the six lexical categories under investigation. Our analyses revealed that for native speakers of the two languages, *mug* and *kruzhka* were overlapping categories, which included ceramic objects for hot drinks with vertical sides, wide bottoms and a handle (e.g. Figure 7.1, stimulus 1). The only differences were found in containers slightly tapered toward the bottom – these were named *mug* by English speakers and *chashka* by Russian speakers (e.g. Figure 7.1, stimulus 54). In contrast, in the case of *cup/chashka* and *glass/stakan*, the speakers of the two languages differed systematically in the naming patterns and typicality judgments of the drinking containers.

Cup, in English, was found to be a broad category that includes containers with or without handles, made out of a variety of materials, and intended for hot and cold drinks, as well as for measuring purposes. The prototypical *cups*, i.e. the objects rated most typical of *cup* by English speakers, were tapered containers without handles, made out of paper, styrofoam, plastic, metal or ceramic, intended for cold drinks (e.g. Figure 7.1, stimuli 43, 27, 52; Figure 7.2, stimuli 7, 4). In contrast, prototypical *chashki* were shorter ceramic or porcelain containers with handles, slightly rounded at the bottom, and intended for hot drinks – mostly objects that the English speakers called *tea cup* or *coffee cup* (e.g. Figure 7.1, stimuli 20, 54). The typicality distributions across the 60 objects for *cup* and *chashka* did not correlate significantly, reflecting the fact that the objects most typical as *cup* were very atypical as *chashka*. These two linguistic categories thus share some membership, but appear to be centered on different prototypes and to differ a great deal in their breadth.

Glass, in English, was found to be a category heavily constrained by material (glass) and the absence of a handle, but to include objects with or without a stem, and those used for cold alcoholic and non-alcoholic drinks (e.g. Figure 7.1, stimulus 44; Figure 7.2, stimuli 53, 47, 50, 33, 18). In contrast, in Russian it is a broad category constrained only by shape – it includes tapered containers without handles, made out of paper, styrofoam, plastic, metal, glass or ceramic, some of which, including containers made of glass, can also be used for hot drinks (in this case they are served in a metal glass-holder) (e.g. Figure 7.1, stimuli 44, 43, 27, 52, 19; Figure 7.2, stimuli 7, 4, 10). For these two categories, then, there is some overlap in typical members (tall, glass containers without handles used for cold drinks, such as stimulus 44 in Figure 7.1), but Russian admits a broader range of materials and objects intended for hot drinks while excluding objects with stems regardless of material.

To name containers used for alcoholic drinks, Russian has four lexical categories: tall ones are called *bokal* (with or without a stem) or *fuzher* (with a stem) (e.g. Figure 7.2, stimuli 53, 47, 50), and shorter ones *riumka* (with or without a stem) or *stopka* (without a stem) (e.g. Figure 7.2, stimulus 18). In English, these containers received the dominant name *glass*, sometimes preceded by functional modifiers *wine, champagne, beer, martini, cognac* and *shot*. Smaller wooden or porcelain containers, with or without a stem, received the dominant name *cup*.

This overview of similarities and differences in the structure of the categories *cup, chashka, glass* and *stakan* explains why some containers, most prominently paper and plastic drinking containers without handles, became 'cross-over' objects, called *cup* in English and *stakan* in Russian, with high intra-group agreement (e.g. Figure 7.1, stimuli 43, 27, 52; Figure 7.2, stimulus 7).

The second set of findings involves the performance of the bilingual participants. The comparisons of bilingual name similarity matrices with the one for native Russian speakers show that the age of arrival in the L2 context affects L1 naming patterns: the late bilinguals' naming pattern correlates most strongly with the native speakers of Russian, followed by the childhood bilinguals, and then by the early bilinguals. Nevertheless, all groups differed from the Russian speakers: late bilinguals in the names for 12 objects, childhood bilinguals in the names for 12 objects (plus 4 objects where the use of a different name tied as a dominant name with the word used by the native speakers) and early bilinguals in the names for 31 objects.

The influence of L2 English on L1 Russian naming was visible in all three groups (see also Table 7.3). Late bilinguals, following the English-language use of *glass*, expanded the use of the word *stakan* to containers used for alcoholic drinks whose dominant names in Russian were, respectively, *bokal* and *riumka* (e.g. Figure 7.2, stimuli 47, 18). Another object with a dominant name, *riumka*, in Russian became *chashka* for late

Table 7.3 Study 3: Examples of category shifts in bilingual performance (% refers to the percentage of participants who produced the name listed)

Stimulus number	Native Russian	%	Bilinguals	%	Native English	%
Early bilinguals						
53	bokal	65	stakan	78	glass	90
47	bokal	60	stakan	78	glass	95
50	bokal	45	stakan	44	glass	90
33	vaza	50	stakan	67	glass	95
18	riumka	80	stakan	44	glass	90
13	piala	40	chashka	56	cup	55
43	stakan	100	chashka	56	cup	90
7	stakan	95	chashka	56	cup	100
52	stakan	50	chashka	44	cup	85
Childhood bilinguals						
53	bokal	65	stakan	67	glass	90
47	bokal	60	stakan	78	glass	95
33	vaza	50	stakan	78	glass	95
13	piala	40	chashka	44	cup	55
4	stakan	30	chashka	44	cup	90
10	stakan	30	kruzhka/ chashka	33 each	cup	90
Late bilinguals						
47	bokal	60	stakan	73	glass	95
18	riumka	80	stakan	55	glass	90
8	riumka	65	stakan	55	glass	95
26	riumka	35	chashka	55	cup	75

bilinguals, also consistent with the English preference for *cup*. In references to tall containers used for alcoholic drinks, they were more likely to default to the broader term *bokal*, including in cases where the dominant name for native Russian speakers was *fuzher*.

Childhood bilinguals have further expanded the use of the word *stakan*, to include two objects called *bokal* and a tall container called *vaza* (vase) by native speakers of Russian and late bilinguals (Figure 7.2, stimuli 53, 47, 33). In English, all three objects received the dominant name *glass*. Similarly, in accordance with the English-language preference for the term *cup*, childhood bilinguals extended the use of *chashka* to objects that Russian speakers named *piala* (drinking bowl, common in Central Asia) and *stakan* (Figure 7.2, stimuli 13, 10). These objects violate the constraints on the category *chashka* in Russian, consequently, the usage suggests that a genuine category shift is taking place.

Early bilinguals differed more sharply from the native Russian speakers than the other two groups. A substantial portion of this difference is due to the absence of the category *kruzhka* from the set of names dominant for at least one object (for native Russian speakers, *kruzhka* was dominant for nine objects and the other two groups have expanded that number). While the term does appear in the naming data, its use is restricted to three participants, two of whom left the Russian context at age six, the upper end of the range for this group. Thus, its absence in the data is consistent with Andersen's (1975) finding that in English, *mug* is learned later than *cup*, around age 6. At the same time, their averaged typicality ratings for *kruzhka* were highly consistent with those of native speakers of Russian and the other two bilingual groups, suggesting that they have acquired a passive grasp of the word and its pattern of use, even though the word is not salient enough or activated enough to be used in a production task.

The category *chashka* has expanded in early bilinguals to include nine containers without handles and made out of a variety of materials (two of these had tied the name *chashka* with the name *stakan*). These were the so-called 'cross-over' containers, named *stakan* by native speakers of Russian and *cup* by native speakers of English, and the usage suggests a category shift toward the English *cup* (Figure 7.1, stimuli 43, 52; Figure 7.2, stimulus 7). The category *stakan* in this group also functions in close correspondence with the English *glass* – it has simultaneously contracted to exclude handleless containers made out of materials other than glass and expanded to include some glass containers with stems (Figure 7.2, stimuli 53, 47, 50, 33, 18). Thus, the early bilingual usage displays the restructuring of the category *stakan* and the expansion of the category *chashka*, in accordance with the English-language use. At the same time, early bilinguals do not simply mirror English-language patterns. The production frequency for early bilinguals' naming patterns still has a substantially higher relation to native Russian typicality ratings than to the English typicality ratings, and they continue to differentiate, albeit in a limited manner, between *stakan*, *bokal* and *riumka* as dominant names for certain objects. And in a manner distinct from both groups, they use the word *chashka* to refer to containers with vertical sides and wide bottoms used for hot drinks, named *kruzhka* in Russian and *mug* in English.

To sum up, the study established that concrete word pairs, *cup/chashka* and *glass/stakan*, function as partial translation equivalents in Russian and English. In the context of such partial equivalence, Russian-English bilinguals were shown to display systematic L2 influence on L1 in mapping concrete nouns to familiar household objects. This influence was shown to increase with the decrease in the age of arrival in the L2 context. At the same time, L2 influence was also identified in late bilinguals who arrived in the USA as adults and have been exposed to the L2 for a relatively short time compared to the other two groups.

7.7 Factors Affecting Variation in Word-to-Referent Mapping

The studies discussed above allow us to refine our understanding of factors affecting word-to-referent mapping in monolingual and bilingual speakers. I will discuss these additional factors in terms of four categories put forth earlier: linguistic, referent-specific, individual and context-specific.

7.7.1 Linguistic factors

The three sets of studies examined the effects of two linguistic factors: codability and translation equivalence, i.e. the relationship between linguistic categories of respective languages. Full translation equivalence, operationalized as a large or complete overlap between the two categories, was linked to high levels of intra-group and inter-group agreement. For instance, in the study of emotion vocabulary (Pavlenko & Driagina, 2007), Russian L2 users of English displayed high intra-group consensus (79%) in describing the main character in *The Letter* as *upset*, in the context where 90% of English monolinguals used the word *upset* and 73% of Russian monolinguals its translation equivalents. Similarly, in the study of drinking containers (Pavlenko & Malt, in press), high agreement (range 56–100%, mean = 85.5%) was found in the three bilingual groups on all objects that were called, respectively, *cup* and *chashka* by native speakers of English and Russian with high levels of agreement (range 75–95%). In contrast, in the context of partial or full translation non-equivalence participants' lexical choices displayed more variation and were affected by the context and the age of L2 acquisition (Pavlenko, 2003, 2008b; Pavlenko & Driagina, 2007; Pavlenko & Malt, in press).

The findings also revealed that crosslinguistic differences in codability led to systematic differences in word-to-referent mapping by native speakers of English and Russian. When the category was encoded in the language in question and when its representation was fairly typical (as in the films *The Ithaca Story* and *The Letter*), speakers would map words onto referents with fairly high agreement. When the category was not encoded, as was the case for *privacy* and *personal space* in Russian and *perezhivat'* in English, speakers would not comment – and perhaps even fail to notice – the aspect of external reality captured in the category.

The study by Pavlenko and Malt (in press) also documented the effects of the lexical differentiation in the domain in question on intra-group agreement. English speakers used only 3 dominant names – *cup*, *mug* and *glass* – to refer to the 60 drinking containers, while Russian speakers used 10 dominant names to refer to the same objects. As a result of these differences in lexical differentiation, intra-group agreement levels were higher among native speakers of English (range 45–100%, mean = 82.75%) than among native speakers of Russian (range 25–100%, mean = 62.42%).

7.7.2 Referent-specific Factors

The study by Pavlenko and Malt (in press) also examined the effects of typicality and found a correlation between typicality judgments and naming consensus among native speakers of Russian and English: objects judged to be highly typical of a particular lexical category elicited high naming agreement, and objects judged to be less typical, elicited higher levels of individual variation. For instance, one medium-size, wide and somewhat tapered container had a dominant name of *glass* in English (70%) and *stakan* in Russian (25%). Because its typicality as a *stakan* was judged to be low, speakers of Russian also named this drinking container *bokal* (wine glass), *fuzher* (wine glass), *riumka* (shot glass), *sakharnitsa* (sugar bowl), *podsvechnik* (candle-holder), *posuda* (dish) and *sosud* (container). These findings may be interpreted as indicating a relationship between typicality and what Downing (1980) terms low codability: entities with low codability appear to be peripheral or borderline members of two or more linguistic categories.

The films used in the studies discussed here contained several such objects. For instance, in *The Ithaca Story*, English-speaking participants had difficulties naming a concrete border around a flower bed on which the main protagonist sat down. Only six participants attempted any references to this entity, using the terms *bench* (3), *cement wall* (2), *ledge* (1), *step* (1), *railing* (1), *curb* (1) and, in the words of one participant, 'the concrete, whatever that thing is'. Native speakers of Russian ($n = 15$)

displayed somewhat more lexical richness and consistency, referring to the same entity as *porebrik* (brick border) (5), *parapet* (parapet) (4), *skameika* (bench) (2), *bordiur* (border) (1), *barier* (barrier) (1), *bortik* (side, board) (1), *obochina* (roadside, curb) (1), *krai gazona* (side of the lawn) (1), *ograzhdenie klumby* (flower bed fence) (1) and *pristupochka* (step) (1). The terms *parapet*, *skameika*, *ograzhdenie*, *barier* and *bordiur* were also used by Russian-English bilinguals in L1 Russian narratives.

These choices illustrate the phenomenon of referential indeterminacy at the heart of the low intra-group naming agreement and particularly visible in the case of peripheral objects. In the absence of features that place such objects clearly within a particular category, different speakers focus on different object properties in the naming process: some focus on the function (e.g. bench), others on shape (e.g. border) or material (e.g. cement wall, the concrete), and yet others try to situate the object in the context of the overall scene (e.g. railing, side of the lawn, flower bed fence). All these terms, however, elicit very different imagery, suggesting, in turn, that low codability and referential indeterminacy may lead to the loss of lexical precision in word-to-referent mapping and communication.

7.7.3 Individual factors

Individual factors examined in the studies above include: (a) familiarity with the objects, events or phenomena in question; and, in the case of bilingual performance; (b) the context of L2 acquisition; (c) the age of L2 acquisition; and (d) language proficiency. To begin with familiarity, as already mentioned earlier, in the naming process speakers often rely on previously seen exemplars. Low familiarity or lack of familiarity with the object prevents them from doing so and encourages guesses regarding the object's nature and function, thus increasing individual variation. For instance, in the study of drinking containers (Pavlenko & Malt, in press), the object called *beer stein* or *beer mug* by English speakers (Figure 7.1, stimulus 51) was less familiar to the Russian speakers and, consequently, elicited a higher range of naming variation: its dominant name *kuvshin* (pitcher) had a low degree of consensus (25%) and additional names given to this object included superordinate terms, such as *posuda* (dish) and *sosud* (container), as well as different guesses regarding its function: *kruzhka* (mug), *stakan* (glass), *sakharnitsa* (sugar bowl), *grafin* (decanter), *kofeinik* (coffee pot) and *vaza* (vase).

In bilingual speakers, performance on translation non-equivalents and partial equivalents was affected by the context of L2 acquisition. Acquisition in the target language context was found to be critical for internalization of L2-specific lexical categories: some L2 users were able to acquire and use such categories in a target-like manner, while FL users did not use such categories spontaneously, even when they had 'studied' them previously (Pavlenko, 1997, 2002b, 2003; Pavlenko & Driagina, 2007). In contrast, translation equivalents and structural non-equivalents were acquired similarly in and out of the L2 context.

Pavlenko and Malt's (in press) study also showed that in the case of partial equivalents, bilinguals' performance may be additionally affected by three inter-related variables: the age of arrival in the L2 context (which in most cases coincided with the age of L2 acquisition) and L1 and L2 proficiency levels. The L2 influence on L1 in word-to-referent mapping was highest in the earliest arrivals who judged themselves to be native-like in the L2 and weaker in the L1.

7.7.4 Text- and Context-Specific Factors

Last but not least, the studies also provided some insights regarding the role of context-specific factors, such as (a) the language of recall and (b) visual context. The key finding of the studies of *privacy* and *personal space* was the fact that external referents can trigger lexical categories that are not encoded in the language of recall or the language-in-use (Pavlenko, 1997, 2002b, 2003). This suggested, in turn, that the language-in-use does not fully determine how words are mapped to referents. The drinking containers study (Pavlenko & Malt, in press) provided further evidence that word-to-referent mapping in one language may be affected by the categories of another language.

Cultural context, operationalized as the visual context in the films in question, also did not appear to exert a systematic influence on participants' performance. The language-specific terms *privacy* and *personal space* did appear more frequently in narratives elicited by *The Ithaca Story*, filmed in the 'American' context. However, the language-specific emotion term *perezhivat'* appeared more frequently in the narratives elicited by *The Letter*, also filmed in the USA, suggesting that some categories – at least those in the emotion domain – may be judged by bilingual speakers to be universally applicable.

7.8 Discussion and Conclusions

Together, the studies discussed here show that the process of word-to-referent mapping is neither as automatic and immutable as assumed by psycholinguists, nor as variable and idiosyncratic as sociolinguists are apt to believe. Rather, the mapping of words onto external referents is a complex cognitive process that involves selective attention to particular features, functions or properties of the object, event or phenomenon to be named, matching of those properties with internal representations, and retrieval of words linked to these representations. The levels of intra-group agreement and lexical precision achieved in this process will vary based on the interplay of linguistic, individual and referent-, text- and context-specific factors.

These findings challenge the view adopted in many models of the bilingual lexicon (cf. Costa, 2005; De Bot, 2004; Green, 1998), according to which the formulation of a linguistic message begins in the conceptualizer or the undifferentiated conceptual system and activates lexical links in both languages of a bilingual. This view is based on three central assumptions: (a) that a speaker is an individual agent who is at liberty to formulate his or her own messages before they are turned into words; (b) that words of different languages are full translation equivalents linked to the same 'concepts'; and (c) that those 'concepts' or 'mental representations' are bounded and holistic. Clear and elegant on paper, these assumptions do not hold in bi- and multilingual contexts.

To begin with individual agency, humans rarely exist in a vacuum – as interactive beings, we continuously respond to our linguistic and physical environments, which privilege particular languages or combinations of languages. The formulation of a linguistic message, thus, may not always begin 'from scratch' as an independent internal process. Just as often, messages may emerge in response to texts and utterances articulated by others, as seen in the intertextual nature of our everyday communication (e.g. 'How could you say that I don't care?!'). The studies discussed here show that language-specific responses may be triggered not only by verbal but also by non-verbal stimuli, such as films portraying a violation of privacy or an invasion of personal space. In fact, as demonstrated in the privacy and emotion studies, the physical environment may trigger categories that are encoded only in one of the speaker's languages, while an attempt to activate lexical links in the other language leads to code-switching or breakdowns in fluency (Pavlenko, 1997, 2002a, 2002b, 2003, Pavlenko & Driagina, 2007).

These language-specific effects reveal the flaw in the assumption that in the bilingual lexicon undifferentiated concepts are linked to words of both languages. As noted by Epstein (1915) almost a century ago and as demonstrated in the studies discussed here and in the chapter by Malt and Ameel, words of respective languages are rarely fully equivalent. This, in turn, means that word-to-referent mapping processes of bi- and multilingual speakers are likely to be language-specific and not language-independent. This argument fits well with the larger argument in favor of language-dependent cognition made by Bylund and by Schmiedtová and associates in this volume. These findings are also consistent with findings from experimental studies in cross-cultural psychology that point to the context-dependent nature of bilingual cognition, where culture-specific stimuli trigger language- and culture-specific categories and interpretive frames (Hong *et al.*, 2000; Marian &

Kaushanskaya, 2004, 2007; Ramirez-Esparza *et al.*, 2006; Ross *et al.*, 2002; Trafimow *et al.*, 1997).

The metaphor of bounded and holistic 'concepts' or 'mental representations', commonly invoked in models of bilingual processing and the bilingual lexicon, fails to capture this context-dependence and the complexity of word-to-referent mapping in the real world. These phenomena are much better incorporated in approaches that view internal representations as distributed and emergent phenomena that function in a context-dependent manner, so that the same container may be named *cup* if it contained coffee and *bowl* if it contained mashed potatoes (Barsalou, 2003; Labov, 1973; Malt *et al.*, 2003).

To sum up, I have argued that the mind is not a self-contained entity that stores internal representations of everything in the outside world only to match them, flawlessly, to their external referents. The linguistic and physical aspects of 'the outside' constitute an intrinsic aspect of meaning construction, with the mind processing, recreating and (re)naming external reality. The logical corollary of this view is that external reality needs to be incorporated in empirical studies that aim to understand what exactly is processed for linguistic purposes and how the mind comes to construct and use 'internal representations' in the context of referential indeterminacy. Undoubtedly, word-to-referent mapping is only a minor aspect of the larger lexicon puzzle, which, in turn, is only one of the many mysteries of language. Yet, solving it will allow us to understand how, in production, words are used to construct referents (including those that are not immediately visible), how, in comprehension, words activate internal representations, and, how, in communication, we come to construct a joint world. I am convinced that future breakthroughs in this work will come from studies that break disciplinary boundaries in the pursuit of the understanding of things we do with words.

Notes

1. For an example of contemporary usage, see http://www.worsleyschool.net/socialarts/personal/space.html.
2. For examples of such explanations, see http://www.internet-technologies.ru/articles/article_340.html, http://www.homepc.ru/slydecision/13212/, http://www.hist.msu.ru/Labs/Ecohist/OB8/zorina.htm.
3. In descriptions of *Kiev Story*, only two participants referred to *invasions of privacy* or *personal space*.

References

Alderman, E. and Kennedy, C. (1995) *The Right to Privacy*. New York: Knopf.
Ameel, E., Malt, B. and Storms, G. (2008) Object naming and later lexical development: From baby bottle to beer bottle. *Journal of Memory and Language* 58, 262–285.

Ameel, E., Storms, G., Malt, B. and Sloman, S. (2005) How bilinguals solve the naming problem. *Journal of Memory and Language* 52, 309–329.

Andersen, E. (1975) Cups and glasses: Learning that boundaries are vague. *Journal of Child Language* 2, 79–103.

Bamberg, M. (1987) *The Acquisition of Narratives: Learning to Use Language*. Berlin: Mouton de Gruyter.

Barsalou, L. (2003) Situated simulation in the human conceptual system. *Language and Cognitive Processes* 18, 513–562.

Berlin, B. and Kay, P. (1969) *Basic Color Terms: Their Universality and Evolution*. Berkeley, CA: University of California Press.

Berman, R. and Slobin, D. (1994) *Relating Events in Narrative: A Crosslinguistic Developmental Study*. Hillsdale, NJ: Lawrence Erlbaum.

Brown, R. (1958) *Words and Things*. Glencoe, IL: The Free Press.

Brown, R. and Lenneberg, E. (1954) A study in language and cognition. *Journal of Abnormal and Social Psychology* 49, 454–462.

Chafe, W. (ed.) (1980) *The Pear Stories: Cognitive, Cultural, and Linguistic Aspects of Narrative Production*. Norwood, NJ: Ablex.

Costa, A. (2005) Lexical access in bilingual production. In J. Kroll and A. De Groot (eds) *Handbook of Bilingualism: Psycholinguistic Approaches* (pp. 308–325). Oxford: Oxford University Press.

De Bot, K. (2004) The multilingual lexicon: Modelling selection and control. *International Journal of Multilingualism* 1, 17–32.

Downing, P. (1980) Factors influencing lexical choice in narrative. In W. Chafe (ed.) *The Pear Stories: Cognitive, Cultural, and Linguistic Aspects of Narrative Production* (pp. 89–126). Norwood, NJ: Ablex.

Du Bois, J. (1980) Introduction – the search for a cultural niche: Showing the Pear film in a Mayan community. In W. Chafe (ed.) *The Pear Stories: Cognitive, Cultural, and Linguistic Aspects of Narrative Production* (pp. 1–7). Norwood, NJ: Ablex.

Epstein, I. (1915) *La pensée et la polyglossie: Essai psychologique et didactique* [Thought and Multilingualism: A Psychological and Didactic Essay]. Lausanne: Librarie Payot et Cie.

Fast, J. (1970) *Body Language*. New York: MJF Books.

Graham, R. and Belnap, K. (1986) The acquisition of lexical boundaries in English by native speakers of Spanish. *International Review of Applied Linguistics* 24, 275–286.

Green, D. (1998) Mental control of the bilingual lexico-semantic system. *Bilingualism: Language and Cognition* 1, 67–81.

Hall, E. (1966) *The Hidden Dimension*. New York: Doubleday.

Hall, E. and Hall, M. (1990) *Understanding Cultural Differences*. Yarmouth, ME: Intercultural Press.

Hong, Y., Morris, M., Chiu, C. and Benet-Martinez, V. (2000) Multicultural minds: A dynamic constructivist approach to culture and cognition. *American Psychologist* 55, 709–720.

Jarvis, S. (1998) *Conceptual Transfer in the Interlingual Lexicon*. Bloomington, IN: Indiana University Linguistics Club Publications.

Jarvis, S. (2000) Methodological rigor in the study of transfer: Identifying L1 influence in the interlanguage lexicon. *Language Learning* 50, 245–309.

Karasik, V., Prohvacheva, O., Zubkova, I. and Grabarova, E. (2005) *Inaia mental'nost'* [A Different Mentality]. Moscow: Gnosis.

Kaufman, D. (2001) Narrative development in Hebrew and English. In L. Verhoeven and S. Strömqvist (eds) *Narrative Development in a Multilingual Context* (pp. 319–340). Amsterdam: John Benjamins.

Keil, F. (1989) *Concepts, Kinds, and Cognitive Development*. Cambridge, MA: MIT Press.

Kempton, W. (1981) *The Folk Classification of Ceramics: A Study of Cognitive Prototypes*. New York: Academic Press.

Kroll, J. and De Groot, A. (eds) (2005) *Handbook of Bilingualism: Psycholinguistic Approaches*. Oxford: Oxford University Press.

Kronenfeld, D. (1996) *Plastic Glasses and Church Fathers: Semantic Extensions from the Ethnoscience Tradition*. Oxford: Oxford University Press.

Kronenfeld, D., Armstrong, J. and Wilmoth, S. (1985) Exploring the internal structure of linguistic categories: An extensionist semantic view. In J. Dougherty (ed.) *Directions in Cognitive Anthropology* (pp. 91–110). Champaign, IL: University of Illinois Press.

Labov, W. (1973) The boundaries of words and their meanings. In Ch. Bailey and R. Shuy (eds) *New Ways of Analyzing Variation in English* (pp. 340–373). Washington, DC: Georgetown University Press.

Lakoff, G. (1987) *Women, Fire, and Dangerous Things: What Categories Reveal about the Mind*. Chicago, IL: University of Chicago Press.

Malt, B. and Sloman, S. (2003) Linguistic diversity and object naming by non-native speakers of English. *Bilingualism: Language and Cognition* 6, 47–67.

Malt, B., Sloman, S. and Gennari, S. (2003) Universality and language specificity in object naming. *Journal of Memory and Language* 49, 20–42.

Malt, B., Sloman, S., Gennari, S., Shi, M. and Wang, Y. (1999) Knowing versus naming: Similarity and the linguistic categorization of artifacts. *Journal of Memory and Language* 40, 230–262.

Marian, V. and Kaushanskaya, M. (2004) Self-construal and emotion in bicultural bilinguals. *Journal of Memory and Language* 51, 190–201.

Marian, V. and Kaushanskaya, M. (2007) Language context guides memory content. *Psychonomic Bulletin and Review* 14, 925–933.

Mayer, M. (1969) *Frog, Where are You?* New York: Dial.

Mercier, P. (2009) *Night Train to Lisbon* (B. Harshav, trans.). London: Atlantic Books.

Murphy, G. (2002) *The Big Book of Concepts*. Cambridge, MA: Bradford Book/MIT Press.

Olshtain, E. and Barzilay, M. (1991) Lexical retrieval difficulties in adult language attrition. In H. Seliger and R. Vago (eds) *First Language Attrition* (pp. 139–150). Cambridge: Cambridge University Press.

Pavlenko, A. (1997) Bilingualism and cognition. Unpublished PhD dissertation. Cornell University.

Pavlenko, A. (2002a) Emotions and the body in Russian and English. *Pragmatics & Cognition* 10, 207–241.

Pavlenko, A. (2002b) Bilingualism and emotions. *Multilingua* 21, 45–78.

Pavlenko, A. (2003) Eyewitness memory in late bilinguals: Evidence for discursive relativity. *International Journal of Bilingualism* 7, 257–281.

Pavlenko, A. (2008a) Narrative analysis in the study of bi- and multilingualism. In M. Moyer and Li Wei (eds) *The Blackwell Guide to Research Methods in Bilingualism* (pp. 311–325). Oxford: Blackwell.

Pavlenko, A. (2008b) Structural and conceptual equivalence in the acquisition and use of emotion words in a second language. *Mental Lexicon* 3, 91–120.

Pavlenko, A. (2009) Conceptual representation in the bilingual lexicon and second language vocabulary learning. In A. Pavlenko (ed.) *The Bilingual Mental Lexicon: Interdisciplinary Approaches* (pp. 125–160). Bristol: Multilingual Matters.

Pavlenko, A. and Driagina, V. (2007) Russian emotion vocabulary in American learners' narratives. *Modern Language Journal* 91, 213–234.

Pavlenko, A. and Malt, B. (in press) Kitchen Russian: Object naming by Russian-English bilinguals. *Bilingualism: Language and Cognition* 14.

Ramirez-Esparza, N., Gosling, S., Benet-Martinez, V., Potter, J. and Pennebaker, J. (2006) Do bilinguals have two personalities? A special case for cultural frame switching. *Journal of Research in Personality* 40, 99–120.

Reyn, I. (2000) Recalling a child of October. In M. Danquah (ed.) *Becoming American: Personal Essays by First Generation Immigrant Women* (pp. 146–155). New York: Hyperion.

Richmond, Y. (1992) *From nyet to da: Understanding the Russians.* Yarmouth, ME: Intercultural Press.

Ripp, V. (1984) *From Moscow to Main Street: Among the Russian Emigrees.* New York: Simon & Shuster.

Rosch, E. (1973a) Natural categories. *Cognitive Psychology* 4, 328–350.

Rosch, E. (1973b) On the internal structure of perceptual and semantic categories. In T. Moore (ed.) *Cognitive Development and the Acquisition of Language* (pp. 111–144). New York: Academic Press.

Rosch, E. (1975) Cognitive representations of semantic categories. *Journal of Experimental Psychology: General* 104, 192–233.

Rosch, E. (1977) Human categorization. In N. Warren (ed.) *Studies in Cross-cultural Psychology* (Vol. 1) (pp. 1–49). London: Academic Press.

Rosch, E. (1978) Principles of categorization. In E. Rosch and B. Lloyd (eds) *Cognition and Categorization* (pp. 27–48). Hillsdale, NJ: Lawrence Erlbaum.

Rosch, E., Mervis, C., Gray, W., Johnson, D. and Boyes-Braem, P. (1976) Basic objects in natural categories. *Cognitive Psychology* 8, 382–439.

Ross, M., Xun, W.Q.E. and Wilson, A. (2002) Language and the bicultural self. *Personality and Social Psychology Bulletin* 28, 1040–1050.

Scott, G. (1995) *Mind your Own Business: The Battle for Personal Privacy.* New York: Plenum.

Shlapentokh, V. (1989) *Public and Private Life of the Soviet people: Changing Values in Post-Stalin Russia.* Oxford: Oxford University Press.

Smith, H. (1983) *The Russians.* New York Times Books.

Strömqvist, S. and Verhoeven, L. (eds) (2004) *Relating Events in Narrative: Typological and Contextual Perspectives.* Mahwah, NJ: Lawrence Erlbaum.

Trafimow, D., Silverman, E., Fan, R.M-T. and Law, J. (1997) The effects of language and priming on the relative accessibility of the private self and the collective self. *Journal of Cross-Cultural Psychology* 28, 107–123.

Taylor, J. (1995) *Linguistic Categorization: Prototypes in Linguistic Theory.* Oxford: Clarendon Press.

Verhoeven, L. and Strömqvist, S. (2001) *Narrative Development in a Multilingual Context.* Amsterdam: John Benjamins.

Wierzbicka, A. (1984) Cups and mugs: Lexicography and conceptual analysis. *Australian Journal of Linguistics* 4, 205–255.

Wierzbicka, A. (1991) *Cross-Cultural Pragmatics: The Semantics of Human Interaction.* Berlin/New York: Mouton de Gruyter.

Wierzbicka, A. (1992) *Semantics, Culture, and Cognition: Universal Human Concepts in Culture-Specific Configurations.* Oxford: Oxford University Press.

Wood, J. (1994) *Gendered Lives: Communication, Gender, and Culture.* Belmont, CA: Wadsworth Publishing.

Chapter 8

Thinking and Speaking in Two Languages: Overview of the Field

ANETA PAVLENKO

The purpose of this final chapter is to synthesize the findings of recent studies of thinking and speaking in two languages, both those discussed here and ones that did not find their way into this volume. I will begin the overview with a summary of findings in six broadly conceived areas of inquiry: (1) non-linguistic cognition; (2) thinking, seeing and gesturing for speaking; (3) word-to-referent mapping; (4) inner speech; (5) language, thought and autobiographic memory; and (6) negotiation of identities and self-translation. Then, I will examine the implications of these findings for our understanding of the processes taking place in the bilingual mind. I will end with a discussion of predictors of conceptual restructuring that may take place in additional language learning and language attrition.

8.1 Areas of Study

8.1.1 Non-linguistic cognition

The first area of inquiry and the only one that directly addresses the current version of the Sapir-Whorf hypothesis is the study of *non-linguistic cognition*. The focus of this research is on processes considered to be non-verbal, such as visual perception, sorting, matching and remembering, examined through similarity judgments and memory tasks. In the present volume, this strand of inquiry is represented in the chapter by Athanasopoulos that, *inter alia*, questions whether all of the processes listed above are genuinely non-verbal and raises the possibility that some may involve implicit verbal descriptions of the stimuli.

To date, studies with bilingual speakers have focused on categorization of objects and substances in noun class and classifier languages. Noun class languages, such as English or French, encode the count/mass distinction grammatically, with count nouns referring to discrete entities, marked for number (e.g. candle – candles). Classifier languages, such as Japanese or Korean, lack the count/mass distinction; nouns in these languages commonly refer to substances and are accompanied by numeral classifiers (e.g. one long thin wax [= candle]). Speakers of the two types of languages were shown to perform differently on non-verbal tasks. Specifically, the researchers found that in judging similarity of simple objects, speakers of the noun-class language, English, favored shape and speakers of classifier languages, Japanese and Yucatec Maya, favored material, presumably because noun-class languages draw speakers' attention to discreteness of entities and classifier languages to material (Imai & Gentner, 1997; Lucy, 1992). Kasai *et al.* (2008) replicated these results with English and Japanese monolinguals and with Japanese speakers with low levels of second language (L2) English proficiency, but found, unexpectedly, that speakers of Korean, another classifier language, patterned with speakers of English in their shape preferences. The researchers attempted to explain their findings by the English proficiency of their participants, but for now these preliminary results await further inquiry.

Other studies suggest that L2 learning can indeed influence categorization preferences. Research conducted with Japanese-English bilinguals demonstrated that their performance is influenced by their level of proficiency in the L2 English (Athanasopoulos, 2006, 2007; Athanasopoulos & Kasai, 2008) and the length of stay in the English-speaking context (Cook *et al.*, 2006). Speakers with advanced-level proficiency and/or length of stay of more than three years were beginning to resemble speakers of their L2 English in favoring shape over material in similarity judgments.

8.1.2 Thinking, seeing and gesturing for speaking

The next area of inquiry, the study of *thinking, seeing and gesturing for speaking*, draws on Slobin's (1996) definition of linguistic thought as 'thinking for speaking' and examines processes that accompany verbalization of events and actions: (a) segmentation or decomposition; (b) selection of particular components; (c) event structuring (i.e. allocation of topic and focus, perspective taking according to spatial and temporal reference frames); and (d) the ordering of words and grammatical constituents for verbal representation (for a detailed discussion see Habel & Tappe, 1999; v. Stutterheim & Nüse, 2003). Studies in this area commonly rely on elicited descriptions of visual stimuli and, in some cases, also on analyses of accompanying gestures and eye gaze. In the present volume, this research is represented in the chapters by Schmiedtová, v. Stutterheim and Carroll, by Bylund and by Gullberg.

To date, studies of bilingual speakers have exploited three main types of crosslinguistic differences (for a discussion of other differences, see Gullberg's chapter). The first such difference involves the relationship between aspect and event construal. It was shown that in descriptions of the same visual stimuli, speakers of grammatical aspect languages, such as English or Spanish, segment the flow of events in a more fine-grained way and pay less attention to the point of event completion (endpoint) than speakers of non-aspect languages, such as German or Swedish, who tend to discuss events holistically, mention the endpoints more frequently and look at the endpoint area in the visual stimuli for a longer time (Bylund, 2008; v. Stutterheim, 2003; v. Stutterheim & Carroll, 2006; v. Stutterheim & Nüse, 2003). One interesting exception to this generalization involves speakers of Czech, an aspect language, who behave like speakers of non-aspect languages, an outcome Schmiedtová and Sahonenko (2008) attribute to a long-term contact between Czech and German (see also Schmiedtová *et al.*, this volume).

The second crosslinguistic difference that has inspired studies of thinking, seeing and gesturing for speaking involves motion. This research draws on Talmy's (1991) framework that differentiates between two broadly defined types of languages. In satellite-framed languages (S-languages), such as English or Russian, the manner of motion is typically encoded in the main verb and the path of motion in the satellites, such as prepositions, prefixes or particles. In verb-framed languages (V-languages), such as Spanish or Hebrew, the main verb encodes the path of motion and the marking of manner is optional. This is not to say that the marking of manner is obligatory in all S-languages. In Russian, for instance, it is obligatory, while in English it is optional and several high-frequency motion verbs, such as *go, come, leave* or *enter*, do not encode manner, a difference that also has implications for bilinguals' performance (for an expanded discussion, see Pavlenko, 2010). The studies conducted to date have demonstrated that speakers of S- and V-languages focus on different information when talking and gesturing about motion. When describing voluntary motion, speakers of S-languages focus more on manner, and speakers of V-languages on the path of motion (Berman & Slobin, 1994; Slobin, 1996; for a summary see Cadierno, 2008).

The third difference involves the framing of caused motion and more specifically entities that may appear in the subject position. Type A languages, such as Russian or Dutch, restrict the subject position to entities that can initiate events, such as animate subjects or natural forces, whereas type B languages, such as English, allow for a greater range of entities, including but not limited to instruments (Wolff & Ventura, 2009). Consequently, the sentence 'The knife cut the bread' would be semantically acceptable in English but not in Russian. Wolff and Ventura (2009) argue that as a result of such differences, speakers of type B languages take into consideration a greater range of forces that may cause events than speakers of type A languages. Their study of descriptions of caused events showed that monolingual speakers of Russian and English differed in descriptions of situations, where characters showed no sign of being able to accomplish the event on their own: monolingual English speakers favored verbs that stress causality (e.g. make) and Russian speakers favored verbs that stress enabling (e.g. *pozvolit'* [let]) (Wolff & Ventura, 2009).

Explorations with L2 learners at different levels of proficiency show that learning a typologically different language is a challenging undertaking and that the first language (L1) influence may persist in the verbal L2 performance and also in gesturing (Cadierno, 2004, 2008; Gullberg, this volume; Hendriks *et al.*, 2008; Hohenstein *et al.*, 2006; Özyürek, 2002; v. Stutterheim, 2003). For instance, Cadierno's (2004) study of Danish-Spanish bilinguals demonstrated that under the influence of the L1 Danish (S-language), learners of L2 Spanish (V-language) provided more complex and elaborate path descriptions in Spanish than native speakers of Spanish. Hohenstein *et al.* (2006) found that Spanish-English bilinguals speaking L2 English used more path verbs than monolingual English speakers, an influence attributed to their L1 Spanish. In event construals, L1 English and L1 Russian learners of L2 German were shown to rely on the L1 perspective and thus encode significantly fewer endpoints than monolingual speakers of German (Schmiedtová & Sahonenko, 2008; v. Stutterheim, 2003; v. Stutterheim & Carroll, 2006; see also Schmiedtová *et al.*, this volume).

Nevertheless, it appears that, given time and opportunities, L2 learners can internalize new patterns and even experience the L2 influence on the L1 (Brown & Gullberg, 2008; Bylund, 2009; Bylund & Jarvis, in press; Cadierno, 2004; Hohenstein *et al.*, 2006; v. Stutterheim, 2003; Wolff & Ventura, 2009). Thus, studies by v. Stutterheim (2003) and Hohenstein *et al.* (2006) found approximation of the target language patterns in event construals of, respectively, L1 German and L1 Spanish speakers of L2 English. Studies by Bylund (2009) and Bylund and Jarvis (in press) revealed an L2 influence on the L1 in event construals by Spanish-Swedish bilinguals, seen in a significantly higher frequency of endpoint encoding than that of monolingual Spanish speakers. L2 English influence on L1 in motion talk was identified in the manner of motion talk and gestures of L1 Japanese speakers (Brown & Gullberg, 2008), in the use of manner and path verbs of L1 Spanish speakers (Hohenstein *et al.*, 2006), and in caused motion talk of L1 Russian speakers (Wolff & Ventura, 2009). In the latter study, Russian-English bilinguals speaking L1 Russian were shown to pattern with monolingual English speakers in their preference for causal verbs (e.g. *zastavit'* [make]) in descriptions of situations, where characters appeared unable to accomplish the action on their own. In contrast, English-Russian bilinguals performing the same task demonstrated an in-between performance pattern, using similar proportions of causal and enabling verbs. Their frequency of use of causal verbs, however, was significantly lower than that of monolingual English speakers, thus showing a divergence from the L1 pattern and probably the beginning of the restructuring process. Similar divergence from the L1 pattern was found in event encoding by L1 German speakers of L2 English in a study by v. Stutterheim and Carroll (2006).

8.1.3 Word-to-referent mapping

The third area of inquiry, *word-to-referent mapping*, also examines processes that accompany verbalization, but with the focus on lexical, rather than grammatical, categories. These processes include the matching of referents to category prototypes and decisions made regarding category boundaries and borderline exemplars. The main task used in this research is a naming task, which may be accompanied by similarity, typicality, familiarity and confidence judgments. In the case of color, participants may be asked to name separate Munsell chips or to map the focal area and the range of particular terms on a Munsell color chart. In the present volume, word-to-referent mapping is discussed in the chapters by Malt and Ameel and by Pavlenko; research on color naming is briefly discussed in the chapter by Athanasopoulos.

To date, bilinguals' word-to-referent mapping has been examined in several domains: color (Alvarado & Jameson, 2002; Andrews, 1994; Athanasopoulos, 2009; Athanasopoulos *et al.*, in press; Caskey-Sirmons & Hickerson, 1977; Jameson & Alvarado, 2003), artifacts (Ameel *et al.*, 2005, 2009; Graham & Belnap, 1986; Malt & Sloman, 2003; Pavlenko & Malt, in press), emotions (Panayiotou, 2004a, 2004b, 2006; Pavlenko, 2002a, 2008; Pavlenko & Driagina, 2007; Stepanova Sachs & Coley, 2006) and abstract concepts, such as privacy (Pavlenko, 2003). The purpose of these studies was to see how bilinguals perform in cases where monolingual speakers differ either because their respective languages have different category prototypes and boundaries or because one language encodes a category absent in another.

The findings show that performance of beginning and intermediate L2 learners may display L1 influence (Graham & Belnap, 1986), while the categories used by more advanced learners and bilinguals may fall in-between those of monolingual speakers (Alvarado & Jameson, 2002; Ameel *et al.*, 2005, 2009; Jameson & Alvarado, 2003) or begin to approximate the L2 categories (Athanasopoulos, 2009; Malt & Sloman, 2003). Some studies also found L2 influence on L1 object (Pavlenko & Malt, in press), emotion (Pavlenko, 2002a; Stepanova Sachs & Coley, 2006), and color categories (Caskey-Sirmons & Hickerson, 1977). In the latter area, research has documented a weakening of the obligatory contrast between dark and light blue in L1 Russian (Andrews, 1994), L1 Greek (Athanasopoulos, 2009) and L1 Japanese (Athanasopoulos *et al.*, in press) under the influence of L2 English. The studies have also demonstrated internalization of new abstract and emotion categories and possible attrition of L1 emotion categories (Panayiotou, 2004a, 2004b, 2006; Pavlenko, 2002a, 2003, 2008; Pavlenko & Driagina, 2007).

8.1.4 Inner speech

The next three areas of inquiry are not reflected in this volume. The inquiry into inner speech is still in its emerging stage and thus lacks sufficient data for a chapter-long overview. Nevertheless, I find it to be a promising area for future research and thus deserving of inclusion in a general overview. The other two areas, on the other hand, have generated abundant research whose results have been reviewed elsewhere. Consequently, I have opted to include only a brief summary of the findings in these areas, pointing to existing reviews of this work.

While definitions of inner speech differ across studies, for the purposes of the present review, *inner speech* will be viewed as subvocal or silent self-talk, i.e. mental activity that takes place in an identifiable linguistic code and is directed primarily at the self (the dialogic function of inner speech). This mental activity constitutes an important aspect of the language/cognition interface, even though it is not representative of all 'thinking'. The origins of the idea of 'inner speech' are commonly traced to Wilhelm von Humboldt, the forefather of the linguistic relativity hypothesis (Guerrero, 2005). In the 20th century, Vygotsky and his followers articulated the theory of inner speech as internalized social speech, giving rise to empirical studies that appeal to diverse methodologies, ranging from self-reports (e.g. diaries, questionnaires and interviews) to experimental studies (e.g. think-aloud protocols, random sampling) (for a comprehensive and up-to-date overview, see Guerrero, 2005).

To date, only a few studies have engaged directly with the issue of language choice for inner speech in bi- and multilingual speakers. Guerrero (2005) offers a comprehensive summary of the work on development of inner speech in the L2, with the focus on foreign language (FL) learning. Particular attention in this discussion is devoted to her own and others' studies that documented *the din phenomenon*, or the involuntary appearance and mental rehearsal of L2 words and phrases, which is often construed as the initial stage of internalization of a new language. The din phenomenon and L2 inner speech in general were found to be mediated by language proficiency. For instance, Guerrero's (2005) study of 472 L1 Spanish learners of L2 English revealed that the frequency of reported L2 English inner speech increased with an increase in proficiency levels from 75% at the lower level to 98% at the advanced one. The increase in proficiency also led to greater use of L2 inner speech for dialogic purposes and a decrease in its use for mental rehearsal and language play. Students' responses also revealed that 59%

of the participants replayed voices of other people in English, thus confirming the polyphonic or heteroglossic nature of inner speech.

Other studies identified variables that affect language choice in inner speech. Thus, Larsen *et al.* (2002) found that in 20 L1 Polish immigrants who learned L2 Danish on arrival in Denmark, the choice of language for inner speech varied as a function of age of arrival (AOA): later arrivals (average AOA = 34) appealed to L1 Polish in spontaneous inner speech more frequently than earlier arrivals (average AOA = 24). Proficiency in L2 Danish significantly correlated with inner speech behaviors in Danish, while proficiency in L1 Polish did not affect inner speech behaviors in Polish (most likely because all participants maintained high Polish proficiency).

Dewaele's (2006) study of self-reports of 1454 multilinguals about language choice in inner speech found that the L1 is the preferred language of inner speech, yet a later learned language (LX) may also become a language of inner speech. Factors that facilitate that shift included age of acquisition (younger learners of LX used it more frequently for inner speech), language proficiency (more proficient users of LX were more likely to use it for inner speech), context of acquisition (COA; speakers who learned the LX as an FL in the classroom used it less frequently for inner speech), frequency of language use (higher frequency of the general LX use increased the likelihood of its use for inner speech) and the size of the speaker's network (the larger the network, the more likely the use of LX for inner speech). Most importantly, the study established that, according to multilinguals' own perceptions, there is a lag in internalization of inner speech in a new language: a given language is used less for inner speech than for other purposes, such as oral interaction or written communication.

Given the importance accorded to inner speech by bi- and multi-linguals themselves (see Chapter 1, this volume), in future studies it would be interesting to pursue this line of inquiry further and examine closely the nature of inner speech, its relationship with bilingualism, language learning and attrition, and developmental changes that take place in inner speech in different language learning trajectories.

8.1.5 Language, thought and autobiographic memory

The fifth and relatively well-explored area involves studies of *the relationship between language, thought and autobiographic memory*. These studies show that the language of encoding is a stable property of autobiographical memories (Larsen *et al.*, 2002; Marian & Kaushanskaya, 2007; Marian & Neisser, 2000; Matsumoto & Stanny, 2006; Schrauf & Rubin, 1998, 2000, 2004). Recalls appear to be more efficient, accurate, detailed and emotional in the language of encoding of the original event

(Javier *et al.*, 1993; Marian & Fausey, 2006; Marian & Kaushanskaya, 2004). Most importantly, this research suggests that in bilingual speakers, different languages may activate different cultural frames, e.g. individualistic versus collectivist (Marian & Kaushanskaya, 2004; Ramirez-Esparza *et al.*, 2006; Ross *et al.*, 2002) and different visual imagery, e.g. Chinese versus American (Marian & Kaushanskaya, 2007).

8.1.6 Negotiation of identities and self-translation

The last and equally productive area, the study of *negotiation of identities and self-translation*, considers bilinguals' positioning and performance in oral (Koven, 1998, 2006, 2007; Marian & Kaushanskaya, 2004; Panayiotou, 2004a; Pavlenko, 2003) and written narratives (Beaujour, 1989; Besemeres, 2002; Kellman, 2000; Pérez Firmat, 2003), with the former inquiry commonly conducted by linguists and psychologists and the latter by literary scholars. Together, these studies show that bilinguals commonly adopt different stances, interpretive frames and subject positions in their respective languages and, as a result, construct different identities and focus on different themes and associations (for an overview of this research, see Pavlenko, 2006). This line of inquiry most closely addresses bilinguals' own concerns about their relationship with their languages, outlined in Chapter 1 of this volume.

8.2 Linguistic and Cognitive Processes in the Bilingual Mind

8.2.1 Frames of reference approach to the study of bilingualism and thought

To analyze and synthesize the findings of this new wave of studies, we need a new approach to the relationship between language and thought, one that makes bilingualism a meaningful point of departure. Humboldt's (1963 [1836]) and Sapir's (1949 [1924]) comments on bilingualism, cited in the introduction to this volume, provide us with an excellent way of articulating this relationship through the notion of 'frames of reference'. In and of itself, this notion is not novel – there exists a large body of theoretical and empirical work on cognitive, cultural and interpretive frames, and on perspectivization (e.g. Dirven *et al.*, 1982; Fillmore, 1975, 1976; Tannen, 1993) and some studies of bilingual speakers have already adopted the frames of reference or interpretive frames approach (e.g. Marian & Kaushanskaya, 2004; Pavlenko, 2003; Ramirez-Esparza *et al.*, 2004; Ross *et al.*, 2002). What has not been articulated until now, however, is a set of hypotheses that would adopt the notion of frames to capture the relationship between language and cognition in the bilingual mind. The approach proposed here makes two main claims:

(a) *Even unambiguously monolingual speakers internalize multiple frames of reference or perspectives in the process of L1 development.* Crosslinguistic studies of linguistic relativity furnish ample evidence of this multiplicity – sometimes despite their original objectives – because differences between populations in these studies are usually found only in preferences and trends, with some monolingual participants invariably performing just like speakers of the other language (e.g. Cadierno, 2004). These findings challenge simplistic understandings of linguistic relativity, according to which all speakers of a given language should perform in a similar manner. Instead, they reveal variation enabled by the variety of lexical and grammatical options offered by any language (Kay, 1996) and affected by idiolects, individual preferences, geographic or dialectal variation, and socioeconomic background (e.g. Pederson, 1995). Some studies also highlight the task-dependent nature of categorization preferences where the same group of speakers may shift preferences from one task to another (Athanasopoulos & Kasai, 2008) and demonstrate language effects only in specific kinds of tasks (Gennari *et al.*, 2002).

A few studies discussed in this volume also show that speakers of typologically similar languages do not necessarily behave in the same way. Thus, speakers of Korean, a classifier language, were shown to perform like speakers of English, a grammatical number marking language (Kasai *et al.*, 2008) and speakers of Czech, an aspect language, like speakers of German, a non-aspect language (Schmiedtová & Sahonenko, 2008).

In the context of such variation, crosslinguistic inquiry should focus not on categorical differences between speakers of different languages, but on determining what options are available to speakers of particular languages to categorize particular objects, actions, events or phenomena, and which of these are favored and under what circumstances (i.e. Whorf's 'habitual thought'). Taking the relativity of linguistic strategies as a point of departure, this approach recognizes that most of the time individual speakers have multiple linguistic options available to them and focuses on the study of factors that favor particular choices in particular contexts.

(b) *The relationship between monolingualism and multilingualism is a continuum where, in the process of additional language learning, speakers may internalize additional perspectives, frames of reference or interpretive categories, restructure the frames and categories they already have, and shift their patterns of preference, inhibiting those favored earlier.* The purpose of the study of bi-/ multilingualism and thought then is to examine how experiences of language learning and attrition affect verbal and non-verbal behaviors and to identify the processes taking place in the bilingual mind and the predictors and manifestations of conceptual restructuring.

8.2.2 Conceptual restructuring in the bilingual mind

The term *conceptual* (or, alternatively, cognitive) *restructuring* will refer here to changes in speakers' linguistic categories, seen as a subset of cognitive categories. In what follows, I will outline the processes of conceptual restructuring in the bilingual mind within an analytical framework that I have elaborated over the years. In 1995–1996, when I first articulated the notion of conceptual transfer, there was scarcely any empirical work I could consult. My initial ideas about conceptual transfer and restructuring were based on my own research and a few other studies (Pavlenko, 1996, 1997, 1999; for elaborations see Pavlenko, 2002b, 2004, 2005). The notion was then adopted by other researchers (e.g. Jarvis, 1998; Odlin, 2003, 2005). A decade later, an increasing amount of empirical data allows me to exclude studies that are either not sufficiently rigorous or only tangentially related to the topic, to refine this framework and to identify seven processes that take place in the bilingual mind, sometimes sequentially and at other times simultaneously, depending on the speaker's language learning trajectory and the domain in question. These processes are particularly visible in the context of crosslinguistic differences in linguistic categories or frames of reference favored by particular languages.

(1)   The first process, *co-existence*, refers to bilinguals' ability to maintain the categories and frames of references relevant to both languages and to use them in accordance with the constraints placed by particular languages. An example of co-existence comes from a study by Stepanova Sachs and Coley (2006), where Russian-English bilinguals display native-like categorization patterns in both Russian- and English-language emotion categorization tasks.

(2)   The second, and perhaps the most common, process, *the influence of the L1 on the L2*, refers to cases where speakers' L2 performance is guided by L1 linguistic categories, frames of reference or preferences. We may see it as 'thinking in L1 for speaking in L2', with the proviso that such performance is not necessarily an outcome of conscious translation – the influence may be imperceptible to the speakers themselves. To date, evidence of such L1 conceptual transfer has been found in the verbal performance of speakers with beginning and intermediate L2 proficiency in the studies of object categorization (Athanasopoulos, 2006, 2007; Athanasopoulos & Kasai, 2008; Graham & Bellnap, 1986), event construal (Carroll & Lambert, 2003; Hendriks *et al.*, 2008; Schmiedtová & Sahonenko, 2008; v. Stutterheim, 2003; v. Stutterheim & Carroll, 2006) and talk (and/or gestures) about voluntary and caused motion (Cadierno, 2004; Gullberg, this volume; Özyürek, 2002).

(3) Another process involves *convergence* of L1 and L2 categories, perspectives or frames of reference, which results in bilingual participants performing differently from speakers of both the L1 and the L2 in a way often termed 'in-between' performance. This performance has been documented in studies of categorization of colors (Alvarado & Jameson, 2002; Jameson & Alvarado, 2003) and objects (Ameel *et al.*, 2005, 2009; Athanasopoulos, 2007; Cook *et al.*, 2006), in motion talk and gestures (Gullberg, this volume; Hohenstein *et al.*, 2006; Wolff & Ventura, 2009) and in granularity (i.e. degree of event segmentation) of event construals (Bylund, in press). It is important to note here that in-between performance is still poorly understood and may in fact reflect two distinct phenomena: ongoing restructuring in individual bilingual speakers (i.e. beginning divergence from the L1 pattern and convergence with the L2 pattern) (e.g. Gullberg, this volume; Hohenstein *et al.*, 2006; Wolff & Ventura, 2009) and internalization of linguistic categories emerging in language contact situations (i.e. stabilized convergence) (e.g. Ameel *et al.*, 2005, 2009).

(4) The former process, i.e. *restructuring* of linguistic categories, perspectives and frames of reference, is of central interest in the study of bilingualism and thought. As a result of this process, bilinguals perform, verbally and non-verbally, in ways that diverge from the L1 pattern and begin to resemble, albeit not necessarily fully, that of the L2 speakers. To date, evidence of such restructuring in the direction of the L2 has been documented – most frequently in advanced-level L2 speakers – in studies of color (Andrews, 1994; Athanasopoulos, 2009) and object categorization (Athanasopoulos, 2006, 2007; Athanasopoulos & Kasai, 2008; Cook *et al.*, 2006; Malt & Sloman, 2003) and talk and gesturing about events and motion (Cadierno, 2004; Cadierno & Ruiz, 2006; Gullberg, this volume; Hohenstein *et al.*, 2006; v. Stutterheim, 2003; v. Stutterheim & Carroll, 2006; Wolff & Ventura, 2009).

(5) In cases where later learned languages encode categories, perspectives or frames of reference absent in the L1, it is also legitimate to talk about *internalization* of new categories, perspectives, frames and/or patterns of preference that result in target-like performance. To date, studies of late bilinguals have documented internalization in the domain of emotion categories (Panayiotou, 2004a, 2004b) and abstract concepts, where Russian-English bilinguals, for instance, spontaneously use the term *privacy* absent in Russian (Pavlenko, 2003; see also Pavlenko, this volume).

(6) Prolonged exposure to the L2 may also lead to another type of conceptual transfer, namely, *L2 influence on L1* linguistic categories, frames of reference or patterns of preference. Evidence of L2

conceptual transfer has been documented in studies of color categorization as a change in category boundaries and/or foci (Andrews, 1994; Athanasopoulos, 2009), in studies of artifacts as a change in category prototypes and boundaries (Pavlenko & Malt, in press), in studies of motion as the choice of verbs and use of gestures (Brown & Gullberg, 2008; Gullberg, this volume; Hohenstein *et al.*, 2006; Wolff & Ventura, 2009) and in studies of event construals, where Spanish-Swedish bilinguals speaking L1 Spanish paid increased attention to endpoints similar to speakers of their L2 Swedish (Bylund, 2009; Bylund & Jarvis, in press).

(7)   Last but not least, a few studies also indicate a possibility of *attrition* of linguistic categories or preferences. Pavlenko (2002a) found that Russian-English bilinguals living in the USA no longer rely on the Russian emotion category *perezhivat'* (to suffer things through), central in narratives elicited with the same stimulus from Russian monolinguals (Pavlenko, 2002a). In turn, studies of color categorization documented a weakening of the obligatory perceptual contrast between light and dark blue in L1 Russian, L1 Greek and L1 Japanese under the influence of L2 English (Andrews, 1994; Athanasopoulos, 2009; Athanasopoulos *et al.*, in press). Unfortunately, the findings to date do not allow us to differentiate conclusively between the L2 influence on L1 and L1 attrition, and in the case of some participants in Andrews' (1994) study, between L1 attrition and incomplete acquisition. To provide convincing evidence of attrition of linguistic categories and preferences (or absence thereof), future studies need to adopt longitudinal designs that would document an actual shift from target-like to non-target-like performance in bilingual speakers (for further discussion, see also Pavlenko, 2004).

8.2.3 Predictors of conceptual restructuring in the bilingual mind

The findings to date also allow us to identify six predictors of conceptual restructuring that takes place in the process of additional language learning and/or language attrition (for a discussion of these and other predictors, see also Athanasopoulos' chapter).

(1) The first predictor is the age of L2 acquisition (AOA), sometimes also termed the age of onset of bilingualism (see e.g. Bylund's chapter). It has been shown, not surprisingly, that AOA affects target-like acquisition of the L2. For instance, Hohenstein *et al.* (2006) showed that Spanish-English bilinguals who began acquiring L2 English between the ages of 1 and 5 display target-like preferences in the use of English manner and

path verbs, while bilinguals who acquired English after the age of 12 displayed evidence of L1 influence in the use of path verbs.

AOA has also been found to be a factor in L2 influence on the L1. Thus, Russian-English bilinguals who began acquiring English between the ages of 1 and 6 were shown to be most susceptible to L2 influence on L1 object categories (Pavlenko & Malt, in press). Spanish-Swedish bilinguals who started learning L2 Swedish between the ages of 1 and 12 were shown to be most susceptible to L2 influence on L1 endpoint encoding (Bylund, 2009). Andrews (1994) found that Russian-English bilinguals who came to the USA as children or teenagers expanded their category of dark blue (*sinii*) into the territory reserved for light blue (*goluboi*) by monolingual Russians and bilinguals who acquired English in adulthood. Together, these findings suggest that the L2 influence may be strongest in early bilinguals, but it is by no means limited to this population. Studies with speakers who acquired the L2 as teenagers or adults provide evidence of internalization of new categories, such as *privacy* (Pavlenko, 2003) and of L2 influence on the L1 in object category structure (Pavlenko & Malt, in press). Studies of inner speech also show that AOA effects are not limited to puberty: young adult L2 learners may also shift to the L2 as the language of inner speech (Dewaele, 2006; Larsen *et al.*, 2002).

There are also studies where AOA did not appear to affect performance. Thus, in the study of motion talk by Spanish-English bilinguals, no differences were found between early and late bilinguals in L1 Spanish performance (Hohenstein *et al.*, 2006). AOA also did not affect segmentation of events in the two languages of Spanish-Swedish bilinguals (Bylund, in press).

Regardless of their outcomes, all of the studies to date share one important limitation – they were conducted with participants who learned their L2 in the target language context. Consequently, the studies confound two different AOA variables – age of L2 acquisition and age of arrival in the target language country. Future studies need to dissociate the two and determine whether the age of L2 acquisition per se is a meaningful variable, regardless of the acquisition context.

(2) The COA also appears to be a predictor, whereby immersion in the L2 context favors conceptual restructuring. Studies by Pavlenko (2002a, 2003) and Pavlenko and Driagina (2007) showed that in word-to-reference mapping in the domains of emotions and privacy, FL users, living in the L1 context, patterned with speakers of their L1, and L2 users, living in the L2 context, with speakers of their L2. Malt and Sloman (2003) demonstrated that years of immersion are a much better predictor of object naming performance than years of formal instruction. Dewaele (2006) found that instructed learners use their FL less frequently for inner speech than those who acquired new languages in

the target language context. At the same time, FL learning does not appear to preclude restructuring. Brown and Gullberg's (2008) study of talking and gesturing about motion found evidence of L2 influence on L1 also in Japanese FL learners of English.

(3) Length of exposure (LOE) through residence in the target language country also appears to predict conceptual restructuring (but see Athanasopoulos, 2007). Studies conducted with L2 users of English showed that they begin restructuring their categorization preferences in the direction of the L2 after two or more years of LOE in the domain of color (Athanasopoulos, 2009) and after three or more years in categorization of objects and substances (Cook *et al.*, 2006). Wolff and Ventura (2009) demonstrated that English-Russian bilinguals began diverging from the L1 English pattern of causality description after six months in the Russian-speaking setting, while Russian-English bilinguals who resided in the USA for an average of 7.8 years began approximating the L2 English pattern. Notably, the starting point of the restructuring process is easier to identify than the endpoint (if one even exists). Thus, Malt and Sloman (2003) found that the approximation of L2 object naming patterns increases in L2 speakers as a function of years of immersion, but even the most advanced speakers with LOE in the USA of 10 years or more were not fully target-like in their naming patterns. It is also possible that after 10 or so years, LOE ceases to be an important predictor – thus, studies by Bylund (2009, in press) and Bylund and Jarvis (in press) identified no effects of LOE on either endpoint encoding or segmentation of events in participants who had lived in Sweden for longer than 12 years.

(4) Language proficiency may also play a role in conceptual restructuring. Several studies demonstrated that advanced L2 speakers – but not low-level or intermediate ones – approximate L2 categories and preferences (Athanasopoulos, 2006, 2007; Cadierno & Ruiz, 2006; Özyürek, 2002; but see Brown & Gullberg, 2008, where low proficiency speakers also approximate the L2 pattern). Language proficiency was also found to be a significant predictor of language choice for inner speech, with the choice of L2 or LX increasing with the rise in L2/LX proficiency (Dewaele, 2006; Guerrero, 2005; Larsen *et al.*, 2002). The difficulty in conducting any meaningful meta-analysis of these results lies in the fact that only a few studies use formal proficiency measures and those that do, use widely different proficiency measures (for discussion, see also Athanasopoulos' chapter).

An additional predictor in this area is domain-specific proficiency in the speakers' languages. Thus, Athanasopoulos and Kasai (2008) demonstrated that bilinguals' number-marking competence correlated with their object categorization preferences, while Bylund and Jarvis (in press) found a correlation between bilinguals' capacity to detect L1 aspectual errors and their endpoint encoding preferences.

(5) Frequency of language use may also be a predictor of conceptual restructuring. Thus, Athanasopoulos *et al.* (in press) demonstrated that frequency of L2 English use affects the differentiation between dark and light blue in L1 Japanese in Japanese-English bilinguals. Dewaele (2006) found that self-reported frequency of language use correlates with the choice of that language for inner speech. In contrast, Bylund (in press) found no influence of frequency of L1 use on endpoint encoding. Bylund's chapter acknowledges that this finding may be due to the reliance on self-reports and that is a weakness of the other studies as well. To date, however, no other reliable measures have been put forth to substitute or at least supplement self-reports on the frequency of language use.

(6) Another possible predictor is the type of required adjustment, such as, for instance, incorporation of a new contrast versus suppression of an already existing contrast. The study of this predictor requires a symmetrical design where the two languages appear both as the L1 and as the L2. The few studies that implemented such designs suggest that directionality and the type of required adjustment do matter (but see Gullberg's chapter for an argument that difficulties persist regardless of adjustment type). Thus, v. Stutterheim (2003) demonstrated that L1 German learners of L2 English approximated the target language pattern of endpoint encoding and the focus on ongoingness, while L1 English learners of L2 German did not (see also Schmiedtová *et al.*, this volume). This difference suggests that the adjustment required of L1 English learners of L2 German, namely, increased attention to endpoints, may be more challenging than the reverse adjustment required of L1 German learners of L2 English. Schmiedtová and associates also point to the transparency of encoding of the new linguistic category: the English progressive is formally encoded and perceptually prominent, while the holistic perspective in German is not.

Their explanation serves to show that the list above is not exhaustive and there are several other possible predictors, such as linguistic transparency or the frequency or salience of particular categories in the input, which need to be considered in future research. It also appears that the results of conceptual restructuring may differ across conceptual domains within the same speakers. For instance, Bylund (in press) found that Spanish-Swedish bilinguals in his study maintained language-specific patterns in temporality structuring, but displayed convergence between the L1 and the L2 in granularity of event description. Similarly, Pavlenko (2002a, 2010) found that the same Russian-English bilinguals maintained L1 patterns in motion categorization, but displayed L2 influence on the L1 in references to emotions. Athanasopoulos' chapter in this volume offers an informative discussion of the ways in which language proficiency appears to affect object – but not color – cognition, while the length of stay in the L2 context appears to have a reverse effect. Together, these findings suggest that future research needs to pay more attention to domain vulnerability and linguistic and cognitive complexity.

8.3 Conclusions

The purpose of the discussion above – and of the volume as a whole – was to demonstrate that the time has come, at least in the fields of bilingualism and second language acquisition, to discard the narrow search for evidence for or against linguistic relativity and to engage in broad explorations of thinking and speaking in two or more languages. The first stages of this inquiry have already presented us with intriguing findings and promising directions for future studies with bi- and multilingual speakers. Several decades ago, Benjamin Lee Whorf (1956 [1942]: 252) wrote: 'Actually, thinking is most mysterious, and by far the greatest light upon it that we have is thrown by the study of language'. Given his belief in the importance of multilingual awareness, I doubt he would have objected to our adding 'the study of languages in the bilingual – or for that matter multilingual – mind'.

Acknowledgments

I am deeply grateful to Panos Athanasopoulos, Colin Baker, Sarah Grosik, Scott Jarvis, Barbara Malt, Monika Schmid and Barbara Schmiedtová for their critical and constructive feedback on this chapter. All remaining errors are exclusively my own.

References

Alvarado, N. and Jameson, K. (2002) The use of modifying terms in the naming and categorization of color appearances in Vietnamese and English. *Journal of Cognition and Culture* 2, 53–80.

Ameel, E., Malt, B., Storms, G. and Van Assche, F. (2009) Semantic convergence in the bilingual lexicon. *Journal of Memory and Language* 60, 270–290.

Ameel, E., Storms, G., Malt, B. and Sloman, S. (2005) How bilinguals solve the naming problem. *Journal of Memory and Language* 52, 309–329.

Andrews, D. (1994) The Russian color categories *sinij* and *goluboj*: An experimental analysis of their interpretation in the standard and émigré languages. *Journal of Slavic Linguistics* 2, 9–28.

Athanasopoulos, P. (2006) Effects of grammatical representation of number on cognition in bilinguals. *Bilingualism: Language and Cognition* 9, 89–96.

Athanasopoulos, P. (2007) Interaction between grammatical categories and cognition in bilinguals: The role of proficiency, cultural immersion, and language of instruction. *Language and Cognitive Processes* 22, 689–699.

Athanasopoulos, P. (2009) Cognitive representation of color in bilinguals: The case of Greek blues. *Bilingualism: Language and Cognition* 12, 83–95.

Athanasopoulos, P. and Kasai, C. (2008) Language and thought in bilinguals: The case of grammatical number and nonverbal classification preferences. *Applied Psycholinguistics* 29, 105–121.

Athanasopoulos, P., Damjanovic, L., Krajciova, A. and Sasaki, M. (in press) Representation of color concepts in bilingual cognition: The case of Japanese blues. *Bilingualism: Language and Cognition*.

Beaujour, E. (1989) *Alien Tongues: Bilingual Russian Writers of the 'First' Emigration*. Ithaca, NY: Cornell University Press.

Berman, R. and Slobin, D. (1994) *Relating Events in Narrative: A Crosslinguistic Developmental Study*. Hillsdale, NJ: Lawrence Erlbaum.

Besemeres, M. (2002) *Translating One's Self: Language and Selfhood in Cross-cultural Autobiography*. Oxford: Peter Lang.

Brown, A. and Gullberg, M. (2008) Bidirectional crosslinguistic influence in L1-L2 encoding of manner in speech and gesture: A study of Japanese speakers of English. *Studies in Second Language Acquisition* 30, 225–251.

Bylund, E. (2008) Procesos de conceptualización de eventos en español y en sueco: Diferencias translingüísticas [Event conceptualization processes in Spanish and Swedish: Crosslinguistic differences]. *Revue Romane* 43, 1–24.

Bylund, E. (2009) Effects of age of L2 acquisition on L1 event conceptualization patterns. *Bilingualism: Language and Cognition* 12, 305–322.

Bylund, E. (in press) Segmentation and temporal structuring of events in early Spanish-Swedish bilinguals. *International Journal of Bilingualism*.

Bylund, E. and Jarvis, S. (in press) L2 effects on L1 event conceptualization. *Bilingualism: Language and Cognition*.

Cadierno, T. (2004) Expressing motion events in a second language: A cognitive typological perspective. In M. Achard and S. Niemeier (eds) *Cognitive Linguistics, Second Language Acquisition, and Foreign Language Teaching* (pp. 13–49). Berlin: Mouton de Gruyter.

Cadierno, T. (2008) Learning to talk about motion in a foreign language. In P. Robinson and N. Ellis (eds) *Handbook of Cognitive Linguistics and Second Language Acquisition* (pp. 239–275). London/New York: Routledge.

Cadierno, T. and Ruiz, L. (2006) Motion events in Spanish L2 acquisition. *Annual Review of Cognitive Linguistics* 4, 183–216.

Carroll, M. and Lambert, M. (2003) Information structure in narratives and the role of grammaticized knowledge: A study of adult French and German learners of English. In Ch. Dimroth and M. Starren (eds) *Information Structure and the Dynamics of Language Acquisition* (pp. 267–287). Amsterdam: John Benjamins.

Caskey-Sirmons, L. and Hickerson, N. (1977) Semantic shift and bilingualism: Variation in the color terms of five languages. *Anthropological Linguistics* 19, 358–367.

Cook, V., Bassetti, B., Kasai, Ch., Sasaki, M. and Takahashi, J. (2006) Do bilinguals have different concepts? The case of shape and material in Japanese L2 users of English. *International Journal of Bilingualism* 10, 137–152.

Dewaele, J-M. (2006) Multilinguals' language choice for inner speech. Paper presented at the Sociolinguistics Symposium, Limerick, Ireland, July 2006.

Dirven, R., Goossens, L., Putseys, Y. and Vorlat, E. (1982) *The Scene of Linguistic Action and its Perspectivization by Speak, Talk, Say, and Tell*. Amsterdam: John Benjamins.

Fillmore, C. (1975) An alternative to checklist theories of meaning. In C. Cogen, H. Thompson, G. Thurgood and K. Whistler (eds) *Proceedings of the Berkeley Linguistic Society* (pp. 123–131). Berkeley, CA: Berkeley Linguistics Society.

Fillmore, C. (1976) The need for frame semantics within linguistics. *Statistical Methods in Linguistics* 5–29.

Gennari, S., Sloman, S., Malt, B. and Fitch, W. (2002) Motion events in language and cognition. *Cognition* 83, 49–79.

Guerrero, M., de (2005) *Inner Speech – L2: Thinking Words in a Second Language*. New York: Springer.

Graham, R. and Belnap, K. (1986) The acquisition of lexical boundaries in English by native speakers of Spanish. *International Review of Applied Linguistics in Language Teaching* 24, 275–286.

Habel, C. and Tappe, H. (1999) Processes of segmentation and linearization in describing events. In R. Klabunde and Ch. v. Stutterheim (eds) *Processes in Language Production* (pp. 117–153). Wiesbaden: Deutscher Universitätsverlag.

Hendriks, H., Hickmann, M. and Demagny, A. (2008) How English native speakers learn to express caused motion in English and French. *Acquisition et Interaction en Langue Étrangère* 27, 15–41.

Hohenstein, J., Eisenberg, A. and Naigles, L. (2006) Is he floating across or crossing afloat? Cross-influence of L1 and L2 in Spanish-English bilingual adults. *Bilingualism: Language and Cognition* 9, 249–261.

Humboldt, W. v. (1963) *Humanist without Portfolio: An Anthology of the Writings of Wilhelm von Humboldt* (M. Cowan, trans.). Detroit, MI: Wayne State University Press.

Imai, M. and Gentner, D. (1997) A crosslinguistic study of early word meaning: Universal ontology and linguistic influence. *Cognition* 62, 169–200.

Jameson, K. and Alvarado, N. (2003) Differences in color naming and color salience in Vietnamese and English. *Color Research and Application* 28, 113–138.

Jarvis, S. (1998) *Conceptual Transfer in the Interlingual Lexicon*. Bloomington, IN: Indiana University Linguistics Club Publications.

Javier, R., Barroso, F. and Muñoz, M. (1993) Autobiographical memory in bilinguals. *Journal of Psycholinguistic Research* 22, 319–338.

Kasai, Ch., Hasebe, M., Kim, D-J., Lee, H-W. and Chung, H-J. (2008) Bilingual cognition – shape/material preference among Japanese and Korean subjects. Paper presented at the EuroSLA conference, Aix-en-Provence, France, September 2008.

Kay, P. (1996) Intra-speaker relativity. In J. Gumperz and S. Levinson (eds) *Rethinking Linguistic Relativity* (pp. 97–114). Cambridge: Cambridge University Press.

Kellman, S. (2000) *The Translingual Imagination*. Lincoln, NE: University of Nebraska Press.

Koven, M. (1998) Two languages in the self/the self in two languages: French-Portuguese bilinguals' verbal enactments and experiences of self in narrative discourse. *Ethos* 26, 410–455.

Koven, M. (2006) Feeling in two languages: A comparative analysis of a bilingual's affective displays in French and Portuguese. In A. Pavlenko (ed.) *Bilingual Minds: Emotional Experience, Expression, and Representation* (pp. 84–117). Clevedon: Multilingual Matters.

Koven, M. (2007) *Selves in Two Languages: Bilinguals' Verbal Enactments of Identity in French and Portuguese*. Amsterdam: John Benjamins.

Larsen, S., Schrauf, R., Fromholt, P. and Rubin, D. (2002) Inner speech and bilingual autobiographical memory: A Polish-Danish cross-cultural study. *Memory* 10, 45–54.

Lucy, J. (1992) *Grammatical Categories and Cognition. A Case Study of the Linguistic Relativity Hypothesis.* Cambridge: Cambridge University Press.

Malt, B. and Sloman, S. (2003) Linguistic diversity and object naming by non-native speakers of English. *Bilingualism: Language and Cognition* 6, 47–67.

Marian, V. and Fausey, C. (2006) Language-dependent memory in bilingual learning. *Applied Cognitive Psychology* 20, 1025–1047.

Marian, V. and Kaushanskaya, M. (2004) Self-construal and emotion in bicultural bilinguals. *Journal of Memory and Language* 51, 190–201.

Marian, V. and Kaushanskaya, M. (2007) Language context guides memory content. *Psychonomic Bulletin and Review* 14, 925–933.

Marian, V. and Neisser, U. (2000) Language-dependent recall of autobiographical memories. *Journal of Experimental Psychology: General* 129, 361–368.

Matsumoto, A. and Stanny, C. (2006) Language-dependent access to autobiographical memory in Japanese-English bilinguals and US monolinguals. *Memory* 14, 378–390.

Odlin, T. (2003) Crosslinguistic influence. In C. Doughty and M. Long (eds) *The Handbook of Second Language Acquisition* (pp. 436–486). Malden, MA: Blackwell.

Odlin, T. (2005) Crosslinguistic influence and conceptual transfer: What are the concepts? *Annual Review of Applied Linguistics* 25, 3–25.

Özyürek, A. (2002) Speech-language relationship across languages and in second language learners: Implications for spatial thinking and speaking. In B. Skarabela (ed.) *BUCLD Proceedings* (Vol. 26) (pp. 500–509). Somerville, MA: Cascadilla Press.

Panayiotou, A. (2004a) Bilingual emotions: The untranslatable self. *Estudios de Sociolinguistica* 5, 1–19.

Panayiotou, A. (2004b) Switching codes, switching code: Bilinguals' emotional responses to English and Greek. *Journal of Multilingual and Multicultural Development* 25, 124–139.

Panayiotou, A. (2006) Translating guilt: An endeavor of shame in the Mediterranean? In A. Pavlenko (ed.) *Bilingual Minds: Emotional Experience, Expression, and Representation* (pp. 183–208). Clevedon: Multilingual Matters.

Pavlenko, A. (1996) Bilingualism and cognition: Concepts in the mental lexicon. In A. Pavlenko and R. Salaberry (eds) *Cornell Working Papers in Linguistics. Volume 14, Papers in Second Language Acquisition and Bilingualism* (pp. 39–73). Ithaca, NY: Cornell Linguistics Circle.

Pavlenko, A. (1997) Bilingualism and cognition. Unpublished doctoral dissertation. Cornell University.

Pavlenko, A. (1999) New approaches to concepts in bilingual memory. *Bilingualism: Language and Cognition* 2, 209–230.

Pavlenko, A. (2002a) Bilingualism and emotions. *Multilingua* 21, 45–78.

Pavlenko, A. (2002b) Conceptual change in bilingual memory: A neo-Whorfian approach. In F. Fabbro (ed.) *Advances in the Neurolinguistics of Bilingualism* (pp. 69–94). Udine: Udine University Press.

Pavlenko, A. (2003) Eyewitness memory in late bilinguals: Evidence for discursive relativity. *International Journal of Bilingualism* 7, 257–281.

Pavlenko, A. (2004) Second language influence and first language attrition in adult bilingualism. In M. Schmid, B. Kopke, M. Kejser and L. Weilemar (eds) *First Language Attrition: Interdisciplinary Perspectives on Methodological Issues* (pp. 47–59). Amsterdam/Philadelphia: John Benjamins.

Pavlenko, A. (2005) Bilingualism and thought. In J. Kroll and A. De Groot (eds) *Handbook of Bilingualism: Psycholinguistic Approaches* (pp. 433–453). Oxford: Oxford University Press.

Pavlenko, A. (2006) Bilingual selves. In A. Pavlenko (ed.) *Bilingual Minds: Emotional Experience, Expression, and Representation* (pp. 1–33). Clevedon: Multilingual Matters.

Pavlenko, A. (2008) Structural and conceptual equivalence in acquisition and use of emotion words in a second language. *Mental Lexicon* 3, 91–120.

Pavlenko, A. (2010) Verbs of motion in L1 Russian of Russian-English bilinguals. *Bilingualism: Language and Cognition* 13, 49–62.

Pavlenko, A. and Driagina,V. (2007) Russian emotion vocabulary in American learners' narratives. *Modern Language Journal* 91, 213–234.

Pavlenko, A. and Malt, B. (in press) Kitchen Russian: Object naming by Russian-English bilinguals. *Bilingualism: Language and Cognition.*

Pederson, E. (1995) Language as context, language as means: Spatial cognition and habitual language use. *Cognitive Linguistics* 6, 33–62.

Pérez-Firmat, G. (2003) *Tongue Ties: Logo-eroticism in Anglo-Hispanic Literature.* New York: Palgrave Macmillan.

Ramirez-Esparza, N., Gosling, S., Benet-Martinez, V., Potter, J. and Pennebaker, J. (2006) Do bilinguals have two personalities? A special case for cultural frame switching. *Journal of Research in Personality* 40, 99–120.

Ross, M., Xun, W.Q.E. and Wilson, A. (2002) Language and the bicultural self. *Personality and Social Psychology Bulletin* 28, 1040–1050.

Sapir, E. (1949) *Selected Writings of Edward Sapir in Language, Culture, and Personality.* Edited by D. Mandelbaum. Berkeley/Los Angeles, CA: University of California Press.

Schmiedtová, B. and Sahonenko, N. (2008) Die Rolle des grammatischen Aspekts in Ereignis-Enkodierung: Ein Vergleich zwischen tschechischen und russischen Lernern des Deutschen [The role of grammatical aspect in the encoding of events: A comparison between Czech and Russian learners of German]. In P. Grommes and M. Walter (eds) *Fortgeschrittene Lernervarietäten: Korpuslinguistik und Zweitspracherwerbs-forschung* [*Advanced Learner Varieties: Corpus Linguistics and Second Language Research*] (pp. 45–71). Linguistische Arbeiten. Tübingen: Niemeyer.

Schrauf, R. and Rubin, D. (1998) Bilingual autobiographical memory in older adult immigrants: A test of cognitive explanations of the reminiscence bump and the linguistic encoding of memories. *Journal of Memory and Language* 39, 437–457.

Schrauf, R. and Rubin, D. (2000) Internal languages of retrieval: The bilingual encoding of memories for the personal past. *Memory and Cognition* 28, 616–623.

Schrauf, R. and Rubin, D. (2004) The 'language' and 'feel' of bilingual memory: Mnemonic traces. *Estudios de Sociolinguistica* 5, 21–39.

Slobin, D. (1996) From "thought and language" to "thinking for speaking". In J. Gumperz and S. Levinson (eds) *Rethinking Linguistic Relativity* (pp. 70–96). Cambridge: Cambridge University Press.

Stepanova Sachs, O. and Coley, J. (2006) Envy and jealousy in Russian and English: Labeling and conceptualization of emotions by monolinguals and bilinguals. In A. Pavlenko (ed.) *Bilingual Minds: Emotional Experience, Expression, and Representation* (pp. 209–231). Clevedon: Multilingual Matters.

Talmy, L. (1991) Path to realization: A typology of event conflation. *Proceedings of the Seventeenth Annual Meeting of the Berkeley Linguistics Society* (pp. 480–519).

Tannen, D. (ed.) (1993) *Framing in Discourse.* New York: Oxford University Press.

v. Stutterheim, Ch. (2003) Linguistic structure and information organization. The case of very advanced learners. In S. Foster-Cohen and S. Pekarek-Doehler (eds) *EUROSLA Yearbook 3* (pp. 183–206). Amsterdam: John Benjamins.

v. Stutterheim, Ch. and Carroll, M. (2006) The impact of grammatical temporal categories on ultimate attainment in L2 learning. In H. Byrnes, H. Weger-Guntharp and K. Sprang (eds) *Educating for Advanced Foreign Language Capacities* (pp. 40–53). Washington, DC: Georgetown University Press.

v. Stutterheim, Ch. and Nüse, R. (2003) Processes of conceptualization in language production: Language specific perspectives and event construal. *Linguistics* 41, 851–881.

Whorf, B. (1956) *Language, Thought, and Reality. Selected Writings of Benjamin Lee Whorf.* Edited by J. Carroll. Cambridge, MA: MIT Press.

Wolff, Ph. and Ventura, T. (2009) When Russians learn English: How the semantics of causation may change. *Bilingualism: Language and Cognition* 12, 153–176.

Author Index

Subject Index